Colonial Ecology, Atlantic Economy

EARLY AMERICAN STUDIES

Series Editors
Daniel K. Richter, Kathleen M. Brown,
Max Cavitch, and David Waldstreicher

Exploring neglected aspects of our colonial,
revolutionary, and early national history and culture,
Early American Studies reinterprets familiar themes
and events in fresh ways. Interdisciplinary in character,
and with a special emphasis on the period from about
1600 to 1850, the series is published in partnership with
the McNeil Center for Early American Studies.

A complete list of books in the series
is available from the publisher.

Colonial Ecology, Atlantic Economy

Transforming Nature in Early New England

Strother E. Roberts

PENN

UNIVERSITY OF PENNSYLVANIA PRESS

PHILADELPHIA

Published by
University of Pennsylvania Press
Philadelphia, Pennsylvania 19104-4112
www.upenn.edu/pennpress

Printed in the United States of America
on acid-free paper
10 9 8 7 6 5 4 3 2 1

A Cataloging-in-Publication record is available from the Library of Congress
ISBN 978-0-8122-5127-2

CONTENTS

Map 1. The Connecticut Watershed. Adapted from "Connecticut River Watershed Atlas," New England WSC / USGS, accessed May 21, 2018, https://nh.water.usgs.gov/project/ct_atlas/images/LIS_maj_basins.jpg.

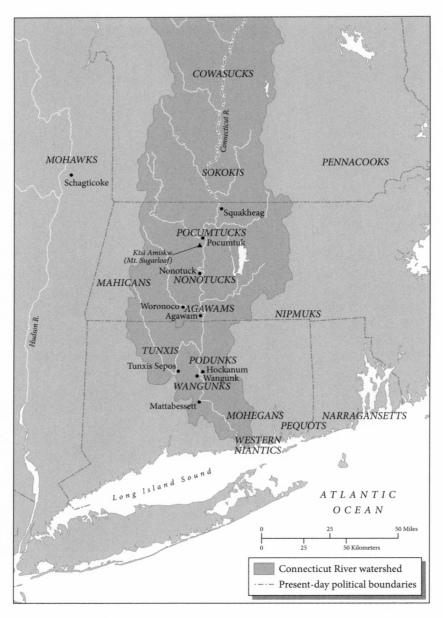

Map 2. Native American Nations Discussed. Adapted from Lisa Brooks,
The Common Pot: The Recovery of Native Space in the Northeast, MAPS,
accessed May 21, 2018, https://lbrooks.people.amherst.edu/thecommonpot/.

INTRODUCTION

Conflict, Choices, and Change

Metaphorically speaking, no ecosystem is an island, complete unto itself. Nature is no more fixed in character and features than are the human beings who inhabit it. And, like human beings, individual ecosystems are defined by their relationships. These relationships include the dense networks of natural processes that tie regions together—the exchange of soil and seeds upon wind and waves, the migration of animal life on flippers, feet, and wings. Just as important are the links that humanity has created between far-flung ecosystems. Ever since the earth's Eastern and Western Hemispheres rediscovered each other in 1492, human networks of commerce and migration have been tying the ecosystems of the world ever closer together. This book is an exploration of how the early modern revolution in world commerce transformed human and ecological relations in the lands touched by European colonialism. At its heart lies the question of how and why, in the seventeenth and eighteenth centuries, the opportunities offered by transatlantic commerce led ordinary men and women—both settlers and Native peoples—to radically transform the ecology of one corner of their rapidly globalizing world.

Origins

The Connecticut Valley, like all landscapes, has not always been as it is now. A tradition kept alive by the Pocumtuck Nation recalls a time when the Kwanitekw, the "Long River," was not a river at all, but a great pond spreading out over the land. Far to the south Ktsi Amiskw, the Great Beaver, had erected a giant dam that held back the waters of the river. The lands to the south of the dam suffered from drought, while those to the north lay drowned. Ktsi Amiskw reveled in his giant beaver pond, devouring its fish and, when these became scarce, coming ashore to prey on the humans who inhabited its shores.

In time, Hobomok, a trickster figure and cultural hero of the Pocumtucks, grew annoyed with the evils committed against the land by Ktsi Amiskw and called on the Great Beaver to take down his dam. When Ktsi Amiskw refused, Hobomok took up a massive tree trunk and waded into the pond. With this mighty cudgel Hobomok slew Ktsi Amiskw and demolished the Great Beaver Dam, setting loose the waters of the Kwanitekw to run freely to the sea. The Great Beaver Pond subsided to form a bounteous valley and the ancestors of the Pocumtucks moved their homes amid the fertile meadows and game-filled woodlands that now bordered the banks of the newborn river.[1]

In this telling the landscape of the modern valley was created through an act of destruction. Hobomok's violence offers a reminder that nature exists as a site of conflict and that every landscape holds multiple possibilities. The valley could not support both Ktsi Amiskw's beaver pond and the woodlands and meadows upon which the ancestors of the Pocumtucks depended for subsistence. In this story, human beings exist within nature and are at the mercy of its often brutal forces. But human beings are also shapers of nature. Like Hobomok, the historical Pocumtucks and their ancestors also destroyed beaver dams to transform the ponds behind them into verdant meadows.[2] The myth of Ktsi Amiskw reminds us that humans are not alone in their ability to reshape the natural landscape. The Great Beaver held the power to reshape the valley to his liking, as did his more diminutive beaver cousins who historically inhabited much of New England. But in the end it was Hobomok, as a stand-in for the mortal humans with whom he dwelled, who triumphed in imposing his own vision upon the natural landscape.

The history of the Connecticut Valley that follows, like the tale of Hobomok and Ktsi Amiskw, is a narrative of conflict, choices, and change. Like many environmental histories, it considers how particular local environments changed over time, the role of human beings in creating those (often unexpected or unforeseen) changes, and the way that market pressures and incentives helped shape those human decisions. It employs instances of historical conflict as signposts to map scarcity along the Connecticut's course and to determine which natural resources were most in demand where and when. Most importantly, the following pages explore the growth of an overlapping network of local, regional, and transatlantic markets in natural resources and studies the impact that local inhabitants' choices within these markets had upon both the land- and waterscapes of the colonial Connecticut Valley. As soon as the river was freed from Ktsi Amiskw's dam, its waters ran down to the sea and mingled with the ocean beyond. No longer held back, the great pond became the Long River, which in time became a commercial highway tying the Pocumtucks, neighboring Native American communities, and eventually Euro-American settlers in the valley to the wider world beyond.

At first, the European colonists who joined the Pocumtucks in the Connecticut Valley recorded and repeated the story of Hobomok and the Great Beaver. But, in time, their descendants developed their own creation narrative for the region. By the early decades of the nineteenth century, Euro-Americans had crafted a creation tale for the Connecticut Valley that was set in the last ice age and began with a glacier moving down from the north.[3] The advancing ice sheet carved out a great channel along the course of the Ammonoosuc Fault that separates the White Mountains in the east from the Green Mountains of the west. Steadily advancing, the glacier took the path of least resistance, plunging through the soft soils that lay between the mountains and finally reaching Long Island Sound around twenty-one thousand years ago. As the earth began to warm, the glacier melted, depositing sand and boulders picked up along its travels. Near present-day Middletown, Connecticut, a large moraine of such debris formed, arresting the seaward journey of melting glacial waters. The result was a great lake stretching over two hundred miles long from what is today Middletown to Littleton, New Hampshire. The pent up waters gradually wore away the moraine dam and the lake drained to create, about twelve thousand years ago, the modern Connecticut Valley. As the waters receded, plants, animals, and the ancestors of the valley's historical Indian communities colonized the newly revealed lands.[4] As rational as this description of natural forces may seem, it remained firmly wedded to a Eurocentric belief in progress and a circumscribed view of what constituted civilization. In this new myth, geology and biology (or what earlier generations referred to as Providence) prepared a "wilderness" to receive the civilizing efforts of America's Puritan forefathers.[5]

Atlantic Economy

In contrast to such narratives—which often identified progress with the triumph of Euro-American technologies over nature—recent environmental history recognizes that human economic activity exists within nature and both shapes and is shaped by the dynamics of natural ecosystems. At its heart, economics is the study of how humanity chooses to manage the scarce resources that nature provides. Consequently, economic activities stand at the forefront of this environmental history of the Connecticut Valley. The book that follows is not the first to consider how the natural environment has shaped New England's history. Nor is it the first to point out the important role that commodity production and exchange played in the development of an increasingly globalized "Atlantic World" in the early modern period. What this history proposes is to tie these two historical approaches together, to embrace the new methodological questions raised by recent transnational histories of commerce and empire in order to breathe new life into the older and increasingly dated environmental history of colonial New England.

Unlike other regions of colonial America, New England famously lacked a single foundational staple commodity—for example, sugar, tobacco, cotton, indigo—around which its early economy could be built. In 1679, only fifty years after the founding of the first English town in the Connecticut Valley, Parliament asked the government of Connecticut for a list of the commodities that the colony produced. In response the colony's general court provided an inventory of "the Comodities of the country" that boasted an array of grains, salted meats, livestock, cider, and timber products. Each of these commodities was important to the economy of the Connecticut Valley, but no single one could be said to underpin the region's economy in the way, for example, tobacco did for Virginia. A portion of these commodities, the general court continued, went directly into Connecticut's small, but growing, trade with the West Indies and the Spanish and Portuguese Wine Islands. The largest part was sold to merchants operating out of the mainland's greatest entrepôt, Boston, where Connecticut Valley products mingled with commodities from all over New England before being resold into the wider Atlantic World beyond.[6] This official exchange highlights Connecticut's role as a colony within a larger imperial system—as a site of resource extraction for the good of the English Empire—and it emphasizes the commercial forces that linked colonial Connecticut Valley residents and their local environments to far-off markets.

For Americans raised on tales of Pilgrim forefathers and New England exceptionalism, it is worth remembering that colonial New England's lack of an economic staple actually made it—as one economic historian recently wrote—"something of a disappointment to those with an imperial vision."[7] It was the Caribbean, not New England or any other mainland region, which provided the economic engine that drove the early modern British Empire in the Americas. As early as 1668, wealthy merchant and political economist Sir Josiah Child asserted that every English subject who immigrated to the West Indies provided for "the employment of Four Men in England, whereas peradventure of ten men that issue from us to New England . . . what we send to or receive from them doth not employ one."[8] On the surface of things, Sir Josiah seems to have had a point. By the second half of the eighteenth century, the West Indies accounted for about 60 percent of the annual value of the exports coming out of Britain's American colonies. The combined value of New England's exports made up only about 7 percent of this total. New England's share of imperial wealth did increase slightly over the course of the colonial period, but the northern colonies never came close to generating the levels of profits or revenue generated by the Caribbean sugar islands.[9]

The "sugar revolution" that began on Barbados in the 1640s transformed the English imperial economy. Over the course of the seventeenth and eighteenth centuries, white planters throughout the Caribbean embraced sugarcane as a crop that seemed to promise instant wealth. European consumers clamored for sugar, turning what had once been a luxury "spice" into a household staple. Sugar replaced other common sweeteners in cuisine, encouraged the invention of new sweet concoctions, and served as a preservative for an array of foodstuffs. It also helped cut the bitterness of other exotic comestibles finding their way onto global markets around the same time, making commodities like tea, coffee, and cocoa acceptable for finicky European palates. English merchants, most in the metropole but also many in the colonies, amassed fortunes. The number and tonnage of English ships plying Atlantic waters underwent an astronomical expansion. Revenues poured into state coffers. By the late eighteenth century, taxes on sugar contributed more to the exchequer than duties on any other imported commodity, and the revenue from sugar and its products trailed only the land tax and taxes on domestic alcohol production in their importance to the imperial budget. Subsidiary trades—most notably the transatlantic slave trade that delivered African laborers into bondage on sugar plantations—flourished as a result.[10]

For those shut out from the rarified business opportunities that offered obscene wealth to a lucky few planters and merchants (which is to say, the vast majority of Britons), the sugar revolution could still offer a chance at increased prosperity. The high profits offered by sugar (and tobacco, indigo, and other tropical crops) meant that planters were often loathe to devote valuable plantation lands to uses other than cultivating their staple. Colonists elsewhere in the Americas, including the Connecticut Valley, seized upon the opportunity to supply the West Indies with what the islands failed to provide for themselves: grain and flour, draft animals and meat, fish, and timber, as well as the barrels and ships needed to carry out the trade of an empire. The British Isles supplied some of these same commodities, as well as tools and the manufactured luxuries craved by the free planter class. The economic actors who supplied the sugar islands may not have grown sugar themselves, and most may not have participated directly in the slave trade, but they nonetheless profited from the sugar revolution and the labor of the enslaved millions who toiled on the plantations of the West Indies.[11]

Historians have long suggested that the wealth generated by the trade in sugar and other slave-produced plantation commodities played an important role in laying the foundation for Britain's industrial revolution and the British-led transition to a modern capitalist economy in western Europe and the United States. Sugar and related commodity trades certainly contributed capital for later industrial investments, but, perhaps more importantly, sugar production undergirded an entire imperial system that fed consumer demand in the British Isles while also creating demand for British produced goods in far-flung regions of the world. Successful colonists—whether they participated directly in sugar production or were otherwise employed in ancillary sectors of production—indulged their tastes for imported British goods and, over time, consumed an expanding array of textiles, household furnishings, and luxury goods produced in or reexported through Britain. British goods, likewise, found their way outside of the empire, filling the demands of African traders engaged in the transatlantic slave trade (a crucial underpinning of the sugar trade) and of Europeans both on the continent and in the often poorly supplied colonies of French and Spanish America. Meanwhile merchants and the owners of capital in Britain invested in new ventures to meet these demands, employing workers who were themselves constituents of the "consumer revolution" of the sixteenth and seventeenth centuries. These workers channeled their earnings into a domestic demand for commodities that had already been increasing in England since the beginning of the early modern era.[12]

If not its centerpiece, commodity production in New England was, nonetheless, integral to this imperial economic expansion, a fact easily overlooked by scholars, such as Sir Josiah Child and his intellectual heirs, who place too much focus solely on the connection between colonies and the metropole. Furs for the European market were New England's first major transatlantic export commodity, tying the region into commercial networks that stretched north into New France and across the Northern Hemisphere to Siberia. However, by the second half of the seventeenth century, the fur trade had been supplanted in importance by New England's trade with the sugar islands. New Englanders played a critical role in creating and maintaining the slave labor–based plantation system of the West Indies.[13] Boston merchants drew on their agricultural hinterland—which included the Connecticut Valley as well as the rest of New England—to establish a steady trade with the West Indies by the 1650s.[14] The food, timber, ships and other commodities produced in New England, and elsewhere on the mainland, allowed Caribbean planters to specialize in cultivating staple crops. Nor did New Englanders limit their commerce to the British sugar islands, but also fed and supported European settlers in the French and Spanish Caribbean as well. In 1679, royal agent and customs official Edward Randolph observed critically that New England merchants were willing to "trye all ports" in search of customers and that Boston had consequently become "the mart town of the West Indies."[15] In the late eighteenth century, the value of New England's commodity exports to the West Indies was over three and a half times that of its exports to the British Isles.[16]

No single leg of Britain's intraimperial Atlantic trade was balanced. The West Indies exported more (in terms of value) sugar and other tropical commodities to the British Isles than they imported back in manufactured and luxury goods. By contrast, a small variety of New England–produced commodities flowed directly to Europe—most notably fish, agricultural goods, timber and wood products, and, early on, furs—but the northern mainland colonies purchased far more from Britain then they exported in return. On the other hand, New England and the Middle Colonies ran a trade surplus with the West Indies. New England, in particular, imported a good deal of sugar, molasses, salt, and some rum from the Caribbean, but these imports fell far short of balancing the interregional ledger. Instead, New Englanders effectively relied on their trade surplus with the West Indies to cover their shortfall with Europe. Trade within the empire roughly balanced, and regional specialization helped optimize productivity in the imperial system as a whole.[17] Over the course of the eighteenth century, goods and services traded to the West Indies facilitated New England's rapid increase in per capita wealth and allowed New Englanders to raise their standards of living by indulging in imported European goods. In the words of economic historian Carole Shammas: "It is difficult to imagine a thriving New England post-1640 . . . without the sugar islands."[18]

Like other works within the developing genre of "commodity histories," *Colonial Ecology, Atlantic Economy* connects commodity production and, to a lesser extent, consumption to the development of new commercial networks that united the emerging transatlantic world of the early modern period. William Cronon justified centering his *Nature's Metropolis* on a study of commodity markets by asserting that "few economic institutions more powerfully affect human communities and natural ecosystems in the modern capitalist world."[19] This project shares Cronon's appreciation for the importance of commodity markets in shaping humanity's relationship to the natural world, but recognizes that the ability of such markets to profoundly alter natural ecosystems predated capitalist modernity. This book goes a step beyond other commodity histories by tying its analysis of commercial networks to a study of ecological change—effectively integrating not only human communities but also nonhuman fauna, flora, and even the nonorganic elements and physical systems of the Connecticut basin into its definition of the early modern British Atlantic economy.[20] The result is a history that explores how markets connected consumers in far-flung communities not only to human producers but also to the natural resources that these producers exploited and the broader ecosystems from which these resources were drawn.

This ecological focus means that *Colonial Ecology, Atlantic Economy* differs from other commodity histories in a second important way as well: Instead of following a single commodity across the globe from its site of production to its site of consumption, this study seeks to understand how the historical production of a number of commodities impacted the societies and ecologies of a single region. The goal of this book is to produce a particular type of "Atlantic World history," what David Armitage has termed a "cis-Atlantic" history. This history will explore the "local particularity" of New England, and more specifically of the Connecticut Valley, while also asking what historical developments in this one corner of the early modern world can tell us about the larger processes at work within the "wider web of connections" that tied together the economies and ecologies of the far-flung lands bordering the Atlantic.[21] Whereas, the two monographs which currently dominate the historiography of early New England's regional environment—William Cronon's *Changes in the Land* (Cronon's *other* seminal work of environmental history) and Carolyn Merchant's *Ecological Revolutions*—give only passing attention to the historical markets that drove environmental change in colonial New England, the new research presented here emphasizes the centrality of Atlantic markets. [22]

Just as Pekka Hämäläinen has worried that "big-picture ecohistorical models" are to blame for "suffus[ing] history with biological determinism," it can likewise be claimed that many existing environmental histories of early America overindulge in a particular brand of economic determinism.[23] Cronon and Merchant, for example, relied heavily on the abstract concept of "capitalism" as the driving force behind environmental change in early New England. This book, by contrast, pushes deeper into historical economic life to explore the way that the growth of specific markets—social networks connecting producers to consumers, often through several layers of economic intermediaries—contributed to a new, increasingly capitalistic, early modern Atlantic World.[24] Capitalism was not an autonomous actor that pulled New England into modernity. Rather, the Indian and Euro-American inhabitants of early modern New England worked with economic actors elsewhere to build the expanding system of social and commercial networks that constituted modern capitalism.

Among other benefits, this new interpretive model highlights the importance of nonagricultural export commodities to New England's economic development and ecological transformation. The previous historiographical fixation on agriculture as the driving force behind economic growth in early modern New England has caused many scholars to overlook or downplay the ecological impact of other forms of commodity production in the region. For example, Cronon and Merchant's interpretive fixation upon capitalism was aggravated by their commitment to the theory (predominant in the historiography of the time) that the transition to capitalism was driven by late eighteenth-century agricultural improvements that encouraged the widespread adoption of commercial agriculture.[25] As a consequence, they and other scholars have misdated the beginning of large-scale ecological change in the region to the late eighteenth or early nineteenth centuries.[26]

The Connecticut Valley's rich soils, diversified colonial economy and strong ties to Atlantic trade recommend it especially well as the focal point of a study seeking to tie together early American economic and environmental history. The Connecticut River itself—the natural highway that connected the producers of these natural resources to the markets of the broader Atlantic World—is the longest in New England at approximately 410 miles. Its many tributaries stretching out to the east and west—embracing a basin of 11,250 square miles—expanded the commercial network of the Connecticut Valley even deeper into New England's hinterlands. The Connecticut River has its headwaters in the unimaginatively named Fourth Connecticut Lake, just 300 yards from New Hampshire's modern-day border with Canada. From its source, the river runs roughly south-southwest through a hard bedrock that keeps the valley walls rocky and steep. Around the modern site of Colebrook, New Hampshire, the river's waters take a more southerly turn, passing through softer rock, the sides of its valley less sheer. But it is not until Stewartstown that the valley begins to open up and meander. It is here that the famously rich meadows of the Connecticut Valley begin.

The commercial potential of the Connecticut River, especially its navigability, shaped the development of the valley's earliest English towns. The wealthy and powerful William Pynchon founded Springfield in 1636 just above the Connecticut's first major cataracts. Here goods coming from the upper valley would need to be unloaded from rafts and portaged around the falls. Springfield's position as the northernmost of the early towns also made it a funnel for receiving the Indian trade coming downriver and from the interior. William Pynchon's son John would build a commercial empire and transform himself into a veritable feudal lord by exploiting Springfield's fortuitous position. Running south from Springfield, the river continued its path beyond the bounds of the Massachusetts Bay Colony.[27]

The river may have formed the far frontier of early New Hampshire and Massachusetts, but in Connecticut the valley formed the very heart of the colony. Long the northernmost township in Connecticut, Windsor had been

Figure 1. This 1761 engraving was based on a sketch by Thomas Pownall, Massachusetts' governor during the Seven Years' War. It offers an idealized view of the colonial project by counterpoising a rough new settlement on the left with a fully improved farm on the right. Small river vessels (foreground) and trading sloops (background) highlight the commercial ambitions of both settlements. James Peake, "A Design to Represent the Beginning and Completion of an American Settlement or Farm," London: 1761. Courtesy of the John Carter Brown Library at Brown University.

founded in 1635 at the confluence of the Connecticut and its largest tributary, the Farmington River. An important avenue for the local Indian fur trade, the Farmington would in later decades provide Windsor access to the produce of new towns founded in its own rich valley. Hartford, also founded in 1635, sat at the highest point on the river navigable by oceangoing craft, ensuring its commercial importance as the northernmost site where commodities from upriver could be loaded on ships bound for Atlantic markets, or goods sent in from England, the West Indies, and elsewhere unloaded and transferred to rafts and carts for sale to customers deeper in the interior. The earliest English settlers in the valley, those who founded "ancient" Wethersfield in 1634, claimed for themselves a site at the southernmost limit of the Connecticut's meandering meadows. Even though it was not settled until 1650, the site of Middletown, too, enjoyed certain advantages. If Hartford marked the absolute limit for oceangoing navigation, Middletown marked the border of convenient navigation. Above Middletown, seated upon its deep river bend, shifting shoals and sandbars plagued any moderately deep-hulled vessel. Below Middletown, the Connecticut once again cuts through a bed of hard rock, passing below steep banks as it turns sharply southeast toward Long Island Sound. Here, Saybrook was founded in 1635 to guard the river's mouth from imperial rivals, rounding out the list of the valley's oldest towns.

Colonial Ecology

Timothy Dwight—travel writer, theologian, and president of Yale University in the early nineteenth century—once described the Connecticut as the "Beautiful River."[28] What he meant was that the Connecticut and its valley corresponded to a Euro-American definition of aesthetics that identified beauty with agricultural fertility and agrarian productivity. Dwight encountered a Connecticut River frequented by cattle and sheep, interspersed with busy grist and sawmills, and everywhere flanked by the luscious meadows that for centuries had drawn both Native American and European settlers alike. For Dwight and his contemporaries, the banks of the Connecticut presented an image of utilitarian beauty. Although ostensibly he took the river valley as his subject, Dwight principally concerned himself with the region's recent human history.

By contrast, an environmental historian can discern the natural processes at work within Dwight's observations.[29] The operations of glaciers had long ago stripped the valley of its best soil. The majority of what remained was the result of silt and sand, which had gradually accumulated at the bottom of Lake Hitchcock, together with a mix of clay washed down regularly from the mountains. Only along the banks of the river, where flooding deposited fresh earth every year, could the soil truly be called rich. Here, in the bottomlands regionally known as the intervales, nature presented a picture of agricultural plenty. Elsewhere crops grew, but not as well as grass or woods. Here were the luxurious green meadows, "which may [be] said literally to glow with verdure," that made the valley such an important site for livestock husbandry.[30] The pastoral beauty observed by Dwight hid the thousands of years of geological activity that had created the soils upon which this human idyll was built.

The ecological transformations of landscapes and waterscapes that occurred in Dwight's time—the turn of the nineteenth century—and afterward have received the lion's share of historians' attention. The most visible human assaults upon the Connecticut River—canal building, industrial waste, electrical dams—were all the products of later decades. In fact, this work takes the 1790s as its endpoint precisely because that decade saw the rise of the large-scale canal building that marked a new ecological era in the life of the valley. But to ignore the equally dramatic changes brought about in the seventeenth and eighteenth centuries is to begin in the middle of the story.

Everything humans do on a river's banks, or on the terraces overlooking those banks, unavoidably impacts the river itself. For every bundle of pelts, barrel of salted pork, or "hundred" of pipe staves produced, something had been taken from the colonial valley's ecosystems. A particular choice, among conflicting options, had been made about how best to exploit its resources. In some way, great or small, the land- and waterscape of the valley had been changed. The valley's ecological history lay bound up in the commodities its human inhabitants chose to produce.

To combine the history of the river and its human inhabitants means to write a history of environmental changes in both the land and water. Consequently, this work is not so much a history of the Connecticut River itself as of the Connecticut *Valley*, of the river's watershed and the many human, animal, and plant communities that dwelled within it. In truth, a river and its valley are ecologically inseparable. The river creates its valley, slowly over millennia carving its way through rock and soil. Large rivers, like the Connecticut, define the climate of the lands that surround them, moderating temperatures and, in northern regions, extending the growing season for both wild plants and human crops. At least in the lowlands, a river determines the soils of its valley and determines which species of plants and animals will inhabit its banks. Rivers create land through the accretion of the sediments that they carry downstream. They also destroy land through erosion, shifting their banks sometimes rapidly—as when floods strike—but always gradually as the years, decades, and centuries pass. The relationship flows the other way as well, especially where human settlements flank the river's course.

This focus on human interactions with a physical, ecologically defined region further sets *Colonial Ecology, Atlantic Economy* apart from previous studies which have instead defined their scope through reference to political abstractions ("New England") largely independent of the natural landscape. Rather than delimiting nature within the political boundaries of a historically defined region, the research presented here recognizes that natural processes (in this case, located within a particular river basin) often shape and define their own logically discernable geographical regions. Nevertheless, the pages that follow (and also some that have preceded) make frequent mention of New England as a discrete region. The watershed formed an important part of this larger geopolitical space, and many of the ecological processes at work in the Connecticut basin in the seventeenth and eighteenth centuries are representative of developments taking place throughout New England (as well as other areas of North America). Taking the Connecticut basin as a spatial focus is not intended as a rejection of "New England" as an important category for historical study, but rather to suggest that an environmental history should, in its scope, be defined by the physical environment.[31]

The Connecticut basin, as a geographical focus, is small enough to allow for detailed analyses of how various ecological changes affected local streams and soils in individual towns. The region is broad enough for generalizations about what those local changes meant for the hydrology and ecology of the river basin as a whole. And, finally, focusing on a discrete ecological unit like the Connecticut watershed offers a case study from which to explore the implications of the expanding ecological, commercial, and social networks in which the Connecticut Valley's inhabitants took part. In short, the book that follows conceives of the Connecticut Valley as a discrete ecological region, but one whose physical ecology was intimately tied to the larger geographical region of New England and to the transatlantic community beyond.

If the valley's earliest English settlers arrived already in possession of an Atlantic-oriented view of the world, its trade-savvy Native communities lost no time in exploring how best to exploit the new economic incentives that the Atlantic World had to offer. The lands of the valley were neither unpeopled nor ungoverned when the first English settlers arrived. For over ten thousand years the Native communities of the valley had traded with other

Native populations living to their north, east, and west. The arrival of the English merely expanded these preexisting trade networks, integrating European markets with Indian ones and slowly reorienting the trade of the valley toward the markets of the Atlantic World.[32]

Early English settlers often rejected the authority of the region's Indian occupants. In part, they did this by ignoring the presence of these earlier proprietors of the valley. The Puritan founders of Windsor referred to the valley as "the Lord's waste": an uninhabited and unclaimed land prepared by God for his chosen people.[33] Even when they took note of Indians' presence and use of the land, these newcomers often asserted that the perceived inferiority of Native cultures and economies undermined the latter's title to territory. The Massachusetts Bay Colony's first governor, John Winthrop, put the English case succinctly: "This savage people ruleth over many lands without title or property; for they inclose no ground, neither have they cattell to maintayne it, but remove their dwellings as they have occasion. . . . Why may not christians have liberty to go and dwell amongst them in their waste lands and woods. . . ?" In English eyes, only settled occupancy and farming could justify the ownership of land. Although Winthrop advocated the usurpation of lands that Indians used for hunting and gathering wild foods, he did recognize the propriety of "leaving them such places as they have manured for their corne."[34] Succeeding English generations were not always willing to make even this allowance for the rights of their Indian neighbors.

The Connecticut basin's Native populations never disappeared. Nor, in the face of increasing rates of environmental change, did they remain static in their practice of "traditional" cultures and economies. Generations of Pocumtucks, Podunks, Wangunks, Tunxis, Nipmucs, and others learned that while English livestock, crops, and weeds often undercut the ecological foundations of long-practiced economic pursuits, these exotic imports, when incorporated into Native practices, also offered the opportunity to create a new material culture.[35]

The imposition of the English system of property rights—through a combination of honest purchase, judicious deceit, and outright force—displaced the collective sovereignty of Native communities and ushered in a creeping tide of usurpation and dispossession. The horrendous toll that disease took upon the indigenous populations of the Connecticut Valley (and of the American continents in general) is well documented.[36] In the valley, tens of thousands of men, women, and children never survived to face the decision of how best to adapt to the new economy and new environment spawned by the arrival of Europeans. Thousands rejected these changes and perished at the hands of English violence in the Pequot War and King Philip's War or were sold into distant slavery, joining other victims of the transatlantic slave trade to supply the labor that kept the plantation system of the sugar islands profitably running. Of those who avoided death or enslavement, many decided relocating was their best option and moved west or north. Despite these losses, many of the valley's Native inhabitants chose to remain and build a place for themselves within this new economy, joining their own labors to the English transformation of the region's land- and waterscapes.

Much ink has been spilled discussing early English settlers' antipathy for the woodland wildernesses that faced them upon arrival in the Americas and which later offered sanctuary to Indian neighbors-cum-enemies.[37] Puritan minister and poet Michael Wigglesworth, in a much quoted line, described the New England woods as "a waste and howling wilderness where none inhabited but hellish fiends and brutish men."[38] But the woodlands of New England, and of the Connecticut Valley, were more than simply a symbol. Historical discussions of the *imagined* wilderness of the Puritan mind has led to too little consideration of the role that the *physical* landscape played in shaping the everyday lives of colonial New Englanders.[39] Early Americans expressed their understanding of the world not just through what they wrote on paper but also by what they wrought upon the land. For the Puritans and for the later generations of Euro-American settlers who followed them, it was the mundane chores of economic production that most intimately defined their relationships with the woods and waters surrounding their New England homes. The ecological history of the valley can best be seen here, where human labor married itself to the natural world.[40]

All too often violence tinges the outlines of these stories. For instance, tales of Indian attacks—of neighbors kidnapped and killed—fill the pages of the journal kept by farmer William Heywood of Charlestown, New Hampshire, in the years surrounding King George's War. Here, in the northern valley, western Abenakis committed to maintaining their access to hunting, fishing, and agricultural territories clashed repeatedly with the settlers at the vanguard of English expansionism. Heywood kept his entries short and stoic: "June 20th, 1749—about 3 o'clock the Indians fired on Ensign Sartwell and Enos Stevens as they were harrowing corn, killed Sartwell and took Enos, & killed the horse." Heywood never recorded the emotions that such events aroused, but the reader cannot help but imagine the fear that must have gripped him and his neighbors day in and day out. They would have warily eyed the woodlands of their frontier home, familiar from long habitation but now threatening, never knowing when danger might emerge from the cover of the trees. Still, even at the height of their danger, the woodlands could not be avoided.

Heywood joined the local militia and spent each growing season during the war standing guard over his neighbors as they tended crops and cut hay ominously close to the threatening presence of the woods. Nor could the products of the woodlands themselves be dispensed with. Less than a month after the raid that resulted in Obadiah Sartwell's death and Enos Stevens' capture, Heywood ventured into the woods to chop firewood and cut poles to fence in a new turnip yard he was planting.[41] As generations came and went, a lingering fear of the woods and the unknown dangers that they held may have lingered in the darkest corners of the minds of these Puritan descendants, but it was the mundane concerns of subsistence and commerce that truly defined early Americans' lived experience of their wilderness homes.[42]

It is important, when considering the effect of transatlantic trade on the Connecticut Valley, to not regard the dispossession of New England's Indians or their eventual economic marginalization in the region as a foregone conclusion, or, to cite another popular trope, to see Indians as inherently backward and doomed to be eventually replaced by a more industrious/technologically savvy population. For instance, Cronon's *Changes in the Land* concludes by identifying "two central ecological contradictions" that explain environmental change over the course of the colonial period. The first insists that "the ecological relationships which European markets created in New England were inherently antithetical to earlier Indian economies."[43] This is— as Cronon would likely admit—an oversimplification of the economic transition that took place in seventeenth-century New England. The assertion that the economic choices introduced by Euro-American merchants and settlers in the seventeenth century were "antithetical" to Native American economies undervalues the dynamism of those economies and belittles the adaptability of Indian societies.

The environmental history of the New England fur trade is not the simple story of a "traditional" Indian economy displaced by a European/ Euro-American capitalist system. Far from seeing the expanding European economy as incompatible with their own existing commercial networks, Native communities often enthusiastically embraced the opportunity to partner with European traders. The existence of the seventeenth-century fur trade (among other cross-cultural economic exchanges) proves as much. Rather, seventeenth-century New England witnessed the rise, operation, and ultimate decline of a new economy—one that encompassed European merchants and supplied European consumers, but that was, on its production side, just as much of an "Indian" economy as that which had preceded it. The history of early New England is not the story of an economic system imposed from outside, but rather a process by which Indians and Europeans cocreated new economic and ecological systems.[44]

The eventual decline of Native American economies in New England at the end of the seventeenth century can more appropriately be attributed to the historically contingent and culturally defined political and commercial choices that Indian communities made in the face of the fur trade and the ecological transformations it triggered. The abstract big-picture econohistorical models (to paraphrase Hämäläinen) of capitalist expansion embraced by Cronon, Merchant, and other scholars of early America downplay both human and nonhuman agency while obscuring regional historical processes.[45] It was not, as Carolyn Merchant concludes, the simple introduction of "diseases and property rights" by Europeans that "destroyed [the] traditional patterns of subsistence" practiced by seventeenth-century New England natives. Certainly, Native American communities in the seventeenth and eighteenth centuries suffered tragically high mortality rates following the introduction of foreign pathogens through commercial contact with Europeans.[46] But it was Indian communities themselves who *chose* how best to *adapt* their subsistence strategies in response to ecological, economic, social, and political forces that included new diseases and Euro-American demands for land, as well as the "traditional" demands of Native networks of diplomacy and exchange.

The second of the "two central ecological contradictions" that Cronon identifies at the heart of the colonial economy was the tendency of Euro-American colonists to engage in "ecologically self-destructive" modes of production due to their assumption of "the limitless availability" of natural resources. For Cronon, colonial expansion was fueled by "the temporary gift of nature" and after "that gift was finally exhausted . . . expansion could not continue indefinitely."[47] While such an interpretation of early American environmental and economic history contains a germ of truth, it nevertheless misrepresents the historical attitudes that it claims to explain. To put it another way, Cronon's final analysis of the early American economy—and the analyses of scholars that have followed him—better represents the viewpoint of a late twentieth-century environmentalist than it does the ecological perceptions of New England's seventeenth- and eighteenth-century Euro-American inhabitants.[48]

To begin with, colonists did not assume "the limitless availability" of natural resources that they depended upon the New England landscape to provide. In fact, English settlers from the early decades of the seventeenth century forward remained ever mindful of the finite nature of locally available resources, continuously bemoaned the risk of shortages facing their settlements, and repeatedly drafted laws for conserving these resources. The historical irony at the heart of colonial resource exploitation is, in fact, the exact opposite of that presented by Cronon: even as colonists worried about impending resource shortages, these shortages rarely manifested themselves. (The one exception explored in this book is the regional exhaustion of fur stocks.)

The expansion of transatlantic markets into the North American mainland meant, in a very important sense, that the "gifts of nature" were not, in fact, "temporary" as Cronon claimed. The economic expansion of New England has continued, with some interruptions, from the seventeenth century through the twenty-first. Euro-American communities in New England never faced any prolonged or meaningful shortages of firewood, timber for construction, foodstuffs, or even agricultural lands. Commodity imports and population exports (outmigration) perpetually prevented (or at least took the sting out of) any impending shortages in these resources. Even after beaver disappeared from their own region, New Englanders could purchase hats and coats made from furs trapped around the Great Lakes or Hudson's Bay. In the nineteenth century, New Englanders who had formerly cut lumber for sale to far-off markets (or whose forebears had) became consumers of lumber sawn in the Midwest. Historical efforts at resource conservation slowed exploitation and, in most cases, prevented the absolute exhaustion of natural resources, but it was the continuous expansion of markets that transformed relative local resource scarcities into a purchasable abundance.[49] Cronon was, of course, correct that natural resources are *globally* limited and exhaustible, but this is a realization born of modern ecology. The lived experience of early modern New Englanders was one of feared local shortages repeatedly avoided through market participation. Just as colonial New England offered England and its West Indies colonies access to resources scarce in those regions, New Englanders gradually came to depend upon territories elsewhere in North America to supply them with their furs, lumber, meat, and so forth.[50]

This is not to say that many natural resources, readily available from the local environment in 1600, had not become scarce by 1800. Nor is it to deny that many ecological changes occurred which may justifiably be identified as examples of environmental degradation. The history that follows does not endorse the contention of Julian Simon and others like him that markets, in partnership with human ingenuity, can continue perpetually to overcome the limits placed upon humanity by a finite global environment.[51] If market participation allowed New Englanders to avoid the hardships they might otherwise have faced from local resource exhaustion, this should be taken as a statement about the historical operation of commercial networks, not a prediction of the role that commodity markets might play in the future.

A focus on commerce and commodity production necessarily emphasizes the roles of some historical actors over others. This book's five chapters revolve around five commodities which were especially important for networks of local, regional, and/or transatlantic trade in the colonial period: furs, agricultural crops, firewood, timber, and livestock. The choice of these particular commodities dictates which groups of historical human actors have received the most analytical attention. Native American economic actors, for example, occupy a central role in Chapter 1's discussion of the Connecticut Valley fur trade and Chapter 2's study of valley farming but make only intermittent appearances in later chapters. This is not because Indians or Indian communities disappeared from the Connecticut Valley after the decline of the fur trade in the late seventeenth century. Indeed, there continued to be— indeed has always been—an Indian presence in the valley. Rather, Native Americans play a smaller role in later chapters because the most widely traded commodities coming out of the valley in the decades after the 1670s were overwhelmingly produced by Euro-American labor. Native Americans continued to participate in the production of these commodities, raising livestock or becoming wage laborers in the larger Euro-American economy, but their role in resource exploitation decreased markedly compared to the role of incoming settlers. Likewise, the essential role that women played in colonial society is only occasionally mentioned, not because women's labor was not crucial to maintaining the colonial economy, but because colonial society considered the production of each of these particular market commodities to fall within the realm of male labor.

An Ambiguous Legacy

Timothy Dwight wrote in an era when New England was already well on its way to becoming the commercial and industrial heart of a nascent American empire. With its furs depleted, its woodlands scarce, and its soils in decline, the nineteenth-century Connecticut Valley epitomized a region that had shed its past as a colonial site of resource extraction and was now embracing the new opportunities offered by millwork and manufacturing. Meanwhile, the southern states and the Midwest functioned, in effect, as colonies providing New England's workers and mills with the food, timber, and other raw materials that their own region had once produced for export.

Within this historical context, Dwight and most of his turn-of-the-nineteenth-century contemporaries looked at the valley and saw a narrative of economic progress written upon the landscape. Twentieth- and twenty-first-century historians have more often looked at the same economic processes and written, instead, of an environment in decline.[52] This book aims to retire this declensionist narrative, not to replace it with a triumphal narrative of economic progress, but rather to examine how historical commodity producers in the region responded to market incentives to create a new landscape that offered both ecological challenges and opportunities. Progress and decline are ultimately in the eyes of the beholder, and the historical inhabitants of colonial New England who came before Dwight most often saw both in the changing environment around them. For New Englanders producing and consuming commodities in the seventeenth and eighteenth centuries, the incentives offered by a globalizing Atlantic economy wrought an ambiguous legacy upon the land- and waterscapes of the physical world around them. This lesson—the inherent ecological ambiguities of commercial production and consumption—is perhaps the most important lesson about the power of global markets that an environmental history of early modern New England can present to a twenty-first-century reader concerned about the fate of the global environment.

CHAPTER 1

Hunting Beaver

The Postdiluvian World
of the Fur Trade

The seventeenth-century introduction of European trade goods, especially firearms and metal weaponry, into existing Native American networks of trade, warfare, and diplomacy transformed both the politics and the ecology of the Connecticut Valley. Seeking to gain an advantage over rivals, Indian nations competed to exploit the furbearing wealth of the region. Over the course of a century, hunters killed hundreds of thousands of beaver to satisfy the demands of consumers living in Europe. With beaver extirpated from the region, their dams collapsed, and the ponds and wetlands they had created drained. In all, up to nine hundred thousand acres of wetlands may have disappeared. This drying of the Connecticut watershed brought certain advantages. Swamps and marshes gave way to lush meadows and fertile croplands, saving English settlers the hard labor of improving agricultural land through ditching and draining. The loss of breeding habitat for mosquitoes spared valley inhabitants the ravages of malaria. But the destruction of wetlands also brought a range of negative consequences for the valley's human inhabitants. Indian communities faced food shortages as biodiversity declined. English farmers suffered increased flooding and erosion in their fields, accompanied by the silting up of the river that they relied upon for trade with the world beyond the valley. By 1700, the land- and waterscapes of the Connecticut Valley would have been unrecognizable to the Indian communities living there when the first Dutch explorers arrived in 1614.[1]

* * *

In the spring of 1631, a party of Indian diplomats arrived in Boston to meet with the leaders of the Massachusetts Bay Colony. Among them was the Podunk sachem Wahginnacut, who had traveled five days overland from the west to bring an invitation to the English. Wahginnacut offered land to the English for a new settlement near his own people's villages along the banks of the "River Quonehtacut." The Podunks called their homeland Nowashe, "the land between the two rivers." It lay in the triangle of land formed where the Hockanum River joins its waters to the Connecticut. The lands of the valley, Wahginnacut assured Puritan leaders in Boston, were "very fruitful," and to further encourage settlement, the sachem offered both corn to feed new settlers and a tribute of eighty beaver skins to be paid annually.[2]

John Winthrop, Massachusetts' governor, refused Wahginnacut's offer. He was more than aware that the Podunks chafed under the authority of the powerful Pequots, who dominated the territory between the bay and the Connecticut River, and that hostilities had recently broken out between the two nations. Trade with New Amsterdam and with Dutch ships along the northern shore of Long Island Sound had given the Pequots an advantage in the trade for firearms, powder, metal weaponry, and the other European goods that had come to dominate Native commercial and military relations. Since the 1610s, the Pequots had exploited this advantage to assert their political hegemony over neighboring Indian peoples. The Podunks, living just north of present-day Hartford, found themselves cut off from access to this trade by Pequot middlemen. By recruiting English settlers for the Connecticut Valley, Wahginnacut hoped to gain a European ally and trading partner. Winthrop, though, had no desire to antagonize the powerful Pequot nation or to see a vulnerable English town planted amid thousands of "warlike Indians."[3]

The governor's caution in turning down Wahginnacut's hospitality only deferred the showdown between the English and Pequots. As Winthrop himself bemoaned in his journal, the godly Puritan settlers of Massachusetts had little desire or intention to forego the consumer items they had enjoyed in England.[4] And if consumers living in the Bay Colony were to continue importing goods from across the Atlantic, then Massachusetts would need a marketable commodity to make good its balance of payments. Thanks to the high demand for beaver hats, coats, and cloaks in Europe, the pelts of these semiaquatic creatures were by far the most lucrative natural resource available to early New Englanders, and a steady supply of them seemed to beckon from just up the Connecticut River.[5] Despite Governor Winthrop's trepidation, more than eight hundred English settlers moved to the Connecticut Valley over the next five years.[6] Their presence undermined the already fragile balance of power between the Native American nations of New England, contributing to the outbreak of the Pequot War in 1637.

For the Podunks, and for Native nations living elsewhere in the Connecticut Valley and New England, the arrival of European settlers in the seventeenth century merely contributed to the ongoing social adaptations undertaken by Native American communities who had always lived in an environment defined by change. The first Paleo-Indian communities had arrived in New England approximately twelve thousand years earlier, at the tail end of the last Ice Age and just as the great megafauna of the Pleistocene era were disappearing from the landscape. Societies to the southwest introduced maize agriculture to the region about 1000 AD, during a period of mild climactic warming that lengthened growing seasons. Four centuries later, many New England Indian communities decreased their reliance on farming, returning to an economy dominated by hunting and gathering as cooling temperatures made agriculture less tenable in the northeast. Only the villages of the Connecticut Valley, where the river helped moderate temperatures and extend the growing season, continued as agricultural centers. The river villages consequently became hubs of trade, sending corn both to the coast and farther inland in return for dried fish and shells on the one hand, and copper, furs, and other commodities on the other.[7]

Of course, the greatest disruption to New England's early modern Native communities—greater even than shifting temperatures or the regional extermination of beaver on which this chapter focuses—was the introduction of new, devastatingly deadly diseases as a result of European trade and settlement. Trade with northeastern coastal communities—which by the 1520s were themselves engaged in sporadic trading with European fishing vessels— may have introduced some Eurasian pathogens, such as influenza, to the valley during the sixteenth century, but these early outbreaks seem to have led to relatively few deaths.[8]

They certainly never triggered the sort of catastrophic epidemics that would become all too familiar in later centuries. In 1600, New England's indigenous peoples numbered well over one hundred thousand.[9] Their populations plummeted precipitously over the seventeenth and eighteenth centuries as an influx of European traders and settlers introduced diseases with which Native Americans had no previous cultural or immunological experience.[10] An epidemic of mysterious identity—generally referred to simply as "plague" by European witnesses—ravaged southern New England from 1616 to 1619, but largely spared the communities of the Connecticut Valley. In 1633, a smallpox epidemic, this time centered on the villages along the Connecticut

River, swept through the region. Mortality estimates for interior villages are hard to come by, although Pilgrim leader William Bradford recorded the intense suffering experienced the by Indians living near the Plymouth colony trading house at present-day Windsor, Connecticut—"ye poxe breaking and mattering . . . their skin cleaving . . . to the matts they lye on; when they turne them, a whole side will flea [flay] of[f] at once . . . they will be all of a gore blood, most fearfull to behold"—and offered the tragically high estimate that among a tribe living farther north in the valley (likely Pocumtucks) 950 died out of 1,000.[11] Scholars have estimated that the coastal Pequots may have suffered losses of as high as 75 percent, falling from a population in 1600 of about 16,000 to only 4,000 by 1637. The Connecticut River Indians, whose villages held perhaps 12,000 before the epidemic, likely suffered similarly.[12]

Such massive losses of human life dramatically undermined the social and political stability of Native New England. Introduced European diseases often carried off male hunters and female farmers in the prime of life, undermining food security in Native communities. If an entire village, or even a large portion, were incapacitated by disease at a crucial season for planting, harvesting, or hunting, the result would be famine. Hunger and malnutrition left those who avoided the first wave of an epidemic more susceptible when the disease returned, as with the recurring plague of 1616–1619, or when a new disease struck.[13]

Entire villages disappeared and new ones formed as survivors of epidemics banded together to form new societies from the wreckage of the old. Former regional powers declined or competed with emerging powers as they exploited circumstances to expand their regional authority at the expense of rivals. John Smith, for example, wrote of "civill wars" rending Native New England during the plague of the 1610s.[14] Trade with Europeans offered new weapons in this struggle for regional power, driving Native nations into the fur trade. At the same time, competition for trade and unequal access to European merchants further destabilized an already volatile diplomatic environment. Seeking advantage in these shifting political and economic times, New England Indians, including leaders like Wahginnacut, worked to integrate European traders into preexisting Native American networks of diplomacy and trade at the same time that the region's European settlers sought to integrate both Indian labor and the natural resource wealth of New England into an expanding network of transatlantic markets. Together, Native communities and European newcomers created a new economy and political system that would redefine human interaction with the natural world for much of the seventeenth century.

Over a surprisingly short period of time—less than a century—Native American hunters, pursuing the wealth and military power offered by the fur trade, destroyed the beaver populations of southern New England. As beaver pelts flowed into the hands of English (and Dutch and French) traders, the waters of beaver ponds flowed past the decaying remains of the beaver dams that had once held them in place. Hundreds of thousands of acres of wetlands disappeared over the course of just a few decades. Indeed, for most areas of the valley, the landscapes first encountered by English settlers were not in any sense "natural." Nor were they the same landscapes that Native Americans had carefully crafted and cultivated for generations prior to the arrival of Europeans. Rather, the first English settlers of the Connecticut Valley were greeted by a new landscape—what could be termed a postdiluvian landscape—already in the throes of major ecological and hydrological upheavals.

Beaver Ecology

In Pocumtuck legend, Ktsi Amiskw, the Great Beaver, possessed the power to reorder nature. His giant dam halted the course of a mighty river (the Connecticut), flooding what had been dry land and transforming it into a great pond stretching up the length of the Connecticut Valley. Although terrible in life, Ktsi Amiskw left a rich legacy for the ancestors of the Pocumtucks. Slain by the hero Hobomok, the Great Beaver's dam gradually drained to reveal a verdant valley, full of game and soils far more fertile than the surrounding lands. Modern understandings of the ecological role played by beaver echo this older Pocumtuck understanding. Biologists refer to beaver as a "keystone species"—one whose behavior affects the presence and relative abundance of multiple other species within an ecosystem. Unlike in the story of Ktsi Amiskw, however, beaver historically played an overwhelmingly positive role in Native American economies.

Like human beings, beaver possess the ability to profoundly reshape the physical world by applying their labor to the natural resources around them. Beaver transform the hydrology of rivers and streams by constructing dams from tree trunks, limbs, stones, and mud. As the water backs up behind the dam, a pond forms. The beaver of the colony then construct a separate lodge in the midst of their pond. Underwater passageways provide access to the lodge's interior and the encircling waters of the beaver pond provide protection from predators. When ice forms in the pond and over the top of lodges in winter, this protective shell provides insulation against the cold air outside.

The aquatic plants that flourish in beaver ponds provide the colony with a portion of their sustenance, the remainder coming from the bark of trees felled for construction and repair work on the lodge and dam. In sum, beaver engineer their own habitat and, in so doing, reengineer the land- and waterscapes which they inhabit.

Prior to the seventeenth century, beaver inhabited almost every body of water in New England. Beaver dams dotted the landscape, impounding and slowing the flow of the countless brooks and streams that eventually came together to form the Connecticut. Every major tributary housed multiple beaver colonies. Only the smallest brooks, those with too little flowing water to produce a proper pond, escaped their attention. Even the Connecticut River itself, too powerful for most of its length to be held back by the timber, mud, and stones that make up a beaver dam, would have housed a few intrepid beaver colonies in the slack waters of its more tranquil elbows and meanders.[15]

The approximately eleven thousand square miles of the Connecticut drainage basin likely supported upward of half a million beaver prior to the fur trade. The ponds sequestered behind the dams built by these half million beaver—maybe as many as one hundred thousand individual impoundments—would have varied in size from a few square feet to hundreds of acres. These beaver colonies formed a dense mosaic of nearly contiguous ponds and wetlands stretching along the length of most rivers and streams. One of the early settlers of Massachusetts provided a glimpse of these vast interior wetlands, writing in the 1630s of "swamps, some be ten, some twenty, some thirty miles long."[16] Taken together, beaver ponds may have engulfed up to 40 percent of the length of each of the Connecticut's tributaries.[17] While not quite on the scale of Ktsi Amiskw's engineering handiwork, early seventeenth-century beaver ponds likely covered hundreds of thousands of acres within the basin—perhaps as much as nine hundred thousand acres, approximately 12 percent of the total Connecticut watershed.[18]

Beaver not only lived within the natural landscape of the Connecticut Valley, to an appreciable extent they *created* it. Long-term beaver occupation engineered much of the fertile bottomlands lining the Connecticut and its many tributaries, the very lands that first attracted English settlers to the valley in the 1630s. In the absence of beaver ponds, swiftly flowing streams would have gradually eaten away their beds and banks. The valleys of the watershed would have grown deeper and their banks steeper. Beaver dams slackened the flow of waters both within the ponds they impounded and in downstream stretches of river, decreasing stream bank erosion.

Indeed, the engineering skills of beaver actually reversed the process of stream bank erosion. Over time, beaver habitation built up rich meadowlands along the banks of tributary waterways.[19] Rain and snowmelt runoff from the mountains, hills, and uplands of the watershed carried gravel, sand, silt, and soil into the streams of the region. As these waterways entered beaver ponds and their flow slowed, suspended sediment settled to the bottom of the pond. Individual beaver dams remain in operation for decades, sustaining multiple generations of a beaver colony and multiplying the effects of sediment retention over time.[20] Deposited sediment gradually raised the floor of these ponds, until grasses and swampland brush could take root and the pond site became too shallow to house a beaver lodge. When this happened, the beaver would move on in search of a new dam site. Abandoned by its engineers, the old dam would decay, and the last shallow waters impounded behind it would drain away to reveal a lush meadow. Given sufficient time—the several millennia beaver thrived in New England following the last Ice Age—the aggregate action of beaver colonies throughout the Connecticut watershed resulted in the painstakingly gradual aggradation of valley floors.

Beaver ponds played an important role in determining the species composition of the woodlands that, at least in part, came to cover these newly formed valley lands. The presence of beaver ponds raises the water table in a landscape. In the long term, those trees poorly adapted to life in wet soils— primarily pines and firs—slowly lose out to trees more tolerant of higher water tables. Most notable among these latter are aspens and birches, the two species most preferred by beaver for construction material and food. The cumulative effect of the hundreds of thousands of acres of beaver-engineered wetlands in pre–fur trade New England meant that birch and aspen stands would have been far more common than they are today.[21] In essence, the beaver could be said to have farmed their own preferred tree species.

By engineering new ponds and wetlands, beaver also created habitat for numerous other species. Beaver ponds and the semisubmerged wetlands that often lay along their edges support a biomass that ranges from two to five times greater than comparable undammed stretches of stream. Species that call beaver ponds home tend to be extremely rare or nonexistent in other stretches of a watershed. Fish, bird, amphibian, reptile, mammal, aquatic invertebrate, and aquatic plant species that require ponded or slow moving waters to grow, breed, and/or feed proliferate in the ponds and wet meadows that beaver engineer.[22] As a consequence, the pre-seventeenth-century Connecticut Valley, with its thriving beaver population, supported far more species and a greater overall biomass than did the eighteenth-century watershed.

Figure 2. This vignette from a 1715 British map of North America greatly
exaggerates the size of beaver colonies (which usually contained no more than
six individuals), but does show that turn-of-the-eighteenth-century Europeans
possessed some awareness of the beaver's impact within a landscape. Hermann
Moll, "A View of ye Industry of ye Beavers" (1715). *A New and Exact Map of
the Dominions of the King of Great Britain on ye Continent of North America*,
London: 1715. Courtesy of the John Carter Brown Library at Brown University.

Despite the hostility ascribed to the legendary Ktsi Amiskw, the Pocumtucks and other Native Americans living in New England prior to the seventeenth century enjoyed a largely symbiotic relationship with the region's
beaver. Although beaver was considered a delicacy among many of the
nations of the northeast, their meat never formed a staple of Native American
diets. Instead, beaver contributed to Native American food supplies by creating novel habitats in which numerous other species could flourish. Multiple

species of fish, frogs and toads, tortoises, and freshwater mussels made their homes in beaver ponds and contributed to the dietary diversity and seasonal food security of Native communities.[23]

Beaver also transformed streamside woodlands in ways that supported Native American hunting and foraging. As they cut timber, beaver ranged up to one hundred yards beyond their dams. Selectively cutting down trees, beaver created gaps in the canopies of woodlands bordering their ponds. These new parklike stretches of woodland promoted the growth of myriad plant species whose growth was otherwise held in check by a lack of sunlight.[24] The growth of new succulents, in turn, attracted game animals like deer and moose, which also browsed the aquatic plants of the beaver pond. Native American communities made use of these new parklands both by harvesting edible plants, like blueberries, and by hunting the game they attracted.

Finally, the beaver meadows that emerged at the end of a pond's life cycle provided perhaps the most important benefit to local Indian communities. Just as beaver ponds trapped sediment, they also became a holding site for organic material. Streams and rivers swept along leaves, branches, grasses, animal carcasses, and other decaying matter and deposited them as they entered the slack waters of the beaver pond. Algae and bacteria decomposed this natural compost, returning nutrients to the soil at the pond's bottom. As sediment and organic detritus accumulated, the pond floor slowly rose and eventually gave way to a lush meadow. Wild food plants and other succulents flourished in the rich soils of these newly emerged meadows. This flora, in turn, continued to provide excellent browsing for the deer and moose that had formerly fed upon the pond's aquatic vegetation. The fertile soils of former beaver ponds also made excellent planting grounds for the horticultural nations living in southern New England. Because beaver ponds acted as natural nutrient traps, soils in beaver meadows would have contained over four times the nitrogen of soils in surrounding areas.[25] And since maize draws heavily on nitrogen in soils during its growth cycle, beaver meadows could offer Indian agriculturalists far better yields than surrounding planting sites.

For their part, Native Americans set seasonal fires to preserve meadows against the encroachment of forests and to maintain parklike woodlands for hunting. As a side effect, Native American landscape management promoted the growth of certain tree species at the expense of others. Many of the fast-growing tree species best able to take advantage of the seasonal recycling of nutrients through burning—like aspen and birch—happened to be those most favored by beaver as food and construction material.[26] In the long term, Indian burning practices created habitat more favorable to beaver colonization at the same time that beaver engineered a landscape that favored human hunting, foraging, and farming.

As they worked to engineer their environment, beaver also served as an important buttress against ecological disturbance. Ponds and wetlands acted as reservoirs during periods of drought. They provided catchments in seasons of heavy rains or especially heavy snowmelts, reducing torrential flooding. When high waters overflowed or swept away a dam, surviving beaver or new colonizers would eventually repair or replace it, restoring the landscape to its predisturbance state.[27] In the beaver's absence, the landscape of New England would have contained more swiftly flowing waterways, deeper gullies and valleys; more dry land, but less fertile soils. Open meadows and parklike woodlands would have been less common, as would game animals like deer and moose, which thrive in such habitat. Overall biodiversity would have been greatly lessened, and some species which rely on ponds for breeding or feeding may have been almost completely absent.

Echoes of the beaver's ecological role in creating the Connecticut Valley can be easily discerned in the legend of Ktsi Amiskw, but instead of a single giant beaver creating the fertile lands of the valley, the rich soils of the watershed were the product of tens of thousands (and, over generations, perhaps millions) of smaller dams. And if the story of Hobomok's slaying of Ktsi Amiskw seems to run counter to the symbiosis that actually characterized the human-beaver ecological relationship prior to the seventeenth century, it seems all too appropriate when viewing this same relationship through the prism of the transatlantic fur trade. In the Pocumtucks' geography, the body of the slain Ktsi Amiskw became a mountain ridge that loomed over their historic heartland. The English who founded the town of Deerfield within sight of the ridge saw something different in its distinct shape. In an act of toponymical dispossession, they renamed the ridge Mount Sugarloaf. The Great Beaver was symbolically transformed into a manifestation of the desire for imported luxuries—an apt metaphor for the seventeenth-century fur trade.

The Fur Trade

Furs, including those of the Eurasian beaver (*Castor fiber*), were a staple of elite fashion throughout medieval Europe. Members of the royalty, nobility, and upper clergy drove a demand for fine furs that, by the high middle ages, contributed to a bustling trade between trappers, furriers, and their wealthy clients. Gradually, the most popular furbearers—sables, ermines, beaver—began to disappear across much of their former ranges. The beaver, for example, had disappeared from England by the end of the thirteenth century and from the whole of Great Britain by the beginning of the fifteenth, a victim of overhunting for its fur (and, likely, of habitat loss in the face of efforts to drain and improve agricultural lands).[28] This process of beaver destruction was not limited to Great Britain, but instead proceeded upon approximately the same schedule throughout northern Europe. By the late middle ages the aristocratic classes of western and southern Europe had become increasingly dependent upon trade with the Rus to their east to supply them with the luxurious furs that helped mark them off from their social inferiors.[29]

By approximately the mid-sixteenth century, overhunting for export had led to the near extermination of beaver, sable, and other furbearers even in Russian lands. To hold onto the lucrative state revenues generated by the fur trade, Ivan IV (known as "the Terrible") of Muscovy sent his armies east to drive the Tartars from Siberia and subjugate the native hunters of the region. The Muscovites would eventually—after eight decades—win their wars and extend their fur trading empire to the Pacific. The hostilities that ensued in the meantime, together with growing fur shortages in Russia, led to rising international prices in the late 1500s.[30] As Russian armies marched east, the same historical forces driving Ivan the Terrible's conquest of Siberia encouraged merchants in the Netherlands, France, and England to look west for a new, cheaper supply of furs at just the historical moment that maritime explorers were introducing the lands of northeastern North America to an expanding world economy.[31]

The availability of American furs to western European consumers contributed to a larger consumer revolution taking place during the Age of Exploration. As European traders increasingly integrated producers in the Americas, Africa, and Asia into an expanding world economy, luxury goods once available only to the most elite members of European society began to move down market. As furs streamed across the Atlantic, prices fell, and this luxury once reserved for kings and nobility increasingly appeared in the wardrobes of the gentry and professional classes. Besides their appeal as a traditional marker of social status, garments of beaver retained the same qualities that made their former owners so successfully adapted to semi-aquatic lifestyles in often frigid climes. Beaver fur was warm, water resistant, and—once it had been felted—strikingly soft. For Europeans gripped in the throes of the Little Ice Age, beaver pelts held an obvious appeal. By the seventeenth century, lawyers, clerics, clerks, military officers, and their wives in England sported cloaks, capes, mittens, pantaloons, and, especially, hats made of North American beaver (*Castor canadensis*). By the 1640s, beaver hats had become the preferred headwear of a broad economic and political cross section of English society, sported by king and cavaliers, and Puritans and parliamentarians alike.[32]

Consequently, the Dutch and English who arrived in the Connecticut Valley in the seventeenth century looked out at the extensive beaver dams and ponds spread across the countryside and imagined the wealth that their architects' hides might fetch. Strong demand and good prices in Europe meant that a cargo of New England beaver pelts guaranteed welcome profits for European merchants and settlers trying to finance their new colonies in America. As one nineteenth-century New England historian observed: "The colonist desired Indian corn and venison, but all the world desired beaver."[33] Or, at least, all the European world.

Indian hunters in the Connecticut basin and elsewhere desired the metal kettles, pots, knives, and firearms that they received in payment for their beaver pelts. Prior to the fur trade, Indian communities in eastern North America had utilized the beaver for meat and clothing, and had used its impressive incisors to make cutting tools. But for Native communities living in New England in the seventeenth century, beaver and the other furbearing mammals of the American north came to represent a much wider range of newly available commodities. Consumers in Europe may have provided the commercial demand, but it was Native American hunters (themselves also consumers) who formed the sharp spear point of the fur trade. As Massachusetts settler William Wood observed in 1634, "These beasts are too cunning for the English. . . . All the Beaver which the English have, comes first from the Indians."[34]

European fishermen pioneered the fur trade with New England's coastal communities in the first decades of the sixteenth century. For the sailors on these early fishing vessels, bartering furs from coastal Indians represented a lucrative sideline to the cod fishery, the primary economic motivator for their cross-ocean ventures. These sixteenth-century fishermen offered small bits of metal—nails, fishing hooks, and, perhaps, knives—and in exchange Indians often, literally, sold them the beaver coats off their backs. By the closing decades of the century, however, it had become apparent to many European merchants and statesmen that the financial returns from North American furs justified pursuing that trade in its own right.

In 1614, Dutch explorer Adriaen Block captained the first ship to sail up the Connecticut River while exploring the Long Island coast in search of trading opportunities. Block's ship, the *Onrust* ("Restless"), penetrated upriver perhaps as far as present-day Hartford. Sailing east from the mouth of the

Figure 3. The mid-ground of this vignette from an early eighteenth-century map depicts Indians using metal-headed axes and spears to hunt beaver with the assistance of dogs. Elsewhere, two hunters have treed a bear while another pair course a moose in the background. Henri Abraham Chatelain, "Vignettes of Indians Hunting Beaver" (1719). *Carte Tres Curieuse de la Mer du Sud*, Amsterdam: 1719. Map reproduction courtesy of the Mapping Boston Collection at the Norman B. Leventhal Map Center at the Boston Public Library.

Connecticut, Block established the first trade contacts between the Dutch and the powerful Pequot nation, whose territory centered on the Thames River. Over the course of the next two decades, the Pequots' commercial relationship with the Dutch would transform the political and ecological landscape of southern New England and draw the Native nations of the Connecticut Valley firmly within the transatlantic network of the fur trade. Over the course of the late 1610s through early 1630s, the Dutch operating out of New Netherland exported approximately ten thousand beaver skins a year.[35] Many of these the Dutch obtained from Native trappers operating along the Hudson River, but a sizable percentage likely came from the Pequot trade, and most of these latter furs (perhaps a few thousand) would have come from subordinate villages lying within the Connecticut watershed.

At first, the Pequots may have taken advantage of their fortuitous placement along Long Island Sound merely to act as middlemen between the Dutch and Native communities lying farther inland. Pequot traders exchanged cloth and metal implements obtained from the Dutch and acted as a funnel through which the beaver pelts of southern New England flowed into the hands of Dutch traders. Soon, however, the Pequots sought to turn their commercial advantages into political hegemony. Direct access to Dutch firearms and other metal weaponry gave the Pequots a military advantage that allowed the nation to extend its authority over neighboring tribes.[36] In 1626, Sequin, the sachem of the Wangunks, an Indian village near present-day Middletown, led a coalition of Connecticut Valley Indians against the Pequots in an attempt to break the latter's monopoly on the Dutch trade in the region. Sequin and his allies were defeated after a series of "three desperate pitched battles" and thereafter required to pay an annual tribute to the Pequots. The Pequot demanded that a substantial portion of this tribute be paid in beaver skins.[37]

The strategic benefits that arose from the beaver trade spawned competition and then violence farther inland as well, in the territory lying between the Connecticut and the Hudson River. The Five Nations of the Iroquois Confederacy had been attempting to establish their control of the beaver trade in this stretch of lands since at least the first decade of the seventeenth century. In 1628, a military offensive by the Mohawks, the easternmost of the Iroquois nations, defeated the Mahicans, whose territory had formerly encompassed the interriver region, along with their allies among the Pocumtuck, Sokoki, and Pennacook villages of the middle and upper Connecticut Valley. Reeling from this defeat, the Mahicans withdrew from the Hudson watershed to concentrate on the portions of their hunting territory that lay closer to the Connecticut. Intermittent violence followed for the next five decades. The Mahicans, Pocumtucks, and Sokokis repeatedly clashed with the Mohawks as both sides sought to control the beaver trade of the lands west and north of the Connecticut River.[38] As the milliners of Europe ramped up their production of the beaver hats that had recently become the height of European fashion, violence engulfed the frontiers of Native New England.

Throughout the 1620s–1630s the Indian nations of the middle and upper Connecticut watershed—the Mahicans, the Pocumtucks, the Sokokis, and, one could add, the Nipmucs and Pennacooks—straddled three separate spheres of influence within the broader fur trade of the northeast. To the west were the lands that by 1628 had become dominated by Mohawk hunters trading with the Dutch operating out of the Hudson River. The growing political hegemony of the Pequots lay to the south. But trading opportunities also presented themselves to the north. The French founded their first

permanent trading post at the mouth of the St. Lawrence in 1615, just one year
after Adriaen Block opened Dutch commercial relations with the Pequots.
The Wabanaki nations inhabiting what would become Maine and southern
Quebec maintained close commercial and political ties to the French from
the early sixteenth century forward and participated actively in the fur trade.
Western Abenaki nations like the Sokokis and Cowasucks maintained ties
with the French and with other Native American middlemen in the north,
providing their regional allies with an alternative market for their Connecticut Valley furs.

The fur trade tied the Indian hunters and trappers of the Connecticut Valley not just to European merchants and, through them, European customers and producers living across the ocean, but also to Indian manufacturers
living to their south.[39] Following their victory in the Mahican War of 1628,
the Mohawks began extracting annual tribute from the defeated nations of
the middle Connecticut Valley, a large portion of which had to be paid in
wampum. Wampum was produced in largest quantities along the shores of
Long Island Sound. During the 1620s, the Pequots began consolidating their
control over these wampum-producing communities as a means of monopolizing trade with the Dutch. In the 1620s and the early 1630s, Iroquois tribute
demands forced the middle and upper valley Indians to integrate themselves
into the Dutch fur trade system by providing pelts to the Pequots in exchange
for wampum. As a result, the tribes of the middle Connecticut Valley found
themselves between the proverbial rock and a hard place; militarily and politically envassaled to the emerging hegemony of Iroquoia to the west and com-
mercially beholden to growing Pequot power in the south. Consequently, the
nations of the valley welcomed the appearance of the English in the east, first
at Plymouth in 1620 and then along Massachusetts Bay in the 1630s, as an
opportunity to free themselves from the control of their powerful neighbors.[40]

As they settled the New England coast in the early seventeenth century,
English adventurers began to view the fur trade of the Connecticut Valley
as theirs for the taking. Edward Winslow, the governor of Plymouth, led a
successful trading expedition up the Connecticut in 1633.[41] A second group
of Plymouth traders, seeking to follow their governor's example, founded
a trading house on the future site of Windsor in the same year. The Dutch
responded to these English incursions by establishing the House of Good
Hope, a trading fort built on Podunk lands but granted to the Dutch by the
hegemonic Pequots.[42] Many Bay Colony leaders and merchants also began
to agitate for a trade route into New England's interior and access to the fur
wealth that could be found there.[43] A 1634 petition from a group of settlers

eager to take up lands in what would become Hartford laid the matter bare: the Massachusetts Bay Colony needed to secure control of the Connecticut or risk losing out to either Dutch competitors or rival English colonists from Plymouth.[44]

A breakdown in relations between the Dutch and their erstwhile trading partners, the Pequots, finally triggered a shift in Bay Colony policy. In early 1634, a band of Pequots, jealous of their nation's commercial monopoly in the southern Connecticut Valley, attacked a group of Narragansett Indians traveling to trade with the Dutch at the House of Good Hope. Incensed at this interference with their trade, the Dutch retaliated by imposing an embargo on their former commercial partners. In all likelihood, the Dutch reasoned that weakening the Pequots would allow them to establish a more direct commerce with the other Indian peoples of the region. In fact, this attempt to shake up the distribution of power within the fur trade of New England merely drove the Pequots into the arms of the English, with whom they sought to negotiate a new treaty of friendship at the end of 1634. In exchange for this friendship, Governor Winthrop recorded, the Pequots offered "all their right at Connecticut."[45]

With the Pequots now in an uncertain position, the Massachusetts General Court moved to supplant Dutch influence in southern New England. In 1635, the court reversed its position and allowed the settlement of Newtown (later Hartford) on the north bank of the Little River (today's Park River) at its junction with the Connecticut. This placed the Dutch House of Good Hope, located on the Little River's southern bank, under the watchful eyes of English colonists. Also in 1635, the general court formally approved settlements at Windsor and Wethersfield (both of which had been founded without the Court's sanction at the end of 1634). Adventurers backed by two wealthy Puritan lords founded Saybrook toward the end of 1635. Finally, wealthy merchant William Pynchon founded Springfield, the last of the original English Connecticut Valley towns, in 1636. Each of these towns owed its early settlement, at least in part, to English ambitions to dominate the beaver trade of the New England interior.

For the Pequots, the chance of a treaty with the English offered the hope of maintaining the status quo—trade with the English would replace trade with the Dutch and allow the Pequots to continue in their role as middlemen and regional hegemon. The English, however, viewed the treaty as an opportunity to bring the Pequots under their political heel. In exchange for peace and commerce, the Massachusetts Bay Colony required the Pequots to pay forty beaver skins, thirty otter skins, and four hundred fathoms of wampum.

This small fortune would have given Massachusetts a strong advantage in competing for the trade of those more northerly Connecticut Valley nations who required wampum as tribute payments for the Mohawks. The Pequot delegates at Boston promised to bring the proposal to their sachems.[46]

Such a demand represented a double insult to the Pequots. It would likely have beggared the nation to gather such a wealth of wampum, forcing the Pequots to lean heavily upon their tributary networks and likely stirring resentment. In Indian diplomacy such a one-sided payment of wampum held strong symbolic meaning, marking the paying nation as a political subordinate of the recipient. In effect, the Bay Colony's leaders, through their demand, had declared the Pequots a dependent nation of the English. In the face of these insults, and despite the risk of being shut out of the fur trade, the Pequot council rejected the treaty's terms.[47]

Their commercial and political rivalry with the Pequots shaped how English colonial officials reacted to the deaths at Indian hands of two English traders, the first in 1633 and the second in 1636.[48] In late 1633, Captain John Stone of Virginia—a man who had formerly been banished from Boston for drunkenness and suspicion of piracy—kidnapped two Western Niantics, whom he forced to act as pilots for his pinnace while trading up the Connecticut River. The next night, while at anchor, a party of Niantics boarded Stone's ship to rescue their captive comrades. Stone and the other Englishmen aboard were killed during the rescue, and the powder stores of the ship were accidentally set alight, causing it to explode. News of Stone's death arrived in the Bay Colony in January of 1634. Many in Massachusetts and Plymouth took the view that Stone deserved his fate—one Massachusetts colonist even suggested that the Niantics had acted as God's divine retribution against the sinful Captain Stone. Publicly, however, Massachusetts blamed the Pequots— to whom the Western Niantics were tributary—for Stone's death and for sheltering his killers. The Pequots insisted that the Niantics were justified in their actions and, besides, had not known that Stone was English and instead thought they were killing Dutchmen. Within the context of the Anglo-Pequot trade negotiations taking place in 1634, English insistence on restitution for Stone's murder provided the Pequots one more reason to reject the Bay Colony's extortionary demands.[49]

In July of 1636, another English trader, John Oldham, was discovered dead upon his pinnace, which had run aground on Block Island, off the Rhode Island coast. Oldham had been exiled from Plymouth Plantation in 1624 for conspiring against the colony's government, but had subsequently settled in Massachusetts and prospered through trade with the Indians and other English colonies. Massachusetts officials strongly suspected that Old-ham's murder had been engineered by a group of Narragansett leaders angry that the Englishman had been trading with their Pequot rivals. However, Narragansett ambassadors insisted that these conspirators had fled Narra-gansett territory and been given sanctuary among the Pequots. English lead-ers proved surprisingly willing to accept this somewhat unlikely story, and the fallout from a Narragansett plot became the Pequots' problem.[50]

A force of 90–120 men from Massachusetts first launched a retaliatory raid against the Indians of Block Island, and then, after being joined by troops from Connecticut, continued on to a large Pequot village at the mouth of the Thames River. The English demanded that the Pequots surrender those responsible for Oldham's murder. In the process they also renewed their demand that John Stone's killers be turned over and further insisted that the Pequots accept the extortionary terms of the 1634 treaty of friendship. Unable to satisfy these demands (the Narragansett Indians guilty of Oldham's death were beyond their reach, the Niantics who had led the assault against Stone's ship had since all either died of smallpox or been killed by the Dutch, and the demands of the 1634 treaty remained infeasible), the Pequots prepared for war. Their demands unmet, the English attacked the Pequots at the mouth of the Thames only to find their village deserted.[51]

These hostilities came at an especially disastrous time for the Pequot nation. Their villages had been particularly hard hit by the smallpox epi-demic of 1633–1634, in which three out of every four Pequots died. Then, in the summer of 1635, a hurricane made ground in southern New England, destroying crops as they stood in the fields. Hunger stalked New England from 1635 to 1636, striking European and Indian communities alike. Short-ages in maize harvests may have placed further strain on subordinate villages who owed tribute to the Pequots, and the specter of famine likely contrib-uted to the English rush to war. Raiding parties, especially those coming out of the hard-hit Connecticut Valley, made the seizure of Pequot corn supplies a wartime priority.[52] Finally, the wealth and authority that came from the fur trade had not been evenly distributed among the villages and sachems of the Pequot nation. By the 1630s, a group of Pequot leaders who had been shut out of the inner circles of power, led by the sachem Uncas, had formed a splinter nation, the Mohegans, who sought their own commercial and mil-itary alliance with the English at the expense of the larger Pequot confeder-acy.[53] Reeling from natural disasters and beset by enemies both without and within, the Pequots had, by 1636, reached the nadir of their military and political power.

Despite now being outnumbered by the English, the Pequots retaliated in 1637, leading to a full-scale war for political control of southern New England. Rival nations (most notably the Narragansetts), eager to see the Pequots defeated and their hold over the regional fur trade destroyed, allied with the English. Meanwhile, many of the Indian communities whom the Pequots had reduced to political subordination, and upon whom the Pequots depended for military assistance, abandoned their erstwhile political masters. The Mohegans became key allies of the English, while many Connecticut Valley villages chose to remain neutral in the conflict. English colonists waged a campaign of fire and wanton slaughter against the hopelessly outnumbered Pequots. The majority who survived the war were either taken captive by their Indian opponents or enslaved by the English. Many of the latter were sold to the West Indies, joining other victims of the transatlantic slave trade to toil on tobacco and cotton plantations, and perhaps contribute their labor to the development of the still nascent sugar economy. Only a small fraction of the nation escaped to reconstitute a community on the Thames River. Having violently expelled the Pequots from their position in the New England fur trade, English traders eagerly began a direct commerce with the Indian nations of the lower and middle Connecticut Valley.

English entry into the valley fur trade quickly disrupted relationships between competing Native American nations in the region. Competition between European traders—both between individual English traders and between the English and the Dutch—led to a sharp uptick in the quantity of manufactured goods flowing into the hands of Indian traders. At the center of this new English fur trade in the valley sat the town of Springfield. William Pynchon and the other founders of Springfield located their town at the site where the Connecticut River was joined by the Westfield River; the latter's basin being especially renowned among early traders for the density of its beaver populations.[54] The town's location to the north of the other Connecticut Valley towns granted William Pynchon, and later his son John, an advantage in wooing Indian traders traveling down the Connecticut from the north. Since Springfield was located just above what became known as Enfield Falls, the Pynchons were well-situated to intercept Indian traders who otherwise would have needed to portage their canoes around the rapids. Writing in 1645, Edward Johnson, author of the first printed history of New England, declared that the fur trade at Springfield had already become "of little worth" through the practice of competing merchants "out-buying one another."[55] In 1650, the Dutch director-general at New Amsterdam wrote to the commissioners of the United Colonies of New England to complain that

English terms of trade were far too generous. As a result the Dutch found their trade "damnified and undervalued."[56]

Local Connecticut Valley Indian nations proved the winners—at least in the short run—in this competition between colonial European merchants. For English and Dutch merchants in New England, and the French farther north, their bidding war represented yet another front in the commercial contest being waged by their respective empires in the early seventeenth century. Indian nations in the northeast willingly and shrewdly exploited these interimperial tensions to their own gain. In doing so, they parleyed access to European goods—especially firearms and other metal weaponry—into military and diplomatic power within the shifting network of Indian alliances that defined political relationships in the region.

Local Indian leaders established new trading relationships with first William and, later, his son John Pynchon. The majority of the furs acquired by the Pynchons at Springfield came from hunters and traders operating out of the Pocumtuck villages of Pocumtuck, and Norwottuck, from the Agawam (today's Westfield) River watershed, from the Sokoki town of Squakheag, and from hunters (other western Abenakis and likely Mahicans, as well) operating farther north in the Connecticut basin. The Indians of the valley also provided the Pynchons with maize, upon which the survival of Springfield and the other Connecticut towns depended in the early years of settlement.[57] Wampum obtained for furs and maize paid off the tribute demands of the Mohawks and could, potentially, buy the support of new Native allies. Meanwhile, direct access to English tools and weaponry increased the military power of those tribes who called the middle Connecticut home.

The fur trade of the Connecticut watershed, and of New England more generally, continued to revolve around the shifting military and diplomatic relationships between the Native nations of the region. The fur trade between the Pynchons of Springfield and the Indians of the Connecticut Valley reached its apex in the early 1650s, peaking in 1654 before declining precipitously. During these years, the Iroquois redirected their hunting and military efforts to the west and north, toward the lands of the Hurons, Petuns, and Neutrals. This realignment of Iroquois imperial interests freed Pocumtuck, Nipmuc, and Sokoki hunters from competition both in the northern Connecticut Valley and in the lands lying immediately westward. It also lessened the risk of renewed warfare with the Mohawks. The conclusion of hostilities following the Mahican War in 1628 had brought an uneasy peace. The Connecticut Valley nations resented Mohawk demands for tribute, and their acquiescence was ensured only by the threat of superior Iroquois military might. As long as Mohawk hunters ranged the same territories as hunters from the Connecticut Valley villages, the potential existed for misunderstanding and violence. This threat kept valley hunters close to home during the 1630s–1640s. But in the 1650s, with the Mohawks distracted farther west, valley hunters expanded their hunting efforts northward and westward along Connecticut tributaries and, consequently, increased their take of beaver and other furbearing species.[58]

Although the volume of pelts traded to English merchants during the seventeenth century fluctuated with the political climate, the overall trend was clearly one of declining fur yields.[59] Conflict in any given year could divert hunters and trappers to more martial pursuits, or else make them fearful of venturing into hunting territories that lay too far from the relative safety of fortified villages. As a long-term process, however, the incessant warfare that surrounded competition over the fur wealth of New England, and of northeastern North American more generally, created conditions that encouraged the extirpation of beaver from the region. French agents operating to the northeast of the Connecticut Valley had noted as early as the 1630s the tendency of Indian fur traders to "kill all, great and small, male and female" when harvesting beaver from a colony.[60] A similar practice seems to have prevailed among nations operating in the Connecticut basin. Mohawk hunters ranging eastward threatened Mahican, Sokoki, and Pocumtuck hunting territories in the Connecticut Valley. Indeed, Iroquois pressure culminated in a series of raids in 1664 and 1665 that resulted in the destruction of Pocumtuck and Squakheag, the two most populous villages in the central valley.[61] Under such conditions, not harvesting as many pelts as possible became tantamount to handing them over to the enemy; an enemy who would exchange their poached beaver for new weapons that might be turned against one's own community. The logic of conservation broke down and incentives to exploit—or, one might say, overexploit—furbearing species prevailed.[62]

Records from the earliest years of the trade are hard to come by. But the account books of John Pynchon show that in the five-year span from 1652 to 1657, this premier trader of the valley received the pelts of nearly 10,000 beaver. From 1658 to 1674, Pynchon shipped another 6,500 beaver skins from the valley.[63] To these sums should be added the unknown thousands of beaver pelts collected by merchants active in other parts of the valley. Each of the Connecticut colony towns, for example, granted a single merchant the monopoly on the beaver trade with Native Americans operating in its hinterland, and most of these merchants' records have not weathered the ravages of time and chance as well as have Pynchon's accounts.[64] Other English land-owners in the valley may have been legislatively prohibited from trading with the Indians, but nothing prevented them from hunting and trapping themselves on a small scale—further increasing the number of beaver that were likely taken in the early decades of settlement. And, finally, the Mohawks funneled an unknown number of pelts into Dutch hands.

As a result of these commercial pressures, beaver populations in the Connecticut watershed collapsed. The beaver trade of the lower and middle valley had entered decline by the 1650s, as evidenced by John Pynchon's account books. When Pynchon's trade rebounded, slightly, in the late 1660s it was only because his Indian trading partners had taken advantage of Mohawk distractions farther west to push their hunting into the Hudson River watershed.[65] In his 1677 history of New England, the Reverend William Hubbard wrote that beaver, which once had inhabited the lands lying between Casco Bay and the Piscataqua River, had been "gleaned away" as a consequence of the French and English fur trades.[66] Although Hubbard concerned himself primarily with the coastal trade, trading ties between the Abenaki nations living here and those living along the Connecticut meant that the latter region had been heavily depleted as well. By the turn of the century, beaver had disappeared from southern New England and only vestige populations survived in the northern valley.[67]

For the Pocumtucks, the legend of Ktsi Amiskw kept alive a folk memory of a time when their ancestors had waged war not just against their Mohawk rivals, but, in a sense, against the beaver of their valley as well. The ancient Pocumtucks had called upon Hobomok to destroy the Great Beaver. Their descendants, encouraged by European traders, dealt with Ktsi Amiskw's lesser cousins themselves. Over time, beaver disappeared from the Connecticut basin, their dams fell, and their ponds drained. The mutually beneficial environment that the beaver and Native Americans of New England had maintained for thousands of years disappeared in a few short decades. In this sense, Ktsi Amiskw's fate has offered Pocumtucks (and, for that matter, any Euro-American who should stop to reflect on this appropriated tale) living from the eighteenth century until the present day a parable on the wages of greed. The Great Beaver, in his gluttony, sought to claim the land and resources of the Connecticut Valley for himself. His heedless actions threw the natural environment out of balance. That natural balance was eventually restored, but only after Ktsi Amiskw was forced to pay for his environmental misdeeds.[68] The humans living in the valley would likewise have to endure the ecological consequences of their economic actions.

A Postdiluvian Landscape

Colonial New Englanders were ignorant of the ecological role played by beaver. Nor could they imagine the impact that removing beaver from an ecosystem might have upon the ecology and hydrology of an area. Hunters, likely in concert with farmers attempting to claim wetlands for agriculture, had driven the Eurasian beaver to extinction in Great Britain at least a century before the first English colonists settled in North America. Even before this, knowledge of the beaver was extremely limited among Britons. Illuminated English bestiaries from the thirteenth century—when a dwindling number of beaver colonies may have still persisted in the more remote streams of the kingdom—depicted beaver that more closely resembled dogs, foxes, or even horses than they did actual specimens of C. fiber.[69]

Edward Topsell's *Historie of Four-Footed Beastes*, published in 1607, offered the most complete description of beaver available to England's earliest American colonists. The book's woodcuts provided important corrections on details of beaver anatomy (Topsell's beaver actually looked like beaver), but its text did little to explicate the beaver's relationship with the environment. Topsell presented beaver as piscivores who, when fish became scarce in their ponds, would "leave the water and range up and downe the land, making an insatiable slaughter of young lambes untill . . . they have fed themselves full of flesh, then returne they to the water, from whence they came." Topsell also repeated the medieval belief that when pursued by hunters for its scent glands (from which beaver produce castoreum, a highly prized component in medieval and early modern medicine) the beaver would chew off its own "stones" and throw them to its pursuers in exchange for its life. For Topsell, and for the medieval bestiaries that preceded his text, the veracity of these accounts of beaverly bargaining was less important than their allegorical value. By casting away its own glands, the beaver set an example for humans "to give our pursse to theeves, rather then our lives, and by our wealth to redeeme our danger."[70]

The seventeenth-century chroniclers of New England combined the colonial booster's interest in furs as an exportable commodity with a new appreciation for the beaver's engineering prowess, now on display to the English settlers beginning to push up the river valleys of North America.[71] William Wood, writing in the 1630s, noted the value of beaver as a source of furs and castoreum while also marveling at the creatures' teamwork. He judged their dams and lodges to merit "admiration from wise understanding men."[72] Such sentiments would eventually develop into a new allegorical role for the beaver. In the eighteenth century English artists and authors anthropomorphized the beaver as a paragon of industriousness, and held up their colonies as models of well-ordered efficiency. In a similar vein, French anti-Cartesians pointed to the beaver's engineering genius as proof that animals could possess souls.[73] Unfortunately, such representations did little to advance knowledge of the beaver's broader role in the landscape.[74] Even those colonial authors who eschewed discussing the moral dimensions of beaver behavior focused instead on describing how best to hunt the creatures while showing little interest in the environmental impact of fur harvesting.[75]

Knowledge of the important role that beaver played in creating and maintaining land- and waterscapes was slow to develop. For the English, the fact that most beaver hunting and trapping was done by their Native American trading partners in areas far removed from colonial settlements meant that it was hard to draw a direct link between the removal of beaver from a stretch of stream and the myriad environmental changes that followed. As late as the 1790s, Harvard-educated minister Jeremy Belknap was able to remark in his *History of New Hampshire* that the beaver's capacity for constructing its own environment was "not mentioned by any of the writers of natural history which I have had the opportunity to consult."[76]

It was one of Belknap's correspondents, New Hampshire Congressman Joseph Peirce, who helped make up this scientific shortfall. In a short essay on natural history, Peirce praised the benevolence of "that Being by whom the universe is so wisely governed" whose "design in this little animal [the beaver]" had in the two previous centuries created a landscape providentially suited to the pioneering efforts of English colonists. Precolonial beaver had, by Peirce's account, transformed great stretches of swamps and marshes—the "worst of lands"—into verdant meadows. By creating ponds, beaver had drowned off trees and brush. At the same time "the leaves, bark, rotten wood and other manure, which is washed down by the rains, from the adjacent high lands . . . spread over this pond . . . making it smooth and level." Then Indian hunters, "subservient to the great design of Providence," destroyed the beaver and its dam so that "the whole tract, which before was the bottom of a pond, is covered with wild grass, which grows as high as a man's shoulders, and very thick." These newly formed, lush meadows attracted game animals like deer and moose for Native hunters. They were "of still greater use to new [English] settlers" who found "a mowing field already cleared to their hands . . . and without these natural meadows many settlements could not possibly have been made." Beaver meadows provided early English settlers in New Hampshire and elsewhere in New England sufficient grass for their cattle until they had "cleared ground enough to raise English hay." For Peirce, then, it was the hand of Providence—acting through the teeth of the beaver and the industry of Indian hunters—that had made successful English colonization possible.[77]

Setting aside the role of "Providence," Peirce presented an astute early understanding of the importance of beaver to colonial landscapes. Beaver had historically played an important role in converting woodlands bordering streams into first ponds and wetlands, and then broad, verdant meadows.[78] These meadows provided Native American hunters with game and, later, fed the cattle of the English settlers who appropriated their lands. But while astute, Peirce's late eighteenth-century tribute to the utility of the beaver fell far short of accounting for all of the creature's myriad impacts upon New England's land- and waterscapes.

As beaver ponds disappeared from the landscape in the wake of the fur trade, species diversity declined apace. Bird species that nested in water-logged trees—the blue heron, osprey, woodcocks, and various types of eagle—disappeared or saw their regional populations decline precipitously. Species of woodpecker that fed upon the insects living in these decaying trees also would have declined in number and, as a consequence, birds like black-capped chickadees, nuthatches, tree swallows, and screech owls that live in the holes excavated by woodpeckers would have become scarcer. As the populations of insects associated with ponds and wetlands—like dragon- and damselflies—declined, so too did the populations of birds like the tree swallow and kingbird, which fed upon them. While the declining numbers of many of these bird species would likely not have dismayed early English settlers, or even their Native American neighbors, they may have felt differently about the loss of waterfowl habitat within the Connecticut basin. Duck species—like the wood duck and hooded merganser—lost many of their summer feeding and nesting sites in the region, reducing their numbers and forcing them to concentrate in the watershed's lakes and remaining ponds.[79]

Other pond species also suffered. Frogs, toads, tortoises—all of which local Native American communities relied upon seasonally to supplement their diets—and other species of amphibians and reptiles lost a large percentage of their breeding habitat. Freshwater crayfish continued to thrive in lakes and free-flowing rivers, but their numbers likely declined as the overall amount of freshwater habitat fell. Most obviously, fish populations faced declining habitat as a result of disappearing beaver ponds. Some species suffered more than others. Since beaver ponds are dynamic ecosystems, gradually transitioning from free-flowing stream to pond and back again, different fish species benefit from different stages in the pond lifecycle. Brook trout flourished in the still, well-shaded waters of new beaver ponds. As rising water tables and tree harvesting by beaver opened up the woodland canopies bordering ponds and waterways, yellow perch and sunfish flourished in the warmer, sunbathed waters and fed on the proliferating species of aquatic plants. With the disappearance of beaver dams and the ecological dynamism they fostered, fish of all species became less abundant, and local Native American and Euro-American communities faced declining opportunities for including fresh fish in their regular diet.[80]

This decline in the availability of freshwater fish may in part explain English colonists' later focus on the springtime runs of anadromous fish (those species that live and feed in the ocean but spawn in freshwater streams) like salmon, shad, and alewives. The relationship between beaver and salmon, especially, is an ambiguous one. While young anadromous fish can often pass downstream through the loose weave of limbs that forms a beaver dam, these same dams can pose an obstacle for adult fish attempting to ascend a river to breed. With each subsequent beaver dam on a stream, fewer spawners would have been able to pass. However, placing such geographic limits on anadromous fish actually protected the biodiversity of the river system. Shad and alewives head out to sea within a few months of hatching, but juvenile salmon can linger to feed in their native streams for up to five years, significantly decreasing the population of freshwater fish with whom they compete for food and space.

If beaver dams limited the geographic distribution of anadromous fish, beaver ponds provided important spawning habitat and more abundant food sources to help ensure the survival of the newly hatched fry. As beaver dams disappeared, anadromous fish would likely have expanded their range upstream in each of the Connecticut's tributaries, but their overall numbers may have suffered, just as this new source of competition would have increased the pressure on freshwater fish populations already undergoing habitat loss.[81] Still, the salmon, shad, and alewives would have retained one key advantage. Once their young had passed downstream and made it out into the ocean, the diets of these far-traveling fish no longer relied on the declining resources of the inland river environment. They could feed on the ocean's bounty before returning to their native waterways to spawn, offering a bonanza to the humans who anxiously awaited their annual runs.

A broader phenomenon of nutrient loss within the river system as a whole meant that filter-feeding freshwater mussels also declined, further impoverishing the foraging options available to local Indian communities. Prior to their destruction, beaver ponds had functioned to conserve nutrients within the waters of the Connecticut basin by acting as nutrient sinks.

Filter-feeding mussels and aquatic plants benefitted most directly from these impounded nutrients, but their good fortune reverberated throughout the food chain. Undammed stretches of waterways also felt the impact of beaver ponds. By slowing the overall pace of waterways beaver ponds significantly increased the likelihood that nutrients carried by streams and rivers would be utilized within the drainage basin, rather than being carried out to sea. Detritus in slow moving water was more likely to fall out of the current, to be decomposed and returned to the soil. In this way, beaver ponds not only increased the extent of aquatic habitat in a watershed but also increased the biomass that it was able to support. Without beaver dams holding back these ponds, the overall ability of the watershed to support life declined.[82]

Concurrent species loss meant that the extermination of beaver from New England was a double catastrophe for Indian communities. Beaver provided the most lucrative pelts, but were far from the only furbearers harvested. Minks, river otters, and muskrats contributed a considerable amount to the profits earned by merchants like John Pynchon. As beaver numbers declined, these other species took on new importance for Native hunters. Unfortunately, the population levels of mink, muskrat, and otter were directly linked to the presence of beaver in the landscape. Both minks and otters fed on the fish, amphibians, and invertebrates that thrived in beaver ponds. Muskrats exploited beaver ponds to build their own aquatically protected limb-and-mud lodges. Each of these species suffered an extensive loss of habitat as beaver ponds gave way to meadows. Reduced numbers of these species, added to the loss of the beaver, exacerbated the economic distress faced by Native communities that, by the second half of the seventeenth century, had become increasingly dependent upon the fur trade.[83]

If, from the 1630s to the 1650s, the terms of the fur trade favored Native American hunters, by the 1660s onward, the long-term consequences of the trade had begun to severely undermine Native American claims to the lands of the Connecticut Valley. The Indian nations of the valley continuously reduced the quantity of cropland they cultivated over the course of the seventeenth century. In part, this represented a decline in population occasioned by outbreaks of European diseases, many introduced through contacts in the fur trade. A decline in land under cultivation may also have occurred as a direct result of the fur trade. As Indian men harvested more beaver, women needed to exert more labor cleaning and processing beaver skins into marketable pelts. Since women provided the agricultural labor in Connecticut Valley Indian communities, this new demand may have cut into efforts to plant and maintain crops. With less land under cultivation, and facing declining fur yields, many Connecticut Valley communities chose to sell off territory in order to maintain access to European commodities.[84]

From the mid-1650s forward, the Pocumtucks, and neighboring communities, sold off great chunks of territory, a practice encouraged by English merchants who willingly advanced goods to Indian leaders on credit and then encouraged land cessions to clear these debts. Many of the deeds transferring these lands into English hands contained clauses in which the former Indian owners retained the right to hunt in the ceded lands—often explicitly mentioning beaver among the list of prey that Indian hunters should be allowed to pursue. Still, these land deals likely followed the extirpation of beaver from a given territory, the retained hunting rights representing a claim on any new beaver colonies that might someday return to local waterways. As such, the land cessions that spread through the Connecticut Valley in the 1660s–1680s represent Indian leaders' efforts to market the only merchantable commodity left to them—their land.[85] By the late seventeenth century, the Indian communities of the Connecticut Valley faced the end of the fur trade at the same time that they faced a decline in food security due to declining populations of numerous species of edible plants and animals as an ecological consequence of this trade.

Little wonder that most of the Connecticut Valley Indian nations—including the Mahicans, Pocumtucks, Podunks, and Pennacooks—chose to side with Metacomet during King Philip's War in 1675. The English victory a year later forever broke Native American power in southern and central New England, ensuring English political hegemony in the region. In the decades following this military defeat many Mahicans, Pocumtucks, Podunks, and Pennacooks chose to abandon their Connecticut basin homes to join either the Wabanaki nations to the north or the new Schaghticoke nation along the Connecticut/ Massachusetts/New York border. Other members of these nations integrated themselves within New England's increasingly English-dominated economy as crafts artisans, wage laborers, or European-style farmers.[86]

While the tragic economic and ecological consequences of the fur trade fell disproportionately upon the Native communities of the Connecticut Valley, the region's new Euro-American inhabitants also suffered from the beaver's disappearance. The dynamic life cycle of beaver impoundments— from free-flowing stream, to pond, meadowland, and, after the erosion of streambeds, often back again—provided for the long-term, perpetual rejuvenation of large swaths of fertile meadow and woodlands.[87] The fur trade brought this process to a halt. The overall fertility of soils along waterways would have slowly declined as the cycle of rejuvenation achieved through ponding was brought to an end. The spring freshets continued to annually overspread their floodplains, depositing silt and refreshing the fertility of the broad bottomlands bordering the Connecticut River and its larger tributaries. But lands along lesser streams would have slowly deteriorated. Even the intervales of the Connecticut River itself received less regenerative organic matter than in previous centuries due both to the more rapid flow and the general decline in the nutrient load of the river system as a whole. In the centuries that followed the fur trade, Euro-American farmers had to rely on manuring to rejuvenate soils.[88]

The drainage of beaver ponds by the thousands in the decades of the seventeenth century also had impacts beyond the biology of the Connecticut Valley. The very hydrology of the watershed was transformed. Vast stretches of ponded water and wetlands—perhaps as much as nine hundred thousand acres—would have disappeared from the Connecticut watershed along with the beaver.[89] In many cases, this transformation to dry land brought negative environmental impacts that would plague the new English settlers of the region.

The increased amount of sediment borne all the way downriver to Long Island Sound directly threatened the commerce of the valley.[90] The Connecticut, at its mouth, had never been deep. The first European explorer to visit the river, the Dutch explorer Adriaen Block, declared the river's mouth to be "very shallow" as he sailed upstream. The disappearance of beaver ponds and the loss of wetlands upriver would have only made this problem worse. In the river's tidal zone, waters rushing downstream collide with the incoming tide, slowing, swirling, and dropping their load of soil and silt. Such encounters are most dramatic just south of Hartford, at the far upper reaches of the river's tidal flows. Here the increased sediment load of the Connecticut formed a series of shifting shoals and sandbars that came to plague the maritime trade of what had in its earliest years been a promising port with easy access for small oceangoing vessels. By the late eighteenth century, a traveler on business in Hartford complained that thanks to "these inconveniences the inhabitants are not only compelled to make use of smaller vessels than they could wish, but are also obliged to send them out partially loaded, and to complete their lading at New-London."[91]

Falling local water tables would have followed the collapse of a beaver dam, resulting in a decline in local biodiversity among tree species.[92] Still, it would have taken several decades of forest succession for pines and other wetlands-intolerant species of trees to begin making up the ground lost to beaver dam impoundment. This means that when colonial lumbermen went north in the eighteenth century in search of pine for regional and Atlantic markets, they would have encountered a scarcer supply than if beaver had never inhabited New England. It also means that many second-growth pine forests in those regions may be the result not just of colonial-era lumbering, but also of declining water tables in the wake of collapsing beaver populations.

English settlers were also denied the long-term flood control benefits that beaver dams convey. During heavy rains, ponds acted as a catchment for flood waters. Beaver dams (which one noted environmental historian has eloquently compared to "leaky sieves") then released the waters at a near steady rate. The large-scale transition from ponds and wetlands to dry land that prevailed in the seventeenth-century Connecticut Valley decreased the watershed's ability to deal with flood waters. Where once beaver ponds had helped to sequester rising waters and beaver dams impeded rushing torrents, flood waters now ran freely. In the absence of such wetlands and forest cover, streams and brooks ran swifter and their height fluctuated more dramatically over the course of the year. When the weather was dry, these waterways ran lower and the colonial-era grist and sawmills they powered ceased to run. When seasonal rains came or when an unexpected downpour struck, the streams overran their banks and spread across areas where their new English inhabitants would have preferred they not go.[93]

Writing from the perspective of the late eighteenth century, Jeremy Belknap declared that the beaver "is now become scarce in New Hampshire," but noted that that "the vestiges of its labours are very numerous." Although scarce, Belknap makes clear that New Hampshire did host a beaver population in the 1790s. In the volume of his *History of New Hampshire* devoted to natural history, Belknap recorded his observations on the life and industry of the beaver he encountered along the banks of New Hampshire's streams and ponds. Belknap even recorded the "frequent" practice of laying out new roads in the more rural parts of the state so that they might incorporate beaver dams as crossing points for streams and brooks, thus allowing localities to forego the labor and expense of building a bridge or causeway.[94]

Belknap's observations suggest that at least relict populations of beaver in the Connecticut watershed had survived the commercial onslaught of the seventeenth- and early eighteenth-century fur trade. Perhaps along the secluded small streams of the White and Green Mountains in the north, or the Berkshires in the west, individual colonies had survived unnoticed by hunters. In the absence of countervailing forces within the ecosystem, surviving lodges in the far north or west of the watershed could have recolonized the entire Connecticut Valley in just four decades.[95] Of course, countervailing forces *did* exist (and were multiplying) throughout the Connecticut watershed in the seventeenth and eighteenth centuries.

For example, in Hampshire County, Massachusetts, in the eighteenth century, three successive generations of artisans and their apprentices combined the trades of furrier and hatter and sold their wares to their neighbors in the valley. They purchased most of the furs for their work from the markets in Albany and Boston. A small part of their supply, however, came from local farmers and hunters. Throughout the eighteenth century, this included a small number of beaver, trapped either in Hampshire County or in the territories lying farther to the north in New Hampshire and what would become Vermont.[96] Although the sale of locally trapped beaver was rare in this period, their occasional mention suggests that relict beaver populations from the far north of the Connecticut Valley, or perhaps the sparsely settled Berkshire Mountains, were attempting to recolonize the middle valley. Only continued pressures from hunting, likely supplemented by farmers' efforts to prevent flooding on valuable grazing and croplands, prevented beaver from recolonizing the whole of their former territory in the Connecticut basin.

The Benefits of Extermination

For the English settlers who dispossessed the Native peoples of the Connecticut Valley in the seventeenth and eighteenth centuries, the disappearance of beaver, with their dams and ponds, from the landscape did bring certain benefits. To a degree, the successful establishment of English agriculture in New England depended upon the prior removal of the beaver, a fact that Joseph Peirce first grasped in the 1790s. Had Indian hunters not removed beaver through the fur trade, the English farmers who settled the seventeenth-century valley would have had to exterminate them. This would have only added to the time and effort that colonists were already expending to drain and improve the marshes and swamps of the region, a task that environmental historian Brian Donahue has likened to "the labors of Hercules."[97]

Throughout the seventeenth century, English efforts to "improve" lands by draining them reinforced the general drying out of wetlands due to the annihilation of the beaver. As the waters impounded behind beaver dams drained, the formerly high groundwater tables that they had helped to maintain began to gradually fall. As the water table fell, wetlands dried out and many small streams disappeared. English settlers, meanwhile, worked hard throughout the seventeenth century, and later the eighteenth century, to drain what swamps and marshes remained. In the process, they destroyed the few refuges left to wetland dwelling wildlife, including the beaver.

Some of the earliest town regulations in the Connecticut Valley centered on ditching and draining the commons. Springfield boasts the earliest extant record of town-mandated efforts at swamp draining. In 1639 the town passed a law requiring all landholders to dig a ditch along the side of the highway as it passed through their lands, each inhabitant linking his ditch to his neighbor's. Landowners were enjoined to keep this ditch clear to help ensure "the ready passadge of ye water yt it may not be pent up to flowe the meddowe."[98] A year later, Hartford ordered landholders in its Little Meadow to dig a three-foot wide "dreyne" along the border of their lands to facilitate the draining off of seasonal standing waters into the nearby Little River.[99] The town records of Wethersfield for 1640 mention the arms of a "three-way lete" converging in that town's centrally located common meadow. (The early modern English word "leat" refers to an open drainage ditch.) Such efforts continued for decades. In 1667, Springfield parceled out extensive new tracts of "swampy meadow" from its commons on the condition that the new owners would "improve" (presumably meaning drain) the land.[100] Numerous other drainage efforts, especially those undertaken on private lands, went unrecorded.

Changing nomenclature can help illustrate the combined impact of the mutually reinforcing processes of agricultural improvement and declining water tables. In Hartford, for example, much of the vast swamps recorded in the earliest land divisions had transformed into dry land within just a few short decades. The large parcels of swampland originally granted to town founders Nathaniel Ward and John Haynes, and referred to locally as Ward's Swamp and Haynes' Swamp, came over the seventeenth century to be known as Ward's Meadow and Haynes' Meadow, respectively. Hayne's Swamp may have begun the process of drying out in the 1640s when Haynes sold five and a half acres described in the records as "sometime swamp, now mowing land." The drying out of swamps occurred elsewhere as well. One two-and-a-quarter-acre parcel recorded simply as "swamp" by George Wyllys in 1639 had become "dry swamp" by the time it was resold to James Ensign later in the 1640s. A parcel of land registered as "meadow & swamp" by William Parker in 1639 became merely "meadow" by the time it was sold to Edward Stebbing in the 1660s.[101] All of this points to the gradual draining and drying out of the former wetlands that had bordered the Connecticut River and its tributaries.

While the expansion of arable land, pastures and meadow benefitted the English husbandmen of the watershed, the disappearance of wetlands was not without its economic downside. The increased propensity to flooding that accompanied the large-scale loss of beaver ponds in the landscape would have only been exacerbated by the efforts of husbandmen to drain the other wetlands of the valley. Without these wetlands to act as a catchment for seasonal and other unexpected storms, colonial streams and rivers often overflowed their normal banks. The disastrous flooding that the lower Connecticut Valley endured in the early 1680s was likely an early portend of inundations that in later decades would come to be taken as unavoidable acts of nature.[102] Usually this meant floodwaters overflowing the same lands that had formerly been swamp, marsh, or pond. The eighteenth-century residents of Hartford accepted with resignation that the northern half of Main Street, built along the course of a swampy stream that was redirected in the seventeenth century, would turn to a mass of mud and standing water following any heavy rain.[103] The Great Meadow in Springfield continually reverted to its former marshy state, drawing repeated calls from the town assembly for landowners to keep their ditches "well scowred."[104] English landowners in the valley learned time and again that water had to go somewhere, and, especially during the spring freshets, it could not always be contained. The persistence of waters to find their own way to the waiting banks of the Connecticut and its tributaries, and then downriver to Long Island Sound, would continue to frustrate its human inhabitants throughout the colonial period and, indeed, can still cause problems today.

Even as the valley's eighteenth-century inhabitants continued to wrestle with the increased hazards of periodic flooding, they benefitted from the absence of an even greater scourge to their health and well-being. The disappearance of large areas of standing water reduced the breeding habitat for, and thus the numbers of, mosquitoes in the region.[105] This in turn spared the valley's human residents both the annoyance of being bitten and the very real dangers associated with mosquito-borne illnesses. Malaria, for example, was a common affliction throughout the early modern Atlantic World. The disease's near-complete absence in the eighteenth-century valley suggests the wide-ranging ecological impacts of beaver extermination in the Connecticut Valley, and New England more generally.

Plasmodium vivax, the species of malarial microbe that made up the vast majority of cases in New England, seldom proved fatal in itself. This species is less deadly than *Plasmodium falciparum*, which can lead to organ failure and which came to predominate in the American south. But the symptoms of *P. vivax* could still be quite debilitating for sufferers, and could expose their hard-pressed immune systems to other diseases that might result in death. Malaria afflicts sufferers with recurring fevers interspersed with severe cases of the chills. Seventeenth- and eighteenth-century writers commonly referred to malaria as the "ague" (a general term for fevers, although it was especially associated with malarial symptoms), "remittent" or "intermittent fever" (a reference to the chills that interspersed spiking malarial fevers), or as "tertian" or "quatrain fever" (depending on whether the periods between fevers averaged three or four days). Although early modern theorists commonly blamed malarial outbreaks on the presence of "miasmas" ("bad airs" usually associated with marshes and other areas of stagnant water) the exact nature of the disease and its transmission remained a mystery. This was at least partially because malaria is a recrudescent disease—one in which the invading microbes can lay dormant for a period of years between the outbreak of symptoms. Malaria sufferers who seemed to have been cured of their fevers could quite suddenly fall ill again many miles, or even an entire ocean, away from the areas of "bad air" where they first contracted the disease.[106]

Three factors are required for malaria to persist as an endemic disease within a region: the presence of the protozoa which causes the disease, a sufficiently large human host population to maintain the microbe and allow it to multiply, and a sufficiently large *Anopheles* mosquito population to transmit the microbes to new hosts. Prior to 1600, the lands that would become New England housed a large number of populous human communities as well as a substantial *Anopheles* mosquito population—the latter a source of considerable complaint for early European explorers in the region. However, like so many of the deadliest and most debilitating diseases to afflict humanity, malaria had evolved in the eastern hemisphere. To gain a foothold in New England, malaria plasmodium first needed to hitch a ride across the Atlantic. Beginning in the 1620s, thousands of English emigrants unwittingly volunteered as carriers.

Malaria was endemic to many areas of southeastern England in the seventeenth century. The very counties which contributed the majority of emigrants to the first wave of Puritan settlement in New England also experienced some of the highest rates of malarial fever.[107] Malaria was also widespread in the Netherlands, where many leaders of the Pilgrim and Puritan migrations lived in exile prior to their departure for America. For example, Thomas Hooker, Hartford's first minister, contracted the "ague" in 1633 (or earlier) while living in Rotterdam.[108] After recovering from his initial illness, Hooker, along with many of his coreligionists, carried dormant *Plasmodium* protozoa in their bloodstreams when they crossed the Atlantic. Any recurrence of symptoms turned infected migrants into transmitters of the disease, as native mosquitoes spread malaria from the initial host to his or her neighbors.

Malarial fevers plagued New Englanders from at least the 1640s forward, and recurred region-wide throughout the remaining decades of the seventeenth century.[109] One scholar has suggested that an outbreak of malaria helps explain symptoms ascribed to some of the supposed victims of the Connecticut witchcraft craze of 1647–1653.[110] John Winthrop Jr., Royal Society member and governor of Connecticut, recorded numerous new cases in the colony from 1657 forward—including one especially virulent outbreak he witnessed firsthand during a visit to Hartford in the summer of 1672.[111] Indeed, in the 1680s and early 1690s, the towns of the Connecticut Valley gained a reputation as particularly bedeviled by the scourge of malaria.[112]

Then, after approximately 1700, malaria almost completely disappeared from both the Connecticut Valley and New England more generally.[113] New England's climate is usually credited for malaria's eighteenth-century disappearance.[114] Unlike the warmer southern colonies, the greater length of northern winters limited the annual number of days during which mosquitoes were active at the same time that greater severity of cold reduced the survival rate of adults and larvae. However, a climactic explanation fails to account for malaria's persistence in the first decades after English settlement or for the disease's decline just as average temperatures began to rise from the seventeenth-century low point reached during the depths of the Little Ice Age. Nor can it explain the persistence of malaria in areas like New York City, which shares, roughly, the wintery conditions of southern New England. Even more puzzling is the case of Deerfield, the one exception to the general disappearance of malaria from the eighteenth-century Connecticut Valley. In the neighborhood immediately around Deerfield, new cases of malaria continued to appear throughout the 1700s. Locals blamed these persistent outbreaks, so exceptional in New England as a whole, on a group of undrained marshes and stagnant pools that persisted on the unimproved lands east of Deerfield, on the far side of the Connecticut River.[115]

In this, the inhabitants of Deerfield offer a clue both to the persistence of malaria as a health concern in their own locality and the disease's disappearance from the larger region after 1700. Since the pool of human hosts continued to increase as the population of the valley grew during the eighteenth century, and the *Plasmodium* microbe remained in the region, at least, in Deerfield, then a decline in the number of available disease vectors, of *Anopheles* mosquitoes, must explain malaria's disappearance. As water tables throughout the valley slowly fell, no longer maintained by the presence of beaver dams, related ponds and wetlands dried up and mosquito-breeding habitat disappeared. Euro-American settlers, intent on draining lands and improving them for agriculture, contributed to the process. Only in the lands east of Deerfield—in an area that had, at the time of first settlement, been a lake bed—did sufficient standing waters persist to provide adequate breeding grounds for a mosquito population capable of maintaining malaria as a local health threat. Deerfield's own population, likely supplemented by migrants passing through town, some of whom likely had experience in the West Indies trade, provided a reservoir from which the *Plasmodium* could spread, via mosquito intermediaries, to new hosts.

That the drainage of lands following the decimation of beaver ponds lay behind malaria's post-1700 retreat from New England is further evidenced by the conditions that eventuated the disease's return at the end of the eighteenth century. The millponds associated with the saw- and gristmills of the colonial era provided insufficient breeding habitat to reestablish mosquito populations capable of maintaining malaria outbreaks. The much grander engineering projects of the last decade of the eighteenth century, and of the nineteenth century, were another matter. Malaria returned to the valley (outside of Deerfield) in 1792, striking at the towns of Northampton and nearby Hadley. Local residents had little doubt as to the cause of the new outbreak. They pointed to the waters backed up behind a recently constructed dam—a part of the lock system for the new South Hadley Canal then being erected by a construction crew of migrant laborers, "the most of them Hollanders."[116]

Contemporaries blamed the miasmas produced by these new standing waters as the source of their illness. Interpreting the outbreak from the perspective of twenty-first-century epidemiology, it seems that these new waters provided new breeding habitat for mosquitoes at the same time that the presence of Dutch skilled laborers offered a new reservoir of *Plasmodium* microbes. Malaria's prevalence in the valley only increased over the following decades as new engineering projects sequestered waters for lock operation, to power industrial water mills, and to provide urban drinking water. As malaria outbreaks proliferated, contemporaries continued to identify new construction projects, and the miasmic waters they produced, as the source of their malarial woes.[117] By the end of the nineteenth century, the towns lying on either side of the Connecticut Valley had once again gained a notorious reputation as regional hotspots for malarial infection within New England.[118] If the postdiluvian landscape yielded by the fur trade spared eighteenth-century valley residents from the scourge of malaria, the reflooding of the watershed's nineteenth-century industrial landscape placed their descendants once more at risk.

New Markets, New Landscape

Native Americans did not merely act within European commercial networks, they engaged with Europeans to actively construct the commercial networks and economic system that dominated and defined the seventeenth-century New England landscape. The economy that defined New England's ecology up through the late seventeenth century was neither European nor Native American, but a hybrid system coconstructed by cultures with roots on both sides of the Atlantic. In many ways, and for most of the century, this economy was more Indian than European. The most significant changes to the Connecticut Valley land- and waterscape between 1600 and 1700 were the result of a Native American market revolution and the political and diplomatic transformations that accompanied it.

When Wahginnacut first urged the English to settle in the Connecticut Valley in 1631, he was inviting them to build their homes amid a landscape experiencing substantial ecological and hydrological changes. As English settlers pushed up the Connecticut Valley in the seventeenth century, they continually encountered lands that Indian communities had depleted of beaver and then traded away for as great a profit as possible. The ecosystems that greeted these new homesteaders were, in terms of biodiversity, far simpler than they had been mere decades before. And they were still in the process of becoming simpler yet. In many ways the "natural" environment that English settlers found in the Connecticut Valley in the mid- and late seventeenth century was actually a recent invention. Human actors, driven by the incentives of the fur trade, had destroyed the former ecological and hydrological systems that beaver had engineered over the course of millennia. By the end of the seventeenth century, the Connecticut Valley was a postdiluvian landscape diminished in its biodiversity, but "providentially" well-suited to the demands of English agriculture.

CHAPTER 2

Raising Crops

Feeding the Market

The seventeenth- and eighteenth-century English appropriation of Indian lands—a process sped along by the declining fortunes of the fur trade—radically transformed the ecology and economies of the Connecticut Valley. Native communities, who had formerly traded their agricultural surplus to feed ill-prepared English colonists, gradually found themselves displaced by aggressive (and often violent) English traders and settlers. A long-established Native American trade network was supplanted by a new English agricultural system that tied the valley into an imperial commercial network that stretched throughout the Atlantic. English farmers exploited the fertility of the bottomlands to turn the region into a breadbasket for empire, raising wheat and a myriad of other crops for export to the other mainland colonies, Europe, and, most importantly, the Caribbean. This transition introduced new plants, animals, and diseases to the valley, and redefined how human farmers managed the region's landscape.

* * *

In 1639, Captain David Pieterszen de Vries, acting on behalf of the Dutch West Indies Company, sailed his fluyt up the Connecticut River to call upon Governor John Haynes of the newly established Connecticut Colony. De Vries' mission was to warn off the English, who by 1639 had planted four towns along the southern Connecticut River in lands that the Dutch considered their own by right of exploration. The Dutch had strengthened their title by purchasing these lands from the conquering Pequots with the (likely coerced) approval of the local Wangunk Indians and their sachem,

Sowheage. Governor Haynes could have responded to de Vries' accusations by pointing out that the English had also been granted land for their towns by local Indian communities eager to break the fur trade monopoly of the Pequots. Hartford, for example, had been founded upon lands provided by Wahginnacut, sachem of the local Podunks, while Sowheage himself had also sold lands to the settlers of nearby Wethersfield.

Instead, Haynes chose another tack. The governor upbraided de Vries and his Dutch countrymen for having left the lands of the Connecticut Valley "lying idle." "It was," Haynes insisted, "a sin to let such rich land, which produced such fine corn, lie uncultivated."[1] Implicitly, Haynes criticized not only the Dutch West Indies Company's decision to curtail agricultural settlement for fear it might disrupt the corporation's monopoly on the fur trade, but also the Indian system of agriculture that had supported the peoples of the valley for centuries. For Haynes and most of his fellow English colonists, proper agriculture required plowed fields, livestock to produce manure, and fences all around. The Indians' failure to exploit their lands in accordance with such a model supposedly invalidated any title they may have otherwise claimed to their homelands and invited—perhaps even required, in the view of Puritan leaders—their dispossession by new settlers.[2] The English may have first come to the valley to exploit the opportunities offered by the fur trade, but they would stay to become farmers.

Just as John Winthrop had, in 1633, bemoaned his fellow colonists' continued addiction to "foreign commodities," de Vries predicted that the Puritans of the Connecticut Valley would, despite the strict religion of their leaders, maintain a taste for many of the imported luxuries they had enjoyed in the commercial world of old England.[3] During his short visit in Hartford, de Vries witnessed an English trading ketch arrive carrying, among other imports, a cargo of wine from the Portuguese Madeira islands. When a servant of the town was shortly afterward discovered to have overindulged in this luxury, he was sentenced to be flogged for his drunkenness. Horrified by what he considered an excessive punishment, De Vries interceded on the servant's behalf and convinced Haynes to forgo the whipping. De Vries later warned the English governor "that it would be impossible for them [the colony's Puritan authorities] to keep the people so strict, as they had come from so luxurious a country as England."[4]

These two factors, the region's rich soils and its inhabitants' desire for imported goods, ensured that the Connecticut Valley remained firmly tied to Atlantic markets even following the failure of the fur trade. Writing a little over a decade after de Vries' unsuccessful mission to Hartford, Captain Edward

Johnson of Massachusetts observed that although the valley had originally been settled because it was so "fitly seated for a Bever trade with the Indians," the decline of that trade had already encouraged enterprising settlers to shift their focus and "caused them to live upon husbandry." [5] Although this new focus on husbandry—a mixed agricultural system combining raising field crops with keeping livestock—initially aimed merely at subsistence, English farmers had by the time Johnson was writing already begun to export their agricultural surpluses beyond the valley.

In this, the new English settlers of the valley followed the example of the region's Indian agriculturalists, although the cultural chauvinism of men like Haynes likely prevented them from appreciating the fact. Agricultural commodities had flowed from the valley for time immemorial. The River Indians exported corn, squash, and dried beans to their nonagricultural neighbors farther north and to coastal communities which specialized in exploiting marine resources. Indeed, the earliest English colonists in the valley depended on these surpluses to provision their own poorly planned efforts at settlement. But over time this reliance shifted toward a desire to dispossess the Native communities of the valley. As fur supplies declined, English merchants instead demanded land in exchange for their goods and Native leaders—facing devastating mortality from disease, stiff and sometimes hostile competition from rival nations, and the intimidating power of expanding English settlements—often saw trading away land as the best path forward for their communities. English traditions of agriculture replaced Indian practices. New crops were planted and, in time, the English began exporting the products of their own fields: apple cider to quench the thirst of neighboring New Englanders, flaxseed to supply the linen industries of Ireland and Britain, wheat and other grains to feed the slave plantations of the West Indies. Indeed, by 1660, one knowledgeable merchant was able to declare to the King's Council for Foreign Plantations that the provisioning trade of New England, of which the produce of the Connecticut Valley made up an important part, was "the key to the Indies, without which Jamaica, Barbadoes and ye Charibby Islands are not able to subsist."[6] From a Native American trading nexus supplying the regions all around, to a production site for empire sending its produce into an Atlantic marketplace, the ecology of the valley shaped and was shaped by the economics of trade.

Native Agriculture

Maize had spread to the Connecticut Valley around 1000 AD, a relatively short six hundred years prior to the arrival of the first Europeans in the region, and disseminated throughout southern New England at roughly the same time. Indian women adopted this new crop and planted it in their fields alongside earlier arrivals—multiple species of beans and squash.[7] Throughout the region, Native communities enjoyed broad diets. Native women raised crops and collected wild plant foods like berries, nuts, and tubers, while men hunted for game and fished. Along the coast, plentiful shellfish further expanded Native diets. The arrival of maize roughly paralleled a period of mild climatic warming in the northern hemisphere known as the Medieval Warm Period. Together, warmer temperatures (which in turn produced longer growing seasons for both cultivated and wild food plants) and the arrival of an important new dietary staple led to a gradual increase in the human populations of New England as a whole.[8]

This period of agricultural plenty proved fleeting. Within four centuries, warmer temperatures gave way to a period of global cooling—the Little Ice Age—that would stretch from roughly the mid-fourteenth to the early nineteenth century. By the end of the fourteenth century, lower average temperatures in the spring and autumn had shortened the agricultural growing season to the point where most communities throughout southern New England were forced to abandon cultivating crops. Even in communities where women continued to plant and tend to their fields of maize, squash, and beans, they cut back significantly on the amount of land planted and on the amount of time and labor spent in tending crops relative to their efforts at collecting wild plants and game. Only in the Connecticut Valley—where the waters of the Connecticut River and its larger tributaries acted to moderate local temperatures and slightly extend the growing season—did communities remain committed to a largely sedentary and agriculturally centered lifestyle. Elsewhere, New England communities returned to cultivating crops only as average temperatures rose (slightly) at the turn of the sixteenth century. As the earliest European explorers pushed into New England in the mid-sixteenth century, then, they encountered many Native communities that had only just recently readopted farming to supplement their continued reliance on hunting and foraging.[9]

The villages of the fifteenth- and sixteenth-century Connecticut Valley took advantage of their climatically fortuitous placement to become a breadbasket to the rest of New England, trading their surplus agricultural produce to communities living to their north, east, and west. Native traders traveling amid multiple interregional commercial networks traded agricultural foodstuffs and ceramics from the Connecticut Valley for copper coming from Nova Scotia and the Great Lakes, stone for toolmaking from areas in present-day Pennsylvania, and shells, wampum, and seafood from New

England's coastal communities. Historical sources show that Connecticut Valley communities continued to produce large agricultural surpluses for trade to northern and coastal New England even after the return of (again, slightly) warmer temperatures led to the readoption of crop cultivation elsewhere.[10]

The earliest English colonists in North America invariably relied upon the preexisting Indian provisions trade for the survival of their settlements. For example, the settlers of England's first permanent American colony, Jamestown, at first proved notoriously bad at feeding themselves. Those who survived the colony's early years relied on the flow of agricultural surpluses that undergirded Powhatan's empire, receiving food as gifts, trading for corn, and eventually using violence to extort provisions from the Indians of coastal Virginia. Captain John Smith believed that subsequent colonies could likewise rely on America's Native communities to supply them with food. In 1616, he assured English readers that settlers in the "New England" which he had recently returned from exploring would be able to purchase corn from neighboring Indians "for a few trifles," and thus sustain themselves until their own plantations had been firmly established. For Smith, New England agriculture was not an end in itself. Rather, Indian corn, and eventually the provisions that the colonists grew for themselves, would support the production of "merchandable fish" and "other commodities."[11]

Whether intentionally or not, the early settlers of New England followed Jamestown's lead by relying on local Indians for their initial subsistence. Perhaps taking Smith's advice too much to heart, the Pilgrims who landed at Plymouth four years later relied on Indian corn to get through their first winter—although their decision to ransack abandoned Wampanoag villages and gravesites for grain caches likely alienated their would-be trading partners and contributed to the deaths of about half of the *Mayflower*'s passengers. Luckily, an improvement in relations with the Wampanoags early in 1621 allowed the foundering colony to trade for seed corn. A decade later, Podunk leader Wahginnacut recognized the potential of appealing to English bellies in his search for a European trading partner, offering the leaders of Massachusetts Bay both land for a new settlement along the Connecticut River and corn to feed its settlers.[12] As John Smith had recommended, the founders of the Connecticut Valley's first English towns hoped to rely on Indian neighbors for provisions while extracting the region's "merchandable" furs for sale to Europe.

Self-sufficiency was not easily achieved by settlers accustomed to an agricultural system developed in a society where labor was plentiful and most fields and meadows had been cleared generations ago and kept plowed, fenced, and manured annually ever since. Even given the great fertility of valley lands, and despite the fact that they were often able to take advantage of abandoned Indian fields for their early crops, there was no chance that the eight hundred English men, women, and children who moved to the banks of the Connecticut in the 1630s would be able to feed themselves without the support of local Indian communities. As at Jamestown, this dependence on the Indian provisioning trade left Connecticut Valley colonists ill at ease when famine threatened, eventually contributing to the outbreak of violence in the Pequot War.

Imperial competition and the English desire to dominate the fur trade provided the overarching impetus for the war, but hunger and a fear of famine helped to trigger the descent into violence. The two men whose deaths ostensibly sparked the war, John Stone and John Oldham, made for unlikely martyrs. Stone was a drunkard, a blasphemer, a kidnapper, and probably a pirate. Oldham lived in Plymouth only about a year before the colony's leaders exiled him for his tendencies toward violence and rebellion. Unlike Stone, Oldham did eventually achieve a degree of respectability as a trader in the Bay Colony, but his slaying under unclear circumstances by Niantics on Block Island seems a poor justification for English colonists' subsequent campaign to eliminate the Pequot as a nation. A number of ulterior motives—land hunger, the lure of fur trade profits, and a desire to wrest regional political hegemony from the Pequots and Dutch—better explain the English rush to war. To these may be added one further factor which helps to explain both the war's timing and the importance that Stone's and Oldham's deaths likely played in English calculations: access to Indian corn.[13]

Recent scholarship suggests that the specter of famine stalked the communities of southern New England—native and colonist alike—in the years 1635–1636. The prospect of hunger loomed especially dire in the newly planted English towns of the Connecticut Valley. Native Americans in New England had first seen their food security threatened by the smallpox epidemic of 1633–1634. The disease devastated Indian communities, incapacitating and killing hunters and agriculturalists in the prime of life. Survivors, many still recovering from the ravages of illness, struggled to maintain their subsistence as best they could even as they mourned their dead. To compound problems, a hurricane struck southeastern New England in the summer of 1635, destroying crops as they stood in the fields. Only a few years old, many English towns in Massachusetts and, especially, in the Connecticut Valley still struggled to achieve self-sufficiency in food and relied heavily on trade with Indian villages to stave off starvation.[14]

Although they may not have always been welcome in polite society, trad-ers like Stone and Oldham served as linchpins within this nascent regional commercial network. Few other colonists possessed the experience, knowl-edge, and contacts needed to strike deals with Indian villages while also suc-cessfully navigating the often-treacherous waters of the New England coast. The waterborne trade carried on by a handful of merchants like Stone and Oldham provided a lifeline to the early settlers of the Connecticut Valley. In the 1630s, English settlements still only hugged the coast of what these new-comers aspirationally labeled "New England." The territory separating the Massachusetts Bay from the Connecticut Valley belonged to communities of Massachusetts and Nipmucs and was crisscrossed by Indian paths too rough for English carts. The deaths of Stone and Oldham threatened to cut the English towns of the Connecticut Valley off from both Indian corn suppliers and any assistance that might otherwise be forthcoming from the English settlements of eastern New England. Worse yet, if the murders of Stone and Oldham signaled a new unwillingness on the part of Indian communities to trade away their own (likely diminished) supplies of corn, then the English towns faced the prospect of a hungry future.[15]

War offered the beleaguered towns of the Connecticut an immediate solution to their food shortages. As the corn trade floundered amid wors-ening relations with the Pequots, settlers instead filled their cellars with food raided from Indian stores. Early raids against the Niantics of Block Island and the Pequots at the mouth of the Thames, ostensibly to chastise those commu-nities for their roles in Stone's and Oldham's deaths, yielded large caches of corn that the English hauled back to their towns. Connecticut militiamen continued their raids for corn into 1638, long after Pequot power had been effectively crushed. Along with captives/slaves, corn was one of the princi-pal spoils that the victorious English divided up among themselves and their Narragansett and other Indian allies at war's end.[16]

This victory bought the fledgling Connecticut Valley towns a respite, but did not free them from their dependence on the Indian corn trade. In early 1638, the English—riding high after their victory over the Pequots—sought to impose greater control over the provisions trade of the Connecticut Valley by fixing the price at which corn could be purchased from Indians at five shil-lings a bushel.[17] Unfortunately, when William Pynchon, acting as broker for the Connecticut towns, attempted to buy provisions at this rate, he encoun-tered few willing to sell. He came away empty-handed from successive vis-its to the villages of Agawam, Woronoco, and Nonotuck. It was only after pushing farther north to Pocumtuck that he was able to secure five hundred bushels of corn in exchange for three hundred fathoms of wampum. Despite his having saved the residents of Hartford from starvation, the Massachusetts government fined Pynchon for overpaying. A few months later, Captain John Mason of Connecticut (a leader of the previous year's Mystic Massacre of almost five hundred Pequots, mostly women and children) managed to procure fifty canoes loaded with corn from Indians upriver "at a reasonable rate," but only by approaching his Indian trading partners with an armed militia at his back. The Pequot War may have laid the foundations for English hegemony in the valley, but as long as the English remained at least partially dependent upon purchased corn to feed their growing towns, the Indian communities of the valley possessed a bargaining chip with which to oppose the unwanted encroachment of English authority.[18]

As mid-century approached, however, the bargaining power of Indian villages in the valley began to decline. Indian traders found they could no longer rely on what had historically been their most important exports to the English towns—food and furs. After peaking in the early 1650s, fur yields in the valley began a precipitous decline until the 1670s when the regional trade effectively came to an end.[19] At the same time, the early English towns of the valley, after twenty years of building and plowing, finally achieved self-sufficiency in feeding themselves. After forty years of trading with Europeans, valley Indians had to find a new commodity to offer if they were to maintain access to the European goods to which they had become accustomed (kettles, blankets, coats, knives, hatchets, guns, etc.) and thereby maintain their economies, fulfill their diplomatic obligations to powerful neighbors like the Mohawks, and maintain good relations with the English by honoring the debts that many Indian traders had run up by trading on credit. Increasingly, European merchants demanded land—rather than the resources that Native peoples harvested from it—in exchange for their goods.

After the mid-1650s, networks of English merchant credit and declining beaver yields paved the way for divorcing valley Indians from their ancestral territories. Transfers of land had long been tied up with the fortunes of the fur trade. When Wahginnacut, the Podunk sachem, approached the English in 1631 he offered the land for a new English settlement (which would eventually become Hartford) as part of the entry price he was willing to pay to break into the fur trade. Similar transfers, and numerous smaller sales, provided for the founding of the other Connecticut River towns. After midcentury, however, land went from a relatively minor, supplemental commodity in the larger fur trade to the central focus of Anglo-Indian trade and credit relationships.[20]

A number of considerations made land sales an attractive choice for the Indians of the valley. Decades of epidemic diseases and warfare encouraged by the fur trade had led to depopulation and the abandonment of small scattered farming communities in favor of larger, centralized village sites. Land that had fallen out of cultivation and that lay far from the village center was of little immediate use to these smaller, consolidated communities. Hunting lands, too, declined in value as there were fewer hunters to exploit them, as beaver populations declined, and as conflicts with the Mohegans and Mohawks made them unsafe to venture into. Despite these circumstances, land deeds with Europeans often included clauses stipulating that the Indian sellers could still return to deeded lands to hunt, fish, collect wild foods, and sometimes even to plant crops. With such stipulations, Indian communities worked to protect their agricultural heritage and adapt to changing conditions in the valley even as they yielded to English demands. For example, when Chickwallop and his fellow sachems among the Norwottucks sold the lands that would become Hatfield, Massachusetts, to John Pynchon in 1653 they did so with the express understanding that they would "have liberty to plant their present corn fields" and on the condition that Pynchon would "plow up or cause to be plowed up for the Indians sixteene acres of land on ye east side of the Quinnoticott River."[21]

Trading away lands that were not currently under use or that were being used suboptimally made sense for Indian traders and village leaders under pressure to maintain access to both European goods, which their communities had come to enjoy and depend upon, and to wampum, which was crucial for treating with Native neighbors and for demonstrating the trader/leader's own social preeminence. Land sales brought immediate, bulk payments of wampum and European goods equal to several years' worth of proceeds from the fur trade into a community without the uncertainty that came from harvesting an increasingly scarce resource like beaver. In 1659, for instance, Umpanchela, a sachem of the Norwottucks, leased (and later sold) a parcel of farmland along the Connecticut north of recently founded Northampton, Massachusetts, in exchange for goods worth about 250 pounds of beaver pelts. This was in a year when the entire fur trade of the valley amounted to only 291 pounds of beaver. For traders and leaders like Umpanchela, the short-term benefits of land sales were obvious.[22]

The details of the deal Umpanchela made with John Pynchon help illustrate why land sales proved so attractive for Native leaders despite their negative long-term consequences, which seem so obvious in hindsight. In 1659, Umpanchela had purchased a variety of items on credit from Pynchon. The fur trade had been a source of great wealth for valley communities as recently as the early 1650s, and Umpanchela doubtlessly hoped to pay his debt off quickly. But by 1659, changing circumstances—renewed tensions with the Mohawks, often-violent competition with the Mohegans to the southeast, and rapidly declining regional beaver populations—emerged to stymie the trade.[23] Umpanchela carried his debt over into 1660 and, in a gamble that the beaver trade would bounce back, ordered even more items from Pynchon. The variety of items purchased by Umpanchela—several fathoms of cloth, shirts, coats, breeches, knives, and even wampum—suggest he may have been acting as a middleman in the regional fur trade. Pynchon, however, was not convinced that Umpanchela would be able to make good on his climbing debt and demanded that the sachem mortgage three parcels of Norwottuck planting land as collateral. In December of 1660, Umpanchela departed upriver on a high-stakes trading venture to the Sokokis at Squakheag, while Pynchon gloated in his account book: "If I am not paid in Bever when he comes from Heakeg all his land is to be mine." In the end, Umpanchela was unable to obtain enough pelts from the Sokokis to clear his accounts, and the Norwottuck lands transferred to Pynchon to be resold and incorporated into the English town of Hadley.[24]

While land sales offered immediate benefits to valley Indian communities under growing pressure from both their English and Native neighbors, this strategy also brought important long-term drawbacks. Land sales slowly undermined a village's capacity for growth. As Indian populations in the valley gradually rebounded from the smallpox epidemic of the 1630s, the women farmers of the new, consolidated villages had to plant crops on ever more acres. Without the agricultural lands which had been sold to the English, these farmers were unable to allow their fields to lie fallow or to shift cultivation to outlying fields when those nearest villages began to lose their fertility.[25]

Continuous encroachment by English settlers exacerbated this problem. The Indian communities of the valley quite naturally chose areas of prime agricultural land when situating their villages along the course of the Connecticut River. No likely location went unoccupied. When the English arrived in the valley, they too sought out these fertile farming lands, often founding their towns adjacent to existing Indian villages. The founders of Wethersfield built their town alongside Wangunk, and within a few years had displaced their Indian neighbors farther south to Matabessett (which was, in turn, encroached upon by the settlers of Middletown two decades later). Hartford was settled across the Connecticut from the Podunk village of Hockanum, Windsor just south of Namferoke, another Podunk settlement. The Agawam River, a Connecticut tributary, separated the village of Agawam in the south from Springfield in the north. As English settlement progressed up the valley in the 1650s–1670s, new towns grew up that pushed against and often hemmed in the planting grounds of villages in the central valley: Northampton and Hadley founded on lands formerly belonging to the Norwottuck villages of Nonotuck and Norwottuck, respectively, Deerfield near the reoccupied village of Pocumtuck, and Northfield beside the remaining inhabitants of Squakheag. Moving into the broader watershed, this same pattern was often repeated along the tributaries of the Connecticut, such as on the banks of the Farmington River where the English settlement of that name was founded alongside Tunxis Sepos, the largest of the Tunxis villages.[26]

English settlers often chose to ignore terms written into land deeds that granted neighboring Indian communities the rights to continue hunting, fishing, gathering plants, and planting crops on territory that had been incorporated into English towns.[27] Free-roaming English livestock displaced game animals like deer and wreaked havoc in those planting fields Indians still retained. Pigs even competed directly with Indian communities for wild foods like acorns and other nuts, groundnuts, and birds' eggs.[28] At the same time, freshwater fish and mussels, waterfowl, and riverine mammals grew markedly less abundant following the eradication of beaver and the drying up of beaver ponds and associated wetlands. The end result of all of these pressures was, by the 1670s, a landscape where the various Indian communities of the Connecticut Valley found it increasingly difficult to secure a livelihood.

Like other Native nations throughout southern New England in the 1670s, many River Indians gambled that war might halt English encroachment and joined their efforts to the growing coalition centered around the Wampanoag sachem Metacomet (known to the English as King Philip). In the southern valley, where the English presence was larger and more entrenched, some Indian communities either chose to aid the English or had their men conscripted into service by English forces. Farther north, however, most Mahicans, Norwottucks, Pocumtucks, Nipmucs, and even some Podunks allied with the Sokokis, Pennacooks, and other Abenakis to drive the English from the valley. At first, their efforts met with success. Deerfield was destroyed and Springfield burnt. The English abandoned Northfield rather than wait for it to also be put to the torch. But as the English recovered from these initial setbacks and went on the offensive, Native supplies of powder and shot ran low. When the powerful Mohawks entered the war on the side of the English, any hope the allied Indians of New England still held for victory was lost.

English patrols, along with their local Indian allies, raided settlements and burned crops in an attempt to starve out any opponents they could not capture through battle. Thousands died and hundreds more were enslaved. Hundreds of the latter were sold to the West Indies, forced to board ships which followed the regular routes of New England trade to disperse their human cargo among the sugar islands of the English Caribbean. Many surviving Indians whose communities had allied themselves with King Philip either chose to leave or were driven from the Connecticut Valley after the war. Most either moved north to live among the Abenakis or west to Schaghticoke and other communities in lands claimed by New York.[29]

Individuals who chose to remain in the valley faced renewed challenges. The valley's remaining Indian communities found themselves hemmed in by the expanding population and economy of Anglo New England. At the same time, prejudice pushed them to the margins of this society. With beaver gone and the populations of other game animals in decline from habitat destruction and competition from settlers' livestock, hunting became an increasingly untenable occupation for Indian men. The same market considerations that had encouraged Indian communities to sell lands in the seventeenth century persisted into the eighteenth. Court proceedings over debts and issues of trespass slowly chipped away at the reservations of land that were left in the hands of the valley's Native communities. An Indian farmer who could not pay his or her debts to a local English storekeeper often saw his or her lands seized, as did any Indian unlucky enough to be convicted of even minor offenses, such as trespass or petty theft.[30] Denied ownership of their former lands, many men undertook what had formerly been women's work and became seasonal laborers on English farms. Women more often became domestic servants in English households. Many from both sexes turned to traditional handicrafts as a means to engage the English market. As English farmers claimed the best farming lands, the region's original agriculturalists turned to the resources available in the remaining wetlands to produce mats, brooms, and baskets crafted from reeds and marsh grasses.[31]

Although Indians never disappeared from the valley, most did slowly "vanish" from the historical record. As they integrated themselves into the English economy and society, or traveled between Native communities both within the valley and without, they were either ignored by the official gaze of English town and colonial governments whose greatest interests lay in the more sedentary and more prosperous white population or else were recategorized as poor whites or blacks when they intermarried with the region's more recent immigrants and the small, but still significant, number of slaves they brought with them. While many Indian communities and individuals chose to leave the valley in search of better circumstances elsewhere, especially in the wake of King Philip's War, hundreds (if not thousands) remained in the lands of the Connecticut watershed largely hidden from historical view.[32]

The experiences of the Wangunks of the lower valley encapsulate this long and drawn-out process of agricultural dispossession. At the beginning of the seventeenth century, the Wangunks had occupied the bend of the Connecticut River at what would become Wethersfield. Subjugated by the Pequots sometime early in the century, Wangunk Sachem Sowheage (also referred to as Sequin) sent one of his sons to Boston alongside the Podunk sachem Wahginnacutt in 1631. Sowheage's goals mirrored those of his northern Podunk neighbor. His son offered land in the Connecticut Valley if only the English would agree to plant a settlement there. The English would acquire prime, fertile lands along a large navigable river stretching deep into the New England interior, and the Wangunks (Sowheage hoped) would gain an ally, trading partner, and counterweight to Pequot power.[33] Although the Massachusetts government initially reacted with hesitance, in 1634 a small vanguard of English traders led by John Oldham established an outpost along the Connecticut at a location adjacent to Sowheage's capital at Pyquag. A year later, several families of settlers followed. Although the details remain lost to time, these first settlers quickly alienated their Wangunk neighbors, committing "divers Injuryes" that convinced Sowheage to remove his village south to Matabessett, in present-day Middletown. The English retained possession of the fertile fields and meadows of Pyquag—now Wethersfield—and the Wangunks were left with a grievance that led Sowheage to aid the formerly despised Pequots during their war with the valley's newest settlers.[34]

By 1650, encroaching English settlers had begun planting their own crops in Wangunk fields in Matabessett. Rather than alienate the English, Sowheage sold the lands lying closest to the river to the founders of Middletown. In the following decades, similar encroachments by settlers and the failing beaver trade led to further land sales and created tensions between the Wangunks and their English neighbors. When King Philip's War came, Sowheage's son-in-law and successor, Massecup, led a small party that raided the farm of Major John Richards of Hartford. Captured and imprisoned, Massecup spent the rest of the war as a hostage for the peaceful behavior of his fellow Wangunks, many of whom were pressed into military service alongside the English. After the war, pressure from the growing English population of Middletown led to the gradual sale of further lands until only about fifty acres remained to the tribe in the uplands west of the river at "Indian Hill."[35]

In 1760, a group of Wangunks—at the instigation of two Middletown land owners—complained to the Connecticut General Court that these acres had become "used, worn out, and left useless" and petitioned for the right to sell their reservation. Following the sale, those Wangunks who did not find a place within the Middletown economy moved to live with kin among the Tunxis near Farmington or dispersed to join Native communities elsewhere. In 1774, the composite Indian community at Farmington also chose to sell out and the vast majority of its members left the Connecticut Basin to settle on Oneida lands at Brothertown.[36]

Throughout the seventeenth and eighteenth centuries, the original farming communities of the valley were largely displaced. As the examples of the Wangunks and Tunxis suggest, those families who remained were increasingly denied access to the best lands along the intervals, forced onto lands either farther inland from the Connecticut Basin or else farther north in the valley where the growing season was shorter and agriculture more tenuous.[37] Many refugees remembered their connections to the lands of the southern and middle valley, returning to harvest resources that lay outside of English towns and to visit relations even well into the nineteenth century. Some even later chose to return to their ancestral homes.

For example, in 1665, Nipmuc sachem Shattoockquis (also referred to in the records as Shadookis or Sadoques) sold a large parcel of land along the Quabaug River to Thomas Cooper of Springfield. The Quabaug flowed west into the Chicopee River, which in turn emptied into the Connecticut a little above Springfield. This purchase allowed Cooper—who immediately turned around and sold the land to other Englishmen—to speculate in new farmlands lying deeper within the Connecticut basin. The sale likely followed the disappearance of beaver and other furbearers from the waters of the Quabaug. In exchange, the Nipmuc village received three hundred fathoms of wampum, which Shattoockquis likely spent negotiating a peace with the Mohawks who had recently been raiding Native communities in the area. A little more than a decade later, in the wake of King Philip's War, Shattoockquis led a group of 150 River Indians north in search of new homes among the Abenakis.[38]

A further two centuries passed before Israel Sadoques, one of Shattoockquis' descendants, returned south down the Connecticut River. Some unknown setback in the 1870s drove Sadoques, a hunter and trapper, to leave his home in the Abenaki village of Odanak, Quebec, and seek his fortunes in his ancestral home. He was accompanied by his wife, Mary Watso, who was herself a descendant of displaced Pocumtucks and Sokokis. The couple traveled almost the length of the Connecticut in search of a livelihood, without luck. On their return trip north, they encountered an itinerant Indian sales-man who encouraged them to settle in Keene, New Hampshire, a town located just beyond the eastern uplands of the valley on one of the Connecticut's trib-utaries. Here Sadoques and Watso initially made their living weaving and sell-ing baskets for the English residents of the town. Once he had raised enough money, Sadoques paid a neighbor to teach him to handle a plow and eventu-ally bought his own farm. Sadoques emulated his Euro-American neighbors by planting grain crops, keeping a small number of livestock, and even start-ing a fruit orchard, while Watso tended the family's large garden plot and their growing number of children.[39] The landscape in which Sadoques and Watso settled had changed, as had the economy in which they sought a living, but their return to the valley illustrates the enduring, if often overlooked, presence of the region's original inhabitants in its environmental history.

Like Sadoques and Watso, most River Indians who remained in the valley chose to settle among the incoming English, to farm as they did. In most cases, their Euro-American neighbors eventually ceased to recognize the Indian identities of these persistent residents, largely forgetting that they and their descendants were anything other than white. English landowners increasingly defined the new agricultural system of the region, and English merchants controlled its interactions with the larger Atlantic world. Indian farmers continued to work the land, but made their way within an economy that was overwhelmingly controlled and defined by newcomers.[40]

Wheat, an English Staple

For the valley's English settlers, membership within an expanding empire encouraged a degree of regional specialization. New England would develop to supply raw materials or commodities that required only limited processing to other economic centers within the English (and later British) imperial sys-tem. The impressive fertility of the Connecticut Valley allowed its farmers to outshine their fellow New England colonists in their efforts to provision this commercial system. For instance, in 1753, the Irish-born Reverend Dr. James McSparran spared a few words of praise for the "Industry" of Connecticut farmers amid his otherwise condemnatory account of the American colo-nies, their unwholesome climates, and the dangers that "multifarious wicked and pestilent Heresies" posed to their inhabitants' souls. "No place this way can boast of larger Exportations, in proportion to its Extent and Inhabitants," McSparran wrote of Connecticut, adding that "the Markets in the other

Main-land Provinces, as well as our West-Indian Islands, owe a good deal of their Supply to the Butter, Beef, Mutton, Pork, Indian Corn and Wheat, of this Colony."[41] Surviving customs records from the late colonial period bear out McSparran's impressions. From 1768 to 1773, Connecticut was the single largest exporter of hogs, horses, cattle, preserved beef, onions, flax, rye, and oats among all of Britain's mainland colonies. Much of the colony's success as an exporter rested upon the remarkable fertility of the Connecticut Valley and its role in reexporting the agricultural produce that flowed down the river from the interior regions of Massachusetts and New Hampshire.[42]

Colonial agricultural success was, of course, founded upon the displacement and dispossession of the valley's original farming communities. When the English bought (or seized) Indian territory, they obtained not just *any* land. Rather, they often gained access to *prime farming* land. They received from its original inhabitants a landscape superbly suited to agriculture. First, there were the considerable natural benefits offered by the Connecticut River and its tributaries, which moderated the climate, extended the growing season, and annually overran their banks to deposit new, fertile soils during the spring freshets. And then there were the changes made by human hands. The first few generations of English settlers moved into a valley replete with open beaver meadows emerging rapidly in the wake of the fur trade. Elsewhere, the best agricultural lands in the valley had already been cleared for Native fields, many abandoned following losses to disease or in the wake of land sales. Even the woodlands were more open and inviting thanks to the careful management of River Indian communities. Nature had created fertile lands in the valley, but the region's Native American communities had created lands ready for farming. English settlers took these lands and made them their own.

Fire was one of the most important tools employed by the Native agriculturalists of the valley. Men set seasonal fires to prevent woodlands from encroaching upon the open fields where women planted their maize, squash, beans, and other crops. New fields were cleared through "girdling," the practice of cutting away the bark and outer wood of trees in a continuous ring near their base. This process severed the trees' phloem—the inner layer of bark responsible for distributing carbohydrates produced in the leaves down to the roots—causing the trees' root system to slowly starve and die. The resulting stand of dead wood was then set aflame and the resulting ash left to fertilize the soil of the new planting fields.[43] Controlled seasonal burning was also used to clear underbrush and fallen timber from woodlands, creating extensive swaths of open forest that made hunting, foraging, and travel easier. Fruit-bearing bushes such as the wild strawberry, huckleberry, and

gooseberry thrived in these open woodlands, while fire-resistant tree species—many of them mast-producers like oak, hickory, and chestnut—proliferated at the expense of less fire-hardy types. Indian communities enjoyed
berries and mast as parts of their seasonal diets and hunted the game that
each attracted.[44]

The earliest English settlers in the valley were the beneficiaries of this
regime of seasonal burning and recognized many of its benefits. At first the
English followed the example of valley Indian communities, setting fire to
fields and woodlands on an annual basis. The practice seems to have been
widespread in the valley for much of the seventeenth century.[45] In 1671, for
example, a body of settlers from Northampton petitioned the Massachusetts
General Court to establish a new town (Northfield) at the site of a former
Pocumtuck village, warning that the benefits of Pocumtuck burning in the
area were already coming undone from "the want of inhabitants to burn
the meadows and woods, whereupon the underwoods increase, which will
be very prejudicial to those that shall come to inhabit, and the longer the
worse."[46] Despite the benefits they conferred, English settlers viewed seasonal
burns with skepticism, fearful of the cost to property and life that might result
should fires stray where they were not wanted. As settlement progressed and
the number of fences, barns, and wooden homes in the valley increased, so
did the risks associated with fire. Small-scale burning on the peripheries of
towns continued as an annual practice in some areas up through 1743 when
the Massachusetts General Court passed a law prohibiting the firing of lands
in order to protect fences and other property and under the (mistaken) belief
that burning impoverished the soil.[47]

As annual fires disappeared from the valley landscape, their environmental effects gradually came undone. The numbers of insects and snakes
in the region—formerly kept in check by burning—would have jumped. The
composition of woodlands began to change as the mast-producing hardwoods most valued by colonists for firewood, building materials, and livestock feed lost their advantage and more fire-sensitive and shade-tolerant
species (hemlock, beech, and maple) seized the opportunity to flourish. This
shift toward shade-tolerant species reinforced changes in woodland diversity
already under way as a result of the selective harvesting of trees for firewood
and timber. Most immediately and most noticeably, the woodlands became
increasingly impassable for travelers, hunters, and those seeking timber and
firewood. Bushes, brush, and brambles began to encroach on the highways
and paths that connected the valley towns. Meadows and planting fields came
under siege by woody intruders.[48] In place of burning, farmers were forced

to hack through encroaching brush, uprooting saplings and bushes as they went. [49] In this they were aided by their cattle, horses, and other livestock, which were often allowed to graze at the edge of woodlands, consuming or trampling new growth as they went. [50]

By limiting burning, building fences, and planting their fields with European crops, English colonists attempted to replicate to as great an extent as possible the material culture they had enjoyed in old England. In terms of food, this meant a strong cultural preference for wheat bread to accompany daily meals. Colonists from the Massachusetts Bay, to the Plymouth Plantation, to the coastal towns of Connecticut experimented with English grains from the earliest days of settlement, but were often disappointed that their imported crops did not seem to grow as well in New England's rugged soils as they had back home in England.

Most New England soils were poorly suited to wheat. Woodlands sheltered rich, but thin, soils beneath their branches. Once cleared, woodland soils might yield farmers a few good years of crops before exhaustion led to declining harvests. Uplands tended to be stony, bedeviled by rocks churned up as the Laurentide Ice Sheet had advanced across northern North America during the last Ice Age, only to be deposited at the ice sheet's southern edge as it began retreating some twelve thousand or so years ago. Soils in the lowlands, smaller river valleys, and in the terraces that bordered them contained much sand and smaller sediment, which had settled at the bottom of the many lakes filled with meltwater that the glaciers had left behind to dot the landscape as they receded. These stony and sandy soils held water poorly, and as rainwater ran through them it carried away nutrients like nitrogen that field crops required to thrive.[51]

As wheat cultivation faltered farmers turned to rye, which produced a darker bread less preferred by English settlers, but which required less nitrogen and could be successfully grown in drier, sandy soils. One Bay Colony settler summed up the experience of most New Englanders when he wrote that "wheat and barley are not thought to be as good" at thriving as they had been in England, although he added that "Rye and Pease are as good as the English."[52] The English would be able to partake of familiar grains in their new homes, but apple cider would have to replace beer made from barley and rye bread (or more commonly bread made from a mix of rye and maize) would take the place of wheat. Although initially wary of "Indian Corne," John Winthrop Jr. observed that New England settlers quickly "found by much Experience, that it [maize] is wholesome and pleasant for Food."[53] Rye and Indian corn also enjoyed the advantage of being more cold hardy than wheat, a definite plus in a seventeenth-century New England landscape gripped by the Little Ice Age.[54]

The most pronounced exception to the general rule of poor New England soils was the Connecticut Valley, where the loamy soils of the intervals provided colonists with the opportunity to raise wheat in quantities that settlers elsewhere in New England could only envy. The broad stretch of the Connecticut's waters also served to moderate the microclimate of the valley, increasing the growing season and keeping late and early frosts at bay. Together, superior soils and a more moderate climate turned the Connecticut Valley into, as more than one historian has dubbed it, "the bread basket of New England."[55] Wheat was as close as Connecticut Valley farmers ever came to finding a staple export crop that could anchor their local commerce in the way that tobacco, cotton, and sugar did for other regions within the English Empire.[56] Indeed, one much-read historian of New England agriculture, Howard S. Russell, labeled the Connecticut Valley "the continent's first wheat belt." In some years during the seventeenth century, the Pynchons of Springfield alone were able to ship as much as two thousand bushels to market in Boston.[57]

In the 1640s, continuing purchases of maize from valley Indian communities coincided with the beginnings of an export trade in so-called English corn, a term that included wheat, rye, barley and other European grains as well as peas. In 1642, Connecticut's general court lowered the price fixed for corn to two and one-half shillings per bushel, suggesting that shortages had eased since the hungry years of the late 1630s.[58] By 1644, merchants buying grain from the Connecticut River towns had even begun exporting to neighboring Massachusetts and Plymouth in such quantities that leaders in those colonies accused Connecticut of "overfilling their markets" to the detriment of their own local farmers. To appease their fellow colonial leaders, the Connecticut General Court limited agricultural exports to a monopoly formed by a group of prominent Hartford merchants. However, later acts aimed at preventing smuggling by ships sailing down the river and out into Long Island Sound suggest that official attempts to curtail grain exports from the valley may not have been entirely successful. In 1648, the court bemoaned the fact that diverse merchants continued "drawing away Corne from amongst us, out of the River," and ordered local constables to visit all farms in their jurisdictions during harvest time so that farmers could not avoid their taxes by exporting grain before the annual rates were laid. It was not until 1663 that the Connecticut government finally relented in its failing efforts to enforce export restrictions and "set at liberty the transportation of Corne" out of the colony.[59]

In 1660, Connecticut Governor John Winthrop Jr. wrote from Hartford to a friend in England who was contemplating a move to the colonies. He assured his friend that "through the great blessing of the Lord," settlers were producing "a comfortable supply of all sorts of corne & provisions . . . not only for themselves . . . but also for many others." "The country," Winthrop continued, "doth send out great store of biscott, flower, peas, beife, porke, butter & other provisions to . . . Barbados, Newfoundland, & other places, besides the furnishing out many vessells & fishing boats of their owne." Winthrop advised his friend that he had only to bring money with him and he would be able to purchase in the colonies anything he might need—although Winthrop did suggest that any "English goods" his friend chose to have shipped with his belongings would likely fetch a handsome price.[60]

If New England as a whole was "comfortable" in its food supply by 1660, this general regional self-sufficiency was based upon considerable trade between colonists. Grain and other foodstuffs flowed from rural areas to urban and, in particular, from the Connecticut Valley to areas blessed with less fertile soils. The challenges posed by King Philip's War helped make this intraregional dependence clear. In the autumn of 1675, fearful that the newly begun war might threaten their colony's food supply, the Connecticut government passed a law to again prohibit the export of foodstuffs. The general court soon began receiving "many complaynts and urgencies . . . of the want of corn in the neighbor Colonys," which could no longer adequately support their growing populations without grain from the Connecticut Valley. Attitudes toward the grain trade had obviously changed among the leaders of Massachusetts and Plymouth. Far from opposing Connecticut Valley exports, as they had in the early 1660s, Connecticut's neighbors now protested that the grain trade needed to be reopened. The Connecticut General Court relented in the spring of the following year and agricultural produce once again flowed out of the valley to feed the inhabitants of neighboring colonies.[61]

Agriculture's importance to the economy of the Connecticut Valley only grew following the war. In 1680, in response to a query from the Privy Council's Committee for Trade and Foreign Plantations (a forerunner of the Board of Trade), the Connecticut General Court provided a list of the "Comodities of the country" which was headed by "Wheat, Peas, Ry, Barly, [and] Indian Corn." The list also included four other agricultural products (hemp, flax, apple cider, and pear cider) along with livestock-related products (pork, beef, wool, and horses) and forest products (boards, pipestaves, and tar).[62] The Connecticut towns had obviously grown and developed beyond their fur-trading roots. Fur did not even make it onto the court's list (nor had it appeared in Winthrop's 1660 letter), suggesting how deeply in decline the trade was by the last quarter of the seventeenth century. From the end of the seventeenth century forward, the demands of market-oriented English agriculture, rather than the Indian fur trade, would provide the primary driving force behind the major ecological changes in the valley.

Most of the agricultural exports of the valley were shipped to Boston, the largest city in mainland English America. At approximately 4,500 residents in 1680, Boston was not large by European standards (or by the standards of Spanish America), but its population was 40 percent larger than its next nearest rival (New York City). Approximately one in ten colonists living in the Massachusetts Bay Colony called Boston home.[63] The city's growth as an urban center, as well as its growing importance as a port for outfitting fishing boats and merchantmen for trade with Europe and the West Indies, meant that it required an expanding hinterland from which to draw provisions. Its role as an exporter of grain—and later flour and biscuit—tied the Connecticut Valley firmly to the success of New England's fishing fleet and carrying trade.[64] New England's fishermen and merchant sailors, whether they sailed from Boston or some other regional port town, depended upon the fertility of the Connecticut Valley to keep them fed (if sometimes poorly so) during their voyages. But Boston, especially, was more than just a provisioning port; it was also an entrepôt through which produce from the valley entered a wider Atlantic market.

By the 1680s, the plantation islands of the English Caribbean, Barbados chief among them, presented a growing market for provisions from New England.[65] If Boston, by 1680, had largely outgrown the hinterland around Massachusetts Bay and relied on foodstuffs (and lumber, etc.) imported from farther afield, this was even more true of the English Caribbean. In 1680, the nonindigenous population of English Barbados was approximately 59,000 (around 20,000 Europeans and 39,000 African slaves), handily surpassing the largest mainland colonies of Virginia (at approximately 43,500) and Massachusetts (≈40,000).[66] Planters increasingly devoted the limited tillable acreage on the island to profitable exports like tobacco, cotton, and, above all, sugar, leaving them dependent upon imported provisions. The plantations of Barbados and the other islands of the English Caribbean provided a ready market for the agricultural produce of the Connecticut Valley, most of it transshipped through Boston although a limited trade was carried on directly between the valley and the West Indies.[67]

Without this intraempire trade, it would likely have been impossible for the settler economies of either the West Indies or New England to have grown at the rate which they did. New England exports made the slave plantations of the West Indies possible. Slaves repeatedly faced starvation when warfare or politics disrupted trade. Tens of thousands may have died as a result of malnutrition during and immediately after the American Revolution, when the islands became cut off from their erstwhile provisioners. The farmers of the Connecticut Valley thus participated in and made possible a highly specialized—and, for some, highly lucrative—imperial economy built on slave labor and regionally specific agricultural production. England's Caribbean possessions fed Europe's taste for sugar—with Barbados generating more tax revenue for the English exchequer than all of the empire's other American possessions combined—while the farmers of the mainland colonies, those in the Connecticut Valley prominent among them, fed the planters and slave laborers on the sugar islands.[68]

The trade of the valley continued on in a similar vein for several decades. In 1709, according to a report by the Governor's Council, grain—"wheat and peas, rie, barly, and Indian corn"—remained the "principall produce" exported by the colony to Boston and New York, importing cloth and other English manufactures in return.[69] By 1730, the most important goods that Connecticut shipped directly to the West Indies were its horses and its timber. The colony still sent most of its "provisions" to Boston, New York, and Rhode Island, where commodities were either sold locally or transshipped elsewhere. The trade of Connecticut itself, however, was growing. A report for the Board of Trade listed forty-two oceangoing commercial vessels owned by Connecticut merchants in 1730, slightly over a quarter of which were registered to one of the lower Connecticut River towns. This number, however, underestimated the shipping coming out of the colony. For example, the report noted a sloop recently completed in Hartford that was collecting a cargo for a one-way trip across the Atlantic to the English port of Bristol. There the owner planned to sell both the ship and its cargo—presumably provisions for the port's famed fishing fleet. Such one-way trips were even more common in Connecticut's trade with Boston, where the newly built ships would add to that port's fleet, and the West Indies. Land clearing for sugar plantations had left much of the English Caribbean denuded, so sugar planters had need of both the provisions carried in the hulls of Connecticut ships and the timbers from which those ships had been built, with the latter being repurposed for construction in the islands.[70]

This 1730 report from the governor and Council of Connecticut, like those that came before it and those that followed, assured the Board of Trade that colony officials were taking all due pains to prevent any "illegal trade" by ships clearing the coast without paying customs.[71] Despite such protestations, the Board of Trade (and scholars since) remained convinced that Connecticut's small coastal and river towns were carrying out an extensive clandestine trade. Unlike Massachusetts, Connecticut still operated under its original, seventeenth-century charter and thus had no royal governor to police its domestic affairs. Writing on behalf of the Board of Trade, Thomas Fane, the Earl of Westmorland, drily observed that under such a government "it is not surprising, that Governors . . . should be guilty of many irregularities, in point of trade."[72] Imperial officials accepted as an exasperating open secret that Connecticut and Rhode Island, the other remaining corporate colony, carried on a considerable illicit trade with the Caribbean.[73]

Nor were English planters in the West Indies the only Atlantic customers for Connecticut Valley provisions. Boston merchants, and some shipowners operating directly out of Connecticut, did a thriving business with French, Dutch, and Spanish possessions in the Caribbean. Here, as in the British sugar islands, many planters and landowners chose to specialize in profitable export crops, leaving them just as dependent upon imported New England food and lumber as were their British competitors.[74] In the early 1730s, as Parliament mulled placing a heavy import tax on foreign sugar products, the government of Connecticut joined with other northern colonies in decrying what such legislation would do to New England's commercial farmers. New England's trade with the French, Spanish, and Dutch sugar islands, the 1731 petition insisted, in no way harmed planters on the British islands, since New England (along with the middle colonies) exported sufficient provisions and timber to supply the whole needs of the British planters besides also supplying foreign plantations. In contrast, an onerously high tax on foreign sugar products, the items that New Englanders most often received in return for their provisions, might ruin the commerce of New England farmers. A tax "would be of the most fatal consequence to the Northern Colonies," whose farmers would then lack "proper encouragement for clearing their lands and a proper vent for their lumber and provisions." Agricultural exports from New England, the petition predicted, would plummet since the British sugar islands would have no need to purchase surplus grain and other provisions that had formerly gone to the French and Dutch.[75]

In the end, the 1733 Molasses Act, which sought to impose a prohibitively high tariff on French and Dutch sugar products (including molasses), did little to change things, other than driving the provisions trade to the foreign plantations of the Caribbean underground. Smuggling increased, if only because a formerly legal trade had suddenly become illicit. Grain and other provisions from the Connecticut Valley and elsewhere in the British mainland continued to feed the slaves working on French, Dutch, and British sugar plantations. Likewise, legal British sugar and molasses, as well as smuggled sugar products from both Britain's Caribbean islands and their foreign counterparts, continued to flow to New England distilleries where they were turned into rum. This cheap and plentiful rum, in turn, contributed to Britain's slave trade in western Africa and helped ensure Britain's continuing dominance in the still lucrative North American fur trade, which by the eighteenth century had moved inland far beyond the frontiers of the Connecticut Valley to center on Hudson's Bay. Official imperial policy failed to stamp out a commercial network that benefitted enormously from the framework of empire but that had grown beyond imperial boundaries.[76]

By the 1760s, Connecticut's fulltime merchant fleet had grown to 114 ocean-worthy vessels, still mostly trade sloops and other small ships. Connecticut continued to ship provisions to Boston, New York, and Rhode Island, there to feed residents, provision fishing and merchant vessels, and be resold elsewhere in the Atlantic. The colony's direct trade with the West Indies had also grown and developed. Flour and bread (probably in the form of hard biscuits), rather than unprocessed wheat, now flowed from Connecticut ports into Long Island Sound, out into the Atlantic, and from there to the slave plantations of Barbados and the other sugar islands.[77] Towards the end of the colonial era, Connecticut was exporting/reexporting well over eight hundred tons of flour a year. Much of this was milled from grain grown in the Connecticut Valley, including on lands stretching north into New Hampshire and what is today Vermont.[78] Grain cultivation secured valley farmers a place in a trade network that tied them to the West Indies and from there to Europe and Africa, and wheat provided them with the closest thing to a staple crop that the region would ever achieve.

The fact that wheat never quite established itself as a true staple crop capable of undergirding the economy of the Connecticut Valley can be attributed to ecological constraints, on the one hand, and economic incentives, on the other. The first limited the degree to which farmers could rely on wheat alone to support their desire to participate in the market, while the second encouraged them to diversify in pursuit of new opportunities to profit from the variety of commodities their landscape could provide. Not even the moderate climate and natural fecundity of the valley could sustain bumper crops of wheat indefinitely. The constant removal of nutrients, particularly nitrogen, from the soil through farming successive wheat crops in the same field eventually left soils worn out. Along the intervales, seasonal flooding helped to renew soils, but ultimately did not return as much as English farming took out. At the turn of the eighteenth century, livestock raisers would begin penning their animals and collecting manure for fertilizing fields, but while this delayed soil exhaustion, colonial farming always represented a net loss of nutrients from the soil.[79]

A number of strategies had prevented Native American farmers from too badly depleting the soils of the valley. First, Indian agriculturalists depended upon an almost ideal mixture of crops—maize, various types of beans, and squash—all grown in the same field. Maize, like wheat, can be hard on soils and requires large reserves of nutrients, most especially nitrogen. However, beans (and legumes in general) fix nitrogen from the air and return it to the soil. Planting beans and maize in the same field helped replace the nitrogen that maize consumed. Also, whereas Europeans plowed their fields, overturning soil and exposing its nutrients to erosion, Indian farmers hoed their fields and only minimally disturbed soils. Planting their crops together also meant that the vines and leaves from squash and bean plants overspread the cleared ground between corn stalks, further limiting the effects of erosion from wind and rain. When soils did begin to become exhausted—the second law of thermodynamics dictates that all agricultural systems, no matter how efficient, result in a net removal of nutrients from the soil—valley Indians would shift fields, and occasionally even shift village sites, to bring new lands under cultivation and allow old fields to rest. Add to these factors a greater reliance on wild foods and game collected from far-flung uncultivated lands as part of their regular diet and the nutrient cycling benefits of regularly burning fields and woodlands, and it becomes clear that the valley's Native American communities, in contrast with early European settlers, placed far less stress on their local soils.[80]

As wheat yields fell in older fields, farmers often looked to newly cleared woodlands to provide them with fresh soils. These new fields would produce good harvests for a year or two, but soon the thin soil that underlay most woodlands would become worn out, or erosion would expose the sandy/stony earth below the topsoil, and wheat yields would once again fall to be replaced by rye. Far better to seek richer soils in the smaller river valleys of the Connecticut's tributary rivers. English land purchases on the Farmington beginning in 1640s, the Quabaug in the 1660s, and any number of tributaries as the decades progressed were driven by those who had come too late to claim prime lands along the Connecticut or by residents of older towns who were in search of fresh fields. They carried within them a commitment to English models of agriculture that introduced new crops and animals deeper into the New England interior and that linked these new crops to markets elsewhere in the region and beyond.[81]

Commercial wheat production moved steadily up the valley over the course of the seventeenth and eighteenth centuries, moving to fresher soils as yields declined in more established towns: from the original towns in the lower valley, to the towns north of Northampton in the middle valley at the turn of the eighteenth century, and then even farther north.[82] Sylvester Judd, the nineteenth-century historian of Hadley, Massachusetts, recorded that farmers immediately began planting wheat upon the alluvial lands near the river upon the town's founding in 1659. Yields on these lands had dropped noticeably by the 1680s, and farmers in the town had begun to shift away from wheat by 1700. They moved to rye or meslin on these old lands and planted wheat on newly cleared uplands. By midcentury, these too were used up, and the town almost completely abandoned wheat as a crop.[83] Instead, wheat was embraced as a staple export by new towns settled farther north in New Hampshire and what would become Vermont in the 1760s. From the twin river towns of Haverhill and Newbury north through the Connecticut's great northern oxbow, these new settlements yielded bumper crops of wheat, becoming for New England, as another nineteenth-century historian put it, "what the granaries of Egypt were to Canaan."[84]

Disease also proved a problem for farmers who may have otherwise pinned their hopes on wheat as a staple crop. Europeans imported from back home not only the crops with which they were familiar, but also many of the diseases that had historically afflicted those crops. The most notable and destructive for colonial New England was the wheat "blast" or "rust" that could leave entire fields destitute of harvestable grain. John Josselyn, writing in the 1670s, complained of wheat fields "smitten with a blast" that spread quickly to infect healthy plants nearby. The rust first attacked the stems of the plant, leaving them "spotted." From there, Josselyn observed, the infection "goes upwards to the ear making it fruitless." The origins of this "blast" remained a mystery. Josselyn suggested several theories, including "a vapour breaking out of the earth," or an ill "wind [from the] North-east or North-west, at such time as it flowereth." (References to the disease as "the blast" come from this common early modern notion that the ears of grain were blown, or "blasted," from the stalk by gusts of bad air.) Finally, Josselyn suggested that the blast might have originated in wheat fields struck by lightning.[85] This last theory can, perhaps, be seen as fitting most nearly with another cause commonly ascribed to the blast in seventeenth-century New England: the "solemne afflicting hand of GOD."[86]

The disease (which still plagues farmers today) is caused by a fungus that likely arrived in New England on wheat stems harvested and then packed aboard ships as hay, or on bits of stem mixed in among wheat seed. Arriving in New England, apparently in the 1660s, "the blast" found a hybrid environment that provided all that it needed to thrive. *Puccinia graminis*, the fungus that causes the blast/rust, requires two separate host species to thrive: wheat and barberry. In Europe, the spores of *P. graminis* had moved between wheat fields and the so-called common, or European, barberry (*Berberis vulgaris*), which grew wild and was also cultivated for its roots (used to make a yellow dye) and edible berries. In New England in the 1660s, the fungus colonized the wild American barberry (*Berberis canadensis*), a close relation of the European barberry. English colonists may also have compounded their problems with the blast with another effort to reproduce English agriculture in America. Josselyn mentioned the European "barberry tree" as one of many useful transplants successfully cultivated by early New England settlers.[87]

The blast took a significant toll on the grain trade of the colonial valley. In 1664, John Hull, a successful Massachusetts merchant, recorded in his diary that the wheat in the Bay Colony was "generally blasted and the blast this year took hold of Conecticot and New Haven."[88] John Winthrop Jr., writing in 1668, spoke of "thousands of acres . . . every year" blasted in Massachusetts, Plymouth, and his own colony of Connecticut. Thankfully, he recorded, "the peas, barly, rye & Indiā corne were not touched."[89] In 1680, the Connecticut legislature complained to the Privy Council's Committee for Trade and Foreign Plantations that "our wheat haveing been much blasted and our pease spoyled with wormes for sundry year's past, abates much of our trade."[90] By the early eighteenth century, Connecticut farmers had begun to work out the connection between the recurrent blasting of fields and the presence of nearby barberry bushes. In 1726, the general court cited "plentiful experience" proving that "the abounding of barberry bushes . . . do occasion, or at least increase, the blast." To battle this scourge, the legislature ordered town governments to oversee "the utter destroying" of all barberry bushes within their jurisdictions.[91] Massachusetts followed suit three decades later, suggesting the greater importance of wheat in the Connecticut economy.[92] But even with these preventive measures, the blast lingered on and, in conjunction with declining soils and the introduction of the so-called Hessian fly as a pest during the Revolution, contributed to the decline of commercial wheat cultivation in the valley around the turn of the nineteenth century.[93]

To a degree, seventeenth- and eighteenth-century valley farmers may have actually benefitted from the presence of the blast in New England. Governor

Edmund Andros reported to the Lords of Trade in 1687 that the economy of Massachusetts had "sustained great loss of late," pointing to the ravages of King Philip's War, two great fires that had struck Boston in the last decade, recent shipwrecks suffered by local merchants, and, finally, to "blasting of the wheat for some seasons past." Andros found the people of Massachusetts to be "generally but poor . . . and they are wholly supplied by Connecticut with provisions, without which they could not carry on their trade."[94] Writing three years later, after his unceremonious removal from office, Andros again lamented that "all wheat has been blasted there [Massachusetts] for thirty years past," adding that the colony's inhabitants were unable to raise sufficient food for their own subsistence but instead got "their meat from Plymouth, Rhode Island, and Connecticut," and their "grain from Connecticut, New York, Maryland and Pennsylvania." Massachusetts may not have been able to feed itself, "but," Andros added, "they build many ships and are the store-house of the Colonies."[95] Despite Massachusetts' own agricultural shortfall, much of the grain it imported from the Connecticut Valley and elsewhere went on to feed the West Indies. Indeed, New Yorkers complained in the first decade of the eighteenth century that Boston merchants were exploiting their prominence in the West Indies market to shut out New York flour.[96]

Ultimately, the Connecticut Valley's commerce with the Caribbean—whether conducted through Boston or another New England port—allowed the region to participate more fully in the trade of the British Empire and the Atlantic world more generally. New England exported more to the West Indies—grain and flour, but also lumber, preserved meat and fish, and a multitude of other commodities besides—than it imported in return. Consequently, the most important thing New Englanders received from the West Indies in exchange for their provisions was undoubtedly a positive balance of payments—manifested through merchants' notes, credits in the account books of transatlantically connected traders, and some specie. This allowed New England merchants, and the consumers they served, to afford the utilitarian and luxury items that they imported from the British Isles, with which New England ran a trade deficit. In terms of physical commodities, New England's main imports from the Caribbean were exactly what one would suspect: sugar, molasses (a sugar by-product), and rum (distilled from molasses). Most of what was imported was consumed in New England, but some of the Caribbean rum, along with New England rum produced from the imported molasses, was exported to Africa as part of the slave trade. The sale of slaves in the West Indies, in turn, further improved New England's balance of payments and allowed its merchants to further participate in transatlantic and global markets. In multiple ways, then, the trade of the Connecticut Valley was inexplicably tied to the slave plantations of the West Indies.[97]

Diversifying

Wheat cultivation, with its susceptibility to the blast and its tendency to wear out soils, could not, on its own, offer a reliable foundation for the lucrative West Indian trade. Most valley farmers diversified by also planting rye, barley, and /or other grains, and maize. Unlike the region's Indian agriculturalists, the English preferred to plant only one crop to a field. Squash, beans, and some root vegetables were relegated to garden plots alongside the home lots that lay in the center of English towns. In time, orchards of apple and pear trees joined this agricultural landscape, usually on sandy hillsides where grains grew poorly. Other parcels of land ill-suited to crops, but able to grow grass, became pastures for grazing or meadows for cutting hay. Marshes, for example, were often referred to in early records as "wet meadows." Livestock provided the majority of protein for the English diet. Game and wild plants played only the most peripheral role. English farmers diversified their crops and livestock to guard against disease and adverse weather, but still drew on a far more limited number of plant and animal species for subsistence than did their Indian neighbors.

Their greater commitment to grain agriculture had important consequences for the soils of the Connecticut Valley. The more diminutive seeds of wheat, rye, and so forth, when compared to corn, meant that successful farming required that fields be plowed before planting. Overturning the soil through plowing increased erosion through wind and water runoff. The traditional English affinity for bread made of wheat, which is far more demanding of soils than other grains, meant that nitrogen was leached from soils far more quickly than had been the case under the tenure of the valley's Indian agriculturalists. With beans and other legumes banished to other fields, no nitrogen was returned to the soil. Crop rotation with peas (the only legume that was widely grown as a field crop by seventeenth-century English settlers) did not become common until well into the eighteenth century. The same is true of rotating fields between wheat and other nitrogen-fixing imports like clover and turnips. As soils declined, even within the floodplains of the Connecticut, farmers saw their wheat yields fall and often switched to other crops.[98]

Usually this meant rye. The characteristics that helped rye thrive in the problematic soils of other New England regions made it an excellent choice for farmers in the valley looking to replace wheat. Rye was less demanding of soils, in particular requiring lower levels of nitrogen, and grew tolerably well in loose, sandy soils. As wheat harvests fell, valley farmers sowed wheat and rye together in the same furrow (an exception to the general rule of mono-cultured fields), rather than abandon wheat altogether on worn out lands. This mixed crop was referred to as meslin, as was the flour and bread pro-duced when rye and wheat were harvested and milled together. Meslin was a common food in England for those who could not afford pure wheat bread. In the valley it was consumed locally and may have been exported, folded within the broad categories of flour, bread, or biscuit.[99]

Grains were not the only crops that valley farmers chose to cultivate in pursuit of marketable commodities. A whole host of other plants, most imports from their old homes in England, marked the colonists' efforts to reproduce in New England the lives and economy they had previously known. For example, planting fruit orchards helped transform the alien envi-ronment of New England into a landscape more reminiscent of what colo-nists had left behind. Some of the very first settlers of the valley brought apple and pear seeds—or more likely saplings—with them for planting. At least three Hartford landowners boasted small orchards by 1639.[100] A landowner in Saybrook established what was purported to be the first nursery in New England by 1640 or earlier. Henry Wolcott, one of the founders of Windsor, established his own nursery in 1641 and by the early 1650s was able to sell five hundred saplings to a neighbor in a single transaction.[101] The settlers of the other river towns were presumably just as efficient in establishing their own orchards, if not out of a love of fruit for its own sake, then because apple and pear hard cider offered a convenient source of alcohol in a land where barley and other grains remained in short supply.[102] Fruit orchards complemented the broader framework of New England crop agriculture. Fruit trees grew well on the sandy uplands and hill terraces where other crops failed to pros-per, and since livestock could graze on the grasses that grew beneath their branches, farmers were able to put otherwise unprofitable soils to dual use. While most farmers likely produced just enough cider for their own house-holds, others produced a small tradable surplus, and still others specialized to an extent that allowed them to forgo other economic activities in pursuit of a comfortable subsistence.[103]

By the 1650s, locally produced cider had begun to play a small, but possibly important, role in the fur trade of the valley. English traders likely welcomed the chance to offer their Indian trading partners a relatively low-cost, locally produced commodity in place of expensive imported goods—a product that

was, moreover, quickly consumed and addictive, thus helping to create a continued demand. Fearful of hard cider's effects, the Connecticut General Court
banned its sale to Indians in 1654 (as did Massachusetts in 1657), although
court records prove that the trade persisted.[104] In 1680, the general court listed
"cider" and "perry" (hard pear cider) as two of the commodities that Connecticut was exporting to other colonies, a trade that persisted up through the
Revolution, by which time apples, too, were being exported.[105]

In the eighteenth century, farmers in Wethersfield became famous for
growing and exporting the town's signature red, flat onions. By midcentury,
Wethersfield onions had become a regular part of the cargoes carried to the
West Indies aboard trading vessels putting out from Boston, New London,
and the ports of the Connecticut, each ship carrying thousands of ropes of
onions with about three to four dozen onions to the rope. At the height of its
onion trade, an early nineteenth-century gazetteer estimated that Wethersfield was exporting about a million and a half onions a year. Unfortunately,
whatever mysterious quality of the soil made Wethersfield so prodigious a
supplier of onions does not seem to have been shared by towns elsewhere
in the valley, where farmers were forced to seek out other crops to diversify
their household economies.[106]

In an exception to their general reliance on European crops, valley farmers
began growing tobacco in the mid-seventeenth century, although this seems
to have been primarily for local consumption.[107] Connecticut was exporting
small amounts of the noxious weed by the end of the century, and farmers from
the Connecticut and Massachusetts stretches of the valley slowly increased
their exports through the eighteenth century. However, Connecticut Valley
farmers could never compete in quantity or quality (except for leaves for cigar
rolling) with growers in the Southern colonies, and these exports seem to have
been smoked only by particularly undiscerning customers within Connecticut, Massachusetts, and neighboring colonies.[108]

Crop diversification provided households with the opportunity to afford
imported luxuries (and, in some cases, necessities) that otherwise would
have been denied them while also achieving a degree of economic security.
Unlike the sugar and tobacco colonies where a single staple crop undergirded
the regional economy, the New England landscape required settlers to pursue
multiple avenues for engaging with the Atlantic market. Crop diversification
also provided a degree of what could be seen as ecological security. Some
crops survived drought or flooding better than others, and the threat posed
by the blast meant that it was always wise to have fields planted in crops
other than wheat. Besides crops diseases, of which the blast was merely the

most notorious during the colonial era, insect pests also threatened farmers' fields. For example, "worms" plagued the pea fields of Connecticut in the late 1670s, although other crops seem to have escaped harm.[109] A century later, in 1770 "an army of worms" devastated the farmlands of the upper Connecticut Valley in a long swath of townships that stretched from Northfield, Massachusetts, north to Lancaster, New Hampshire. Wheat, corn, and other grain crops were devoured, but the worms left fields of squash, peas, potatoes, and flax untouched.[110]

This last crop, flax, offers perhaps one of the best examples available of New England farmers' quest for financial security through crop diversification. Flax highlights, as few other commodities can, the intricate networks of commerce that tied the eighteenth-century British Empire together. Initially, Connecticut Valley farmers grew flax with an eye to household and local needs. Flax fibers provide the raw material for linen cloth, and early settler families depended upon domestically produced linens—spun and woven by the female members of the household—to provide them with clothing, bedding, and so forth. In 1641, the government of Connecticut, recognizing the importance of this necessity, required every family owning a team of oxen to plant at least a quarter acre of hemp or flax so that "we myght in tyme have supply of lynnen cloath amongst orselves."[111] Laws passed in 1645 and 1646 in Hartford and Springfield, respectively, show that settlers were soaking (or retting) flax stalks in local waterways to soften their fibers prior to spinning the flax into linen. These 1640s laws sought to limit where such retting could take place since the foul-smelling and (unbeknownst to seventeenth-century legislators) bacteria-laden organic matter given off by the process was polluting the water that locals used for drinking and food preparation.[112]

By 1680, Connecticut merchants were exporting raw flax from the valley to Boston. The single most important import they purchased in return was cloth. In the same year, in a report to the Board of Trade, the colony noted that despite the surplus of flax being produced, shipwrights and ships' owners still found it cheaper to import their linen rigging (rope, duck canvas, etc.) from England than to rely on local supplies.[113] During the eighteenth century, flax produced in both the Massachusetts and Connecticut reaches of the valley and shipped through Connecticut ports helped make that state the single largest exporter of flax among all of Britain's American colonies.[114] However, as Connecticut's Governor Thomas Fitch made clear in the middle of the century, New England homespuns simply could not compete with cloth imported from Europe. Fitch dismissed linens produced from Connecticut flax as "the Coarser sort for Laboure[r]s and Servants" and, in 1762, wrote to the Board of Trade that local households produced and traded their own cloth only to "supply the Deficiencies of what our produce Enables us to purchase from abroad."[115] Connecticut flax and linens may have found customers in the colonies, but they could never compete in the broader imperial marketplace.

New England ultimately failed to produce flax in adequate quantity and quality to supply weavers in the metropole, doubtlessly disappointing imperial planners who had long hoped that the region could be cultivated as a source of flax and hemp to relieve English reliance on foreign imports.[116] Writing in late 1698, Richard Coote, Lord Bellomont—who was about to take over as governor of the Massachusetts and New Hampshire colonies—was one of the few dissenting voices of turn-of-the-eighteenth-century plans to supply Britain with flax from its American colonies. Lord Bellomont dismissed New England as poorly suited to hemp and argued that while the soils of the colonies could support flax, he did not believe the crop could be developed into an important export. Both of these crops, Bellomont argued, were "fitter productions for the soil of Ireland . . . to be manufactured there where labour is cheaper."[117] Events in the following decades proved Bellomont's comments on Ireland to be well-founded, as the island became an important site for flax cultivation and linen manufacture. The success of Irish farmers in growing flax did not, however, preclude its becoming an important commercial crop for Connecticut Valley farmers. British and Irish weavers may have had little use for New England flax, but they proved eager to purchase the flax*seed* that colonial farmers had to offer.

The life cycle of flax, and the physical changes that the plant undergoes as it matures, explains the existence of a transatlantic flaxseed trade. The optimal time to harvest flax fibers is while the plant is still "green," before it has matured to produce seeds. This is when the fiber is at its finest and most supple.[118] Flax is a finicky plant, and Connecticut Valley farmers lacked the proper climate and the surplus labor to produce a truly superior fiber, even if they did manage to grow the crop in abundance. For instance, as late as 1795, Timothy Dwight recorded that flax he saw being harvested in Greenfield was "fitted only for the rope walk." When Dwight later visited a mill in New Bedford, Massachusetts, that imported flax from the Connecticut Valley he found that it used the fibers to produce twine, rather than linen.[119] The quality of the flax fibers themselves, however, was of secondary interest to New England farmers who purposely let their crops go to seed, both literally and figuratively. It was flaxseed, not the linen, thread, or rope that could be produced from flax fibers, that was big business in eighteenth-century New England. This was most especially true in the Connecticut Valley where farmers often sowed a few acres of flax alongside other crops to provide themselves with a commodity that was readily tradable with regional merchants.[120] New England merchants' eagerness to deal in flaxseed had little to do with the commodity's value in local markets, since farmers usually carried over seed from year to year to start their next crop, and everything to do with New England's role as a purveyor of raw materials for the broader British Empire.[121] The trade connections fostered by empire allowed flax growers in the British Isles to specialize in fiber production while outsourcing seed production to the colonies.[122]

Flaxseed from the Connecticut Valley found its way onto Irish farms as early as the 1720s, but exports really began to climb during the 1730s, when the British Parliament lifted trading restrictions between Ireland and the Americas and began offering bounties on domestic flax cultivation within the British Isles as a means to wean the empire from a dependence on seed imported from the Baltics and Low Countries. Both policies increased the profits available to Irish farmers and weavers and helped make linen one of Ireland's most important export commodities. The success of Ireland's linen industry and flax farms, in turn, created a demand for flaxseed that market-savvy farmers in the American colonies proved eager to supply. By the 1740s, 80 percent of the flaxseed being brought into Ireland was coming from the American colonies.[123] In 1751, Jared Eliot, a Connecticut minister and improving agriculturalist, clearly stated the appeal of this new Atlantic commodity: "Flax Seed is constantly in so good a Demand to send to Ireland, and fetcheth so good a Price," it reliably allowed colonists to "make returns to Europe . . . [and] thereby increase our Export[s]."[124] A little over a decade later, in 1764, Connecticut merchant Joseph Trumbull echoed this sentiment, writing that: "Our Flaxseed . . . is the readiest of any [article] we have in the Colony, to make remittances to London."[125] In 1774, a board of inquiry convened by the General Assembly characterized Connecticut's foreign trade as focused almost entirely on supplying the islands of the West Indies. The most prominent exception, it noted, was the colony's direct trade in flaxseed with Ireland.[126]

Most Connecticut Valley flaxseed was not carried directly from the colony to Ireland. Instead, traders in New London and the ports of the lower river—primarily Lyme, Middletown, Wethersfield, Hartford, and Windsor—collected seed from local farmers and growers upriver and then shipped their cargoes to merchants in one of the three great port towns of British mainland America—Boston, Philadelphia, or New York.[127] By the mid-eighteenth century, the colony of Connecticut was annually exporting (and reexporting from colonies upriver) flaxseed worth an estimated £80,000—most of it drawn from farms within the valley.[128] In 1774, Silas Deane, a Wethersfield merchant and soon-to-be delegate to the Continental Congress, estimated that the colony exported thirty thousand bushels of flaxseed a year to the port of New York, whose merchants had by the 1760s come to dominate the trade between Ireland and New England.[129]

Linseed oil, produced from flaxseed, also played a small role in the export economy of the Connecticut Valley. Entrepreneurs built at least three linseed mills in the valley between 1735 and 1795—the first in Hatfield, one in Wethersfield, and a third in North Hadley. The oil produced in these mills served as a lubricant in varnishes and/or as a binding agent in locally produced paints. Linseed oil not used locally was exported, alongside so many other commodities of the country, to the plantations of the West Indies.[130]

The market in flaxseed undoubtedly helped facilitate the eighteenth-century spread of English agriculture within the Connecticut Basin. Most households starting out on new lands depended upon homespuns for daily wear and consequently grew their own flax for fiber. The ready marketability of flaxseed offered the added benefit of a commodity that could be sold or traded to help finance the early years of land clearing and construction that were often required to turn a new farm into a sustainable venture. As English settlement in the northern reaches of the valley accelerated in the waning years of the Seven Years'/French and Indian War, settlers brought with them the full array of crops that had been so successfully cultivated farther downriver. This included flax, although the New Hampshire government proved loath to leave the introduction of so important a commodity to the whims of private enterprise. Beginning in the 1760s, when the New Hampshire government began granting charters to individuals seeking to found new towns in the upper Connecticut Valley, town proprietors were required to identify any "Tract appearing to be well adapted to the growth of Hemp or Flax" and ensure that at least five out of every hundred acres in these areas was cultivated every year with these "beneficial Article[s] of Produce."[131] How well these provisions were enforced is hard to say, but merchants' records offer anecdotal evidence that flaxseed was an important commercial crop for farmers in the New Hampshire reaches of the Connecticut Valley (including in what would later become Vermont) throughout the 1760s–1770s.[132] The Connecticut Valley's flaxseed trade with Ireland continued to expand up to the outbreak of the American Revolution, after which wartime disruptions encouraged Irish growers to develop a domestic supply of seed.[133]

Apart from providing capital for farmers seeking to bring new lands under cultivation, the profits from flaxseed helped New Englanders afford the manufactured goods they desired from Europe. Chief among these were the better-made linens that they imported from Britain and Ireland to supplement their homespun.[134] New England consumers thus completed a great circle of imperial commerce, sporting linens produced abroad with English or Irish labor, woven from Irish flax that was grown from Connecticut Valley seed. Two advertisements placed in the *Connecticut Courant* a year apart take this circular trade network even further. In 1765, Middletown shopkeeper Benjamin Henshaw advertised his intention "to purchase more than a thousand Bushels of Flax-Seed" and promised to pay any sellers "the highest market Price . . . either in Goods, Salt, or Cash."[135] A year later, another Middletown merchant promised to pay "Ready Money" for "clean Linen Rags, of any Kind," presumably to be resold to one of the paper mills in the region.[136] These advertisements present a scenario where one merchant could solicit Connecticut Valley flaxseed, which would be sold to New York for transshipment to Ireland, where it would be cultivated for fiber and woven into linen. Many of these linens would then be shipped back to the colonies, often on the accounts of the same merchants who facilitated the seed's export, and some sold to customers in the Connecticut Valley (including many flax-growing farmers), who would wear the life out of their new fineries before selling their rags of Irish linen to be recycled by a regional paper mill. Finally, the linen rag paper produced would provide the medium upon which local newspapers would print new advertisements by merchants seeking flaxseed for export. Thus flowed the commerce of empire, tying markets that might otherwise seem exclusively local into the vast transhemispheric networks of exchange that grew to increasing prominence over the course of the early modern era.

While cloth was perhaps the most notable manufactured item that the Connecticut Valley received in return for its flaxseed, one raw material— salt—may have been even more important to the reciprocal, if often indirect, trade that valley farmers carried on with Ireland. Merchants, such as Middletown's Benjamin Henshaw, commonly offered to trade salt, in particular, for the flaxseed that farmers had to sell. A large part of this salt came, or at least was transshipped, from Ireland and arrived in the colonies aboard the same ships that had previously carried cargoes of flaxseed across the ocean. On other occasions, merchants advertised salt from the Caribbean, often obtained by captains undertaking a triangular trade that carried flaxseed to Ireland and then Irish and British manufactured goods to the West Indies before returning to the mainland colonies. Whatever its provenance, imported salt supplied New England farmers with a resource crucially important to their household economies, one which the region was not yet producing in sufficient quantities to keep up with demand. Salt flavored food, but more importantly it helped to preserve it. Imported salt allowed farmers in the Connecticut Valley and elsewhere to transform the meadows, pastures, and woodlands surrounding them into ready money (or, at least, credit) through the provisioning trade. Cattle and hogs set out to forage, or fed with hay or corn, could be slaughtered, salted down, barreled, and sold to feed the inhabitants of America's growing colonial cities or the slaves toiling on the plantations of the West Indies.[137]

Flaxseed exports thus played an outsized role in the regionally specialized commerce of the eighteenth-century British imperial system. Flax provided New England farmers with the raw material for homespun, but also with seed that could be sold to Irish farmers in support of the growing Irish linen industry. The credit earned with local shopkeepers on the seed's sale offered farmers access to a wide range of imported goods, including Irish linens, British manufactures, and salt. Without the proceeds of the flaxseed trade, English settlers may have found it harder to finance the clearing of new lands, perhaps slowing expansion into the northern valley. The close association of the flaxseed trade with the salt trade, in particular, underscores the relationship between flax cultivation and other economic activities important to the Connecticut Valley and to farmers elsewhere in the colonies. Without additional salt supplies, the English inhabitants of the valley would have had less incentive to raise livestock, and the slave drivers of the West Indies would have had to find new supplies of cheap provisions or, perhaps, limit their operations. With fewer cattle and hogs, the valley's physical environment would have had a very different history. Flax, then, played an important role in weaving the New England landscape into the larger tapestry of Britain's expanding imperial economy (so to speak).

Provisioning Empire

By the turn of the eighteenth century, farmers in the Connecticut Valley had joined a vast web of agricultural producers stretching from New Hampshire through New York and Pennsylvania down to the Carolinas who supplied crops and livestock to markets in the West Indies. Valley farmers fed sailors serving on the merchant ships supplying those markets, on the fishing boats that supplied New England with the closest thing it had to a staple commodity, and on the naval vessels that patrolled this vast commercial network.[138]

Large port cities like, New York, Philadelphia, Newport, and Boston formed the primary nexuses between farmers and merchant exporters. But a significant number of sloops traded directly with the Caribbean after loading in Hartford, Middletown, Wethersfield, and/or another of the river ports, often collecting together a cargo as they moved downriver. Most importantly, from both an imperial perspective and in terms of the simple volume and monetary value of trade, the provisions of the valley fed the plantation system of the West Indies, facilitating a commerce in sugar and other tropical crops that enriched the exchequer, raised the standard of living for New England farmers, and condemned millions to slavery.[139]

But the same market forces that brought commercial success to valley farmers held the potential to undermine that success. At the beginning of the eighteenth century, New England was largely self-sufficient in terms of basic foodstuffs (although the region's consumers continued to demand luxuries like sugar and tea that could only be obtained from far-off markets). This regional self-sufficiency depended upon a large volume of intercolonial trade, particularly between the agriculturally productive Connecticut Valley and the growing urban centers along Massachusetts Bay. By the 1750s, however, New England as a whole was beginning to import grain and flour from other regions—most notably the Middle Colonies and, in the nineteenth century, from the Ohio country. By 1800, even the Connecticut Valley was importing grain and flour to supplement local supplies. New pests, most notably the Hessian fly that began preying on wheat crops in the 1780s, explain part of this shift. But most of the change can be laid at the door of regional specialization within an expanding United States. New England farmers, even in the fecund Connecticut Valley, could not compete with the broad, open, fertile fields of the Middle Colonies and, later, the Midwest. At the turn of the nineteenth century, as New England began to industrialize, the region's farmers could not fully feed its new urban population. Larger producers from outside the region increasingly filled the void while New England farmers specialized in supplying perishable dairy products and fresh vegetables that could not yet be practically imported from afar. Within the British Empire, the Connecticut Valley had been a site for agricultural production, relying on imports from Great Britain for its supply of manufactured goods. In the new American empire, the valley, and New England more generally, would become the manufacturing powerhouse, relying on far-off landscapes to feed its growing cities.[140]

During the seventeenth and eighteenth centuries, though, the success of English agriculture drove a number of changes within the landscape of the valley. While the earliest settlers relied on lands cleared by their Native

American predecessors, later generations were forced to clear new lands. With land burning suppressed and the beaver gone, previous systems of nutrient cycling and soil restoration had to be replaced by manuring. In both cases—the clearing of lands and the raising of livestock for manure—valley settlers would find new commodities to supplement the income they earned from raising crops. Markets in firewood, timber, livestock, and preserved meat would join wheat, flaxseed, and other crops on the ships that carried the products of the valley out into the broader world beyond, and the lands and waters of the Connecticut Basin would be further transformed.

CHAPTER 3

Gathering Firewood

Scarcity Amid Abundance

Firewood, at first glance, may seem an odd choice for inclusion in a study of the Atlantic economy. Firewood from the valley seldom found its way to markets farther afield than Boston and New York. But for the valley's inhabitants firewood was a daily necessity. Without it communities could not have survived, much less produced other commodities for export. Native American firewood consumption shaped the woodlands of the valley for thousands of years. English colonizers brought well-established systems of woodland conservation with them to the Connecticut Valley. Throughout the decades, English settlers remained acutely aware of the inconveniences that firewood scarcities could bring for those seeking to make a home in the chilly climate of early modern New England. Time and again, town governments passed acts to protect against the depletion of woodland resources. And, time and again, these same woodlands were eventually clear-cut to provide wood for the hearth, pasture for livestock, or arable land for agriculture. (Or to achieve all three, since these goals were far from mutually exclusive). It is not that colonial settlers were unaware that they were transforming plenty into scarcity. Indeed, from the mid-seventeenth century onwards, the records attest to an awareness that local woodlands were dwindling and that a dearth of firewood threatened. Despite these fears, the inhabitants of Hartford and other valley towns chose to sacrifice much of their wooded land in order to produce other, more marketable commodities. Instead, they relied on an emerging regional market, rather than local supplies, to satisfy their firewood needs. This decision brought with it a slew of ecological consequences, ranging from increased erosion to decreased local rainfall.

*   *   *

For two tense decades, Hartford's Little River stood as the watery boundary separating two European empires, each vying to become the Atlantic
World's premier commercial and maritime power. When English settlers
from Newtown, Massachusetts, under the leadership of the Reverend
Thomas Hooker, sought a new home in the Connecticut Valley they were
drawn to the neighborhood of what would become Hartford; a valuable
site for commerce because it lay near the river's highest navigable point
for oceangoing vessels. The English settled their new town in 1636 on the
northern banks of the "Little" or "Fresh" River (later referred to as Hog
River, today's Park River) where it flowed into the "Great River," the Connecticut. But these English settlers were not the only newcomers in the
region. Drawn by fur trade profits, the Dutch West India Company had
erected a fortified trading post named Fort Huys de Goode Hoop in the
area in 1633. When the English arrived upon the banks of the Little River
two years later, Dutch traders in the "House of Good Hope" peered across
at them from the tributary's southern bank.

The two settlements coexisted uneasily for the next eighteen years. Arguments over the natural and agricultural resources of their shared valley
home were common. Affairs almost reached a head in 1641 when the English
attempted to build a fence around the House of Good Hope that would have
cut the Dutch off from the woodlots that provided them with fuel. Without firewood, the inhabitants of the House of Good Hope would have been
unable to prepare their daily meals, much less survive through a cold New
England winter. To counter this English plot, the Dutch dispatched fifty soldiers from Fort Orange to reinforce their garrison on the Connecticut River.
Fortunately for the English inhabitants of Hartford, a raid by Raritan Indians
upon Fort Orange resulted in the soldiers' recall. "Thus, possibly," one early
town historian concluded, "the battle of Hartford narrowly missed taking
place." Chastened by their close call, the English left their fence unfinished.[1]

Access to firewood may have provided, nearly, the trigger for this con-
frontation, but larger forces of imperial competition lay at its heart. Anglo-
Dutch disputes over lands and trade in the Americas, at the edge of each
state's empire, reflected a growing competition in the early seventeenth century for Asian markets and the carrying trade of Europe between dominant
Dutch merchants and aspiring English ones. Each nation's merchants enjoyed
the support of its government, and these governments were more than happy
to press conflicting claims to trade rights in both the Indian Ocean and along
the shores of the Connecticut. In the 1650s, this competition would trigger
the first of three Anglo-Dutch Wars fought during the seventeenth century

and force the Dutch West India Company to finally, in 1653, abandon its indefensible position in the Connecticut Valley.

Firewood from the valley played no direct role in these trade wars, and, indeed, never found a market in far-off ports (save for perhaps small amounts that may have gone to the West Indies alongside other goods). As a regularly traded commodity, valley firewood never made it farther than the colonial entrepôt of Boston. It was a regional commodity, rather than an imperial or international one. On the other hand, the production of other resources, for which there *were* lucrative external markets, depended on a steady and reliable supply of fuelwood. The fur trade, farming, and human habitation generally all depended on a supply of wood for cooking and for warmth during cold weather. Which is why English attempts to cut off the Dutch supply of firewood brought such a swift (if abortive) response. As European populations grew, demand for firewood would transform the woodlands of the region.

Which and How Much?

The seventeenth-century settlers of New England devoted entire volumes to the question of how best to navigate one's way into the next life, but comparatively few scraps on how they managed to survive in this one. In 1640, in a sermon titled "The Application of Redemption," the Reverend Thomas Hooker admonished his Hartford congregation that "wood that is knotty" required "sharper wedges, and the heaviest beetle, and the hardest blows to break it." "So it is," the reverend concluded, "with the hard, and stupid, and knotty heart of a scandalous sinner." Heads must have nodded in agreement. Hooker's sermon invoked the tools and demands of a physical chore that would have been all too familiar to the members of his frontier congregation. The resolute sinner resisted Christ's offer of redemption just as knotty wood resisted the axe. To overcome each required special tools and redoubled efforts.

Hooker's intention on that Sunday morn had been to warn the faithful of Hartford against the dangers of sin and to impress upon them the power of redemption. For the historian, Hooker's sermon also provides a glimpse of the physical world that the members of his congregation inhabited the other six days of the week—days devoted not to contemplation of the divine (at least not wholly), but to mundane tasks like the chopping of firewood. Splitting the tough wood of a knotty log required a sharp wedge and a heavy beetle (a block of wood used to pound the wedge into the log). The familiarity of these tools to the parishioners of Hartford provided Hooker's metaphor with meaning. Hooker's familiarity with the wedge and beetle reminds the historian that this was a community where even the most learned of inhabitants was expected to chop his own firewood.

If firewood was an essential and, indeed, strategic resource in the European colonization of New England, it was also a resource that always seemed to be in short supply. During his travels through New England in the early nineteenth century, Timothy Dwight, president of Yale College, offered an elementary system for predicting which of the region's towns were doomed by geography to endure a future of chronic firewood shortages. Good soil was a mixed blessing. It encouraged farmers to clear land for the crops and livestock that could bring them a profit at market. Poor soils, on the other hand, remained in woods. The most fortunate towns were those containing at least some tracts of land that "defying the hand of culture, and incapable of being profitably employed in pasturage," had been allowed to remain as woodlands. Areas of poor agricultural soils were thus "indispensable for the purpose of securing this great necessary of life [firewood] to succeeding generations."[2]

In Westmoreland, New Hampshire, on the eastern bank northern Connecticut River—known in the early days of its settlement as "the Great Meadow"—Dwight recorded that "the soil is excellent . . . it contains very little land which is incapable of cultivation," a fact that he feared "may hereafter prove a misfortune to the inhabitants" since "few farmers have forecast enough to preserve lands in a forested state." Farther south in Greenfield, Dwight observed "the ground is so rich, and so capable of easy cultivation, that the inhabitants have cleared it too extensively, and rendered wood for fuel scarce and dear." Doubly blessed were those towns that enjoyed both access to the rich meadowlands bordering the Connecticut River and nearby highlands that could act as a natural preserve for woodlands. Near the Massachusetts/New Hampshire border, Mt. Toby provided wood for the inhabitants of fertile Northfield. Farther south, the inhabitants of Hadley settled among rich meadow lands but could depend upon the "inexhaustible supply of wood" growing upon the rocky and sandy slopes of nearby Mt. Holyoke and Mt. Warner.

Hartford provides a useful case study of the effects of firewood harvesting upon the land, since it was neither cursed with good soil nor blessed with bad; most of the town occupied ground that was of an intermediate quality for agricultural pursuits. The meadows bordering the river were as rich and fertile as anywhere else along the Connecticut. Indeed, Dwight declared them "very rich; the intervales and the uplands being both very productive."

But farther in from the river the town's soil consisted primarily of stony loam and sandy clay, soils that often proved better suited to growing grass and trees than crops.

The woodlands of Hartford were far from virgin when the first English settlers arrived in the 1630s. The ancestors of the historical Podunks, Tunxis, and Mahicans all played an influential role in shaping local woodlands. Native communities managed their landscapes by the regular use of fire. Setting fire to meadows and the fringes of woodlands brought a number of advantages for New England natives. Burning dead grass, timber, and underbrush recycled nutrients back into the soil. Firing brush, combined with the girdling and chopping down of trees, provided arable lands for growing crops like maize, squash, and beans. Burning also produced open, parklike expanses of woodland and encouraged the growth of fresh grasses and berry bushes. These in turn attracted whitetail deer and other game animals. Together, Indian fires and agricultural clearing reduced the extent of woodlands below what would have occurred naturally.

Indian land management also shaped the species composition of regional woodlands. So long as fires did not get out of control and burn too intensely, regular burning favored fire-resistant trees like oak, chestnut, hickory, walnut, and pine over other regional species. The nuts (referred to as "mast") of these first four species provided an important seasonal food supply for both game and Indian communities themselves. Indians further promoted these mast-bearing trees by planting their seeds, both as a purposeful act of horticulture and by burying caches of nuts that sometimes were never recovered. They also cut down or girdled trees that threatened to compete with these more desirable mast producers. The end result was that by the seventeenth century, the woodlands of New England were home to far more oaks, chestnuts, hickories, and walnuts than would have been present without human intervention.[3]

The Podunks and other Indian peoples who called the Hartford area home relied on these hardwood forests for firewood, just as would later European settlers. The construction of Indian wigwams and lodges generally favored air circulation over insulation, explaining the early explorers' and settlers' reports of New England Indians as prodigious consumers of firewood. The collection and felling of firewood placed further pressure on local woodlands and likely played a role, alongside seasonal burning, in maintaining sections of cleared land and open parklands surrounding local villages. As both firewood supplies and soil fertility declined, individual valley villages, whose populations could number into the hundreds, relocated to new areas. One scholar has estimated that a village in the Connecticut Valley required about

2,300 acres of cleared land every fifty years to maintain its subsistence. In the populous valley of the early seventeenth century (prior to the assault of European epidemics) most favorable town sites would have been home to a village within the recent past. Well-watered sites along major rivers and their tributaries (sites such as Hartford) would have been especially attractive.[4] The woodlands surrounding Hartford in the 1630s, rather than being pristine, may well have been well-picked over by the Podunks who had invited the English to settle there.

It took the inhabitants of Hartford about fifty years to begin to feel the pinch of dwindling fuel supplies. Beginning with those woods lying closest to the town center, Hartford's inhabitants gradually cleared the woodlands around them, venturing farther and farther afield in their search for fuel. By the last decades of the seventeenth century, they had begun to push up against the borders of neighboring towns. To stave off increasing scarcity towns passed laws to regulate use and conserve resources—slowing, if not stopping, the depletion of woodlands. Ultimately, the inhabitants of Hartford turned to a developing local market that connected increasingly denuded urban centers to their still-wooded hinterlands. As the decades of the seventeenth century rolled by, the destruction of woodlands spread slowly from Hartford's center, into lands on the town's periphery, and then farther outwards to the smaller settlements that made up its hinterlands. Through the market, urban dwellers exported the environmental impact of firewood consumption to other less-populated localities lying beyond the town's border.

Even as the town grew, winters in Hartford—just like elsewhere in New England—meant learning to live with the tyranny of seasonal cold. In a literary scene drawn in part from her own memories growing up in the early nineteenth century, Connecticut native Harriet Beecher Stowe painted a rather inhospitable portrait of the New England winter: "There was always something exhilarating about those extremely cold days, when a very forest of logs, heaped up and burning in the great chimney, could not warm the other side of the kitchen; and when Aunt Lois, standing with her back so near the blaze as to be uncomfortably warm, yet found her dish-towel freezing in her hand while she wiped the teacup drawn from the almost boiling water."[5] Although fictional, Stowe's Aunt Lois offers an image of the life of colonial women who stood or stooped, tending the kitchen fire all day, year-round, to ensure that it kept burning—stoking it higher in cold weather to keep away the chill. This continuous source of warmth made the kitchen the center of wintertime life in the colonial home once the first rude one-room houses had been replaced or improved upon. Other rooms were often closed off during the cold weather months. In homes with multiple fireplaces, the kitchen fire often subsisted for routine activities, with auxiliary fires only being lit when entertaining company. As the decades passed, some wealthier inhabitants found that they could afford to keep fires burning in multiple rooms on a regular basis, but it is unclear how common this practice may have been. After all, the fuel demands of even a single continuously burning kitchen fire could be significant.

Spurring this huge demand for firewood was the grossly inefficient design of colonial fireplaces. Broad and cavernous, these fireplaces conformed to an English tradition of open-hearth cooking and heating. Some colonial Connecticut Valley homes contained fireplaces six feet in length and with a ceiling as much as five feet in height.[6] These fireplaces functioned as a part of the room to which they belonged. As they cooked, women would actually enter the fireplace, stooping beneath the raised ceiling to hang pots from chains suspended over the fire. Periodically, they would return, stooping once again and leaning close to the flames to check on a dish.[7] On cold evenings, children (and in larger fireplaces, their parents) would seat themselves on settles placed *within* the fireplace to take extra advantage of the warmth.

The 1685 will of Hartford resident William Randall offers a glimpse into the material culture that surrounded these immense open-hearth fireplaces. After providing for his two step-sons, Randall left his step-daughter Rachel Grant "the rest of my household Stuffe," including "an Iron Pott, Trammells, Spit, Slice & Tongs."[8] Upon marriage, Rachel would need all of these implements for the maintenance of her own kitchen. Kitchen fires required constant attention. Using the tongs and slice (a type of fire shovel), Rachel would have regularly stirred the ashes and rearranged logs in her kitchen fireplace to keep the fire burning evenly and prevent the embers from going out. The spit allowed her to roast meat over the open fire. Large iron pots were the workhorses of the colonial kitchen, used to prepare stews and pottages. Rachel would have used her newly inherited trammel (a series of rings or chains hung from a metal bar and mounted on a crane within the fireplace) to suspend her meals over the fire, occasionally slipping into the fireplace to stir them.[9]

Though well-adapted to traditional English culinary culture, these fireplaces proved a poor fit for the harsher winters English settlers encountered in New England. Traditional English fireplaces and chimneys followed simple designs and were cheap and easy to build. Early on, the relative abundance of woodlands and scarcity of labor discouraged innovation. Settlers could compensate for the colder climate by consuming firewood on a level almost undreamed of back in England. As late as 1776, a New Englander visiting

London during the winter opined, "The fires here [are] not to be compared to our large American ones of oak and walnut, nor near so comfortable; would that I was away!"[10]

Change had to wait for the arrival of new technological options. Much of continental Europe used more efficient stoves for home heating during the seventeenth and eighteenth centuries, but most New Englanders had little or no direct knowledge of this alternative technology. In 1744, Benjamin Franklin summed up the disadvantages of these "large open fire-places used . . . generally in the country, and in the kitchen." The continuous upward motion of heated air toward the fireplace's spacious ceiling, and then back and up the chimney, created a chilling draft by sucking cold air into the room in its place. "The greatest part of the heat from the fire is lost," Franklin complained, "so that people are continually laying on more [wood]," and "thus five sixths at least of the heat (and consequently of the fuel) is wasted."[11] A workable new model did not arrive in the American colonies until the arrival of large numbers of German immigrants in the first half of the eighteenth century and even then diffusion of the new technology proved slow.[12]

The question of just how much firewood the average colonial household used is a difficult one. Surviving records offer many tantalizing clues about the importance of a sufficient firewood supply to New England households, but frustratingly few concrete figures with which to work. Conventional wisdom, reproduced in numerous monographs, suggests that the average colonial New England household burned somewhere between twenty and forty cords a year.[13] (A cord equals a pile of firewood stacked four feet high, four feet wide, and eight feet long, or 128 ft^3 of wood.) Local sources from the Hartford area suggest that the upper bound of this estimate might be a little high, at least for the seventeenth century, while the figure of twenty cords a year represents a good working minimum. A better practical estimate (and the one used henceforth in this chapter) would be twenty to thirty cords, with anecdotal evidence suggesting that actual per-household consumption of firewood in the seventeenth-century Connecticut Valley may have fallen closer to the lower bound of this range.[14] This average consumption probably increased over time as homes became grander and some residents more well to do, but also because the very best firewood (from species with the greatest heat values) in a town was likely used up first. As the decades progressed, inhabitants would have had to make due with inferior varieties that provided less heat when burned. As a consequence, an increase over time in the number of cords burned may represent not just a growing absolute demand for firewood, but the relative scarcity of the superior fuel woods enjoyed by previous generations.

Averages for cords burned per year obscure a variety of particulars: most notably the question of which woods colonial settlers were choosing to burn. The earliest surviving account books of the Hartford area can give the impression that for the English settlers of the Connecticut Valley, wood was wood. For example, an account book used by three generations of farmers from the Francis family of Wethersfield, spanning the eighteenth century, contains 152 entries related to the cutting, carting, sledding, and selling of wood to neighbors.[15] None of these specify the species of wood involved in the transaction. The turn-of-the-eighteenth-century account book of farmer Joseph Olmsted contains four dozen firewood-related entries. Only one identifies the species of wood: in 1704 he sold two loads of "walnutt wood" to his son Joseph Olmsted Jr.[16]

Of course, all wood was *not* created equal, a fact certainly recognized, if not always commented upon, by Hartford's seventeenth-century settlers. Hardwoods burned the longest and warmest. Of those species locally available, hickory possessed the greatest heat content, followed by oak, maple, birch, and beech. Softwoods, like locally available white and pitch pines, could still be used to warm the home and cook meals, but did so less efficiently. A home would need 20 percent more white pine by volume to produce the same amount of heat that could be obtained through burning oak. Pitch pine ignites and burns fiercely but produces prodigious amounts of thick black smoke that can befoul chimneys with soot, making it less than ideal as fuel wood. Its high resin content, the source of its high reserve of potential energy, would also cause the fire to sputter, possibly spitting out sparks that could ignite clothing, floorcoverings, or furniture.[17] In short, pine burned hot and fast; it might serve well as kindling but New England winters demanded hearth logs of hardwood that would provide ample heat all day long and still leave smoldering embers to light the next morning's fire. By fortuitous coincidence, the fuelwood species that English settlers came most to rely upon were the very same species that Native Americans had for generations been selecting for through their agricultural and land burning practices: oak, chestnut, hickory, and walnut.

The New England environment required a certain degree of adjustment from immigrants used to heating their former homes with the woods of old England. Oak remained a mainstay in the fireplaces of America, just as it was in England, although English settlers had to learn which New England oak species burned better than others. The preferred wood in English fireplaces was white oak, a species also found in New England. Red oak, an exclusively American species, was more abundant and burned almost as well.

The black oak of New England, however, retained moisture more than other woods even after seasoning, burning poorly and releasing less heat.[18] Eventually, hickory and walnut emerged as the favored fuels for New England fireplaces, surpassing even white oak in popularity. Early English writers—unfamiliar with hickory, which has no European relatives—often confused these two trees, lumping them together under the same name. William Wood recognized the value of New England "walnut" early on, praising it as superior to English walnut in a longer description of the tree that strongly suggests he was actually describing hickory.[19] In his 1749 history of the British settlements of America, William Douglass told his English readers that the "Hickory or white Walnut" is "our best wood."[20] Timothy Dwight categorized the walnut tree as a type of hickory and "the best wood for fuel."[21] This broad walnut/hickory category likely also embraced the chestnut tree, another nut-bearing hardwood common to New England but conspicuously absent from colonial records.

Surviving account books offer some idea of the high value placed on "walnut" in eighteenth-century Hartford. Like most in this era, landowner Samuel Catlin's accounts for the first two decades of the eighteenth century fail to distinguish among species when recording wood that he sold. Some of Catlin's later entries, those dated during the 1720s, do single out walnut and oak from other woods. By Catlin's accounts, a cord of walnut cost six pence more than a cord of oak (nine shillings versus eight shillings and six pence, or about a 5½ percent markup for walnut), while a general cord of "wood" sold for a full shilling less than walnut (eight shillings for "wood," so that walnut sold at an 11 percent premium).[22] Daniel Wadsworth's accounts from the 1740s also separate out walnut, and in one case oak, from the general category of wood. A load of "wood" cost fifteen shillings by Wadsworth's accounts, a load of oak eighteen shillings, and a cord of "walnught" one pound and ten shillings.[23] Even assuming that a "load" amounted to only about three-quarters of a cord, this would still price walnut wood at about one pound and two shillings; 20 percent higher than the price for oak and a third more expensive than wood in general.[24] This distinction between walnut, oak, and other woods—as well as the climbing prices of all wood, no matter the species—suggests that growing scarcity might have led to a greater discernment among firewood sellers and consumers as the eighteenth century progressed.

This scarcity was fed not just by household consumption, but also by a myriad of other demands on Hartford's woodlands. Buildings and fences were sometimes constructed of the same hardwood species that went onto the hearth, although softwoods were often substituted to take the strain off of

firewood supplies. Indeed, pine became a favorite building material for colonial homes. Shipbuilding and barrel making, on the other hand, demanded
large quantities of hardwood—oak, in particular—placing these industries
in direct competition with firewood harvesters. Indeed, alternative uses for
oak may explain why New Englanders preferred to burn hickory and walnut
despite oak's heavy usage as fuel in England. The tanning of leather—bath-
ing hides in a solution of ground bark to make them supple and workable—
placed further demands on New England oaks. Although a variety of tree
barks could be used, the bark of the multifaceted oak was the tanner's traditional favorite.[25] Tanners in Hartford often collected their bark from live
trees, although they also likely utilized the bark of trees felled by neighbors
for other purposes.[26] Removing bark threatened the health and life of trees,
making it easier for insect and fungal infections to enter the wood. In 1697,
to avoid such destruction of valuable wood, the town prohibited inhabitants
from collecting bark from trees standing on the town's commons.[27]

Nor were private households the only consumers of firewood in colonial
towns. The local blacksmiths who made and mended tools relied on charcoal
to fire their forges. Charcoal was obtained by piling logs in an earthen pit or
kiln, setting them ablaze, and then covering them over with dirt and leaves.
The goal was to achieve a slow, "dead" fire that would char the wood without
consuming it. The process burned off water and superfluous elements, leaving a carbon-rich residue that would burn hotter than regular firewood. A
skilled collier with an efficient kiln could produce thirty to forty bushels of
charcoal from a cord of fuelwood. (Most colonial charcoal pits, especially in
the early period, were probably not so efficient.) A busy smithy might require
upward of one thousand bushels a year.[28]

New England towns also required what one study of America's early
woodlands has described as a "seemingly limitless supply of firewood for
baking clay into bricks."[29] The earliest buildings were constructed almost
wholly from timber, which was plentiful and required less labor than building in either stone or brick. But even early settlers demanded bricks for laying
flooring and walks, and for constructing the hearths and chimneys within
their homes—a purpose for which wood was particularly poorly suited. From
its earliest founding, Hartford could boast at least one brick kiln, located
between the central home lots and the pinelands of western Hartford along
the banks of what became known as Brick Kiln Brook. As the city expanded,
and timberlands receded, brick became increasingly in demand for larger,
more stylish buildings. A second brick kiln was built on the south side of the
town in the 1680s and a larger brickyard built to the west of town in 1702.[30]

The Woodlands of Hartford

Which raises the questions of just how extensive local demands for hardwoods would have been and how well-equipped the woodlands of Hartford may have been to accommodate them. Originally settled by the English in 1635, 119 households called Hartford home in 1640.[31] Ignoring other demands—such as smithing, brick and stave making, and so forth—and assuming 20–30 cords as the average amount of firewood consumed by a household in a year, the town would have required between 2,380 and 3,570 cords just to keep its hearth fires burning. Working from the rule of thumb that a single acre of woodlands hosting a moderately thick stand of good hardwood species can "sustainably" yield approximately one cord of firewood per year, then approximately 2,380 to 3,570 acres (or somewhere between three and one-quarter to five and one-half square miles) would have been needed to keep the town adequately wooded.[32] By 1670, Hartford's population had grown only slightly, to 135 households, raising the town's firewood demand and the acreage of woodlands required to sustainably support it to somewhere between 2,700 cords/acres and 4,050 cords/acres. The woodlands of Hartford could most likely have supported this demand—although it is difficult to come by hard figures with which to work.

For example, Hartford in 1639 contained no woodlands—at least, to judge by surviving official records. By that year, the proprietors of Hartford had parceled out over 4,500 acres of land to private owners. Hundreds of acres entered the town's record book under the labels of meadows, pastures, swamps, uplands, and home lots. Woodlots, however, are conspicuously absent. This absence in the original allotments of land speaks not to scarcity, but rather to the abundance (at least in the short term) of wood for fires and timber for building. In the earliest days of settlement, wood and timber were available in such plenty that they did not warrant special attention. Much of the fuelwood burned by settlers during their first four years in Hartford likely came from lightly wooded private lands which bore the misleading titles of "meadow," "home lot," or "pasture" in the town book. Hartford's early inhabitants could also depend on access to expansive stretches of woods in the still undivided lands lying immediately west of the town center.

Grassy meadow dominated the intervales, the lands lying nearest the Connecticut River and regularly nourished by floodwaters during the river's spring freshets. Here, standing water lay only a little way below the surface, and any increase in the river's flow, especially the spring freshets, brought the water up over these flat bottomlands. Too moist for the deep roots of trees and shrubs, these low meadows remained mostly in grass broken up by only a few scattered trees.[33] Hartford's first settlers quickly set about converting the rich soils of these riverside meadows to croplands. In the process, what trees did dot the meadows were systematically cut down, and either burned where they fell to provide fertilizer for the already rich soil or else chopped up for firewood and timber.

Moving west from the river, the land slowly rose. Beyond those areas washed by the waters of the Connecticut lay lands less suited to growing crops. Here the first generation set aside pasturelands for grazing their livestock and home lots for the construction of houses. Hartford's founders set their city's center upon a promontory of land near the confluence of the "Little River" and "the Great River." Home lots provided ground for a family's dwelling house, promoting community cohesion by clustering inhabitants together within convenient walking distance of the town's meetinghouse. These small lots, usually about two acres, also provided families with land for a vegetable garden and maybe a few fruit trees. In the distant past, this piece of high land had been an island in the great glacial lake that had been the Connecticut Valley's immediate geological ancestor. Sitting above the lake's waters, the soils of the townsite did not receive the effluvial silt that made the intervales so fertile. In their soil, most of the home lots resembled another tract of land laying slightly to the west that the early settlers came to know as "the Pine Lands."[34] The good drainage offered by the stony silt loams of these areas favored the growth of pines, mostly pitch pine, possibly with a few white pines, mixed with oaks and other hardwoods that could tolerate moderately dry soils. Both building and gardening required that these lots first be cleared. Trees useful for timber went toward construction; remaining wood went to the hearth.

Given the opportunity, woodlands held the potential to renew themselves, offering the possibility of a sustainable fuel source for at least a portion of early Hartford's growing population. After being felled, the stumps of most hardwood species, including those most desirable for firewood, put out new shoots. After as little as fourteen years the coppice growth sprouting from felled hardwoods might yield a respectable harvest of firewood, though this new growth would not equal the amount of fuel originally cut.[35] Of course, a woodlot's actual ability to renew itself depended on a multitude of factors—most notably soil quality and a lack of disturbing influences.

Hartford's English settlers, as Timothy Dwight's nineteenth-century observations suggest, first targeted those trees occupying the best soils. Where they converted meadows and drained swamps into farmland, Hartford farmers felled trees and grubbed out stumps, while regular plowing and hoeing uprooted any new saplings that might otherwise have taken hold. The pasturing of livestock did not require the same efforts at land clearing as were devoted to arable lands and garden lots and was thus, theoretically, compatible with sustained wood harvesting. Cattle, hogs, and even sheep were turned loose to feed beneath the far-spaced trees lying along the southern and northern perimeters of Hartford's central cluster of home lots. In practice, however, livestock stripped the leaves and bark of saplings and either ate smaller shoots or trampled them underfoot.[36] Efforts to provide the best grazing and fodder for cattle, sheep, and horses led landowners and commoners to undertake annual brush clearings to prevent trees from repopulating pasturelands.[37] As a consequence, wooded pastures became steadily less woody.

Even where farmers and their animals did not altogether thwart the renewing power of Hartford's colonial woodlands, human influence wrought a shift in the types of trees to be found. The best hardwood species fell first to the settler's axe. If their stumps were left intact, these trees would put out new shoots to renew themselves. But these fragile new buds would then have to compete with other, sometimes more aggressive species, whose growth had previously been inhibited by the shade cast by newly felled trees. Less desirable hardwood species became more numerous. The biggest winners would have been softwood coniferous species like the red cedar (a notorious "weed" tree), the pitch pine (one of only a small number of softwood species capable of sprouting from its own stump), and, in far fewer numbers, the white pine. New growth tended to be smaller and less dense than the old growth that it replaced. New trees might be ready for harvesting in only a couple of decades, but it would have taken perhaps a century, and likely much longer, to truly replace what had been lost. As the decades passed, Hartford's inhabitants would face growing difficulties in finding a good load of firewood.

By the 1640s, access to wood in Hartford had become enough of an issue to merit the mention of woodlands in the town's land records. Most of the woodlands recorded during the 1640s were not new allotments; instead old lots gained new labels as the community's priorities shifted. References to "woodland lying in cow pasture" and parcels of upland that were relabeled as "woodland" after being sold make clear that woodlands were more widespread in the original allotment of Hartford lands than the records attest.[38] As the availability of wood in the home lots and meadows nearest the town center declined, Hartford's inhabitants and the town's clerk placed a new emphasis on woodlands—writing them, for the first time, into the town records.

The Hartford assembly passed its first act governing the wood supplies of the town commons in 1639, only four years after founding. The act required all inhabitants to seek a license from the town's selectmen before felling any trees from the common or undivided lands. The town assembly in January of 1640 assembled a list of ninety-five original settlers who were to have free use of the commons and undivided lands for the collection of firewood and the grazing of livestock. The assembly granted a further forty-one newer arrivals the liberty to "fetch wood & keepe swine or cowes . . . on the common," but "onely at the Towne's Courtesie."[39] The message was clear: even at this early date, Hartford's residents foresaw a day when the wood supplies of the township might not be enough to satisfy the demands of all its inhabitants. Even amid the abundance of the early American woods, scarcity, at least at the local level, was considered enough of a threat to require government intervention.[40]

The continuous and growing firewood demands of Hartford's expanding population also began to threaten timber supplies. In 1686, the town assembly complained of "the greate spoyle" made of young timber by town dwellers cutting firewood. Such young saplings, if "suffered to grow, in a short time would be fit to make posts and rayles," which were "like to be much wanted in a short time." To prevent this spoilage of young timber, the assembly chose by "unanimous vote" to set aside designated parcels within the commons specifically for the gathering of firewood and to impose a fine of twelve pence upon anyone cutting down young growth. Commoners cutting firewood in legally designated areas were told that they "shall cutt and clere all the wood as thay go, boath greate and small."[41]

This last portion of the act thus ran counter to traditional English practices for conserving woodlands. In the village and town commons of England and in the woodlands and pastures of private estates, trees such as the oak which put out a wide crown of branches from a central trunk could be "pollarded"—their branches removed but the trunk left standing to sprout new growth. Likewise, the long-standing practice of "coppicing," common in England and elsewhere in Europe, took advantage of the shoots put off by the stumps of felled hardwood trees, allowing these shoots time to mature to a sufficient girth before cutting them for use as poles, fencing, or cord wood. About once a decade, the assembly felt compelled to revise its prohibition on the "spoyle" of young timber and to redouble its efforts at enforcement.[42] Hartford's 1686 act points to the conflicting interests driving policies toward colonial woodlands. At the same time that the act sought to protect some areas of the commons for timber growth, it also provided for the complete clearing of other areas. In these stretches of the wooded commons, land clearing for farming and livestock raising won out over woodlands conservation.

Even the protections offered to designated timberlands was limited. An exception was made in the 1686 act for anyone clearing woods on the commons with the intention to build. The town may have been facing pressure on its supplies of timber and firewood, but this was no reason to stand in the way of economic growth. Even on the commons, progress required roads, fencing, and the occasional outbuilding or workshop. Private inhabitants could petition the town assembly to be given special use of lands within the commons and at various times trees shared this erstwhile forest reserve with sheep pens and pastures, a tanning yard, and a stone quarry.[43]

In 1714, the assembly increased to ten shillings the fine imposed upon any person who "cut down out of the Commons and use or sell for firewood any Young Tree"—increasing by a factor of twelve the fine put in place in 1686.[44] This new act suggests, first, a growing dearth of locally available firewood on Hartford lands, while also highlighting the existence of a market for firewood in colonial Hartford. Account books and probate records prove that a market had existed for at least two decades prior.[45] In all likelihood, a local market had always existed for this essential commodity. As the decades passed, increased pressure on public woodlands encouraged a growing and increasingly visible trade in firewood.

The Search for New Supplies

Slowly the tyranny of distance asserted itself and Hartford residents were forced to range farther and farther afield to secure the wood needed to keep their hearth fires burning. By the beginning of the 1650s, Hartford had parceled out only 575 acres of explicitly identified woodlands to private owners. Some lay along the western edges of the North and South Meadows, some in the Pinelands, some along Rocky Hill in the southwest, some scattered throughout the town's pasturelands, but most lay toward the banks of the Little River's two branches on what was then the town's western boundary. Added to this were a further 647 acres of swampland from which inhabitants might have drawn their firewood supplies. A total of something over 1,200 potentially wooded acres, then, lay in private hands—far too little to provide firewood for the 120-plus households living in the town at the time. For the remainder, inhabitants would have needed to rely on the town's common woodlands, which were becoming increasingly scarce near Hartford's inhabited town center. New woodlands, distant from the town center, would need to be opened to exploitation.

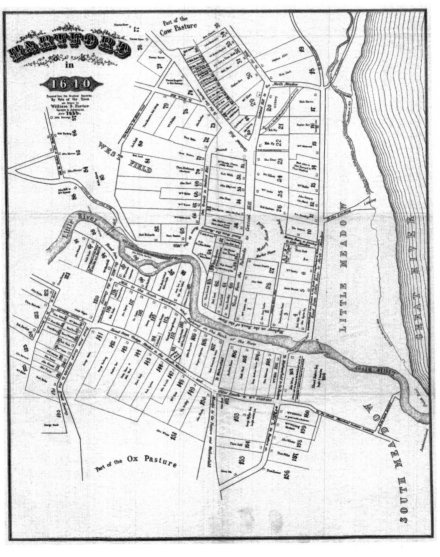

Figure 4. "Hartford in 1640," William S. Porter, March 22, 1851, Lithograph, 2012.312.210, Connecticut Historical Society. Courtesy of the Connecticut Historical Society.

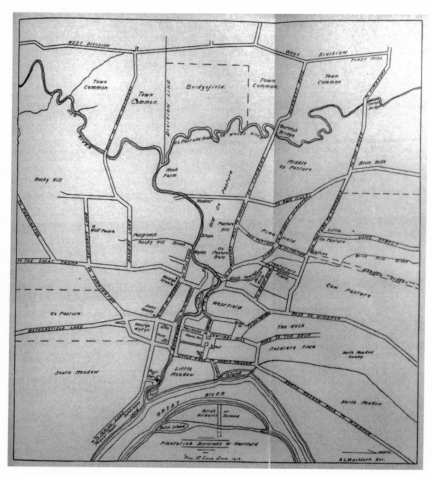

Figure 5. As the Hartford grew, its residents sought building sites, arable, grazing lands, and wood supplies ever farther from the original town center along the banks of the Connecticut. A. L. Washburn, "The Plantation Divisions of Hartford" (1914). William DeLoss Love, *The Colonial History of Hartford: Gathered from the Original Records* (Hartford: W. D. Love, 1914), 134. Courtesy of the Connecticut Historical Society.

Hartford's lands on the east bank of the Connecticut offered one possibility. In 1666, the town assembly voted to divide the eastern uplands, which lay primarily in woods, stretching from the town's border with Windsor in the north to Wethersfield in the south. These eastern lands, separated from most of the town's residences by the Connecticut River, offered a less than ideal solution to any present or impending firewood shortages. The Connecticut often froze during the winter months but not always for its entire width and not solid enough to support the weight of a team of oxen hauling a sledge full of firewood.[46] Rafting logs across during the warmer months may have been the most convenient solution, but still presented challenges.

These practical difficulties aside, the eastern division provided access to new firewood supplies for only a fraction of the town's inhabitants. In 1666, Hartford contained approximately 135 households, but only 55 men received lands in the eastern division.[47] The division excluded Hartford's younger sons (who had the right to inherit their fathers' lands but not always their fathers' rights in the commons) and the town's newer arrivals (unless they bought out the estate and rights of one of the town's original proprietors). Those already facing constrained access to firewood likely benefited little from the division of the east side lots. Instead, over 4,500 acres of new lands were concentrated into the hands of less than half of the town's householders. As the decades passed, the ownership of these eastern woodlands became even more concentrated. By the 1680s, over half of these woodlands were concentrated into the hands of just three men—all of them sawmill owners and all of them active in Hartford's timber trade. For these men, the woodlands of the eastern division likely represented not a new source of firewood to supplement the dwindling supplies on the town's west side, but a timber reserve to feed their sawmills.[48]

This explains the need for the next substantial division of lands, the so-called West Division, that took place only seven years later in 1673. This division embraced almost 5,200 acres that stretched from the banks of the Little River's north and south branches in the east to the foot of Talcott Mountain in the west, and ran the length of Hartford from north to south. Not all of these lands lay in woods. Like Hartford proper, the lands of the West Division were divided between woodland, meadow, pastureland, fields, and (by the mid-1680s) home lots. Tellingly, Timothy Dwight later effused that "for the fertility of its soil [and] the pleasantness of its situation" the West Division was not excelled by any other site in Connecticut.[49]

Once again not all householders participated in the division. In the 1670s, 97 household heads, out of a total of 135, received land in the West Division.

In the southernmost tier of lots, accounting for just over 600 acres of the total, the assembly prohibited grantees from selling their lots before they had been "fenced in & improved."[50] No such restrictions encumbered the 4,500-plus acres lying north of the split in the Little River's two branches. The new owners of these lots were free to sell any time they wanted, whether they had improved their lands or not. That so few did suggests that inhabitants found these lots to be of greater practical benefit than their east side woodlands. By the 1680s, three highways connected the West Division to the home lots in Hartford's center, each with a bridge spanning the Little River that allowed teams of oxen pulling sledges of firewood to deliver their loads to the very doorsteps (or at least to the woodpile stacked out in the yard) of Hartford's growing number of inhabitants.

In 1672, the same year that the town assembly voted to partition the West Division, boundaries were for the first time established for a formal Town Commons. In previous decades, Hartford's residents, at least those granted liberty, could depend upon the undivided lands of the township to provide them with fuel, with building timber, and with forage for their livestock. Gradually, however, the town had divided all lands east of the branches of the Little River into private hands. Year by year, the limits of unimproved woodland had receded. The trees of the town center had been cut down for fuel and timber and the land cleared in favor of frame houses, gardens, and orchard trees. Much of the meadows and pasturelands stretching to the north and south had been cleared for agriculture. To the east, the Connecticut River formed an effective barrier, discouraging the exploitation of the woodlands beyond for firewood. The West Division, meanwhile, butted against Hartford's western boundary and marked the limit of the town's westward drift in search of firewood.

Those with lands in the west, depending on the quality of that land, might enjoy access to firewood for the foreseeable future. But over a quarter of resident households were denied a part in the division. Another twenty-eight heads of household, about 20 percent of the total, received fewer than the twenty acres that would be necessary to maintain sustainable access to the minimum twenty cords that a New England household annually required.[51] These households, about half of the town, would still require access to common lands if they were to supply their own fuelwood needs. The town's assembly, recognizing this fact, paired the West Division with the establishment of a permanent Town Commons lying along the branches of the Little River between the previously divided lots in the east and the lands of the new West Division. This commons, the assembly declared, "shall be & remain a common forever for the use & benifitt of the inhabitants of Hartford."[52] (In this case, "forever" ended in 1754, when—after decades of encroachment by private interests—the last of the Town Commons was finally divided and parceled out.)[53] The total area of this newly bounded commons, most of which lay in woodlands, was about 750 acres.[54]

Assuming it was fully wooded (which is unlikely), this commons would have been barely adequate to supply the minimum fuel needs of those excluded from the West Division. The added demands of those allotted only small parcels, or who had larger but poorly wooded parcels, would have exceeded what the commons could sustainably supply. The wet and marshy lands lying nearest the branches of the river would have favored hardwoods of inferior fuel value over the more desirable varieties of "walnut" (i.e., hickory and chestnut). Early eighteenth-century regulations governing the harvest of turpentine on the commons suggest that pitch pines were a common feature of these woodlands; if not from the time of settlement, then as a result of the opportunistic growth of pines following the felling of species more desirable for fuel and timber.[55] In a 1702 act, the town assembly protected the increasingly scarce oaks and chestnuts from the axes of its inhabitants. At the same time, the town capped the amount of wood that could be taken from the commons to one tree per householder per week during the winter, suggesting that even less desirable species were becoming scarce. By the mid-eighteenth century, Hartford's assembly had enacted a great jumble of regulations restricting the size of trees which could be felled (in order to protect saplings) and prohibiting the cutting of all species of wood excepting only birch, alder, witch-hazel, boxwood, and hardbeam (all subpar fuel woods) to give more preferred species a chance to rebound from overharvesting.[56]

Tension between Hartford and neighboring towns suggests that the wood supplies of the new Town Commons were proving inadequate long before this. In 1686, when the town of Wethersfield granted one of its inhabitants, Sergeant John Stedman, a tract of land on its northern frontier, it did so on the condition that he protect its woods "from all intruders . . . especially from inhabitants of Hartford."[57] As ominous as this charge may sound, the Wethersfield town assembly probably had legal protection in mind. Should intruders from Hartford continue to poach Wethersfield's woodlands, the town would need someone to represent them by bringing charges against the guilty parties at the county court. Sgt. Stedman's new lands likely represented a down payment for his future legal services. Seven years later, the town of Windsor, Hartford's northern neighbor, took similar action. The town assembly reinstated an old law "to prevent Strangers from taking timber and wood out of the town bounds of Windsor."[58] In 1697, the Windsor assembly identified the targets of this revised law. The town voted to "impower" three townsmen "to secure our wood & timber to the extent of our bounds towards Hartford from any intruders."[59] In 1701, complaining that "the town of Hartford & severall of the Inhabitance there doe still continue to seeke ways & meanes to impose upon this town & to prejudice & hurt the publick interest thereof," the Windsor assembly provided for the regular election of officers to act "in any such lawful means" as they might see fit to protect the lands of the town and its inhabitants from further encroachments.[60]

Hartford's woodlands had proven unequal to the task of supplying fuel for its ever-expanding population. By 1761, approximately 283 households lived within the original bounds of Hartford proper.[61] Even by a low estimate (20 cords per household per year), Hartford's mid-eighteenth-century population would have required approximately 5,660 cords of firewood per year, and thus an equal number of acres in healthy hardwoods to support a sustainable fuel harvest. Even by a generous interpretation of the term woodlands (one including all lands listed in the town records as woodlands, swampland, "uplands," lands lying in "meadow & swamp," the whole of the town's "pine lands," and the entire acreage of the Town Commons), something less than 3,500 acres of Hartford remained wooded by the late seventeenth century.[62] Most of what lands were still wooded would have contained new growth—dominated by pitch pines, scrub oak, and immature samples of what preferred hardwood species did remain—which would have yielded far less quality fuel wood per acre than old growth or managed hardwood stands. Over 11,000 acres of these inferior woodlands might have been needed to furnish the firewood needs of Hartford's population in 1761. The core of the township of Hartford (what went on to be incorporated as the city of Hartford in 1784) encompassed only about 10,880 acres of land in total.[63] If the inhabitants of eighteenth-century Hartford were to keep their home fires burning, they would have needed to find new sources of wood outside of their own town bounds.

Just how a regional market grew up to connect Hartford to these new firewood sources is difficult to piece together. One scholar has complained of "the mystery of fuel wood marketing," wondering at the historiographical "lacunae" by which great attention has been lavished upon diverse aspects of colonists' spiritual, political, and economic life but "surprisingly little on the means whereby they have kept warm in their dwellings."[64] An internal market for firewood seems to have existed in Hartford at least as early as the 1660s. In 1661, the town voted eight pounds for the encouragement of William Pipkin to teach school. Each scholar who attended the school was also required to deliver to Mr. Pipkin a load of wood or else to pay three shillings for its procurement, suggesting a preexisting market for the commodity.[65] In early years, this probably represented an internal trade where Hartford residents bought fuel from their neighbors. For example, the account book of Samuel Catlin, a Hartford farmer, shows that he was selling small amounts of firewood (a few cords here and there) to others in town as early as 1700.[66] Other surviving account books record small amounts of wood being purchased from outside Hartford, but do not represent a large enough proportion of the fuelwood needed annually by the town to get a clear picture of the market. In the 1720s, for example, general store owner John Smith imported small quantities of wood, accepting loads of wood in payment for goods purchased by several of his Windsor and West Hartford customers.[67] But most Hartford residents seem to have acquired their wood not from merchants or shopkeepers, but through individual transactions with either neighbors or out-of-towners.

Swedish agricultural reformer and travel writer Pehr Kalm's description of the Philadelphia firewood market in 1750 probably offers a fair representation of how the Hartford fuelwood market operated in the early eighteenth century. During his tour of North America from 1748 to 1751, Kalm wrote of "peasants who lived at great distance from the town" carting in wood to sell in Philadelphia's public market.[68] Similarly, in central Connecticut, "peasants"—farmers and landowners from less developed towns upriver and from upland towns like West Hartford and Farmington—traveled to Hartford to purchase imported goods and market the products of their lands. This trade, in turn, supplied the urban households of the Connecticut capital with the wood needed to keep their fireplaces burning. Unfortunately, for the historian, such transactions leave few, if any, records.

Fuel wood from the Connecticut Valley was also finding its way to slightly more distant markets—New York and Boston—in this period, although it is impossible to determine the wood's precise provenance. Both of these port towns had outgrown the wood supplies of their immediate hinterlands by 1700, and, over the course of the eighteenth century, increasingly relied upon fuel imported by small "wood boats." Landowners from the lower valley joined their peers from coastal Connecticut, the Narragansett country, Long Island, and New Jersey to send cord wood to New York City, while the even larger port of Boston drew its fuel wood from many of these same territories, as well as from lands as far away as coastal Maine. Sellers were drawn by the high prices offered in these growing colonial metropolises. Depending on the month and the severity of the winter, a cord of firewood could be expected to fetch anywhere from one pound twelve shillings to two pounds ten shillings in New York and Boston in the 1730s–1740s, the same period when Daniel Wadsworth was receiving only fifteen to nineteen shillings for the wood he sold in Hartford. While Wadsworth chose to sell locally, at least some of his regional neighbors decided that big-city prices offset the extra cost, time, and effort required to sell their wood outside the valley.[69]

The well-documented life of lawyer and Windsor native Oliver Ellsworth offers a brief glimpse into this mysterious market. In the 1760s, the young Ellsworth took advantage of the firewood market to help pay down the debts accrued during his legal education. During his first few years in practice, when clients proved scarce, Ellsworth turned for his living to a parcel of unimproved woodland lying near the Connecticut River that he had acquired earlier in life—probably through inheritance. With just his axe, other woodsman's tools, and his own labor, Ellsworth set about felling trees, cutting them into cordwood, and finally rafting them downriver for sale in Hartford.[70] Admittedly, Ellsworth—who went on to participate in the drafting of the United States Constitution and serve as chief justice of the U.S. Supreme Court—was hardly representative of the "peasants" who supplied the bulk of eighteenth-century Hartford's firewood. Still, this struggling young lawyer offers a picture of the mixed economy of American farmers and other landowners who often relied upon their woodlands and the markets of nearby urban centers to supplement household income.

A Climate of Change

The seventeenth-century settlers of New England (at least those who stopped to consider such matters) were, in all likelihood, firm believers in human-induced climate change. Early modern theorists of climate believed that local environmental actions—most notably the clearing of wooded land—could transform first local conditions, then regional weather patterns, and finally the climate of entire continents. In part, this belief in the malleability of nature rested on early modern systems of thought that tied political morality firmly to the physical environment. Put simply, savage peoples inhabited savage climates while civilization thrived in civilized climes. In part, this represented the geographic/environmental determinism that underlay premodern systems of race. On the other hand, early modern writers saw the relationship between environment and race, civilization, and climate as dynamic. This meant that "savage" landscapes could be "civilized." They presumed that the moderation of harsh, savage climates would proceed as a natural consequence of a program of civilization.[71]

In 1634, English writer William Wood, who had spent four years traveling in Massachusetts and Plymouth, imagined that he could already discern evidence that the weather of New England was changing to become more like that of old England. Indian informants had told him, Wood wrote, that thunderstorms had become less common, winters were less cold, periods of drought had grown shorter. Wood credited these changes to the land clearing and cultivation of English settlers, few though they may have been at the time. Wood's words betray a belief that the actions of just a few might transform the climate of an entire region. Two decades later, in 1654, when more towns had sprung up but the New England interior still remained largely empty of English farmers, Edward Johnson confirmed Wood's earlier assessment. English agriculture, Johnson declared, had wrought a "change in the very nature of the seasons," moderating the burning heat of New England's summers and the blistering cold of its winters.[72]

As early as 1664, John Evelyn, a founding member of the Royal Society, offered up a physical mechanism to explain some of these changes. In his *Silva, Or, A Discourse of Forest-Trees*, Evelyn explained that "thick standing Forest-Trees and Woods . . . as is found in our American Plantations" prevented the evaporation of excess moisture and rendered those landscapes "more subject to *Rain* and *Mists*." This, in turn, made such lands "musty and noxious," incapable of supporting agriculture and unhealthy for anyone living too close. As a solution, Evelyn proposed that forested land be "improved by felling and clearing" so as to "[let] in the *Air* and *Sun*, making the Earth fit for Tillage and Pasture, [and] those gloomy Tracts . . . *healthy* and *habitable*."[73] Land must be cleared, firstly to allow for successful field agriculture, and secondly to clear up the mists and miasmas blamed for any number of early modern maladies. This, then, is an outline of the complex theory of landscape, bodily health, and civilizational progress that early English settlers carried with them across the Atlantic.

These seventeenth-century climatologists were right to emphasize the importance of deforestation as an ecological process, even if they failed to properly forecast its results. One of the greatest changes wrought upon the land- and waterscapes of the Connecticut Valley by Euro-American settlers (perhaps second only to the draining of ponds and wetlands as a result of the fur trade) came about as a result of deforestation. The lost woodlands of a single town, such as Hartford, may not have had much of a demonstrable effect upon local climate had it not been representative of trends elsewhere.

The timing and details of the particular story of land clearing and lost woodlands presented in this chapter is unique to Hartford, but it was repeated in many details up and down the Connecticut Valley and throughout New England as a whole.

The woodlands of another Connecticut Valley town—as coincidence would have it another Hartford (but in Vermont)—stand witness to this continuing tale of deforestation. Founded in 1761 in lands then claimed by New Hampshire, the town's first historian drew a picture of the rapid denudation of the local landscape and the climactic consequences that this was to have. "Since the hills have been literally scalped of trees," this nineteenth-century scholar wrote, "drouths are more frequent. . . . Most of the streams have diminished in size as the forests have been cleared up, and some are entirely dry in the summer time."[74] This nineteenth-century perspective on deforestation stands in sharp contrast to the theories of land clearing espoused by seventeenth-century writers. The triumphal taming of a savage wilderness is replaced by lamentations on the creation of a landscape of drought.

Modern understandings of the relationship between climate and landscape bear out this nineteenth-century author's observations on the causal link between deforestation and drought. Trees, through their roots, sequester rainfall and store water in their tissues. This water transpires back into the atmosphere through the tree's leaves during photosynthesis, helping create a feedback loop that encourages steady rainfall patterns. Trees also encourage local rainfall by disrupting wind patterns, in turn contributing to cloud formation. If sufficiently large sections of woodland are cleared, these processes stop, rainfall becomes more erratic, and local levels of precipitation decline.[75]

This modern understanding was first developed in the eighteenth century. The naturalist John Woodward, in 1708, published a paper suggesting that transpiration from leaves contributed to the humidity of a country and arguing that a relationship existed between the amount of tree cover in a region and its levels of rainfall. Should woodlands be removed, Woodward predicted, this "clear'd up space" would assume "a temper more dry and serene than before." Stephen Hales' *Vegetal Statisticks*, published in 1727, built upon Woodward's observations and went even further in suggesting a link between deforestation and the drying up of a country. Though Hales' work received a great deal of attention in France, his theories largely languished among the English-speaking intelligentsia. It was not until the 1780s that British administrators in the West and East Indies, seeking to explain the declining levels of rainfall that they were seeing in the empire's far-flung colonial possessions, rediscovered the work of Woodward and Hales. Building

on these two British thinkers, and the previous work of the French philos-
ophes Duhamel de Monceau and Pierre Poivre (both of whom published in
the 1760s), colonial officials across the British empire began to call for tighter
regulations on woodland and for the replanting of forests as a way to fight the
desertification and erosion taking place on the numerous island territories
under British control.[76]

At roughly the same time, inhabitants of the Connecticut Valley were
beginning to recognize this same relationship between woodlands and rainfall
in the changes they were observing locally. In 1794, Samuel Williams—minister
by training, newspaperman by profession, and amateur naturalist by inclina-
tion—summarized how valley residents had come to understand their impact
on the local climate in his *Natural and Civil History of Vermont*. "When the
settlers move into a new township," Williams observed, "their first business is
to cut down the trees." Such widespread transformation of the landscape was
not without its ecological consequences, for Williams declared it a matter of
"common observation" that where trees had been stripped away "the lands and
roads become dry and hard," and "small streams and rivulets dry up."[77]

In fact, the inhabitants of the valley had begun to connect the destruction of woodlands with changes taking place in the waters around them as
early as the 1750s—a full decade before French thinkers would publish their
theories. Valley residents blamed the loss of tree cover in the valley and the
surrounding uplands for decreasing rainfall, and lamented that as a result "a
vast number of little brooks are quite lost, and the mills upon them by this
loss rendered useless," the same sentiment echoed by the town historian of
Hartford, Vermont, a century later.[78] The impact of this reduction in precipitation was so great that even the "Great River" itself was not immune. William Burke, the English author of a geographical text published in 1757, told
his readers that he had learned from residents of the valley "that this cutting
down [of] the woods has affected the river Connecticut itself, the largest in
New England, and that it has grown distinguishably shallower."[79] Burke dismissed the negative impacts of this change, stating that "whatever they [the
inhabitants of the valley] have lost in water . . . where there is such plenty, is
no great loss." Local farmers, as have been seen, were far less sanguine about
the climate changes they observed, worrying about the impact of "drouth"
and the loss of power for grist- and sawmills that provided necessary services for their communities. In recognizing the link between deforestation
and patterns of rainfall and erosion, Burke's anonymous Connecticut Valley
informants anticipated by about twenty years the widespread acceptance of
such a theory by natural philosophers in Britain.

Valley residents, observing firsthand the ecological changes taking place around them, conceived for themselves the link between deforestation and desiccation—and by and large they seem to have done so independently of the intellectual trends in Europe. Williams himself, although his views were undoubtedly influenced by the various national and international scientific societies to which he belonged, pointed to the practical observations of locals as the surest source of information about the natural world. "The husbandman," Williams declared, "from the nature of his occupation, is obliged to contemplate a greater variety of things and objects. . . . His information becomes a practical and experimental science, far more improving to the mind and beneficial to society, than the theoretic tables or speculations of philosophers on such subjects."[80] Indeed, it was the same causal link between deforestation followed by reduced rainfall that would, decades later, encourage imperial officials elsewhere in the British Empire to impose limits on the clearing of woodlands.

Worst yet, the same deforestation-driven atmospheric changes that brought drought also had the power to bring more and increasingly powerful floods. The surface contours produced by deforestation led to new wind patterns that brought rainfall more infrequently, but that resulted in torrential downpours when rain did come. Rain, when it did fall, was more likely to contribute to floods and erosion. As small streams and brooks dried up, the larger waterways that remained became raging torrents during storms, eating away at their banks, carrying away large loads of soil and sediment, and threatening buildings and bridges. Without the spreading leaves of trees overhead, valley soils in abandoned fields, in fields lying fallow, or on recently cleared building lots baked in the sun and felt the full fury of storms. Timothy Dwight described the effect of such conditions on the clay soils of late eighteenth-century Hartford. In the uplands, Hartford soils were a loamy mixture of sand and silt "strongly impregnated with clay." This loam, Dwight observed, "not unfrequently is changed entirely into clay," through the processes of erosion wearing away the layer of fine sand that overlay it. "In dry weather," Dwight continued," the dust, formed of this clay, is so light as to rise with the slightest breeze, and often to cloud the atmosphere. . . . A dry season bakes the soil into clods; a wet season converts it into mortar."

Equally disturbing, given the Connecticut Valley's interests in trade, was the effect that erosion was having on the Connecticut River itself. No longer sequestered behind beaver dams, silt washed into the waters of the Connecticut basin made its way inexorably toward the river's mouth. By the 1750s it was apparent to those living in the valley "that the River in the Tide

Way grows shallower by Accretion of the soil brought continually down from above."[81] This silting up of the tidal area would have been especially troublesome if the Connecticuters with whom William Burke conversed were correct and the Connecticut River itself had, at least seasonally, "grown distinguishably shallower."

The Connecticut, at its mouth, had never been deep. The first European explorer to visit the river, the Dutch explorer Adriaen Block, declared the river's mouth to be "very shallow" as he sailed upstream in his New Amsterdam–built sixteen-ton yacht, the *Onrust*. At low tide, waters coming downstream would flow unimpeded, finally reaching the wide still waters of the Long Island Sound, where they would contribute their load of sediment to the great sandbar lying across the river's mouth. At high tide, waters coming downstream would collide with the incoming tide—slowing, swirling, and dropping their load of soil and silt on the spot. Such encounters are most dramatic just south of Hartford, at the far upper reaches of the river's tidal flows. Here deposits of sediment formed a series of shifting shoals and sandbars that came to plague the maritime trade of what had in its earliest years been a promising port for small oceangoing vessels. As a result, merchants in Hartford and the other river port towns often had to send ships out only partially laden, to complete their cargos at New London or other coastal towns.[82]

Trading Away the Woodlands

By the last decades of the seventeenth century, local market networks for firewood connected the populous sections of the Connecticut Valley, linking older and increasingly denuded urban centers such as Hartford to their still heavily wooded hinterlands. Although firewood would not become an important export commodity for the Connecticut Valley until the eighteenth century, when coasting vessels would carry cordwood from the lower valley to markets in Boston and New York, these early local markets intersected with the growing demands of the Atlantic. The much-sought-after oak, the hard, dense hickory, and the workable elm and maple all had their place in the construction of furniture, homes, and ships. As the focus of early Hartford's firewood demands shifted from the woodlands of the town's center, toward its periphery, and finally beyond, the ecological effect of that demand shifted as well. By the late seventeenth century, the woodlands of neighboring towns began to experience the impact of this demand as their landholders felled trees to sell in the Hartford market. Nor was Hartford alone in feeling the early impact of lost woodlands. Rather Hartford represented the rapid denudation of the landscape that overtook each new town in the valley, and in New England more generally.

As tempting as it is from the perspective of twenty-first-century environmentalism, the clearing of valley woodlands should not be seen as an unmitigated misfortune. At both the individual and the communal level, colonists in the valley made the conscious choice to fell the woods around them. Despite much legislative hand-wringing over the decades, settlers chose not to embrace pollarding, coppicing, or the other woodland management techniques that undergirded the preservation of woods on the commons of early modern England. Valley farmers and husbandmen decided that they preferred lands cleared for crops and livestock over a locally secure fuel supply, while the pioneering settlers of new towns chose to sell wood to their more established neighbors. For settlers living in the valley in the seventeenth and eighteenth centuries, the felling of woodlands represented environmental improvement rather than degradation.

On the other hand, there *were* unforeseen consequences. As a result of this rampant deforestation, the eighteenth-century inhabitants of the Connecticut Valley lived in a natural environment dramatically different than their pioneer forbearers experienced at the middle of the seventeenth century. The denudation of the valley changed the very climate of the region—disrupting rainfall patterns and increasing the likelihood of drought at that same time that flooding became an increasing problem. Erosion increased, as the roots that once held valley soils in place disappeared. Increased amounts of silt and sand washed down into the Connecticut and its tributaries. Without the dense system of beaver dams to hold back this sediment, it washed down to the tidal zone, where it created shifting shoals that plagued the oceangoing vessels that sailed the waters south of Hartford and continuously built up the sandbar that threatened to close the Connecticut River off from the sea at its mouth. The desire to exploit the natural wealth of the valley for trade with distant markets drew the first Euro-American settlers to the region, and the environmental consequences of that exploitation perennially threatened to choke off the commerce of their descendants.

CHAPTER 4

Felling Timber

Profits and Politics

Demand for Connecticut Valley timber came both from home and abroad. While the market for firewood centered on local towns and never expanded beyond regional urban centers like Boston and New York, valley timber regularly found its way to the West Indies and elsewhere in the Atlantic. While colonists relied on regional timber resources to fill a myriad of local needs, the Connecticut and its tributaries also offered an ideal transportation network for floating felled logs to sawmills and for shipping sawn lumber out into the wider world. As settlement proceeded up the valley, new sources of timber—particularly of the coveted white pine—became available. Lumbering cleared lands for agriculture, as did the harvesting of firewood, while also offering greater profits in the process. This quest for profits eventually brought valley settlers into conflict with imperial officials determined upon conservation of naval timbers, influencing the region's politics on the eve of the American Revolution. Local lawmakers, too, worried about the depletion of building timber even as ever-larger swathes of woodland were cleared for the market. As timber crews pushed onto new lands deforestation followed in their wake. With trees gone, erosion increased and rainfall patterns shifted. Meanwhile sawdust from sawmills polluted local streams and threatened fish species.

*   *   *

In the spring of 1753, Daniel Whitmore of Middletown, Connecticut, struck a personal blow against the authority of the British Crown and Parliament. When Whitmore discovered Daniel Blake, a deputy surveyor for His Majesty's Woods in America, lurking around a local sawmill, he seized Blake and hurled him into the millpond, where the imperial agent later complained he had been "in great danger of being drowned."[1] As a deputy surveyor, it was Blake's duty to enforce the White Pine Acts, which reserved all white pines in New England over twenty-four inches in diameter to the Crown and the Royal Navy. By performing his official duties, Blake threatened the livelihood of both Whitmore and others in his community who relied upon the mill to saw their lumber. (Whitmore also had a more direct financial interest in the mill, which was partially owned by members of his immediate family.) As an integral component of the mill itself, the millpond stored the waters that could be released to turn the mill wheel, which in turn powered the sawblade as it sliced through illicitly felled pines—each newly sawn board a challenge to imperial authority. As it turned out, the pond also proved a convenient receptacle for obnoxious imperial officials. William Blake, by performing his duties as deputy surveyor of His Majesty's Woods, threatened Whitmore's livelihood. In response, Whitmore introduced Blake to one of the tools of that livelihood.

This act of not-so-civil disobedience highlights the importance of lumbering and the timber trade—a trade which by 1753 was well established—to the economy of the valley. Most sawmill operators, laborers, and landowners engaged in the timber trade managed not to run afoul of the authorities. Like the colonial smugglers, merchants, and consumers who flouted the Molasses Act of the mid-eighteenth century, most opposition to the Pine Acts took the form of mundane market transactions occurring beyond the gaze of imperial agents.[2] Sometimes, however, when the official gaze proved too sharp and efforts at enforcement annoyingly persistent, popular resistance could descend into physical violence.[3] This resistance took place within the context of a broader culture that supported individual and crowd actions as a legitimate means of protecting local economic rights against the encroachment of government power—a tradition that in the ensuing decades would shake the foundation of British New England as colonists expressed their outrage at new imperial laws designed to appropriate colonial revenues and regulate colonial commerce.[4] For Connecticut Valley colonists, resistance to the White Pine Acts offered practice in the popular politics that, by the 1760s, were already beginning to drive a wedge between Britain and her American colonies.

Meanwhile, sawblades continued to spin and colonial lumbermen progressively laid low the timber of the valley. Over the course of the seventeenth and eighteenth centuries, shipyards in Connecticut and Massachusetts launched growing numbers of vessels built from valley lumber to join New England's fishing and commercial fleets. These merchant vessels transported sawn boards from the valley to the West Indies and farther afield, providing construction materials to increasingly denuded corners of the British empire. Barrels, crafted from valley oaks, carried a myriad of New England commodities out into the Atlantic world, and often carried back the imported goods that New Englanders demanded in return. As this commerce flowed up and down the Connecticut River and its tributaries, the woodlands along their banks retreated, leaving behind a deforested landscape and new environmental challenges for the region's inhabitants to overcome.

The Beginnings of the Connecticut Valley Lumber Trade

In the earliest years of colonization, a scarcity of available labor limited the extent of the Connecticut Valley's lumber trade. English settlers split logs into boards and planks by using wedges, a practice that continued to be used throughout the colonial period in frontier areas and in producing boards for household use. In most areas, however, this crude method was quickly replaced by the traditional English practice of cutting boards in sawpits. The log was suspended over a hole dug in the ground and two men, one below the log and one standing upon it, would slice off boards using a long double-handled saw.

Sawmills, buildings housing water-powered vertical saws, were almost completely unknown in seventeenth-century England. A sawmill had been built outside London in 1663, but was abandoned in the face of violent opposition from city sawyers who objected to the competition. Popular opposition likely played an important role in discouraging sawmill construction in other parts of the kingdom as well. The abundance of labor available in England made sawmills unnecessary and, for those who stood to lose their jobs to this new technology, unpopular. Sawmills also produced more waste than did sawpits; the mechanized saws were less precise than the handsaws of the sawyers. In England, where timber was increasingly scarce, this helped make sawpits a more attractive option, and sawmills did not become popular there until the early nineteenth century.[5]

Far different conditions prevailed in England's American colonies. New England found itself blessed with an abundance of timber and cursed with an enduring shortage of labor. The Dutch built the first sawmill in northeastern North America in 1623. John Mason hired Danish carpenters to construct New England's first sawmill at his plantation on the Piscataqua River in 1634. The first sawmill in the Connecticut Valley seems to be the one built in Hartford in 1654 or shortly before. John Pynchon built his first sawmill in Springfield in 1666. Windsor had its first by 1670 and even Deerfield (Massachusetts' oft-threatened and occasionally abandoned frontier outpost) had a sawmill by 1690.[6]

Sawmills drastically decreased the amount of time needed to saw a log into boards, increasing a community's capacity for processing timber. The limited productivity of the sawpit had formerly acted as a bottleneck, limiting the amount of timber that an individual could effectively market. Now that local inhabitants could take their logs to the sawmill and pay the miller to cut them into boards, the supply of lumber in towns jumped. In Springfield, for example, the price of boards fell by a third in the year following the construction of John Pynchon's first sawmill.[7] Settlers with enough land in woods and enough capital could even begin to think about exporting their boards. And by the 1680s, the sugar islands of the Caribbean presented a lucrative market.

The sea-bounded ecosystems of these sugar islands presented the most clearly finite timber supplies in any of England's American holdings. The insatiable demand of the sugar mills for firewood combined with the continual need to replace wooden structures suffering from tropical rot led to the denudation of first Barbados and later the other sugar islands under English dominion. By the 1660s, imperial officials warned the Board of Trade in London that the sugar economy of Barbados was threatened by the near-complete destruction of the island's timber. By the 1680s, English timber crews from Barbados were traveling to nearby St. Lucia to obtain both firewood and building timber. Laboring on St. Lucia, at the ragged edge of empire, English woodcutters faced the constant threat of attack by French crews—themselves driven to St. Lucia by the deforestation of Martinique—or by the Carib natives of the island who had allied themselves with Martinique's governor in exchange for trade goods.[8]

The gradual deforestation of the English sugar islands, and the desire to avoid conflict with their French and Spanish imperial neighbors, led the sugar barons and other settlers of the English Caribbean to turn to their mainland neighbors for their supplies of both firewood and building timber. Most imports of firewood came from the relatively nearby Southern colonies. Value-added commodities, like sawn lumber and barrel staves, however, could be profitably exported from farther afield. By the 1690s, New England merchants could claim that the sugar islands were dependent upon the forest resources of New England for their very survival.[9] While such a claim belittles the role that exports from Virginia and the Carolinas also played in providing lumber for the English Caribbean, it does point to the growing interdependence (both economic and environmental) of the sugar islands and the New England colonies.

The unintended consequences of Parliament's 1765 Stamp Act for the colonies present the degree of this dependency in stark relief. Many New England merchants, hailing from colonies where the act had been roundly rejected, refused to trade with Caribbean colonies whose officials had pledged to enforce the new system of taxation. Instead, New England trading captains pointed their bows toward the sugar islands of France and Spain. Deprived of timber imports, the sugar economy of the British Caribbean teetered on the edge of disaster. One Antigua planter wrote to Parliament to complain that "our crop promises well, but we are likely to be Miserably off for want of Lumber and Northward Provisions," for, he worried, "there is not One tenth part of the Lumber in the Islands that will be required for the next crop." The planter continued on to admonish Parliament that "when we are deprived of a Trade from the Northward, the Estates here can never be supported," and warned that "the Merchants in England as our remittances principally center there . . . will feel the Effects severely." Fortunately, for the planters of the Caribbean, the mercantile classes of England shared these very concerns, and the pressure they put on Parliament brought the Stamp Act's swift repeal.[10]

The timber trade, like the provisioning trade, tied the Connecticut Valley into a far-flung imperial economy, and, as with the provisioning trade, colonists' eagerness to meet the market demands of other imperial regions brought consequences for their local environment. Ultimately, the woodlands of the valley proved no more infinite than those of the sugar islands. By the turn of the eighteenth century, the towns of southeast Massachusetts, those lying closest to Boston and to the bay, had almost entirely exhausted their local supplies of timber.[11] The first English settlers along Massachusetts Bay had encountered a landscape already transformed by millennia of human occupation and active environmental manipulation. As elsewhere along the eastern seaboard, the Wampanoags and Massachusetts had used fire to clear underbrush and hold back trees, creating planting lands and the open parklike stretches of woodland habitat favored by deer and other game. This transformed landscape was a mixed blessing for the early English settlers of Massachusetts Bay. Even before permanent English settlement, pathogens introduced by fishermen and traders wrought a deadly holocaust among the region's Native peoples. The meadows and croplands that these devastated communities left behind provided a crucial head start for the English. Early settlers did not have to hack a settlement out of the woods—they had merely to take advantage of what was already there. If not for this providential environment (and many Puritans did see the hand of Providence in it), the Massachusetts Bay Company and the settlements that preceded it may never have survived.

On the other hand, the transformation of the Bay region by its Indian proprietors into a land of meadows and parks meant fewer trees and, consequently, fewer fuel and timber resources. As the English along the bay began to multiply, their demands for firewood and building timber grew, and the woodlands that they depended upon for these resources began to shrink. Since overland transport from the west of the colony was impractical and uneconomical due to timber's bulk, the inhabitants of Boston and neighboring towns—like those on the British sugar isles—became dependent upon the water transport of timber supplies from their colonial neighbors in New Hampshire and Connecticut.

By the 1680s, both sawlogs and sawn lumber had become important exports for the river towns of the Connecticut colony.[12] The largest pines, cut north of Hartford, would be harvested in the winter, hauled across the packed snow by teams of oxen and deposited on the river ice to wait for the spring thaw, when the river would carry them to sawmills downriver. Along the way these logs would smash through the sluice gates of mills, threaten ferries and often destroy fishing stages—bringing a slew of legal suits to Connecticut courts every spring. Smaller trees were harvested year-round, processed into lumber at local sawmills, and sent downriver by raft—a far safer proposal. From Hartford on south, the river was deep enough to allow lumber to be loaded onto oceangoing sloops for the trip to Boston, the West Indies, or across the Atlantic to Spanish and Portuguese ports.

The woodlands of the Connecticut Valley quickly proved to be just as finite as those of the Massachusetts Bay area and the Caribbean sugar islands. As the inhabitants of these denuded areas turned to the Atlantic market to fill their timber needs, they effectively exported the environmental consequences of their timber consumption. In the Connecticut Valley, the demands of these new markets added to the stresses already working upon the region's woodlands. In the 1680s, exports for the new transatlantic timber market competed directly with developing local markets for firewood. While timbering produced some waste wood that could be fed to into local fireplaces, the felling of trees for timber ultimately diminished local woodlots, decreasing the availability of wood for the fire. Land clearing for agriculture exacerbated this problem. Land clearing could be made to complement firewood production and timber sales only up to a point; after that the maintenance of former woodlands as arable infringed upon a local area's potential for timber production.

As early as the 1630s, town governments in the Connecticut Valley sought to conserve regional woodlands by regulating timber usage. From their founding, both Massachusetts and Connecticut rested considerable authority for woodlands regulation in local hands.[13] Some of the first acts passed by the assemblies of newly established New England towns necessarily dealt with the issue of the town commons. Formal commons areas were established and timberlands set aside; acts were passed to regulate the rate of use with an eye toward preserving wood and timber resources for future generations. As the population of towns grew during the seventeenth century, town assemblies were eventually forced to limit access to commons, granting the right to gather timber only to those who possessed a certain level of assessed wealth or who could claim priority through their family's early settlement.

Granting individual town governments the authority to regulate timber use allowed the adoption of conservation legislation that could address local needs. The township of Hartford, which contained relatively little timber when compared with its northern neighbors in the valley, passed an act in 1679 stating that "no boards, timber or plank" could be sold and transported out of the town bounds. The act imposed a fine of ten shillings per one hundred feet for boards and twenty shillings per one hundred feet for any planks exported. However, seven years later, the town relaxed its laws, prohibiting the exportation of only those boards sawn at the sawmills to the north of the Park River and reducing the fine (which could also be conceptualized as a sort of export tariff) to five shillings per one hundred feet for both boards and planks.[14] Concerned that "much damage" and "great destruction" was being done to the forests within its bounds, Windsor in 1698 instated a law prohibiting "strangers," or noninhabitants, from taking timber from town lands, and requiring that timber be "wrought up" (sawn into boards) before being exported out of the town.[15] Just north of Hartford and better timbered, Windsor did not entirely prohibit the cutting of timber, nor end its exportation. Windsor's timber acts may have slowed the rate at which trees were felled, but the primary motivation seems to have been to require local timber to be worked by local lumbermen and sawn at local sawmills.

Suffield, Massachusetts, again just north of Windsor and heavily timbered, passed a law in 1683 stipulating that only dwellers in the town could take timber from town lands.[16] Unlike its less heavily wooded neighbors to the south, Suffield never restricted the export of either timber or sawn lumber. Deerfield, the northernmost English settlement in the valley up through the 1710s, did not even see the need to pass rules limiting access to timber supplies on its town commons until the 1730s and like Suffield never saw fit to restrict timber or lumber exports.

In general, Connecticut played a more active role in regulation than its northern neighbor. Massachusetts was divided between an increasingly denuded eastern region that was far more interested in encouraging imports than in restricting exports, and a western region with plentiful timber and a strong interest in exporting it. Legislators from neither region wanted to see the timber trade interfered with. Connecticut, by contrast, was relatively less well-timbered than the portion of Massachusetts immediately to its north. In 1687, the General Court of Connecticut passed its first "Timber Preservation" act to limit the amount of timber exported from the colony. Proclaiming the current rate of "destruction of timber" to be "prejudiciall to the publique," who might soon no longer be able to acquire timber for shelter or wood for fires, the general court required licensing for all timber exports. This act was regularly reissued and gradually strengthened over the course of the proceeding three decades. In its 1714 and 1715 reenactments of the bill, the general court exposed an ulterior motive beyond simply conserving the colony's woodlands. The export of raw Connecticut timber to Massachusetts was, the court claimed, discouraging the development of Connecticut industries, most importantly shipbuilding and stave making. An act initially pitched in the 1680s as a defense against the depletion of the timber resources necessary for local subsistence proved by the 1710s to be a useful protectionist tool for promoting Connecticut-based industries.[17]

Both of the two colonial industries—stave making and shipbuilding—highlighted in the timber preservation acts of 1714 and 1715 produced commodities that underpinned the very fabric of the Atlantic economy. The 1714 act targeted the producers of staves—the wooden planks that are bound together to construct barrels and casks. Some of these producers were professional coopers, some carpenters dabbling in this otherwise specialized trade, and the remainder were landowners seeking to supplement their agricultural income. The prior two categories sometimes produced fully assembled barrels, casks, and pipes. All three types of producers also turned out staves and heads that could be sold unassembled. These staves were a relatively simple commodity to produce and became an important early export item for settlers in the Connecticut Valley and elsewhere in New England. As early as 1641, stave makers in Hartford may have been producing as many as twenty thousand staves a year specifically for export, to say nothing of local use.[18] In that year, the government of Connecticut took notice of this important commodity by passing an act regulating production. The act appointed inspectors in each town to ensure that staves conformed to standard sizes, simplifying questions of volume for would-be customers of the colony's goods.[19] Indeed, staves—or, more to the point, the barrels, casks, and pipes into which they could be assembled—were an essential component of the early modern economy (analogous to the ubiquitous cardboard box of today). For instance, when Connecticut governor Thomas Fitch created a list of his colony's twenty-nine top exports in 1764, twenty-one (mostly grains, preserved fish and meat, and rum) relied on oaken barrels, casks, or pipes for their transport. Of the remainder, horses, cattle, sheep, and hogs traveled under their own power or were transported live by ship; boards and planks did not require barreling; and staves and hoops were the components from which new barrels could be assembled by customers on the other end of the transaction.[20]

The inclusion of staves as an export in their own right highlights the importance that New England oaks played not only in the regional export trade, but also in the broader commercial network of the English/British Empire. For instance, in 1703, during the disruptions of Queen Anne's War, the English governor of St. Nevis noted that imported barrel staves were selling at the shockingly high price of fourteen pounds per thousand. Even with this generous inducement, he complained that barrels were so scarce in the denuded sugar islands of the West Indies that trade had ground to a halt. Although an extreme example, and one arising from the challenges of wartime, this episode points to the crucial role that stave makers in the mainland colonies played in keeping the English commercial empire running and sugar revenues flowing into the Exchequer.[21] Barrels, and so forth, constructed from New England staves—and the reuse of barrels from that region's export trade—provided exporters in the West Indies and the Spanish and Portuguese Wine Islands (where woodlands were also in short supply) with the containers they needed to ship their own goods out into the Atlantic economy.[22] Sugar, molasses, and Madeira wine often sailed back to America—and to other markets—packed in New England oak.

Stave production depended exclusively on oak as a raw material, putting the demands of this local industry squarely at odds with local firewood needs. In 1641, at the same time that it sought to regulate stave production in the valley towns, Connecticut expressed its concomitant desire to protect local timber supplies. Several more acts were passed over the decades that linked stave production to the destruction of woodlands. Finally, in 1714 the Connecticut General Court passed an export tariff of twenty shillings per thousand on barrel staves and thirty shillings per thousand on pipe staves sold to any neighboring colonies.[23] Significantly, this tariff did not apply to staves exported farther afield. Lawmakers in Massachusetts grumbled to the Board of Trade that this "very unneighbourly" act of the Connecticut General Court amounted to a virtual "Prohibition" on the sale of staves between the two colonies.[24] In fact, this was likely the Connecticut court's intention. While the court worried over the "destruction" of local timber supplies, it also made clear its opinion that stave exports to Massachusetts, New York, and Rhode Island were damaging Connecticut's own trade with the West Indies and the Wine Islands. An export tariff, it was hoped, would have the double effect of promoting the sale of Connecticut goods in Connecticut barrels (while also undercutting the exporting ability of neighboring colonies), and of protecting dwindling stands of oak.

Connecticut's 1715 timber preservation act focused on promoting the colony's shipbuilding industry and by extension stimulating its carrying trade.[25] This carrying trade played an essential role in the New England economy. New England–built vessels formed the vital link connecting settlers in the Connecticut Valley, and elsewhere in New England, with the profitable markets of the Atlantic world. Without the shipbuilding industry, the vessels it produced, and the carrying trade they made possible, New England agricultural and timber production would have faltered. The regional economy would, perforce, have been far more insular, Atlantic trade would have been far less brisk, and the economies of the sugar islands, presumably, would have collapsed. The early modern Atlantic world would have been a very different place, and the colonial American environment would have developed in very different ways.

Thomas Deming of Wethersfield launched the first ship ever built in Connecticut in 1648—a small vessel that Deming appropriately named the *Tryall*. (Tellingly, the *Tryall*'s very first cargo was a load of red oak staves bound for the West Indies.)[26] From that beginning, Connecticut shipbuilding quickly took off. By 1680 the Connecticut River port towns were home to twenty-seven seagoing vessels, most of them built in the colony. By 1700, small shipyards could be found all along the stretches of the lower Connecticut, from Saybrook at the river's mouth to just below the first major falls at Windsor. Middletown, Wethersfield, and Haddam became especially important shipbuilding centers. By the early eighteenth century, Connecticut River shipyards were turning out ships of up to one hundred tons or more, most of them agile sloops that could navigate the rivers of the mainland colonies while still being sufficiently seaworthy to carry goods back and forth to the Caribbean.[27]

Carpenters and shipwrights relied on local and regional woodlands to supply them with the spars, yards, planks and masts they needed to build these ships, utilizing a wide array of species. Tall, straight, and easily worked, white pines were preferred for both masts and planking, while pitch pine was considered a second-best substitute for the latter. Hard and durable white oak was the favorite for framing timbers and was also used for planking. In the early years, a shipwright could go out into the local woods and select an oak with just the right bends to form the ribs and stems for the ship he was designing. Cedar, spruce, fir, juniper, hickory, ash, elm, and beech were often substituted for these preferred materials.[28]

Each hundred-ton vessel required the felling of over two thousand trees, placing substantial pressures on the timber supplies of New England.[29] Softwoods, like pine, could be felled well to the north and floated down the river to sawmills near the shipyards to be processed. Dense, less buoyant hardwoods had to be processed near where they fell, either by hand for specially shaped ribs, bowsprits, and so forth, or in a local sawmill for boards and planking. These products could then be carried to the shipyards by wagon, sledge, or, more likely, by raft or riverboat.[30] The shipyards of the lower Connecticut River thus drove a broader valley market for ship timbers.

Shipyards in other New England ports, too, made use of valley timber, with Boston providing the most notable example. Boston was home to thirty master shipwrights by 1676, and by 1693 the governor of Massachusetts, Lord Bellomont, boasted that there were "more good vessels belonging to the town of Boston than to all Scotland and Ireland." By the 1720s, Boston shipwrights were producing over 150 ships annually: a handful sold to England, slightly less than half to merchants in the West Indies, and the remainder purchased by New England merchants active in the coasting trade and in servicing these other far-off markets. Thanks to the relative abundance of timber in America when compared to Europe, New England shipyards could produce ships for half the price per ton, ensuring that colonial shipwrights could always find customers. By 1760, one out of every four merchant ships active within the British Empire had been constructed in New England.[31]

Despite its own growing shipbuilding industry, Connecticut's leaders obviously felt that their colony was not securing its fair share of the lucrative market for colonial-built ships. The general court's 1715 "Act for the Preservation of Timber and Preventing the Exportation Thereof" sought to keep ship timbers sawn from Connecticut trees within the colony as an encouragement to local industry. The act provided an exemption for timber produced from trees grown farther north in the Connecticut Valley and merely sawn in Connecticut, but the burden of proof fell on ship's captains to provide documentation of the provenance of their cargoes. In the absence of such proof, customs agents assumed all timber shipping from the colony was Connecticut grown, a fact that doubtlessly led to the taxation of much Massachusetts timber as well. Worried for the prospects of their own shipbuilding industry, the Massachusetts General Court passed a formal protest to Connecticut's 1715 act.[32] But the leaders of Massachusetts need not have worried. Though the protest went unheeded by Connecticut's General Court, calls to slow the rate of timber exported from Connecticut's river towns went likewise unheeded. The series of preservation acts, in keeping with legal tradition in the colony, relied upon town assemblies for the issuing of export licenses—and the towns proved perfectly willing to see the timber business thrive and local sawmills continue to run.[33]

The general court itself also proved flexible in enforcement. In 1716, Francis Whitmore of Middletown (father of the Daniel Whitmore whose civil disobedience opened this chapter) and his partner, George Stilliman, petitioned the Connecticut General Assembly for the liberty to export thirty thousand feet of sawn planks from the colony. The men complained that they had been caught unawares by the passage of the 1715 "Act for the Preservation of Shiptimber and Plank." Following the law's passage, Whitmore and Stilliman held back their shipment from the export market and attempted to find customers for their planks within the confines of Connecticut, but without luck. With their finances tied up in merchandise sitting idle by the docks of Haddam and worried that their business would be ruined, they petitioned the assembly for an exception from the act passed in the previous year.[34] The Connecticut Assembly granted the men's petition.[35]

Indeed, despite its declared interest in "preservation" the Connecticut General Court had no intention of abolishing the timber trade. If Connecticut's shipyards could not absorb all of the timber produced in the colony, then the preservation act provided methods allowing for export. Connecticut's timber laws had from their inception been framed with dual goals in mind—preservation of the colony's timber resources *and* the collection of revenue. Connecticut chose not to prohibit timber exports—as was done in the most denuded of England's Caribbean colonies at this time—but rather to license and tax the export of timber and finished lumber products. The fees that merchants paid for export licenses added to the revenues of local town governments while the taxes paid on the value of exported merchandise swelled the colony's coffers. Rather than viewing taxation as a means to encourage conservation, it may be more appropriate to view purported conservation acts as a means of facilitating taxation. Moreover, like the 1714 act regulating stave exports, the 1715 act applied only to timber exported to the neighboring colonies of Massachusetts, Rhode Island, and New York.

Exports to the Spanish and Portuguese Wine Islands and the sugar islands of the Caribbean were again excluded, proving the act was as much about inter-regional rivalry as anything else.[36] The Connecticut government wanted to encourage new industries, and raise some revenue in the process, not cut its lumbermen, landowners, and merchants off from lucrative timber markets.

The fate of the naval stores industry of the valley offers another example of the relationship between "preservation" efforts and the desire of local landowners and governments to profit from the timber trade. Valley production of tar, pitch, and turpentine—which together with mast timbers were often referred to collectively as "naval stores"—peaked in the decades before and after 1700. Pine resin provided the raw material for all three, and pines, particularly the highly resinous pitch pine, were something that grew in abundance in the loose, sandy soils of the uplands that flanked the Connecticut and its tributary rivers. Referred as the "pine barrens" by colonists, these areas had proven impractical for growing crops since their soil failed to retain water. Naval stores production thus allowed colonists to successfully exploit lands that were otherwise economically marginal. Moreover, pitch pines were likely expanding their territory beyond these barrens at the turn of the eighteenth century, as settlers harvested more favorable hardwoods for firewood and offered the opportunistic pines the chance to spread.[37]

Settlers produced tar and pitch by felling pines, burning them in earthen "kilns," and collecting the tar and pitch that oozed out. By contrast, turpentine was distilled from resin collected from live trees. All three commodities served as waterproofers and antifouling agents in naval construction. Although moderate amounts of tar and pitch were produced in the valley throughout the colonial era, these naval stores only became important as export commodities in the last decade of the seventeenth century. Production spiked in the early eighteenth century, driven by increased shipbuilding and an imperial export bounty during the War of the Spanish Succession/ Queen Anne's War. Turpentine, in particular, proved an especially popular export among valley landowners since it required relatively little time and labor to produce. All a producer had to do was cut a "box" at the base of a pine, strip the bark above it, and then visit the trees every couple of weeks to collect the resin that pooled there. A tree could be harvested in this way for several years, but the practice eventually resulted in its death. After undergoing a distilling process, the raw resin became turpentine and was ready for export. As early as 1703, the Massachusetts General Court had begun to worry about the "very great havock and waste of the timber" occasioned by turpentining in the colony's western woodlands. In the years that followed, the Massachusetts General Court and local assemblies of many of the valley towns set limits on the production of turpentine, as well as pitch and tar.[38]

Naval store production in the valley declined in the decades that followed, quite quickly in the case of turpentine, and naval stores ceased to be an important export category for the region—although this was largely a result of market forces rather than any government actions. Demand for naval stores within the British Empire fell off markedly after the 1713 end of Queen Anne's War, and the parliamentary bounty on these commodities was allowed to expire. Moreover, the southern mainland colonies began producing naval stores in increasing volumes around 1720, driving prices down further. Since pines produce more resin in warmer climates, southern producers enjoyed a competitive advantage (amplified by their reliance on slave labor), and New England exporters found themselves squeezed out of the Atlantic market. Valley landowners continued to produce some tar and pitch for regional use (although it often proved more economical to import southern naval stores), but increasingly found that pitch pine could fetch them greater profits when sawn for lumber. In the end, landowners and local governments proved less interested in preventing the environmental "havock" wrought by deforestation than with directing the resources of otherwise unproductive lands toward the most profitable of competing opportunities for exploitation.[39]

Pines, Profits, and Politics

The imperial government's inability to enforce the notorious White Pine Acts offers what is perhaps the most famous example of the important role that timber markets played in the economy of the eighteenth-century Connecticut Valley. The white pine occupied a special place in the lumber trade of the colonial Connecticut Valley, and of New England in general. In a poetical turn of phrase, future Connecticut governor Roger Wolcott once wrote of the "cloud-kissing Pines" that towered above the banks of the Connecticut River, mature stands often topping one hundred feet.[40] The very tallest white pines grew taller still: up to 250 feet in height and as much as five feet in diameter at their base.[41] The wood of the white pine was the most extensively used building material in early America. The ease with which its soft wood could be shaped, worked, carved and run into moldings made it a particular favorite among colonial carpenters. Its durability also made white pine a favorite. When used in housing construction, boards and planks of white pine could be expected to last years and even decades longer, without rot or decay, than other woods available.[42] Indeed, it was just these attributes that made white pine an especially desirable commodity in the denuded tropics of the Caribbean.

White pine was also highly valued for naval construction. In particular, the tall straight pines of New England offered ideal masts for the large warships of the Royal Navy. Throughout the seventeenth century and into the eighteenth, England relied upon the forests of the Baltic countries to mast its navy. The tallest trees had long since been cut from these lands, and the practice at the time was to piece together masts from the trunks of three or four smaller pines. Such composite masts were less sturdy than masts formed from a single trunk, or "stick." Imperial planners had from the very first settlement of New England viewed the region as a possible source of masts. At the end of the seventeenth century, embroiled in wars both in Europe and North America, Parliament and the Crown formalized the Royal Navy's claim to this valuable resource.[43]

The White Pine Acts—first set down in the Massachusetts 1691 charter and subsequently extended to all of New England and strengthened in 1711, 1722, and 1729—reserved all white pines in Britain's New England colonies of twenty-four inches in diameter and greater for use by the Crown. The Pine Acts were perhaps the most notorious of Great Britain's eighteenth-century colonial conservation policies. The first legal challenge to the acts came in 1734 when a New Hampshire man filed a suit claiming that the Crown could not lay claim to trees on lands that he owned and which he asserted were his own private property. The case languished in colonial and English courts for a decade before finally being dropped without the legal issue at its heart ever being resolved. Lacking a legally sanctioned outlet for protesting the acts, many colonists turned to extralegal channels. Colonists set fire to stands of forest where surveyors were known to be working.[44] Surveyors enforcing the acts were on more than one occasion belayed and threatened by gangs of lumbermen, or had their supplies and provisions stolen or destroyed, forcing them to seek the safety of coastal towns.[45]

For instance, in 1734, an armed mob in Exeter, New Hampshire, assaulted a crew of deputy surveyors and chased them from town. To avenge this attack upon royal authority, surveyor general of the King's Woods for New England, Colonel David Dunbar, assembled a posse of deputy surveyors augmented by fifteen hired mercenaries, presumably sailors from Portsmouth. Upon approaching Exeter the colonel's small army was met and routed by a crowd of armed protestors approximately twice its size. After the "Exeter Riot" rumors circulated that a group of mill owners had contracted together to hire three Natick Indians to assassinate the surveyor general. Such a threat was, in all likelihood, apocryphal, and Dunbar survived long enough for Parliament to relieve him of his post in 1740.[46] The best-known example of popular resistance to the acts occurred on the morning of April 14, 1772, when around twenty inhabitants of Weare, New Hampshire, descended on the county sheriff and one of his deputies as they attempted to collect a fine against local mill owners. The sheriff was whipped one lash for every tree on which the local mill owners had been fined, then both men were chased out of town. In a foreshadowing of the Boston Tea Party, the rioters blackened their faces with soot to costume themselves as faux Indians.[47]

In their treatment of colonial opposition to the Pine Acts, previous historians have focused almost entirely on these eastern New Hampshire events.[48] The western portion of the colony, along the Connecticut River, and the conflict that surrounded the enforcement of the acts in communities elsewhere in the valley have often been forgotten. The timber trade's central role in the New Hampshire economy made that colony the center of anti–Pine Act activity, but popular (and sometimes official) resistance to the acts also played an important role in the politics of the eighteenth-century Connecticut Valley. These acts of resistance, in turn, highlight the economic and political importance that inhabitants of the valley attached to participation in the timber trade.

A thriving trade in white pine existed in the valley at least as early as 1698. In that year, twenty thousand white pine boards were sent from Springfield area sawmills to Hartford, where they were sold at thirty shillings per thousand and transshipped to New Haven, from there dispersed to other markets.[49] Records for other localities along the valley are not available for this period. Most likely Springfield and its immediate environs—well situated along the river for transport to market, nestled in a well-timbered part of the valley, and still politically and economically dominated by that redoubtable businessman, Major John Pynchon—exceeded any of its Connecticut Valley neighbors in lumber production. Still, that a single township could supply the market with so sizable a stock of boards (representing about a solid acre's worth of woodland consisting exclusively of white pine) implies the volume of pine boards that might have been produced in the valley as a whole. Such a large shipment suggests that the terms of the Massachusetts charter of 1691 were not being enforced in the western portion of the colony.

Up through the 1750s, peaceful circumvention of the Pine Acts prevailed as Connecticut Valley lumbermen continued to fell pines for both the local and far-off markets. The first acts of violent resistance to the acts in the valley coincided neatly with the first efforts at their serious enforcement. Up to this point, the imperial officials tasked with overseeing enforcement, the succession of men who had served as the surveyor general of His Majesty's Woods in America, contented themselves with battling the lumbermen and sawmill owners of eastern New Hampshire and Maine. But in the 1750s the new surveyor general, Benning Wentworth, broke with this long tradition of official indifference to white pine poaching in the Connecticut Valley.

The growing scarcity of timber in the Piscataqua region of eastern New Hampshire helps explain the timing of this policy shift. As early as the 1690s, colonial customs agent Edward Randolph complained that trees fit for masts had already grown scarce near the coast of New Hampshire, the victims of colonial sawmills. Already in the 1690s, masting teams needed to range seven to eight miles inland along the province's rivers and larger streams to find suitable pines.[50] By the mid-eighteenth century, even the banks of these interior waterways had been stripped of suitable mast pines. During a visit to Exeter, New Hampshire in 1750, Antiguan merchant James Birket commented on the progressive deforestation of the Piscataqua River Basin. "The People here as well as in other branches of Piscataway river complain that their lumber is too far to fetch out of the country and stand them very dear," Birket recorded, "the ground generally Cleared and as far as we could see beyond the town."[51] As New Hampshire had exported its white pines to Boston and the West Indies, these latter areas had, effectively, exported their problems with deforestation back to New Hampshire. The masting trade of New England would soon need to shift elsewhere in search of the large, straight white pines coveted for the warships of the Royal Navy, and as the new surveyor general it was Wentworth's duty to see that the enforcement of the White Pine Acts followed.

Not that duty to the imperial government was the only (or even the primary) motive driving Wentworth in the execution of his office; there was also considerable profit to be had. The son of New Hampshire's long-time lieutenant governor John Wentworth, his father's connections had helped Benning Wentworth make a fortune in the colony's timber trade. The profits from his Piscataqua River sawmills provided the two-thousand-pound price tag that he paid his predecessor Colonel David Dunbar in exchange for his commission as surveyor general in 1743.[52] It was a sound investment. His deputies ranged the woodlands of New Hampshire marking large pines with the King's Broad Arrow and then reported to Wentworth where the best trees for masts and lumber could be found. His new office also put him in contact with the King's Contractors, the men granted the lucrative right of procuring supplies for the Royal Navy.

Benning Wentworth's tenure as surveyor general resembled the proverbial fox guarding the henhouse. Although Wentworth had officially retired from the lumber business upon ascending to the governorship of New Hampshire, his brother, Mark Hunking Wentworth, continued to carry on a thriving business exporting the wealth of New Hampshire's woodlands. During his brother's governorship, Mark Hunking came to control the mast trade coming down the Piscataqua River, the primary source of New England masts during most of the eighteenth century.[53] Continuing this commercial success depended upon two things: maintaining the Piscataqua region's ascendancy in the mast trade over the short term and, in the long term, securing a new source of masts against the day this initial supply was depleted. Both required that the timber trade of the Connecticut River Valley be brought under control.

Wentworth began by hiring Daniel Blake of Middletown to act as his deputy surveyor in Connecticut. Unlike in New Hampshire where Wentworth could rely on his own authority as governor to enforce compliance, it immediately became clear that Blake would not be able to rely upon the support of the Connecticut government in his efforts to enforce the Pine Acts. In response to Blake's commission, Connecticut governor Roger Wolcott wrote to Wentworth expressing his fear of the "Dificulty" that the new deputy surveyor would certainly encounter in dealing with his colony's inhabitants. Indeed, Wolcott expressed (or feigned) surprise at Blake's appointment, assuring Wentworth that "there are no White pine Trees fitt for His Majesties navey as I hear of Growing in this Colony." Wolcott assured the surveyor general that all of Connecticut's white pines stood on lands already apportioned to the colony's townships. The pines therefore belonged either to the commons of the individual towns or else to private individuals.[54] (This, of course, ignored the fact that Connecticut mills sawed pines felled not just locally but also logs floated down from Massachusetts and New Hampshire.)

Wentworth took issue with Governor Wolcott's interpretation of the acts. The mere division of lands into townships and then into private parcels was not enough to gain them exclusion from the protections of the White Pine Acts. "Nothing," Wentworth insisted, "is lookt upon as private property, but Lands under Actual improvement & Inclosures." Firmly dismissing Wolcott's warning of potential difficulties with the inhabitants of the Connecticut, Wentworth expressed his hope that "Mr. Blake will give no unnecessary trouble in your Colony," but insisted that "what is necessary in Support of the Kings interest I must desire your Honours Countenance & assistance in."[55] Blake carried out his duties with diligence. Without the support of the governor's office, however, he faced an uphill battle to convince his lower Connecticut Valley neighbors to respect the Crown's claim to the large white pines of the upper valley.

In 1753, Daniel Whitmore of Middletown interrupted Blake as he carried out his duties. Without provocation (or so goes Blake's version of events) Whitmore laid hold of the unfortunate surveyor and threw him into a nearby millpond.[56] Parliament had designed the Pine Acts to protect the security of the British Empire. But their enforcement threatened the livelihoods of Connecticut Valley laborers, merchants, and landowners. Little surprise that some would strike back against this threat.

For Daniel Whitmore, lumber was a family business. His father, Francis Whitmore, had been active in the lumber trade of the valley since at least 1715. His uncles and cousins felled large amounts of timber on common lands and often assisted the inhabitants of Middletown and nearby towns by felling and hauling away timber to aid in the construction of new highways. Daniel Whitmore may have inherited his father's share of the business and thus been part owner (along with an uncle) of the Middletown sawmill where he encountered Daniel Blake. Or he may have merely been a customer.[57]

Either way, Whitmore clearly did not appreciate Blake's interference with the family business. Perhaps Blake had discovered a collection of unsawn logs (or possibly even sawn lumber) that exceeded the legally damning twenty-four-inch mark. These logs would then have been subject to confiscation and the Whitmores, who owned the mill, required to appear before a judge of the admiralty court to be sentenced and fined. Since Connecticut fell under the jurisdiction of the admiralty court headquartered in New York City, proceeding to trial would require the defendants either to travel to New York or to cover the costs required for the judge to travel to Middletown—both costly propositions. Daniel saved his relatives, and possibly himself, the inconvenience and expense. Whitmore deposited Blake in the sawmill's millpond, where the latter complained that "he was in great danger of being drowned." Once he had made it safely back to dry land, a soggy Blake seems to have abandoned his law enforcement efforts in Middletown.[58]

Some Connecticut Valley businessmen did find ways to profit from the region's white pines and still stay within the limits of the Pine Acts. In 1732, twelve Connecticut Valley merchants formed a company and entered into a contract to provide masts, yards, booms, and bowsprits for the Royal Navy. The white pines collected and marketed to the Royal Navy by these merchants originated almost two hundred miles to the north, near present-day Hanover, New Hampshire. In 1733, the company successfully floated an entire shipload's worth of timber down the river to Saybrook. Petitioning for and receiving a loan to cover operating costs from the Connecticut General Assembly, the company promised its ability to do the same the next year. This venture continued at least until 1739 (when the merchants sued a local Saybrook sawmill owner for the theft of two of their logs).[59]

Further attempts to secure masts from the upper valley were delayed by the interimperial wars of the mid-eighteenth century: King George's War (1744–1748) and the French and Indian War (1754–1763). Indeed, Anglo-Abenaki tensions, including the occasional act of violence, never fully subsided in the northern valley during this period. English logging crews' disregard for Abenaki territory played a role in perpetuating these tensions. Lumbering in eastern New Hampshire had contributed to violence along the Anglo-Abenaki frontier during Queen Anne's War. In 1746, during King George's War, Abenaki raiders specifically targeted the Charlestown sawmill for destruction, setting it and a number of other structures on fire. In 1750, western Abenaki diplomats made their position on the further expansion of English lumbering efforts clear. Speaking to a group of English negotiators, Abenaki spokesman Atiwaneto declared that no new lands would be ceded and warned the English to keep to the settlements that they had already been allowed to found: "We expressly forbid you to kill a single beaver, or to take a single stick of timber on the lands we inhabit." Atiwaneto continued, "if you want some timber we'll sell you some." This intriguing offer for the Abenakis to enter into the timber trade does not seem to have ever been realized. With the outbreak of war between the English and French colonies in 1754, the barely contained tensions between the settler and Native communities of the upper valley descended into full-scale warfare. English victories in New France during 1759–1760 cut the Abenakis off from their French allies and suppliers, ending the war in northern New England, eroding Abenaki military power, and opening the way for further English settlement and lumbering efforts in the region.[60]

Jared Ingersoll, a successful lawyer and businessman of New Haven, became the next would-be entrepreneur to attempt a masting venture in the upper valley. Writing to the secretary of the Board of Trade in 1760, Ingersoll emphasized the growing scarcity of large pines in the eastern woodlands of New Hampshire and Massachusetts. Along the shores of the Piscataqua and Merrimack Rivers, the demands of the masting trade—and perhaps more importantly the constant buzz of the region's sawmills—had already claimed most of the large straight pines of the sort suitable for use as masts by the Royal Navy. Those left lay far from the river or on heights not easily reached by a logging crew and team of oxen and could be "got down to the river" only "with cost and difficulty." The Piscataqua's masting trade was clearly in decline.[61]

Its future, Ingersoll insisted, lay in the Connecticut River Valley. The masting operations of the 1730s had already demonstrated the Connecticut's potential as a route for bringing mast pines down from New Hampshire and western Massachusetts. It was, Ingersoll assured the board, common knowledge among those familiar with the region and with the timber industry that the Connecticut River would soon become the main avenue by which the woodlands of New Hampshire were tapped. Private individuals, he pointed out, were already illicitly cutting logs and moving them down the river.[62]

Ingersoll's venture proved unprofitable. The men he hired—some of whom he noted had prior experience in the white pine trade—initially felled eighty-nine trees.[63] Three broke while falling to earth. The lumbering team was forced to abandon another one after a local settler stole the fodder for their oxen.[64] The Connecticut River itself presented even greater challenges. One of the largest sticks, thirty-seven inches in diameter, broke during its bumpy ride down river. Twenty-one logs, the largest and most profitable of what was left, got stuck on a rapid and could not be dislodged. Men were sent back upriver to secure more logs to replace those stuck upon the rapids, but it was late in the year and the river's water level was low. Any new logs would likely have to await the spring freshets to make the passage downriver.[65]

To make matters worse, Ingersoll received word in May of 1763 that a deputy to the surveyor general, a Colonel Symes, had been busying himself among a group of logs being held near Middletown awaiting shipment farther downriver. Symes impounded a number of the logs gathered by Ingersoll's men, condemning them as too small to fit the parameters stipulated in his navy contract.[66] Meanwhile another of the surveyor general's deputies, Gideon Lyman, wrote to the admiralty court in New York, accusing Ingersoll of using his contract with the navy as cover for smuggling trees down the Connecticut in violation of the Pine Acts. While Ingersoll had been granted a contract for 80 trees, the men he had hired had ultimately felled and sent downriver over 160, to the "great waste of the King's woods." Ingersoll had already explained to Colonel Symes that these trees had only been cut to help cover losses experienced along the drive down the river. The surveyor general chose to press the issue anyway, informing the Board of Trade and the admiralty court in New York of Ingersoll's contract violations.[67] When the navy failed to renew his contract, Ingersoll was convinced that Benning Wentworth, through his deputies, had intentionally sabotaged his efforts.[68]

Like Ingersoll, Wentworth recognized that the future of the New England mast trade lay down the Connecticut River. The two men differed, however, on who they hoped would benefit from the naval contracts supplied through this new avenue of trade. Wentworth began laying the foundation for this new Connecticut mast trade in 1760, as English forces racked up victories in New France. Small ranging parties of lumbermen had been illegally cutting timber in the west of the colony and sending logs down the Connecticut for at least the last two decades (courting the ire of the land's Abenaki owners in the process).[69] To enforce the Pine Acts in the west, Wentworth moved to organize the lands along the river and beyond into townships. Each new town charter contained a clause reserving all white pine to the crown—reaffirming the Pine Acts and explicitly placing mast timber outside the protections of private or corporate town property. The proprietors of each town, men indebted to Wentworth for their land grants, would regulate timber use and see to it that the law was observed. But while Governor Wentworth succeeded in blocking Ingersoll's attempts to challenge his brother Mark Hunking's mast monopoly through the legal avenue of naval contracting, the surveyor general's attempts to halt the illicit traffic in Connecticut Valley timber continued to founder, as evidenced by the unhappy career of Daniel Blake. Indeed, Wentworth's efforts proved largely self-defeating. The establishment of new western townships granted government legitimacy to the several thousand settlers who migrated into the upper Connecticut Valley in the years between England's victory over the Abenakis in 1760 and the outbreak of the American Revolution.[70] As these new settlers looked to turn a profit and improve their new lands, they often looked to the region's pines as the most quickly exploitable commodity. Writing to the new governor of Connecticut, Thomas Fitch, in 1763, Wentworth complained of "the uncommon waste" that continued to be made among the pines in the "hinter part" of the New England woods.[71]

To combat this waste, Wentworth turned his attention away from the sawmills of Connecticut, where logs were processed, to the more prolific pinelands of Massachusetts, where many of the logs were being felled. He commissioned Elijah Lyman of Northampton (younger brother of the Gideon Lyman mentioned above) as deputy to the surveyor general, a post which the younger Lyman held at least as early as 1763. In that year two land owners from Hampshire County, Timothy Nash and Elijah Alvoid, sued Lyman and Elijah Clark, presumably another deputy surveyor, for illegally seizing seven pine logs from them. Lyman explained to the justices hearing the case that Nash and Alvoid had felled the trees in violation of the Pine Acts. Nevertheless, the plaintiffs won their case and Lyman appealed to the Hampshire County court. Here the justices once again sided with the aggrieved landowners. [72]

The Hampshire County court decision may have disheartened Elijah Clark, for in the aftermath he seems to have left the service of the surveyor general. Wentworth chose another Hampshire County man to replace him, Eleazar Burt of Northampton. Lyman and Burt attempted to hire local laborers to assist them with the massive task of measuring and marking every sizable white pine in the woodlands of Hampshire County (which at the time also included the lands that would become Franklin and Hampden Counties). But the two deputy surveyors quickly discovered that few in the area were interested in taking work enforcing the Pine Acts, "almost everyone being against it," as Lyman complained. [73] Still, even without the aid of hired hands, Lyman and Burt managed from 1763 to 1765 to mark 363 standing trees and logs around Northampton and its surrounding towns with the King's Broad Arrow. Despite this visible assertion of imperial authority, all but 37 of these quickly disappeared, fed into local sawmills or else placed in the river and sent downstream. [74]

Worse yet, Lyman and Burt received constant threats against their persons as they went about their duties—warnings that should they continue to enforce the unpopular Pine Acts they would be "beat, knocked down and killed." In 1763, Massachusetts governor Francis Bernard had issued a proclamation "enjoining all and every of his Majesty's Justice of the Peace, Sheriffs, constables and all other Magistrates and Officers" to aid the surveyor general and his deputies in their duties. [75] (Unlike in Connecticut where the governor was popularly elected, the governors of Massachusetts Bay at this time were royally appointed—helping to explain why Bernard proved more amenable to requests of the surveyor general than had Connecticut governor Roger Wolcott.) Despite this, when Lyman and Burt applied to local officials for protection and for help in their duties, they were dismissed out of hand. Dr. Samuel Mather of Northampton, justice of the peace in Hampshire County, refused even to read Governor Bernard's proclamation. When Lyman and Burt pressed him on it, he offered his opinion that the governor "did not understand the affair—if he had he would not have put out such a proclamation." [76] The timber trade, including a lucrative trade in white pine boards, was a thriving business in the Connecticut Valley. In protecting local interests, Mather felt himself perfectly at liberty to ignore what he perceived to be the governor's ill-informed order.

Having failed to obtain Mather's assistance, the two deputy surveyors turned to Colonel Israel Williams, the most politically powerful man in

Hampshire County. From the 1750s through the early 1770s, Williams combined political office—colonel of the militia, justice of the peace, justice of the Court of Common Pleas, judge of probate—with an extensive network of patronage and family connections to dominate the political landscape of late colonial Hampshire County. Dubbed "the River God" by one historian, Williams sat at the pinnacle of political authority in the Connecticut Valley in the decades prior to the Revolution.[77] If anyone in western Massachusetts could aid the deputy surveyors in their duties, it would be Williams.

Unlike Mather, Williams agreed to read Governor Bernard's proclamation. Still, he insisted that it did not place him under any obligation to raise the local militia, as Lyman and Burt had requested, in order to assist and protect the two men in their imperial duties.[78] Among his many other commercial ventures, Williams was a partner in at least one Hampshire County sawmill.[79] One of the Colonel's most important political allies, his cousin Major Elijah Williams, owned several other mills scattered up and down the county.[80] Little surprise, then, that the Colonel proved less than enthusiastic to lend his considerable political influence to the protection of the King's white pines.

Lyman and Burt soon discovered that the threats made against them had not been idle ones. On October 25, 1765, Lyman stumbled upon an unknown number of men in the woods around Northampton. The scene greeting the deputy surveyor was in flagrant violation of the Pine Acts; the men were busying themselves at moving one large pine trunk as Lyman strode up to them and a number of others lay on the ground nearby. Impounding the pine logs in the name of the king, Lyman forbade the men from removing any more timber from the site, ordering them to leave the pine trunk where it was. One of the men—identified in the court records as Stephen Ward, a laborer from Springfield—offered Lyman a clear, direct, and blasphemous response: "By God it shall go!" Four months later, Ward found himself in front of the county court accused of having misused the Lord's name.[81] Fortuitously, the record of Ward's indictment for blasphemy offers the only direct evidence linking Lyman's efforts to enforce the Pine Acts to a "riot" that broke out in Northampton later that night.

It seems that events escalated quickly after Ward's irreverent defiance of Lyman's imperial authority. News of the loggers' run-in with the deputy surveyor spread quickly to surrounding towns. As the day progressed toward evening, a crowd began to gather. Drawn from at least five nearby towns (and including at least one rioter who was visiting from New Hampshire), the men of the mob set out after nightfall to find Lyman and express their extreme displeasure at his enthusiasm for the unpopular Pine Acts. The mob "with force and arms" broke in upon Lyman in the dark of the night and proceeded to beat, bruise, and wound the unwary sleeper, holding him captive in his own home for the space of ten hours while committing various "other Enormities" against his person. At some point during the evening a small contingent broke off from the main mob and sought out Eleazar Burt. Bursting into Burt's home, the rioters repeated their treatment of Lyman. The rioters did not abandon their prey until the break of dawn.[82]

The wheels of justice took time to turn on the eighteenth-century frontier. The first breakers of the king's peace faced indictment for their assault on Lyman and Burt in the February session of the Hampshire County court. The accused faced a panel of judges who likely sympathized with their antipathy toward the Pine Acts. Colonel Israel Williams (also a justice of the peace) sat beside Justice Samuel Mather and five other justices, each a close political ally and kinsmen by either blood or marriage of the colonel. The jurors sitting on the case likely also identified with the rioters. The punishments meted out proved quite mild considering the violence of the offense and the impudence it showed in opposing the Crown's authority. Most were convicted to pay fines of no more than three pounds. Stephen Ward pled guilty to the charge of uttering a profane oath and was fined a further four shillings beyond what he was assessed for assaulting Lyman. By all indications, the indicted accepted their sentences and the prosecutions brought no further violence.[83]

At least one of those indicted in the rioting had traveled quite a distance to express his dissatisfaction with the deputy surveyors. Timothy Bedel, given the honorific title of "esquire" in the court documents, was a resident of Haverhill, New Hampshire—a town situated about 130 miles upriver from Northampton. Bedel, like the Lymans, was a beneficiary of Benning Wentworth's efforts to organize New Hampshire's western lands into townships. In 1763, Wentworth granted Bedel lands first in Newbury, across the river from Haverhill, and then in distant Colchester, along the shores of Lake Champlain.[84] Unlike the Lymans, Benning Wentworth's patronage did not turn Bedel into a proponent of the Pine Acts.

In fact, the acquisition of new lands in Newbury, added to the lands he already owned in Haverhill, likely had the opposite effect. Lumbering offered Bedel the quickest route to turn a profit from his lands in the New Hampshire interior and raise the capital needed to begin farming his new holdings.[85] In newly established townships where sawmills were still lacking, like Haverhill and Newbury in the 1760s, trees were hauled to the river and sent to mills downstream. Landowners then needed to travel downstream to make arrangements to have their timber sawn into boards for sale. Unless of course the enterprising lumberman arrived downriver to find his logs impounded for violation of the Pine Acts, as seems to have been the case for Bedel. Under the circumstances, Bedel chose to add his own voice to the mob decrying the deputy surveyors' actions.

Besides the twenty-two men who faced indictment, the court records speak of "many other persons to the Jurors unknown."[86] The crowd that confronted Lyman and Burt was a large one, perhaps not by the standards of Boston, but certainly for an area that was still something of a frontier for the English. In their enforcement of the Pine Acts, Wentworth's deputies had offended a surprisingly large number of people in Hampshire County. By threatening to curtail local production for the timber market, Lyman and Burt had offended against not just an individual or small group of businessmen. They had successfully stirred up the antipathy of the community—from a profanity-spewing laborer, to a young gentleman seeking his fortune in frontier lands, to an obstructionist justice of the peace and the colonel of the county militia. [87]

Still, most opposition to the Pine Acts was not nearly as dramatic as Hampshire County's riot or Daniel Whitmore's defiant act of surveyor dunking. Year in and year out, colonists defied parliamentary authority by quietly going about their daily business. Pine logs destined for the transatlantic market attracted the attention of imperial enforcers, but represented only one facet of the Connecticut Valley lumber industry. Colonists routinely felled white pines on their own lands or paid for the right to fell them on their neighbors' with little thought of seeking the approval of the king's surveyors. Hauled to the local sawmill, these logs were sawn into boards, split into planks and then carted home. Many ended up providing the floorboards and interior paneling for colonial-era houses. Up through the Revolution, inhabitants of the Connecticut Valley (sometimes consciously, sometimes unknowingly) engaged in a quiet repudiation of the Pine Acts either by felling legally protected pines or by purchasing and consuming the illicit goods produced from them.[88] It was a well-worn yarn among New England's nineteenth-century local historians that many of the surviving buildings from the mid-eighteenth century were built of boards sawn to a width of twenty-two or twenty-three inches—just avoiding the legally-damning twenty-four-inch mark.[89] This careful eye to measurements allowed colonial lumbermen and sawmill owners—as well as housewrights and homeowners—to practice a form of clandestine resistance to imperial authority.

Following the Northampton riots, the lumber trade in the Connecticut Valley returned to business as usual. The crowd action of October 25,

1765, fulfilled its purposes. Elijah Lyman and Eleazar Burt both seem to have thought better of any continued efforts at enforcing the Pine Acts. Neither man makes another appearance in the records performing the duties of a deputy surveyor; presumably they resigned their commissions. Nor did Benning Wentworth or his nephew John Wentworth (who in 1767 took his uncle's place as both surveyor general and governor of New Hampshire) have any luck in finding officers to replace them. In 1769, John Wentworth wrote to Jared Ingersoll, now a judge of the vice-admiralty court, imploring him to use the power of his office to assist the surveyor general's office in punishing the continuing depredations being committed against the King's Woods in the Connecticut Valley. Two decades after Benning Wentworth first attempted to clamp down on timber poaching in the Connecticut Valley, the authority of the surveyor general still proved ineffectual at overcoming popular hostility to and official obstruction of the Pine Acts. Ingersoll demurred from rendering any assistance to the younger Wentworth, only promising that he would refer the matter to his superior.[90]

With the outbreak of the Revolution, the white pines of the Connecticut Valley lost any fiction of imperial protection. But the idea that the woodlands of New England should be pressed into the service of the state—that military security justified a government monopoly on those white pines especially well-suited for masting naval ships—did not die easily. In 1777, the Continental Congress "earnestly recommended" that the state legislatures of New Hampshire, Massachusetts, and Connecticut do as the British Parliament had done and take "effectual measures for the preservation of all pine timber . . . which may be suitable and useful for masts."[91] Despite this earnest recommendation from Congress, none of the states of New England chose to follow the British example. Almost a century of quiet circumvention and outright opposition to the Pine Acts had predisposed New Englanders to view skeptically the proposition that government should continue to enjoy exclusive possession of the region's white pines.

Rather than rely on an unenforceable government monopoly on white pines, the newly independent states embraced a timber market unencumbered by national or state-level regulation. In 1777, Connecticut commissioned two warships to be built, one at New London and one at the Connecticut River port of Chatham (formerly East Middletown). To obtain masts, bowsprits, booms, and yards for these vessels, the state assembly turned to the market. Captain John Cotton of Middletown was voted 250 pounds to travel up the Connecticut River in search of suitable masts and spars.[92] Like the Royal Navy, Captain Cotton would have sought out the tall, straight white pines of the upper Connecticut. Unlike the Royal Navy, this agent of a newly independent state approached the local inhabitants with legal tender—not legal writs—in hand.

The Nature of Lumbering

This victory for the market paved the way for further "waste" (as Benning Wentworth had termed it back in the 1760s) to be made of Connecticut Valley pinelands. The exploitation of white pines and other tree species for the timber trade only sped the deforestation already underway from the ever-growing demand for fuel wood and agricultural land. Throughout the eighteenth century, the timber trade encouraged the geographic expansion of deforestation upriver and onto marginal lands that otherwise might have remained wooded.

The Connecticut/Massachusetts border roughly corresponded to the boundary between two different forest regimes. Oaks and other valuable hardwoods dominated in the south. In the cooler northern region, softwoods, especially white pines, made up a far larger portion of woodlands. Since softwoods, like white pines, were buoyant enough to be floated downstream, their exploitation did not need to wait for settlement and the construction of a sawmill in an area. It is hard to say when the practice of driving large logs down the Connecticut River began. One early historian of the region suggests the practice may have begun shortly after the 1726 conclusion of Dummer's War brought peace to English-Wabanaki relations, making it safe for loggers to venture into the upper valley.[93] The earliest log drive on the Connecticut River that we know of with certainty occurred in 1732.[94] Even this drive may have disappeared from the historical records had it not been accompanied by tragedy. At the end of August 1732, a small crowd from Windsor gathered to watch about twenty-five large pine logs as they passed Enfield Falls. As the logs hurdled through the rapids of the falls, one struck a large rock and was thrown up onto the bank, where it struck a teenage boy in the side of the head. The boy survived the initial impact, though the force of the blow knocked out his right eye. He could not be revived and passed away shortly after.[95] The sad news proved sufficiently sensational to make its way east and appear in Boston newspapers. Earlier log drives, unaccompanied by such dramatic tragedy, may have occurred on the Connecticut, but no records remain.

Log drives continued throughout the following decades, serving to connect the landscape and labor markets of the upper Connecticut Valley to the sawmills and lumber agents below. Traces of this activity (often illicit in the case of white pine logs) can be glimpsed in the account books and journals of men such as William Heywood of Charlestown, New Hampshire. In his diary for December of 1749, Heywood recorded that "six men from Springfield came up after logs." The Springfield loggers remained in the area for three weeks. On four days they hired Heywood and his oxen to haul the logs they had cut, presumably to the Connecticut where they could be placed on the river ice to await the spring thaw. Heywood also logged on his own account, cutting pines on his own land and on the unapportioned lands on the west bank of the Connecticut, then rolling them into the river for transport to the sawmills of the lower valley.[96]

The operation of these transient lumber parties pushed the ecological footprint of the timber trade far beyond the pale of English settlement. The mast pine company founded in Connecticut in the 1730s cut its pines near present-day Hanover, New Hampshire, which would not be settled by the English until 1765. The Springfielders to whom Heywood hired out his oxen were scouring southern New Hampshire (including what would become Vermont) for white pines. Jared Ingersoll encouraged his masting team to seek pines "from Deerfield to the Cowhees [Coos]"—a two-hundred-mile stretch of river that included a few small towns in southern New Hampshire as well as a vast area inhabited by Abenaki communities, parts of which would not be home to Anglo-American settlers until the nineteenth century.[97]

The devastating French defeat in the Seven Years'/French and Indian War undermined Abenaki power, allowing the English to claim and redistribute further lands in New Hampshire and Vermont in the 1760s.[98] The timber trade of the upper valley offered new settlers an incentive to exploit and clear lands that otherwise held little economic value. Northern pines dominated on sandy, dry soils ill-suited to English agriculture.[99] Where early settlers in the south might fell oaks, chestnuts, and walnuts for firewood and then expect to successfully farm the denuded fields left behind, the pinelands of the valley offered neither good firewood nor fertile arable land. Instead, pinelands provided an opportunity to profit from regional and Atlantic timber markets. These markets offered established settlers—like William Heywood of Charlestown—an opportunity to supplement income from farming. They offered pioneering settlers—like Timothy Bedel of Haverhill—the chance to earn capital to clear better lands and begin farming. Lumbermen—landless colonists, those with only small holdings, and Abenaki and River Indians who sought itinerant labor within English society—found the opportunity to earn a day's wage.[100] And, finally, regional and Atlantic markets encouraged sawmill owners living farther south—like the Whitmores of Middletown—to seek ever-new sources of timber to feed their mills.

The destruction of pine forests brought with it all of the ecological consequences of deforestation discussed in the previous chapter. As stumps decayed, the root systems that had helped hold valley soils in place disappeared and erosion increased. Exposed soils proved vulnerable to heavy rains, which became more common even as the overall amount of local rainfall decreased. Torrents of water, no longer absorbed by the trees that had once covered the land, cut gullies through fields and pastures, and produced erratic flooding. In 1797, for example, Timothy Dwight observed while traveling past Bellows Falls that "the river is now much fuller than it ever was before the country above was cleared, the snows in open ground melting much more suddenly and forming much greater freshets than in forested ground." The Connecticut's tributaries also ran more erratically or dried up altogether during parts of the year, rendering any mills built along their banks inoperative. But while the growing volume of lumber exports from the valley certainly exacerbated the ecological consequences of deforestation already underway, the lumber trade also brought its own, unique environmental consequences for the lands and waters of the Connecticut Basin.[101]

The millponds that sawmills depended upon to store logs and provide power to waterwheels often flooded valuable agricultural land. Building a dam to pond the waters of streams and small rivers meant flooding the often fertile lands that surrounded them. Such flooding could often lead to heated legal conflicts among neighbors—something town governments sought to avoid by requiring mill owners to exercise care in the placement of their dams. In 1679, Lyme granted one of its inhabitants liberty to build a new sawmill and dam the Falls River on the condition that the new millpond not "Damnify" a neighboring meadow.[102] In 1726, the town granted four more men the right to dam a local brook for a sawmill on the condition that they "not Infringe on any persons land ... without their leave & Consent."[103] If the dam were ever to break, such as during an especially high spring freshet, pond waters could flood neighboring lands that were usually dependably dry and devoted to farming or grazing. Such untimely flooding could ruin the season's planting or threaten to drown newly birthed lambs and calves.

Mills and milldams also threatened the fish in the rivers along whose banks they stood. Unlike beaver dams, which tended to take advantage of natural areas of slack water and stood closer to the level of downstream waters, milldams tended to be taller and located near rapids that already made upstream passage difficult. To protect the fish of its rivers and streams,

Connecticut began regulating milldam construction in 1764.[104] From that year forward, all new mills were required to include a fish gate that would allow fish to pass through. This law joined a collection of others, passed beginning in 1715, that were aimed primarily at protecting salmon, shad, and alewife populations in the Connecticut watershed and other colonial rivers.[105] All three are anadromous species that live most of their lives in the ocean but return to freshwater to spawn. Their seasonal runs offered colonial settlers a bumper crop every spring when valley residents gathered at favorite fishing spots. A single fisherman could take dozens of salmon and perhaps hundreds of shad or alewives in just a few days. Some of this bounty would end up on the fisherman's table, some would be traded to neighbors, and a significant portion would be barreled and exported to larger urban centers like Boston.[106]

By the early eighteenth century, however, officials began to worry about declining populations of anadromous fish species in some of the streams and brooks that served as their spawning grounds. Towns and landowners located on the upper reaches of Connecticut tributaries complained that their neighbors downstream were overharvesting spawning fish, leaving few for upriver communities. In particular, they denounced as unfair any technology that impeded the course of these anadromous fish in their runs. Stone dams built across the width of a stream, usually in a V-shape with a hole toward the middle to allow the passage of fish into a waiting net, were outlawed. So were weirs, wooden fences erected across streams, and seines, nets so large that they could be stretched all the way across a stream or a significant part of it. Milldams also blocked fish as they tried to make their way upriver and often became popular fishing spots for exactly that reason. Laws requiring fish gates, which were to remain open during the spring months, represent both an awareness on the part of colonial legislators that fish populations—especially salmon—were coming under pressure and their desire to protect these valuable species.

Focusing on river obstructions like seines, weirs, and milldams addressed only one part of the problem. While all types of colonial mills disrupted fish migration, the sawmills that processed timber for local inhabitants and transatlantic merchants were especially detrimental to fish populations. For example, in 1751 locals living in New Hampshire's Great Bay, the site of New England's first great lumber boom, told the visiting West Indies merchant James Birket that area mills had already destroyed the bay's salmon fisheries. "The Sawdust" they told Birket, "is very ungratefull to the fish when Mixed with the Water."[107] Despite this dawning ecological understanding of the relationship between sawmill wastes and fish populations occurring to their east, the inhabitants of the Connecticut Valley seem to have remained largely oblivious to the relationship between sawdust and fish stocks. This is perhaps because the impact in the valley was less pronounced and slower to occur than were the declines in fish populations observed in New Hampshire and later in Maine. Sawmills in the Connecticut Valley, spread out as they were along the river's many tributaries, were not so geographically concentrated as in New Hampshire's Great Bay and, as a consequence, neither was the sawdust that they produced. And unlike the calm waters of the bay, the swift current of the Connecticut could be depended upon to wash most sawmill wastes downriver, away from the polluting community.

Still, sawdust likely played an important role in the declining fish stocks of the eighteenth-century valley. Trees contributed as much as 13 percent of their mass to sawdust during the milling process. Using this estimate, the twenty thousand feet of pine boards that Springfield sawmills sold to the Hartford market in 1698 would have introduced 22,500 pounds (or eleven and one-quarter tons) of sawdust into local streams and rivers over the course of that year.[108] As the quantity of boards sawn in the valley increased steadily throughout the colonial period, the amount of sawdust and other wood wastes dumped into local streams would have increased accordingly. Increased levels of pollution, in turn, placed increased stress on local fish populations already hard pressed by the loss of beaver pond habitat, overfishing, and dam construction.

Sawmill wastes brought a myriad of problems for local fish life. Sawdust suspended in the water of brooks, streams, and ponds blocked sunlight, depressing photosynthetic activity and reducing the availability of plant life on which some fish fed. When it settled, the dust could bury water plants, as well as the eggs and fry of many fish species. The decomposition of wood wastes used up oxygen from the surrounding waters, lowering the amount available for plant and fish life. In spots where the accumulation of wood wastes was especially high, decomposition could produce anaerobic conditions—dead zones where plants and fish could not survive. Where accumulated wood wastes did not use up all the oxygen in an area, their decomposition still leached harmful chemicals and introduced noxious gases into the surrounding waters that could kill eggs and young fry and sicken adult fish. Where sawmill activity was especially intense, sawdust and other wastes might even form shoals large enough to block the migration routes of anadromous fish. Sawdust suspended in water increased the amount of energy that fish were forced to exert to filter water through their gills. So long as an adult fish was strong and healthy, the extra effort required to force sawdust through the gill linings proved negligible. But in fish that were sick or exhausted, this extra demand often proved unsustainable, resulting in sawdust-clogged gills, open sores caused by abrasion, and eventually death. Such a threat would not lead to a collapse of fish populations, but it would contribute to decreases in fish populations already under pressure due to other factors such as overfishing and the other effects of sawmill pollution.[109]

Salmon, because of their life cycle, often proved especially vulnerable to the threat posed by wood wastes. The legendary exertions of salmon fighting their way upstream to spawn in their natal waterways take a tremendous toll in calories, leaving the exhausted fish vulnerable to the effects of sawdust. In this context, the added obstruction of milldams conspired with the constant struggle to force sawdust-choked waters through straining gills to exhaust and suffocate migrating salmon. Should an individual succumb prior to reaching the spawning grounds, his or her chance at producing a next generation would be lost. Even if the salmon did survive to spawn, it then faced the challenge of swimming back downriver (unlike Pacific salmon which reproduce only once and then expire, Atlantic salmon often return to the ocean following reproduction). Along the way, the exhausted fish faced the same obstacles as on its way up, reducing the odds that it would survive to return and spawn in future years.

The seasonal nature of sawmilling posed particular threats to young salmon. Eggs, laid in the autumn, risked being buried by waste materials from the seasonal ramping up of sawmill activity. Hatching in spring, the young fry would have faced a similar threat. Feeding in the waters of their natal streams for the first two to three years of their lives, juvenile salmon—referred to as parrs—faced the same threats from mill wastes as confronted freshwater species. Heading downstream in the autumn, nearly mature smolts needed to navigate both the dangers of anaerobic dead zones and of milldams blocking their path to the ocean. In previous centuries, the small smolts—approximately six inches in length—would have easily passed either over the tops of beaver dams or else through the intermeshed limbs that made these dams resemble nothing so much as "leaky sieves."[110] Although far fewer in number, the colonial milldams that replaced beaver engineering were built to be more impermeable, making them a greater hindrance to young anadromous fish trying to make their way back to the sea. Once they reached the tidal zone, smolts fed in the estuarial waters at the Connecticut's mouth, gradually undergoing the physiological changes that would allow them to make the transition from life in freshwater to life in saltwater.

Here they once again faced increased challenges in the eighteenth century: heavier silt loads from increased erosion upstream increased turbidity and, in turn, made it hard for smolts to find food, placing physical stresses on the young salmon that may have inhibited some individuals' ability to adapt to and survive in saltwater.[111]

By 1800, salmon had disappeared from the Connecticut watershed. Their decline had many causes—from the pressures that colonial freshwater fishermen put on populations, to the loss of wetlands habitat, to runoff from livestock and related industries, to the obstruction of streams by milldams, to the pollution dumped into streams and ponds by colonial sawmills. The salmon's demise thus highlights the complexity of ecological changes taking place in the colonial period, while also pointing out the unforeseen consequences that colonial commerce, like the trade in Connecticut Valley timber, could have on wildlife species. The fate of the salmon also offers clues to how the colonial economy affected the numerous freshwater fish species that called the watershed home. Unless they happen to be salmon, shad, or maybe alewives, fish in the extant records tend to be simply "fish"—making it hard to track changes in individual species. But the salmon, which was much commented upon due to its dramatic annual runs, can serve as a stand-in for numerous freshwater fish species whose populations likely suffered from colonial pollutants like sawdust, but which settlers never mentioned by name in their records. Taking the Atlantic salmon as a stand-in for other species suggests how dramatic an impact seventeenth- and eighteenth-century settlers had upon the freshwater fisheries of the Connecticut watershed. As Timothy Dwight recorded during his journeys, by the early nineteenth century, the salmon had "wholly deserted" the Connecticut River and its tributaries.[112]

Exporting Ecological Consequences

By the eighteenth-century, sloops constructed of Connecticut Valley timber carried boards sawn from valley trees at valley sawmills to Boston as well as the far-off West Indies and Spanish and Portuguese Wine Islands. In their holds, these ships also carried barrels made of valley oak containing myriad other valley-produced commodities. High demand for the coveted white pine sent lumberman north into the pine forests of the middle and upper valley, while homesteaders exploited this profitable commodity to raise capital to clear and plant new lands or to supplement the income they earned from farming. Added to local timber needs, production for regional and overseas markets sped the deforestation of valley lands while busy sawmills polluted local waterways. In both cases, the timber trade exacerbated existing ecological problems set in motion by colonists and Indians pursuing other economic interests. As the eighteenth century progressed, the landscape of the valley became increasingly bare and its waterways increasingly befouled by silt and pollution.

Market production continued and expanded during the eighteenth century despite concerns about dwindling timber supplies. Even in the face of imperial conservation efforts, valley loggers, sawmill owners, and merchants persisted in their trade, sometimes with violent results. Local and colony-level attempts to regulate timber markets may have achieved greater compliance, but seem written more with an eye toward supporting local industries, like shipbuilding, than with the intention of actually preserving woodlands. Nor did deforestation in the valley lead to timber shortages for local communities, as proponents of legislation often feared. Instead, the same market forces that in the eighteenth century encouraged valley inhabitants to export timber to the West Indies and elsewhere provided them with the opportunity to purchase timber in the nineteenth. By the early nineteenth century, as valuable pines and other species disappeared from the banks of the Connecticut and its tributaries, lumber production had moved on to the forests of Maine. Eventually, canal and railroad construction would shift the lumbering frontier farther west, allowing New Englanders to purchase boards, planks, and rails more cheaply than they could make them themselves.[113] As New England became more industrialized in the nineteenth century, similar market forces would hinder New England agriculture, encouraging the abandonment of marginal farmlands. No longer under pressure from logging and land clearing, woodlands in the Connecticut Valley and elsewhere in New England would expand. From the mid-nineteenth century forward, reforestation would claim more and more of the region until, by the end of the twentieth century, the landscape would support more trees than any time prior to European colonization.

CHAPTER 5

Keeping Livestock

A Commerce in Beasts
Domestic and Wild

The introduction of English livestock revolutionized the ecological landscape of the Connecticut Valley. The rich intervales of the Connecticut, fed by the renewing waters of the spring freshets, offered husbandmen some of the best pasture and meadowlands in New England. Settlers eagerly exploited this favorable environment, raising livestock to provide meat, wool, and motive power for their own households and for sale to regional and Atlantic markets. Growing colonial populations in Boston and other colonial urban centers, the provisioning needs of New England's fishing and merchant fleets, British military operations in North America, and the rigors of sugar production in the West Indies provided a constant demand for live animals and preserved meat. Cattle, swine, horses, and sheep turned loose in the pastures and woodlands of the valley multiplied quickly. The region's biodiversity, already in decline from habitat loss, dwindled further as livestock outcompeted wildlife for forage. To protect their animal charges, English settlers strove to exterminate the valley's native predators. Husbandmen introduced new species of grass seed to replace overgrazed native grasses. Landowners cleared woods and marsh for new pasturelands and voracious livestock sped the clearing process by devouring shrubs and trampling saplings. As decades passed and settlements spread, the English practice of livestock husbandry transformed nearly every aspect of the ecological relationships that defined life in the lands and waters of the valley.

* * *

As the winter of 1778 approached, and the War for Independence raged, Colonel Timothy Bedel found his time filled with questions of cattle. In private life Bedel was a respected local leader in the Connecticut's upper valley who combined cattle raising, logging, and farming to earn a comfortable living from his extensive landholdings in the twin river towns of Haverhill, New Hampshire, and Newbury, in what would become Vermont. Bedel had first revealed his rebellious leanings twelve years earlier when he joined the pine riots outside Northampton. When the Revolution broke out, Bedel enlisted in the Patriot cause. By 1777 he had advanced to the rank of colonel in the Continental army and been entrusted with defending New England's northern frontier against the threat of invasion from Canada.

The cattle which occupied Colonel Bedel's mind were not his own. They belonged to neighboring landowners living up and down the northern valley. Annual cattle drives had long connected the valley to the coast, tying rural labor markets to Boston's need to feed its ever-expanding urban population. During the peace of the late 1760s and early 1770s, this trade had provided a source of prosperity for local landowners and helped drive the settlement of the northern valley. Now Bedel feared that the course of war hinged upon whether or not this trade would be allowed to continue along its peacetime course.

Bedel's concerns were twofold. First, should the British or their Indian allies mount an attack, the militia would need to be raised, and these fighting men would have to be fed. The loss of the year's crop of beef cattle to the far-off Boston market would sorely strain Bedel's ability to provision his troops. Second, should the cattle of the northern river towns be driven to market in Boston, many of the military-age men of the region would go with them as drovers. Under the circumstances, Bedel chose to requisition the cattle of the region for the use of the Continental army's northern department. In return he offered "the market Price that is given by the Commissary," presumably in the Continental currency that had been rapidly devaluing since first issued by Congress in 1775.[1]

Not all of the upper valley's inhabitants approved of the Continental army's interference in what had by the late 1770s become an economic tradition in the area. Nor were local cattle sellers necessarily contented with what the commissary considered a fair market price. Some even preferred to trade with the British, rather than sell to Continental or militia forces. A local nineteenth-century historian later recorded that it had been "handed down in tradition that there were those in this section . . . who were willing to turn a penny in furnishing beef without too close a scrutiny as to where it was going or who might eat it." Cattle owners would seclude their animals on out-of-the-way pastures, gather them at night, and swim them across the Connecticut to waiting British agents who purchased the herds and drove them north to Canada.[2]

Timothy Bedel found himself at a watershed in history. From its earliest days, the livestock trade of the valley had tied the farmers of the region to the demands of a growing British Empire. By the late colonial period, thanks to trade down the Connecticut River, the ports of Connecticut exported more live animals than any other colony in British America, more pork than any other colony, and more beef than all of the other colonies combined.[3] From the mid-seventeenth century to the late eighteenth, livestock raising connected landowners in the Connecticut Valley, and the upland towns that grew up around the valley, to the demands of fast-growing colonial urban centers like Boston and New York. The export trades of these colonial commercial centers, in turn, linked the farmers and husbandmen of the valley into the commercial networks of the Atlantic World. Merchants in Boston and other ports sold live animals and barreled meat to the commissary agents that kept Britain's soldiers fed during the colonial wars of the eighteenth century. They also funneled livestock and preserved meat from the valley to the West Indies where sugar plantations offered a steady demand for provisions to feed expanding slave populations and draft animals to power the profitable sugar mills. During the Revolution, Bedel joined Patriot rebels throughout the colonies in an attempt to sever these connections.

The 1770s were a time of Revolution. Colonists tested and eventually repudiated their political ties to the British Empire. Requisitioning cattle that might once have fed the British army comprised only one part of the Patriot struggle for independence, but it was an important one. Throughout the war, officers and statesmen committed considerable attention to provisioning the often ill-supplied men of the Continental army and colonial militias. The livestock trade was far too integral to the success of the Revolutionary cause to be overlooked.

The success of the livestock trade, in turn, rested on the success of another revolution: an ecological revolution that had been under way for over a century and a half by the time of the Revolution. As the economic and commercial networks of the livestock trade had expanded, they had created a new ecological system in their wake. European animals and plants took the place of native New England species. The landscape took on a new look as pastures and meadows expanded. As Timothy Dwight observed while touring the Connecticut Valley in the early nineteenth century, agricultural success almost inevitably led to deforestation.[4] Throughout the colonial period agricultural success depended upon the functioning of a mixed husbandry system that combined growing crops with raising livestock. The result of this system was a new environment shaped by the actions and needs of domestic animals and the efforts of their English masters. English colonial expansion drove this revolution. It was the culmination of innumerable decisions made by individual farmers. It was also, in a sense, a legislated revolution: the result of a multitude of laws passed by town assemblies, colonial general courts, and the imperial government. From the seventeenth century to the end of the eighteenth, livestock were a major motive force shaping the settlement, the economy, the politics, and ultimately the ecology of colonial New England.

The Early Cattle Economy

Livestock occupied a central role in the economy of Puritan New England. When English settlers migrated to the New World, they commonly brought as much as possible of their old lives with them. A large proportion of New England's earliest immigrants hailed from parts of England where the wood pasturing of livestock still persisted as an important economic complement to grain cultivation. The earliest English colonizers of Connecticut brought this traditional commitment to mixed husbandry with them to the southern valley, where it would flourish and later, in the mid-eighteenth century, be carried by their descendants to the frontier towns of New Hampshire and what would become Vermont. The shortage of labor for clearing and improving farmland meant that in frontier areas (which included all of New England in the early seventeenth century) livestock actually increased in importance relative to the raising of crops.[5] As a consequence, acquiring livestock became a priority for English settlers looking to begin new agricultural lives in America.

This demand created a thriving early market. The Great Migration (1630–1640) assured a high demand for livestock throughout the 1630s.[6] Some Puritan émigrés invested great sums to transport their animals with them on the voyage across the Atlantic. Many, however, sold off their English estates completely and arrived in New England with little more than pounds and shillings. They depended on earlier arrivals to sell them the cattle and other supplies they would need both for their immediate subsistence and to begin their new lives as colonial farmers. Those with cattle—previous arrivals who had paid to bring their animals with them and then bred the first generations of New England-born livestock—welcomed the opportunity to secure scarce English currency. A thriving domestic market quickly sprang up and prices soared. Governor John Winthrop, a firm believer in the concept of a just price, recorded with some dismay that cattle were being sold to newcomers for as much as twenty-six pounds a head in 1633. The silver lining was that this trade, exorbitant though its prices may have seemed, provided the specie necessary to support the Massachusetts settlers' early demands for imports. Winthrop admitted that the new colony's trade in foreign commodities "could not have subsisted to this time, but that it was supplied by the cattle and corn, which were sold to new comers at very dear rates."[7] The imported specie brought by immigrants bought local cattle, and local cattlemen turned around and spent their earnings on goods needed (or wanted) from England and other colonies.

   As new settlers continued to pour into the colony, they followed the example of earlier arrivals by taking up mixed husbandry, with special emphasis on the raising of livestock. The pursuit of new meadowlands and greener pastures for their cattle and other animals played a key role in the dispersion of population and the proliferation of New England towns in the first decade of Puritan settlement.[8] The Reverend Nathaniel Ward, minister in the newly established Ipswich, condemned his Puritan countrymen for their propensity "to seeke the good of their cattell more then of [the] com[monweal]th."[9] William Bradford, condemning those settlers who left behind lands which were (in Bradford's opinion) perfectly "well-meadowed and suitable for cattle," worried that the dispersal of settlers "will be the ruin of New England . . . and will provoke the Lord's displeasure against them."[10] Such remonstrances did little to slow the dispersal of New England's settlers or their domestic animals.

   Farther afield, the lush meadows lining the banks of the Connecticut River beckoned to the worldly cattlemen of Puritan New England's founding generation. In 1635, Newtown (later Cambridge), Massachusetts, resident John Pratt found himself in trouble with the colony's general court over a letter he had written disparaging the soils and environment of the Bay Colony. Pratt hailed from a region of eastern England whose economy depended heavily upon sheep raising as a complementary activity to grain agriculture. Looking around at the landscape of the bay area, Pratt complained that he found himself surrounded by nothing but "rocks, sands & salte marshes," lands ill-suited for either grain or grazing. Fearful that such talk might discourage future immigration to their fledgling colony, the general court demanded a written recantation. Pratt, instead, offered an apology that sidestepped the question by suggesting that he merely meant that such soils were deficient only for supporting the number of families who had been settled upon them.

Only the founding of new towns that "will afford good meanes of subsistance for men & beasts" could ensure the prosperity of the Bay Colony. Pratt, who at the time was preparing to emigrate further, looked to the lands of "Coñect-icott" as a promising site for new towns that might provide a living "sufficient for myself . . . also for my posteritie."[11]

Many of Newtown's inhabitants shared Pratt's sentiments. In 1634, the town's inhabitants petitioned the general court of the Bay Colony for per-mission to remove westward and form a new township along the banks of the Connecticut River. The Newtown settlers complained that in their pres-ent eastern settlement they lacked sufficient "accommodation for their cattle" making it "so they were not able to maintain their ministers, nor could they receive any more of their friends." The Reverend Thomas Hooker reproved the Massachusetts government for the "fundamental errour" of having set-tled the towns of the colony "set so near each to other." The solution to their present difficulties, the inhabitants of Newtown insisted, lay in the Connecti-cut Valley. They were drawn to the region by its "fruitfulness and commodi-ousness," a natural abundance capable of supporting them, their cattle, and any of "their friends" who wished to follow from England. They pushed the court for a quick decision, warning of the risk of "having it [the valley] pos-sessed by others, Dutch or English."[12] Although Governor John Winthrop at first counseled against English settlement along the Connecticut, warning that the new towns would be isolated, "weak and in danger to be assailed," the court eventually relented. In 1635, the Reverend Thomas Hooker led his flock overland to their new home upon the Connecticut—a *new* Newtown that was renamed Hartford two years later. Winthrop's journal for the year records the exodus: "About sixty men, women and little children, went by land toward Connecticut with their cows, horses, and swine, and, after a tedious journey, arrived safe."[13]

Similar motives drove the founders of the valley's other early towns. The inhabitants of Dorchester, Massachusetts, who formed the town of Windsor in 1635, were drawn mostly from England's West Country, a region where dairying prevailed as a dominant economic activity. Like their Newtown/ Hartford neighbors, these West Country dairymen placed a high value upon the rich meadowlands lining the Connecticut.[14] A group from Watertown, Massachusetts, founded Wethersfield, the third of Connecticut's original townships, in 1633. Before immigrating to Watertown, most of these early founders had made their homes in Yorkshire and its surrounding counties, a region where cattle and sheep raising dominated the seventeenth-century economy.[15] The name given to the new town (a *wether* is a male sheep) represents the founding generation's hope that the area might prove good land for grazing, even though sheep were destined to play a minor role in the agriculture of the valley until the area could be made safe from predators.

The form of livestock husbandry that prevailed in the early valley depended upon an abundance of open pasture and available forage. Indeed, abundant lands and scarce labor combined to produce a fundamental shift in the English colonists' views on the relationship between livestock and real property. In much of England, livestock lived between fences—secured on common lands or on private pastures. By contrast, New England owners turned their livestock loose to run wild in the region's woodlands and nat-ural pastures. Rather than expending valuable time and effort on fencing *in* this expanse of grazing and browsing land, colonists instead chose to fence livestock *out* of their croplands. English law had traditionally placed the bur-den of preventing livestock damage to crops on the animals' owners. A 1634 Massachusetts law effectively reversed this legal burden by requiring farmers to maintain fences around their crops. If they failed to do so, they would be denied restitution should their crops fall victim to hungry ungulates.[16] The husbandmen of the first Connecticut towns carried this freshly minted legal tradition with them when they migrated to the valley.[17]

The open wood-pasture system of husbandry practiced by early colonists had its drawbacks. Without human care, animals could easily perish. Con-necticut governor Roger Wolcott, remembering his younger days, penned a piece of doggerel that captured the perils of turning cattle loose to graze at their will: "Another calfe I had last yeare / but where he's now I cannot heare. / Which fills my heart with sighs and groans, / for feare the croos [crows] have picked his bones."[18] Generations of livestock improvement through selective breeding by English farmers came undone as animals ran loose on com-mon lands and chose their own mates. Natural selection in the woodlands produced livestock that were leaner, meaner, and wilder—better adapted for survival on the open range, but all-around inferior from the husband-men's perspective.[19] Feral livestock wreaked havoc in unprotected or insuf-ficiently fenced fields. Instances of livestock damaging crops are ubiquitous in the colonial records. For example, in 1660 John Pynchon turned a herd of hogs loose to fatten in the woodlands of what would become Enfield. The hogs promptly broke into a number of maize fields in nearby Windsor and stuffed themselves so full on green corn that they subsequently died from overeating.[20]

Colonists struggled to raise sheep successfully during the early years of settlement. Sheep were far more finicky in their grazing than were other livestock species that managed to make do with the wild grasses native to New England. When they did graze, sheep nibbled grasses down to their very roots, often ruining a pasture for other grazers. Whereas swine, cattle, and horses could usually shift for themselves in woodlands and often fend off would-be predators, sheep had difficulty finding greener pastures without being led to them by shepherds and proved hopeless at eluding wolves and the various other creatures that wanted to eat them. Plus, their wool often snagged on branches and brambles, making shearing more difficult and occasionally snaring a sheep in place until it died of exposure or was happened upon by a lucky predator.[21]

The Massachusetts General Court, citing a fear of impending shortages of cloth, banned the export of ewes from the colony in 1652, suggesting that sheep were somewhat scarce at the time. In 1670, Connecticut passed a law requiring all male inhabitants fourteen and older to spend one day a year removing the underbrush from pasturelands to help make them more amenable to grazing sheep.[22] Still, despite such problems, the benefits of woodland and commons pasturing outweighed its costs and the system persisted. English settlers repeatedly re-created it as they pushed northwards up the valley and outwards onto the uplands beyond. As would-be husbandmen turned to making farms out of the frontier, livestock turned to common pastures and woodlands to seek their subsistence.

Success escaped the first English settlers who tried their hands at cattle raising in the Connecticut Valley. Unfamiliarity with the New England climate, and lingering memories of cattle rearing practices in their more temperate English homes, contributed to the devastating losses endured by the valley's earliest herds. The first settlers of the valley knew that their new homes shared the same latitude as northern Spain and southern France and expected New England winters to be comparably mild. They were not.[23] Limited knowledge of their new environment likely led the earliest settlers of Connecticut to underestimate the toll that New England's harsh winter would take on their herds. Migrants required time and experience to teach them what to expect from the climate of their new environment. And many of those who set out for the Connecticut Valley in the mid-1630s had not been in-country long enough to adjust their expectations.

Most of Hartford's founders, for example, had arrived in New England only in the summer of 1634, settling in Newtown barely a year before setting off for a new home farther west. Many of the founding families of Windsor and Wethersfield arrived at the same time.[24] Still unfamiliar with the New England climate, these newcomers brought more livestock than they could feed. Although the Connecticut immigrants could not have predicted it, poor timing only added to their hardships. The winter of 1635–1636 was an especially cold and snowy one.[25] John Winthrop wrote in early 1636 that the Connecticut settlers "lost the greatest part of them [their cattle] this winter," and estimated the value of this loss at two thousand pounds. Settlers in the other early towns provided better for their herds, but finding enough fodder for the winter months still proved a major challenge. Not all animals survived. Even those that made it through the first winter suffered the lingering effects of near starvation. Winthrop recorded in the autumn of 1636 that "things went not well at Connecticut. . . . Their cattle did, many of them, cast their young, as they had done the year before."[26] Increased rates of spontaneous abortion, a clear sign of severe malnutrition, plagued the cattle of the valley for the first two years of English settlement. Settlers learned the hard way that in New England they would need to set aside significantly more fodder to get their livestock through the winter.[27] Building profitable herds would not prove easy.

To make things worse, the initial source of profits driving the search for new pastures and meadows throughout the 1630s soon dried up. As tensions between Parliament and the Crown intensified in the early 1640s, eventually culminating in the English Civil War, Puritans who may have been considering seeking asylum in New England instead chose to stay in England and press for religious reform at home. As migration from England to the Puritan colonies slowed, the price of cattle plummeted.[28] In 1641, John Winthrop recorded with concern that "a cow which cost last year £20 might now be bought for 4 or £5."[29]

The boom prices that had driven Puritan husbandmen to scatter into the New England wilderness in the mid-1630s never returned, but the livestock market did begin to slowly recover with the development of new markets in the 1640s.[30] Springfield grandee John Pynchon, for instance, sent small herds of cattle from Springfield to Boston each autumn as early as 1655, and perhaps earlier. By 1670 he had begun stall-feeding cattle during the winter to fatten them up before sending them overland to the bay each spring.[31] Landowners elsewhere in the valley followed suit. Throughout the second half of the seventeenth century, with a brief interruption during King Philip's War, drovers from the valley made their way to Boston. Along the road, they encountered other herds coming from the Rhode Island towns, from Plymouth, from the New Haven colony, and even from the towns along the Piscataqua River. Together they descended on Boston, the center of a trade network that even as early as the 1650s had drawn together the far-flung towns of New England into a common market for animals, meat, and provisions. [32]

Pynchon and other husbandmen in the valley also sold large quantities of barreled meat to Boston during the seventeenth century—both beef and pork.[33] Slaughtering, butchering, salting, and barreling meat allowed livestock owners to take advantage of the Connecticut Valley's network of river borne trade. Upriver merchants contracted with traders in the port towns to send their beef downriver. A large variety of other country produce accompanied these meat shipments: grain, lumber, potash, wool, flaxseed—in short, anything the inland farmer could produce that might find a buyer in the broader regional and Atlantic markets. To protect the commercial reputation of the colony, the general court passed an act in 1662 requiring that all towns appoint an official town packer charged with insuring that all barreled meat exported was of sufficient quantity and quality.[34] The town of Springfield had first appointed a town sealer, with similar responsibilities in 1652.[35] Even Deerfield, on the far northern frontier of English settlement, had appointed a packer by 1691—indicating its commitment to exports.[36] The extent of this early trade in preserved meat is difficult to gauge, but the records of John Pynchon offer some idea of its scope. From 1662 to 1683, Pynchon's records show 162 hogs, averaging approximately 170 pounds of meat each for a total of 27,409 pounds of pork, sold out of the valley.[37] This trade only grew in the eighteenth century.

Merchants in Hartford and Middletown funneled the livestock of the valley out into the wider world. Connecticut Valley merchants sent live animals or salted meat to Boston to feed the city's growing population, to provision New England's fast-expanding fishing and trading fleets, and for transshipment to the West Indies and other foreign markets. In exchange, these local merchants received and sold manufactured goods from England and sugar, molasses, and rum from the West Indies to the inhabitants of the Connecticut towns.[38] In the eighteenth century, these merchants also imported salt from Ireland, England, southern Europe, and the West Indies, allowing local husbandmen to preserve quantities of meat beyond the limits of regional salt production. Flaxseed exports helped offset the cost of salt bought from the British Isles, while the surplus meat and fish preserved with this imported salt made up an important portion of the regional ledger in New England's trade with the Caribbean, Spain, and Portugal.[39]

Indeed, livestock, and the meat they yielded, were a key component in the maritime commercial networks that undergirded New England's ties to the rest of the transatlantic world. The sailors of New England's merchant fleet would have sailed with empty bellies if not for the industry of the region's livestock raisers. By the 1670s, Massachusetts alone boasted a fleet of over seven hundred merchant vessels, a number that grew over the decades. These ships carried the produce of New England to distant ports in England, the Spanish and French Wine Islands, and Southern Europe. They also plied their wares in markets closer to home, in the West Indies and Newfoundland. Many of the smaller vessels pursued the coasting trade, drawing towns all along the North American coast, including the towns of the lower Connecticut River, into a single, loose maritime marketplace. The sailors aboard all of these vessels required provisions, relying for protein upon barreled beef and, especially, salted pork. Barreled meat arriving in Boston from the Connecticut Valley, and live animals arriving in the abattoirs surrounding the city, fed not only local Bostonians and end consumers on the plantations of the West Indies, but also made possible the provisioning of the merchant fleet that connected these far-off ports.[40]

Added to the demands of the region's merchant fleet were those of its fishing fleet. Fish were big business in the colonial northeast, providing New Englanders with their single most lucrative export. New England farmers never hit upon a staple crop to rival the tobacco, rice, indigo, or cotton of the southern colonies. Instead it was the region's fishermen who provided New England with what can be considered its only true staple commodity: cod. By the 1670s, there were over four hundred vessels fishing the waters between Boston and Kennebec, with perhaps hundreds more venturing north toward the Great Banks. One Parliamentary report even suggests that New England may have supported a total of thirteen hundred fishing vessels in this period. A century later, over a thousand New England vessels were fishing just the waters of the Great Banks. These vessels employed thousands of sailors, all demanding preserved meat for their daily rations. A single barrel of salted pork was sometimes enough to see the crew of a small vessel through a season of fishing, but larger vessels, or those with more generous captains, often demanded greater quantities and perhaps some barreled beef as well for variety. Nor did the Boston provisions market limit itself to serving only New England ships. Merchant vessels carried supplies to Newfoundland and even French Louisbourg, providing provisions for the fleets operating out of these more northerly regions as well. These demands added up, and Connecticut Valley husbandmen played an important role in supplying the provisioning trade that operated out of Boston while also developing commercial ties to other growing fishing and merchant ports like New York and Newport.[41]

Mixed Husbandry

For the pioneering husbandmen moving west out of Massachusetts Bay and Plymouth, the great appeal of the Connecticut Valley could be summed up in one word: grass. Most of the livestock species brought to the valley in the early days of settlement could, and did, live in the open woodlands surrounding the river—but only swine were able to thrive in such a habitat. Building up and maintaining herds of cattle, horses, and sheep meant access not only to the woodlands, but also to pasturelands and to meadows where hay could be cut to maintain animals through the New England winter. The valley's natural meadows, along the river's edge, and those that had been created by the region's Native American communities, were extensive, but expanding herds called for ever more grasslands. Settlers may have bemoaned the clearing of local woodlands because it meant losing easy access to firewood and building materials, but the flip side was that as woodlands diminished, new pasturelands slowly emerged in their place. Indeed, fears over diminishing woodlands seldom slowed continuing efforts to clear lands for grazing and agriculture.

Like any scarce resource, grass had the potential to spark violence. For instance, in 1672 unclear titles to a four-mile-wide stretch of meadow lying along the boundary between Lyme and New London sparked a brawl between hayers from the two towns. When competing parties showed up to scythe the same stretch of ground, approximately forty men (including constables and a justice of the peace from both towns) "rudely & Barbarously fell to Blowes." The New London mob "knockt one man for dead" before cooler heads prevailed. Both parties agreed to let a court decide the question and "so, drinking a dram together, with some seeming friendship, every man departed to his home." (The unfortunate laborer from Lyme who had been "knockt . . . for dead" presumably recovered—perhaps all he needed was a good strong drink.) The county court fined all involved, but ultimately found for the hayers from Lyme.[42] Having lost their case, the New Londoners begrudgingly agreed to recognize Lyme's right to the disputed meadowlands.[43] This conflict between Lyme and New London revolved around the legal question of how best to divide the existing local supply of grass. At the same time, other English settlers up and down the valley worked hard to increase that supply.

Grass, like most living commodities, is not an altogether "natural" resource. Its growth, abundance, and quality are all contingent on human actions. The earliest English settlers of the valley were fortunate enough to enter a region covered with "mowing field[s] already cleared to their hands" and "natural meadows" with "wild grass . . . as high as a man's shoulders, and very thick." New Hampshire merchant Joseph Peirce saw these grasslands, relics of an older ecology engineered by beaver and swept away by the fur trade, as evidence of "the great design of Providence" in providing for English immigrants and their cattle until the settlers were able to clear "ground enough to raise English hay."[44] Persistent local and regional demands for firewood, along with markets for timber in colonial urban centers and the West Indies, opened up even more land to farming, on the one hand, and mowing and grazing, on the other.

Of course, it was not enough merely to clear woodlands and wait for grasses to move in. Clearing woods for grazing and agriculture required more than just the one-time effort of felling trees. Left to themselves, woodlands would regenerate and even expand. Seeds carried by the wind or by animals would take root beyond the tree line and slowly recolonize pastures, meadows, and fields. Keeping the woods at bay required constant vigilance. Indian communities in the valley had long relied on fire to prevent woodlands from encroaching on fields and to keep the edges of woodlands clear so that game could browse. Timothy Dwight, surveying the Indian history of New England, summarized: "The object of these conflagrations was to produce fresh and sweet pasture, for the purpose of alluring the deer to the spots on which they had been kindled."[45] As much as English husbandmen also sought "fresh and sweet pasture," settlers' fear of property damage from fire led them to abandon this advantageous strategy for recycling nutrients and keeping lands clear of woods. Instead, they relied on their animals to browse to the nub encroaching bushes, strip the leaves and bark of saplings, and generally trample any young vegetation underfoot.[46] Where such efforts failed, husbandmen were forced to invest their own labor in annually uprooting and hacking back woodlands.

English settlers also influenced their grass supply by replacing, directly and indirectly, less desirable grass species with preferable ones. The grasses native to New England—wild rye, broomstraw, cordgrass, and so forth—had not had the advantage of evolving in tandem with domesticated grazers. They stood up poorly against nibbling and trampling by herds of large ungulates. Native grasses also offered inferior nutrition. Husbandmen discovered that, compared to back in England, they required substantially more meadow and pastureland to maintain the same number of animals.[47] As native grasses died off from grazing, husbandmen were forced to look for fresh sources— pushing their livestock deeper into woodlands, cutting down trees to create mowing lands, and striking off to found new settlements farther upriver or amid the uplands that surrounded the Connecticut Valley.

The good news for immigrant husbandmen was that wherever livestock went, English plants, particularly grasses, seemed to follow. Unlike New England species, European grasses had evolved to survive and thrive alongside cattle, sheep, horses, and goats. As livestock slowly killed off native grasses, European grasses moved in to fill their niche.[48] At first, the migration of old world grasses to New England and to the Connecticut Valley was largely unintentional. When livestock were introduced into the Connecticut Valley, first by the Dutch and shortly after by the English, European grass seeds tagged along in imported bundles of hay and in the gastrointestinal tracts of animals.

In time, colonial stock raisers turned to actively seeding European grasses in New England meadows. Seed dispersion by livestock could be slow and haphazard. The intentional seeding of European grasses helped speed the ecological transformation of New England into a prosperous pastoral landscape. In 1650, William Pynchon paid to have thirty bushels of "hay-seed" brought up the Connecticut to Springfield. This reference likely refers to seed imported from England or elsewhere in Europe, otherwise the trouble and expense hardly seem justified. By 1658, his son John Pynchon owned several acres planted in "English grass"—a catchall term used to refer to timothy grass, bluegrass, red and white clover, English bent grass, and a number of other European varieties often grown together. From the 1650s to the 1670s John Pynchon traded in hayseed, acting as a middleman connecting buyers with sellers, as part of his extensive mercantile activities. Pynchon also traded in "Flanders grass seed," likely a reference to separated-out white clover.[49] In 1656, David Wilton of Windsor pledged to sow the town's burying place with "English grass, that it may be decent and comely." In exchange, Wilton was granted pasturage rights in among the graves.[50] In 1664, Nathaniel Bacon (no relation to the Virginia rebel) sold off an acre of land in Hartford that he had "Sown with English grasse."[51]

In the upper valley towns founded in the eighteenth century, land grants commonly came with the stipulation that the recipient should clear a certain number of acres and plant it in "English grass."[52] Such stipulations demonstrated a continued commitment to livestock raising in the valley and highlighted the continuing struggle to transform the New England environment to resemble what had been left behind in old England. Legislative support for the spread of invasive species was just one symptom of this continuing ecological imperialism, one in which domesticated livestock served their masters as highly effective allies.

As the decades passed, valley farmers began increasingly to rely on the croplands that they had cleared, plowed, and planted to help feed their growing herds. The growing of crops and the raising of livestock had long coexisted in the system of mixed husbandry that had dominated the English regions from which the valley's first colonial settlers hailed. The two pursuits complemented each other well, allowing farmers to exploit various landscapes and soil types to their full advantage. Indeed, prior to mechanized farming, animal husbandry was a necessary component of field agriculture. The author of *The New-England Farmer*, an agricultural manual first published in 1790, summarized the importance of livestock to the success of early modern farmers: "It is by the assistance of labouring beasts, such as horses and oxen, that he [the farmer] must carry on his tillage, and send the produce of his lands to market. By the help of milch kine his grass, hay and other fodder are to be converted into butter and cheese. Bullocks, poultry and swine must be fed and fattened with the produce of the farm, that he and his family may be fed with their flesh and the markets supplied with meat. And the sheep must assist him in the transmutation of the fruits of his ground into clothing and food."[53]

In the early years, most grain grown in the new towns went toward human subsistence. As time passed and new fields were cleared and came under cultivation, grain became both an export commodity and an important component of the diets of colonial English livestock. The availability of hay had always been the limiting factor determining the size of colonial herds. Farmers often cut meadows twice a year, and the introduction of European grasses helped increase the yield of haying lands, but many livestock owners still faced the need to cull their herds at the onset of winter for lack of sufficient fodder.[54]

To supplement their animals' winter feed, successful farmers began to use provender—a mix of maize and oats (or whatever other grain grew well locally). Stall-feeding allowed those with the means to fatten cattle in anticipation of changing market prices. Usually this meant sending cattle which had been corn fed through the winter overland to market in Boston in early spring, when meat butchered and stored from the previous year would be running low and prices would be highest. Those with access to the valley's intervales—the rich bottomlands most productive for grain cultivation as well as for hay—could even afford to buy up the excess cattle of their less prosperous neighbors.[55]

Livestock also did their part to help ensure the success of the crops on which they fed. Oxen and later horses provided the muscle power needed to draw the plow across planting lands. They also provided manure for fertilizer. Dung is ubiquitous in the extant diaries, journals, and account books of the seventeenth- and eighteenth-century Connecticut Valley. Farmers carefully recorded the time and labor expended in transferring manure from where it fell to where it was most needed.[56] As long as livestock roamed free in the woods, this important resource went largely to waste. But once animals were confined for stall-feeding, their manure could be collected and spread over fields in the spring, helping to renew the land's fertility. Manure could also be collected from pastures for fertilizing nearby fields. Or cattle could simply be turned out onto the fields themselves. Every autumn from the 1690s onward, in a practice common in other valley towns of the seventeenth and eighteenth centuries, the town of Deerfield encouraged its residents to turn their cattle loose in the common field where they would consume the stalks and chaff of that year's crop, manuring the field as they went.[57] Manuring transferred nutrients from the pastures and woodlands where cattle grazed and the meadows where hay was cut to the arable lands where crops were grown. When cattle were fed provender, manuring helped recycle nutrients right back into the croplands from which they had come. As settlements matured, woodlands receded. Husbandmen were able to expend more time tending their animals, creating an important nutrient cycle: crops fed cattle and cattle (or at least their manure) fed crops.[58]

This economic and ecological system expanded to the north, as migrants from the older Connecticut River towns and from the east founded new towns in the upper valley. When the valley towns to the north of Springfield began providing substantial numbers of fattened cattle to the Boston market is unclear. John Pynchon regularly sent stall-fattened cattle east as early as the 1670s, but the trade does not seem to have become regular until after the relative security that followed the end of King Phillip's War. Northern towns sent small droves of grass-fed cattle to Boston throughout the seventeenth century, and by the turn of the eighteenth century, the practice had become commonplace. In the late eighteenth century, Sunderland, Massachusetts, served as a gathering point for cattle from the southern townships of New Hampshire and what would become Vermont. Farmers in these frontier towns would raise their cattle free range, with limited stall-feeding in the winter, and then sell their surplus animals to farmers farther south. Sunderland farmers, taking advantage of the excellent meadows and arable lands offered by their location along the northern intervals of the river, would fatten the cattle on hay and provender before driving them to market in the towns surrounding Boston.[59]

The rapid proliferation of upland towns after 1740 brought a considerable expansion in the overland cattle trade. The surplus grain raised on the intervales surrounding the Connecticut River allowed the cattle trade to push beyond the valley, into the uplands that surrounded. During the eighteenth century, as the valley towns filled up and available land became scarce, new settlers moved onto less fertile lands lying outside the valley on either side. [60] One such uplands town was Granville, Massachusetts, founded in 1754 along a tributary of Springfield's Little River. A half century later, Justin Hitchcock, a Granville native, reminisced about farming and husbandry in those new upland towns of the eighteenth century, offering at the same time an idea of what life must have been like for earlier pioneers in the valley itself:

> The farm was new and rough and my Father had to labour hard. . . . As soon as the lands was cleared and improved it produced great plenty of grass so that we could keep a large stock of cattle through the summer—but the Winters were long and severe. The consequence was that we scarcely ever had hay sufficient to keep all the stock through and we lost Som almost every spring. We used to make a single path in the snow in March when it was very dep to the woods which was near—and the yong cattle would go in such a path to browse upon the tops of the treis we cut for them.[61]

Hard winters, cattle forced to browse on the leaves and limbs of trees, animals faced with malnutrition and starvation: Hitchcock's narrative portrays colonial husbandry as ever pushing its climatic and ecological limits. Insufficient local resources could mean the loss of part of the herd, as this reminiscence records, but farmers in the uplands and in the valley quickly realized that trade offered an opportunity for both to prosper. During the spring, summer, and autumn, when grazing and browse were relatively plentiful, cattle would be spread widely to take advantage of the pastures and woodlands surrounding the old valley towns and the newer towns of the uplands. In winter, cattle owners would bring their animals into the barn and those with more animals than they could support would either butcher their extra animals or sell them to neighbors with access to sufficient provender. Selling cattle to entrepreneurial husbandmen in the valley offered upland farmers a welcome source of supplemental income. In turn, a ready source of upland cattle meant that valley stock raisers did not have to overburden their own lands and could even convert some pasture and meadow to cropland while still producing respectable herds for stall-feeding and sale to the regional and Atlantic markets.[62]

Besides cattle, settlers also raised horses in the valley and drove them overland to market in Boston at least as early as the 1680s. The Massachusetts stretches of the valley, with their broad grasslands and ample meadows for haying, proved well-suited to horse rearing, as did the lands around Windsor. Many of these horses filled local needs for mounts and draft animals. Still, a considerable number found their way into the export market. Eighteenth-century valley farmers continued to drive their horses to market in Boston, but many also headed their herds toward the port towns of Hartford, New London, or even Newport. In all of these port towns, most arriving horses were traded to merchants who then loaded them onto ships to continue their journey into the Atlantic marketplace. [63]

From the late seventeenth century through the eighteenth, New England merchants found a ready market for their draft animals amid the sugar islands of the West Indies. Plantations required large numbers of horses and oxen to operate profitably. Horses served as pack animals and, along with oxen, pulled the wagons that connected plantations to the ports they relied on for imports of food and other needed supplies. Planters and overseers required horses as mounts from which to patrol their enslaved labor force, and either horses or oxen were needed to power the great sugar mills that pressed the juice from raw sugar cane. The grueling work to which most drivers subjected their animals, coupled with the heat of the West Indies, brought early deaths to most of these draft animals. In 1654, an English seaman recorded his impressions of the new sugar milling technology recently introduced to Barbados from Dutch Guiana. "The mills," he observed, "destroy so many horses that it begors the planters." At the time, horses were still a scarce commodity throughout English America, and the sugar islands relied on imports from Europe to supply their needs. It was only in subsequent decades, as the mainland colonies built up the size of their own breeding populations, that planters were able to rely on cheaper imports from the north. By the 1690s, New England had become the leading supplier of horses to the English, Dutch, and French sugar islands.[64]

The calculus of the market encouraged sugar planters and their agents to rely on importing draft animals, rather than breeding them locally. Successfully breeding livestock in the numbers required to keep the plantation system running would have meant shifting land and labor away from the production of staple crops. In many ways, the decision to import draft animals rather than breed them locally paralleled the inhumane logic by which plantation mangers approached the slave trade. More than any other crop, sugar cultivation is notorious for its effects on enslaved workers. The lure of sugar profits encouraged planters and plantation managers to enforce strenuous work schedules in debilitating tropical heat. At the same time, managers sought to

Figure 6. This early eighteenth-century image illustrates the importance of draft animals for transporting goods and as motive power for operating sugar mills (as seen in the left and background). Grueling work coupled with the heat of the sugar islands brought early deaths to most draft animals, ensuring a steady market for New England horses and oxen. Romeyn de Hooghe, *Les Indies Orientales et Occidentales* (1710). Leiden: Chez Pierre van der Aa, 1710, plate 45. Courtesy of the John Carter Brown Library at Brown University.

keep production costs low and—since staple production encouraged special-ization, leading to the need to import most essentials—this often meant that slaves were underfed, underclothed, and underhoused. Many sugar plantation managers seem to have implicitly reached the conclusion that the best way to maximize profits was to effectively work slaves to death during their most productive years while relying on the transatlantic slave trade to economically replace workers lost through malnutrition, exposure, and exhaustion. In their minds, slave drivers dehumanized enslaved workers to the point that similar market considerations governed decisions over the treatment of both human laborers and draft animals. The result of this inhumane calculus was a steady demand from the sugar islands for both African slaves and New England horses and oxen throughout the colonial period and beyond.[65]

As with cattle and horses, hogs were also sometimes driven overland to market. In 1768, the *Boston News-Letter* reported that twenty-eight fat hogs had arrived in Portsmouth, New Hampshire, having traveled over one hundred miles from the newly founded town of Walpole, New Hampshire.[66] Such occurrences seem to have been uncommon, however. Hogs were far less manageable in large numbers than cattle—more prone to wander off the trail or refuse to move onwards. Hogs also lost weight much more quickly on the trail than did cattle, making it difficult to turn a profit when driving them long distances like those that separated the Connecticut Valley from the major port cities of the east.[67] In most cases the arithmetic of trade seems to have favored butchering hogs locally and sending barreled pork downriver to market.

An anecdote from the late eighteenth century gives an idea of what droving and the Boston market for cattle must have meant for landowners in the Connecticut Valley earlier in the century. In September of 1796, merchant Richard Lang of Hanover, New Hampshire, received a letter from his brothers Daniel and Nathaniel, residents of Salem, Massachusetts. Richard had been buying up cattle from his neighbors in the valley, pasturing them to fatten them for market, and preparing to drive them to Boston or the ring of surrounding towns for sale. Daniel and Nathaniel wrote to approve of their brother's business plans.[68] Some unknown event delayed Richard's departure. Daniel wrote to Richard again in late October, to inquire about the state of their herd. Meanwhile, a mutual acquaintance of the brothers', a Major Samuel Jones of Canaan, New Hampshire, paid a visit to Nathaniel's home while on his way to Boston.[69] Canaan was a small farming town founded along the banks of the Mascoma River—a Connecticut tributary—back in the 1760s. Samuel Jones had been one of its earliest settlers and one of its wealthiest inhabitants, but had recently sold out in anticipation of moving west to New York. Having dispensed with his New Hampshire lands, the major was now looking to unload his livestock.[70] The forty-nine head of cattle that trailed him likely represented his entire adult herd plus a number of additional head purchased from neighbors (the 1793 inventory of taxpayers for Canaan listed Jones as personally owning only twenty-two "animals," most, but not all, of which would have been cattle).[71] The major's stop-over at Nathaniel Lang's may have been a simple social call, but more likely Jones took the opportunity to purchase fodder from his Salem acquaintance and possibly to acquire sleeping quarters for himself. The major's hired help, watching over the herd on the trail, were left to "lay out" in the countryside.

Major Jones rode on to sell his cattle in Mystic. Nathaniel Lang set to inquiring among local merchants to make sure that his brother's delay had not lost him the best prices. As autumn wore on, more and more western merchants and landowners, men like Major Jones, arrived weekly with their herds. Nathaniel's investigations reassured him that beef prices in the Boston area were still holding steady—as were prices on hides and tallow. Still, Nathaniel worried for his brother's profits. (And possibly for his own since his level of interest hints that he may have had a stake in the enterprise.) Nathaniel's lines to Richard belie his concern: "Hope to see you down soon & then you will be informd more particularly respecting the price of Beef."[72] Their correspondence does not reveal if Richard ever made it to market.

Drovers might pack provisions for themselves and their mounts, but they faced the need to feed their herds off of the country along the trail. In part, they seem to have responded by pushing their animals at a grueling pace, minimizing the number of days that they would need to provide hay or fodder. Nineteenth-century accounts suggest that drovers in the western portions of the mid-Atlantic and Southeastern states, in the Northwest Territories, and ultimately on the Great Plains, generally set a rather leisurely pace for their herds. Although opinions varied on the proper rate for moving cattle to market, nineteenth-century drovers working from horseback seem to have preferred to keep their cattle moving at a rate between seven miles and an absolute maximum of fifteen miles per day.[73] At these speeds cattle retained most of their weight. Low levels of exertion meant that browsing during evening stops could replace most of the calories cattle expended on the trail. Setting a leisurely pace allowed drovers to protect the market value of the animals under their care.

A lack of sources makes it difficult to determine what pace early New England drovers, operating a century earlier, set for their herds. The journal of William Heywood of Charlestown, New Hampshire, records a drive of eighteen cattle that covered approximately sixty miles over the course of three days—a relentless pace of twenty miles a day.[74] An agricultural survey by the state of Massachusetts in 1841 estimated that cattle driven from Franklin County (the towns around Deerfield) to the cattle yards at Brighton (about six miles west of Boston) lost approximately one hundred pounds during their time on the trail.[75] Such dramatic weight loss suggests that the animals were moving at a speed significantly above the weight-maintaining maximum of fifteen miles per day set by western drovers. If this practice marked a holdover from the colonial past, then it seems that drovers and cattle owners may have been more interested in getting to market quickly (and thus minimizing the number of days' labor expended in a drive) than in keeping up the weight and market value of their animals.

Reducing the number of days spent on the trail by pushing animals forward might have reduced the impact of droving on the lands passed through, but it could not eliminate it. Individual herds might not have much of an impact—after all, these colonial herds were quite modest in size compared to the great Western cattle drives of the nineteenth century, usually ranging from about twenty to fifty animals—but multiple herds all moving along the same network of trails might do considerable ecological damage.[76] Hay brought along as feed or ingested before animals left the valley spread European grass seed to the lands lying between towns. Grasses, shrubs, and young trees along the trails would become intensively browsed, perhaps leaving behind bare ground. The herds also would have befouled local watering holes, the ponds and small streams that cover New England, by churning up mud and defecating in the water.[77]

Those living in towns along the trails took notice when the ecological impacts of passing herds infringed on their own interests. Local landowners, most of whom would have raised livestock of their own, made up the town legislatures that governed common lands in colonial New England. It is little surprise that these men acted to protect the corporate property of the town.[78] In 1715, the town assembly of Brookfield, Massachusetts (which lay along the road connecting Springfield to Boston), passed an act calling for the town's Great Field to be fenced to protect the crops planted there. Gates at either end of the field allowed town inhabitants and their teams to continue using the highway that passed through it, but all drives of cattle, hogs, and horses were prohibited from entering.[79] Oxford, Massachusetts—which lay along two of the paths linking Hartford to the main Boston-Springfield road—likewise passed a series of laws in the first half of the eighteenth century to protect its lands from the depredations of the cattle trade.[80] In 1726, the town assembly voted that no outside herds should be allowed to feed on town lands. In 1734, this law was amended to fine any inhabitant of the town who allowed outside cattle to graze on town lands ten shillings per head. These laws do not seem to have been entirely successful, for in 1735 the assemblymen were forced to call upon the field drivers of the town to "clear the town of all herds of cattle" and "prosecute the owners" of any animals unlawfully turned out to graze.[81]

The growing commercial network of the livestock trade meant that English grasses and weeds spread beyond the older towns of the lower valley. It meant that deforestation, in the name of firewood and building materials for new towns and pastureland and meadow for livestock, continued apace. It also meant that the soil resources of upland towns and new upper valley towns were flowing away from those communities. Even assuming that manure was used to replenish the fertility of grasslands, grazing still represented a net resource loss.[82] Heavy grazing inevitably meant a diminution of a piece of land's ability to support vegetation. The new upland towns were used as pasture largely because their soils grew grass, but little else, well. In effect, the cattle trade represented a flow of nutrients out of the uplands, into the valley, and ultimately on to the urban centers of the Atlantic World. That farmers in the Connecticut Valley managed to support such a system for over a century can be credited to their success in finding ever more lands on which to feed their stock. The annual renewing floods that swept the intervales along the Connecticut River played a part in keeping the valley fertile, as did the early adoption of stall-feeding and crops such as clover and turnips, which fix nitrogen and serve to renew soils.[83]

Wildlife and a Market in Death

Droving, the sale of barreled meat, as well as the raising of livestock for local consumption, drew the colonial New England countryside into an evolving ecosystem that more and more came to be defined by a desire to remake the natural landscape to accommodate the needs of domesticated animals. This process—from the initial migration to the Atlantic coast in the early decades of the 1600s, to the removal to the Connecticut Valley in the 1630s, to the push outwards onto the uplands and north into the upper valley in the eighteenth century—had profound impacts for New England flora. New species of grasses, trees and bush increased their ranges as other species declined. The same was true of the animal species of the newly colonized region. As new domesticated animals (as well as their feral descendants) grew in numbers, other native species came under pressure.

Hogs likely had the greatest impact, both directly and indirectly, upon the native wildlife of New England—largely because they so quickly became "wild" themselves. The Massachusetts General Court took notice of the problem of feral, apparently ownerless hogs, as early as 1631 when it began licensing private individuals to hunt and/or take possession of "wild swine."[84] In 1636, the Massachusetts government granted all inhabitants the liberty to kill or capture any "wild swine" found running loose.[85] By the 1660s, residents of the Connecticut River towns had begun hiring Indian hunters to provide them with pork from the "Wild Hoggs" that roamed the woodlands.[86]

Wood-pasture regions in England traditionally relied upon a system of earmarking to allow individual owners to assert their ownership over animals allowed to roam at will. Similar to branding, each hog owner in a town would cut a distinct pattern into one ear of an animal. The husbandman would then register his individualized earmark with the town government. The new English settlers of the valley began marking their swine at least as early as the mid-1640s.[87] Still, large numbers of hogs seem to have gone unmarked. If not marked soon after birth, or if born in the woods, it could take considerable time and effort to locate, capture, and mark young piglets. It also quickly became difficult to associate a shoat with any particular sow, making it impossible to assign ownership. Allowing inhabitants to hunt these ownerless, feral, "wild" hogs represented one system for controlling their population and exploiting them for food. It was not until 1666 that the Connecticut General Court banned the hunting of wild swine, concerned that privately owned animals were being destroyed under the pretense of their being wild.[88] The court ordered all unmarked and unidentified hogs impounded and sold off for the profit of the town in which they were taken.[89] Henceforward, every hog would have an owner. No feral hog would be considered legally "wild," despite its woodland abode and independent lifestyle.

Hogs present a notorious menace to any natural system into which they are introduced. Broadly omnivorous, they compete with (and often outcompete) a wide range of native animals. Their famed propensity to root in the ground for tubers and insects means that a pack of hogs turned loose on a meadow can, in just a short time, overturn the soil to such an extent that it resembles a plowed field. Since hogs could wreak similar destruction on croplands, colonial authorities early on passed laws requiring all swine to be yoked and "ringed"—to have a thick piece of wire passed through the membrane of the nose from one nostril to the other, after which the ends were twisted together. The small yokes fitted across their shoulders prevented hogs from pushing their way through fences and the rings restricted their ability to root in the ground. Such laws, first passed by the Massachusetts government in 1637 and Connecticut in 1645, doubtlessly helped mitigate the environmental damage done by free-ranging swine.[90] Still, the fact that these laws were continuously passed and repassed for the next century at both the local and colony level, accompanied by lamentations at the damage done by animals that continued to go about unyoked and unringed, suggests that many colonists were lax in attending to their duties as hog owners.

The diets of deer and free-ranging hogs can overlap by as much as 40 percent and resource competition may have contributed to the dwindling numbers of deer living in English-settled areas in the late seventeenth century. Much of this overlap lay in competition for the seasonal supply of mast (acorns and other tree nuts).[91] Autumn in the New England woodlands commonly brought a bumper crop of these energy-rich foods, and a wide variety of species depended upon the mast yield both to supplement other dwindling food resources during the autumn months and to build fat reserves to help them last out the winter. Population levels of deer, as well as various rodent species and songbirds, are closely tied to the seasonal availability of mast, crashing in years of poor mast production and exploding in good years. The introduction of a new competitor, especially one as efficient at monopolizing wild foods as hogs have historically proven themselves, placed a great deal of pressure on these populations.[92]

Although usually portrayed as foragers and scavengers, and though they will happily dine on carrion when they find it, hogs also actively hunt small vertebrate species (and sometimes larger animals, including the young of other livestock). Animal matter can make up as much as 25 percent of a hog's diet when left to run wild.[93] In the Connecticut Valley, and New England more generally, hogs found ample prey. Rodents—deer mice, gray squirrels, chipmunks, voles, groundhogs, and gophers—would have made up the majority of the meat in the diets of colonial hogs, but young deer likely also fell prey. Snakes and ground-nesting birds, along with their eggs, would have made up the remainder of a free-ranging hog's carnivorous diet.[94] In frontier areas, especially, hogs were much celebrated as devourers of rattlesnakes, a potentially mortal nuisance that increased in numbers as English colonists gradually phased out the practice of seasonal burning.[95]

The environs of English towns would not necessarily have become a quieter place, devoid of the sounds of singing birds. Environmental change inevitably harms some species and benefits others. Increased competition for mast and the loss of woodlands habitat would have caused precipitous population declines for forest species like the blue jay, the scarlet tanager, the pileated woodpecker, and even the wild turkey, as well as many species of hawk and eagle. Ravens, too, which many towns placed bounties on and legally required their inhabitants to hunt, largely disappeared from southern New England. Other species, however, took advantage of the new landscapes created by the English and their livestock. Species that thrive in grasslands and the sort of open woods created by woodland pasturing multiplied or expanded their ranges from other regions. Many of the bird species popularly associated with the "natural" landscape of today's New England—the whip-poorwill, the bobolink, the meadowlark, and a number of species of sparrow—first became common as a result of environmental changes brought about by the spread of English livestock.[96]

In many cases, English colonists' impacts on native species were unforeseen and unintended; in some cases, however, settlers intentionally set out to remove species from the landscape. As soon as English settlers began introducing their livestock into the Connecticut Valley, they had to worry about protecting them. The last wolves had been hunted out of England by about 1500, bears disappeared even earlier, and large cats had not survived the end of the Ice Age. But the New England woodlands, at least in the minds of the early settlers, seemed to be filled with these rapacious predators. Indeed, the populations of New England's large predators, especially wolves, may have grown in the seventeenth century as colonists introduced new forms of prey (cattle, swine, sheep, etc.) into the ecosystems of the region.

Full grown cattle were more than a match for a single wolf or even a pack and often could stand off a bear, although settlers often complained of the depredations that predators committed against calves not yet large enough to defend themselves. Mature swine, especially after a few generations of natural selection in the New England woods, also proved capable of defending themselves against predators, although shoats faced the same risks as calves. By contrast, even mature sheep, with the possible exception of rams, possessed no defense against predation other than the protection of their human keepers.

Which is to say that the flip side of the expanding market for valley livestock was a growing demand for the *absence* of certain other species. Bounties on predators make up some of the earliest extant records that exist for the valley. For example, a bounty on wolves of five shillings appears on page one of Windsor's book of town acts.[97] Hartford's town assembly granted the selectmen "liberty to Improve [pay] men for the killing of woolfs" in 1639, the first year for which records survive.[98] In 1644, Springfield appointed its first committee of selectmen to oversee town affairs. The town assembly charged these men to "prevent anything they shall judge to be to ye damage of ye Towne," an injunction that included overseeing "ye killing of wolves."[99]

Colony governments, likewise, played a part in encouraging inhabitants to kill wolves. Massachusetts offered inhabitants a reward for wolf killing starting in 1630.[100] The Connecticut General Court first passed a bounty on wolves in 1647.[101] Both of these early bounties promised ten shillings to any person who killed a wolf within ten miles of the boundaries of any of the respective colony's townships. Bounties were also placed on other dangerous predators: bears, wildcats and "catamounts" (cougars).[102] Over the proceeding century and a half, new legislation reiterated and increased these bounties. Both New Hampshire and Vermont followed the example of the older colonies. New Hampshire posted its first colony-wide bounty on wolves in 1680, and Vermont, after having declared its independence from both New Hampshire and New York in 1777, posted a bounty in 1779.[103] In these two northern states, lying along the frontier of late-eighteenth-century Euro-American settlement, bounties continued to be actively pursued well into the nineteenth century.

Such acts created a local market in death. Local and regional governments provided a demand that the inhabitants of the valley proved quite willing to supply. Some colonists became semispecialists, farming and raising livestock but dedicating a considerable amount of their slack time to exterminating wild predators.[104] Others acted as middlemen by buying carcasses (or pieces of them) from their neighbors or Indian hunters at a slight discount and then delivering them to authorities and collecting the bounty.[105] As livestock multiplied in the valley and the trade in them expanded, the destruction of predators grew up as an important (and, in the opinion of colonists at the time, necessary) complementary commercial activity.

Hunting with guns was far too time consuming a technique of wolf killing for the labor-starved towns of early New England. English colonists settled on trapping, rather than stalking through the woods gun in hand, as the most efficient way to solve their wolf problem. Pitfall traps are the most ubiquitous trapping technologies in the records of the early Connecticut Valley towns; wolf pits and "wolf pounds" appear commonly as landmarks. Little more than a large hole dug in the ground, covered over with brush, and then baited with carrion, these pits would hold an unlucky wolf either until it died from starvation or until the pit's owner came by to dispatch the wolf with a bullet or swift blow to the head.

Other methods brought even more unpleasant deaths. Shortly before being appointed governor to the new Connecticut Colony, John Winthrop Jr. asked a correspondent in England to make inquiries about wolf-killing techniques. In a 1634 letter, the friend advised Winthrop that he knew of "two devices to kill wolves." The first was to hide pieces of sponge in carrion left out as bait. The second was to spike the bait with "pieces of strong wyer twisted together . . . the ends to be bowed and fyled sharpe, and beards [barbs] cutt in them like fish hookes."[106] The indigestible sponges expanded in the wolf's stomach, causing blockages in the digestive tract that led to extreme pain, tissue necrosis, rupturing of the bowels, and ultimately death. Wire and small hooks hidden in bait tore the wolf's esophagus, stomach, and bowels, resulting in internal bleeding, and again, extreme pain followed by death. Thousands of Connecticut Valley wolves (and, presumably, not a few dogs) would endure both fates over the course of the next century.[107]

As in the fur trade, the English often employed the superior skills, knowledge, and experience of Indian hunters to further this commerce in death. New England Indians had long hunted wolves, both to eliminate a competitor for game and for their pelts. Black wolfskins, in particular, were highly sought after and, through gift giving, played an important role in Native diplomacy in the northeast. Hunters used venison or other meat as bait and either laid in ambush and waited for wolves to approach or set snare traps to capture the predators. As English settlements expanded and livestock increasingly encroached on hunting territories, declining game stocks likely offered further encouragement for Indians to eliminate the competition that wolves presented. And, of course, the opportunity to earn English goods would have only sweetened the deal. Indians in various parts of the valley collected wolf bounties throughout the seventeenth and eighteenth centuries, enduring often tedious bureaucratic regulations to do so. Off and on during this period, local and colonial officials became suspicious of Indian hunters—accusing them of stealing wolves out of farmers' wolf pits or collecting bounties on wolves killed well-outside of town or colonial jurisdictions (both accusations may well have been true). As a result, legislatures occasionally suspended bounty payments to Indian hunters or required Indians to obtain a certificate signed by an English official willing to vouch for the location of a kill. Connecticut, for a long while, paid Indians only half what English settlers earned for bringing in a wolf's head, while, for a short time, Massachusetts stipulated that bounties to Indians be paid only in maize and wine. Despite such biased treatment, many Indian hunters embraced wolf bounties as a means to earn credit for English trade goods.[108]

The pits, hooks, sponges, bullets, and snares did their job. Although the rate of local extinction varied, by fifty years after settlement wolves were becoming less and less a problem for the livestock husbandmen of the earliest valley towns. Springfield paid out its last wolf bounty in 1682.[109] After 1683, the Hartford town assembly no longer found it necessary to offer a town bounty on wolves.[110] Farther north wolf populations persisted well into the eighteenth century. The last wolf in Greenfield (a daughter town of

Deerfield) was killed in 1765.[111] Northampton residents and their neighbors in nearby Westhampton thought they had killed off the last of the wolves in their neighborhood in 1763, only to be disturbed by nocturnal howlings from 1772 to 1775. Hadley, likewise, exterminated its local wolf population in the 1760s only to have the predators return in 1785 and again in 1805 before finally being hunted to a lasting local extinction. The nineteenth-century historian of early Hadley records that the hunters of 1805 "had a merry time" tracking the pack in the snow, then surrounding and killing the last wolves in Massachusetts' stretch of the Connecticut Valley. Bears and panthers, which were never that common, were successfully extirpated from the lower valley about the same time.[112]

In something of an historical irony, once wild predator populations were in decline English husbandmen often found their calves, piglets, and sheep beset by a species of domesticated predator: *Canis lupus familiaris*, the dog. In the seventeenth and eighteenth centuries, indigenous and European dogs likely filled, at least partially, the niche that was being vacated by wild wolves. The Connecticut government complained as early as 1638 of Indian dogs "spoiling" and killing cattle and hogs allowed to roam outside of the newly planted English towns of the valley. Indigenous dogs may have presented an especial threat to livestock in the 1630s as warfare and disease decimated regional Indian populations, leaving perhaps thousands of dogs masterless to shift for themselves. In the long run, however, indigenous dog populations declined alongside Native American populations in the valley and the dogs that preyed on colonial livestock in the late seventeenth and early eighteenth centuries were likely the descendants of European imports. As with other predators, the towns and colonies of New England responded with regulations that authorized and sometimes subsidized the destruction of stray dogs. In fact, several of these dog-management regulations appeared as parts of acts primarily aimed at "Encouraging the Killing of Wolves." In the end, it proved harder to eliminate the depredations of domestic dogs than it had been those of wild predators. After all dogs filled useful roles in colonial society—guarding homes and livestock (at least when not attacking them), tracking and retrieving game for hunters, as well as tracking and making war on Indian enemies—so no one wanted to see them wholly exterminated. Instead, officials focused on destroying only those "unruly and ravenous dogs" that resorted to preying on livestock, managing the problem if never eliminating it.[113]

Perhaps the clearest sign that colonists were steadily bringing predators under control is that sheep began to multiply, a process aided by the continuous clearing of woodlands for new pasturelands and the sowing of more delectable European grasses in place of native species. By 1680, Connecticut governor William Leete listed wool as one of the colony's major export items. In fact, wool production soon grew too great, at least in the opinion of Parliament. In 1699, fearful of New Englanders competing with English wool producers, Parliament banned all wool exports both from and within its American colonies.[114]

If English farmers celebrated the disappearance of predators, declines in other wildlife species were less welcome. Deer, for example, also declined in numbers as European populations expanded in the valley. This is despite the fact that decreased pressures from their three greatest predators should have triggered an expansion in deer populations during the seventeenth century. Wolves, the most important wild predator of deer, had dwindled in number by the end of the seventeenth century. The many Indian communities of New England, and the hunting dogs they supported, had long depended upon venison as an important component of their diet, but Native American populations in the region faced devastating losses to both diseases and warfare throughout the seventeenth century. The new populations of the valley only partially filled the niches of their predecessors. Like wolves, dogs—both survivors left behind in depopulated Indian villages and those allowed to run loose in the new English settlements—preyed upon the young, sick, and old in deer herds, although less extensively. Unlike the Indian communities they displaced, English settlers were both less dependent upon venison for protein and far less effective hunters.

Still, deer populations declined throughout the seventeenth century. In 1693, the Massachusetts Bay Colony passed an act "For the Better Preservation and Increase of Deer" that banned the export of raw hides and skins from the colony. The act also set a closed season on deer, complaining of "great numbers [of deer] having been hunted and destroyed in deep snows when they are very poor, and bigg with young, the flesh and skins of very little value, and the increase thereof greatly hindered." Hunters in Massachusetts would only be able to take deer "from the first day of January to the first day of July following annually, forever hearafter."[115] But deer populations did not recover. Partially this is because laws limiting the hunting season do not seem to have been universally observed. For example, in just the year 1765, the Hampshire County court recorded the names of twenty-one men charged with poaching deer out of season.[116] It is impossible to know how many hunters in the county may have illegally taken deer out of season but successfully evaded discovery.

Far more destructive of deer populations was the role that increased competition from introduced livestock species played in displacing wildlife from
the landscapes surrounding New England's growing English towns. Livestock and deer are not necessarily mutually exclusive in a landscape. Deer are
browsers whose diets take in a wide variety of vegetal matter. Grasses make
up only a small part of a deer's diet, while browse (leaves and coniferous
needles, and the softer new growth of woody plants) and forbs (herbaceous
flowering plants) make up the majority. Woodland mast (most importantly
acorns, but also other tree nuts and seeds) also makes up an important component of the deer diet—as much as 90 percent during the autumn months.
Due to their differing diets, deer can—and in many landscapes today, in fact,
do—coexist in the same space with cattle and sheep.

Turn loose all of the domesticated species commonly found in early New
England towns, however, and competition for grazing and browse quickly
intensifies. Cattle subsist mostly on grasses, but will browse flowering plants
and the fresh shoots of woody plants, especially in the late summer and
autumn. Sheep, even more than cattle, tend to supplement their grassy diets
with considerable browsing on leaves and flowering plants. Hogs are notoriously voracious devourers of mast and will dig up shrubs and other plants
while foraging for roots. Goats will eat anything a deer will, although a toxin
in acorns, which makes goats ill if consumed in large numbers, limited their
ability to compete for mast. Likewise, husbandmen tended to limit the size
of their goat herds since goats proved early on to be far too fond of stripping
the bark from the apple trees upon which the English colonists depended for
their hard cider supply.[117] Nonetheless, taken together the full array of English
farmyard animals tended to crowd out local deer populations.[118] Livestock-
related changes to habitat had an even greater effect as woodlands were
cleared to make room for more pasture and meadow. By the early nineteenth
century, Timothy Dwight was able to say that "bears, wolves, catamounts,
and deer are scarcely known below the forty-fourth degree of north latitude
[central New Hampshire and Vermont]. . . . Hunting with us exists chiefly in
the tales of other times."[119]

Fish populations, too, likely suffered from the growing herd of livestock inhabiting the Connecticut watershed. Besides contributing to deforestation and crowding out wildlife species, livestock, and especially cattle,
have a major impact on the water quality of the streams and rivers along
whose banks they graze. Grazing and the trampling of hooves impede the
growth of bushes and young trees and encourage their replacement by grass
species. Overgrazing laid ground bare to the effects of erosion. Since cattle

tend to congregate near watering holes, both of these processes would have been accelerated along colonial stream and riverbanks. As grass replaced shrub and tree cover, the soils along stream banks would have lost the deep root systems that anchored them into place and been more likely to collapse before the fury of spring freshets. Together with the wind erosion from nearby pastures, crumbling banks would have further increased the silt load carried by the streams of the colonial Connecticut Valley. Cattle dung befouled waters, and in small streams or ponds its decomposition could contribute to anaerobic conditions. As turbidity increased, sunlight reaching aquatic plants decreased, in turn decreasing the waterway's ability to support life. Species of fish favored for the colonial dinner table, like trout, would have experienced especially large reductions in population since they require clear waters for spawning and feeding.[120]

Cattle and other species of livestock continued to have an impact on the environment even after the slaughter. Cattle driven out of the valley on the hoof would be slaughtered at their destination. Any pollution resulting from the process would become someone else's problem. But supplying local needs meant that many cattle (and other livestock) were slaughtered in the valley, most often by private individuals. Most of what an animal provided would be used, but not all. Excess fat, bone, hair, and offal were often thrown into the nearest waterway to be washed away. The leather industry further contributed to the pollution of local streams. Raw hides were transformed into finished leather through the process of tanning, which relied on the tannic acid contained in tree bark to bond with and shrink the pores of the skin, making the hides resistant to moisture and decomposition. Tanners in the colonial valley often farmed and undertook other agriculture work as well. Still, they provided a crucial specialized skill. In the over thirty years (1758–1792) that Matthew Noble of Westfield worked as both a tanner and leather worker he did business with over one hundred other heads of household, the vast majority bringing him repeat business from year to year. His neighbors would bring him hides to tan for them, or offer rawhides as payment for the leather work he did. Noble used the leather he produced to make saddles, bridles, straps, bags, and shoe leather.[121] Colonial tanners like Noble preferred the bark of oak and chestnut trees, especially high in tannin content, for their trade. (Hemlock bark became a popular substitute in the late colonial period.) This added to the demand for those already much-sought-after species, though laws requiring that the entire tree be used, rather than stripped of its bark and allowed to rot, may have helped limit waste.

Tanneries were always located on running streams or brooks, both because large amounts of water were needed in the tanning process itself and also because the tanyard needed some way to dispose of the various chemical and organic wastes that it produced.[122] The first step in preparing hides was to remove the hair and the layer of subcutaneous fat that adhered to the inside of the skin. Soaking in a solution of lime dissolved in water loosened these and scraping both sides with a specialized form of blade removed them. The hide was then ready for tanning: soaking in a solution of pulverized oak, chestnut, or hemlock bark for several months or up to a year. As the tanning process progressed, the hide would be moved from one vat to another with the level of bark increasing with each new solution.[123]

The organic waste (fat, hair, etc.) from both slaughtering and tanning would have contributed to deoxygenation as it decomposed in whatever waterway it was dumped. Runoff from slaughterhouses and tanneries could result in a discolored and stench-ridden waterway that threatened local inhabitants with pneumonia and other respiratory ailments.[124] Large concentrations of tannic acid resulted in increased local acidity in the streams and brooks of the watershed, having a detrimental effect on riverine flora and fauna. The pollution produced by tanning—as well as by saw- and gristmills and a myriad other terrestrial production activities—would have put considerable pressure on fish populations in the Connecticut watershed. Surviving colonial records, however, are ill-suited to tracking this change. In most, fish are an afterthought—a convenient and welcome supplement to the colonial farmer's diet but, until fishponds began to come into fashion in the late eighteenth century, not one the farmer expelled a great deal of time or labor in acquiring except during very specific windows during the year. However, the growing popularity of fish raising in the eighteenth century suggests that wild populations were likely declining.[125]

The Politics of Livestock

The arrival of European livestock had equally disastrous consequences for the Native human communities of the valley. John Pynchon's records from his years as a magistrate in Hampshire County offer a glimpse at the first encounter of a group of Norwottuck hunters with a cow. Sometime during the winter of 1635–1636, the hunters stumbled upon an unknown creature wallowing in a deep snowdrift just east of what would become Hadley, Massachusetts. Shivering and weak from the exertion of walking through the deep snow, the creature had collapsed in a heap. Not knowing what the strange new beast might be, the hunters repeatedly tried to help the animal up, but each time it collapsed back down into the snow. In the end, the creature died from exposure. One of the hunters later described it as having small horns, verifying that this mystery beast was a young cow which had presumably wandered away from the English settlement at Springfield, only to become lost in the snow.[126]

These Norwottuck hunters, and other Connecticut Valley Indian communities who first encountered English livestock in the 1630s and 1640s, could hardly have imagined the changes that these foreign creatures would bring in their wake. Livestock competed with, displaced, and ultimately led to the destruction of habitat for native game species on which Indian communities depended for their subsistence. Hogs competed directly with Native Americans for food by devouring mast, rooting up and destroying berry-producing bushes, and consuming the groundnuts (a starchy tuber) that Indian communities depended upon as a wintertime staple.[127] Free-ranging hogs, cattle, and horses from the river towns also strayed into nearby Native American villages and laid waste to their cornfields. Colonial law offered little compensation for such injuries: magistrates often faulted Indians for not fencing their fields, while Indians that killed trespassing livestock could face arrest and legal action by the animal's owners.

In 1669, for example, Chickwallop, a sachem of the Norwottucks, found himself accused of having killed the "small young beast" that the hunters had encountered over thirty years earlier. The cow's purported owner, Jeremy Adams of Hartford, sued Chickwallop, hoping to gain title to Norwottuck lands farther north in the valley. In this case, the magistrate overseeing the suit— John Pynchon, who had long carried on a lucrative trade with the Norwottucks and may have had a personal interest in seeing Chickwallop retain title to his lands—chose to throw out Adams' complaint.[128] In many other instances, however, colonial magistrates proved more than willing to find against Indian defendants and demand reparations for the destruction of wayward livestock.

Native communities were not complacent in the face of the changing environment around them. Many adopted livestock raising themselves. Hogs were especially popular since they were so capable at fending for themselves in woodlands and therefore interfered least with the hunting practices of Native American men. In 1675, during King Philip's War, the Connecticut government dispatched a raiding party of one hundred Indian allies east into Nipmuc territory with orders to pillage their corn and hogs.[129] For Native communities, feral hogs could become a replacement for the wild species that they had displaced. This often bred tension with the expanding jurisdiction of English law. English courts refused to recognize that earmarks could serve as a sign of Indian ownership as they did for English husbandmen. Indian hogs could consequently not be sold in English markets and could easily be stolen by disreputable English stock raisers. Historian of colonial domestic animals Virginia DeJohn Anderson has even suggested that disagreements over hog ownership helped contribute to the outbreak of King Philip's War.[130]

During the War, Connecticut River Indians targeted English livestock for both practical and symbolic reasons. Livestock often proved vulnerable even when colonists had withdrawn into the relative safety of frontier strongholds. Violence against domestic animals could serve as a cathartic stand-in for thwarted attacks on their English masters. In some cases, attacks on livestock crossed into mutilation and what one scholar has termed "torture" as valley Indians struck back against English creatures that had so often spoiled their fields and driven off their game. Killing or stealing livestock also had the material effect of impeding the colonial project by reclaiming meadows and woodlands for game, at least temporarily. In terms of military strategy, keeping warriors and communities fed was a key part of winning any armed conflict. The market value of livestock, after all, lay largely in the fact that they served as meat on the hoof. Nipmuc and Pocumtuck raiders drove off valley cattle or slaughtered and butchered animals where they found them in order to supply their own wartime needs, or else killed the animals to deny their meat and motive power to the English.[131]

Following military defeat in King Philip's War, many Indian communities in the valley were gradually forced to move either farther north or west, or to concede their native hunting practices and conform to English-style mixed husbandry. Those who stayed did their best to make a living at the margins of the English dominated economy, often taking wage labor employment on English farms or in households. Many relied on itineracy to take advantage of seasonal resources and opportunities for employment. Many of those who moved north joined Abenaki communities who continued to resist English expansionism. Western Abenakis continued to target the livestock of the upper valley throughout their eighteenth-century wars with the English, for the same reasons that had driven more southerly nations in the preceding century.[132]

Despite the losses of livestock suffered by English settlements in northern New England, the imperial wars of the eighteenth century (the War of the Spanish Succession/Queen Anne's War, the War of the Austrian Succession/ King George's War, and the Seven Years' War/French and Indian War) only served to accelerate the region's trade in livestock, along with its ecological consequences. Provisioning agents for the British army in North America found Boston a convenient center from which to make purchases. Beef and pork that had previously been intended for sale to the citizens of Boston, to New England's fishing and merchant fleets, or to the West Indies were redirected to feed troops preparing for invasions of Canada or operating in other theaters. This new imperial market meant higher prices for Bostonians, and New England consumers more generally. However, it also meant opportunity for those able to supply the military's new needs.

Thomas Hancock (the business-savvy uncle from whom the most famed signer of the Declaration of Independence inherited his immense wealth) was one of those who sought profits by provisioning British troops. In the late 1740s, Hancock turned his attention to the Connecticut Valley as a source for barreled pork. Salted pork had been shipped down the Connecticut River to Boston since John Pynchon had pioneered the practice in the 1650s. Now the trade truly boomed, and Hancock, although not the only merchant involved, certainly seems to have been the largest. Hancock sold Connecticut pork to the commissaries of the British army, to ship captains for provisions, and to traders headed for the Caribbean and Nova Scotia. In October of 1752 alone, Hancock received shipments totaling 282 barrels of pork at his Boston wharf. In February of the next year, he took delivery of 305 live hogs from a single merchant living along the Farmington River, the Connecticut's largest tributary.[133] Numerous other Boston merchants during the period placed newspaper advertisements offering "Connecticut Pork" for sale from their dockside warehouses. Over 170 such advertisements filled Boston-area newspapers in the years from 1741 to the beginning of the Revolution.[134]

Cattle, too, came under ever greater demand, though their provisioning was less centralized and therefore harder to track. Many of the merchants advertising pork in the mid-eighteenth century also offered barreled Connecticut beef for sale.[135] An entire specialized industry grew up in the towns around Boston—Brighton, Roxbury, and others—where butchers and merchants would buy up animals from drovers headed to the Boston market. These "forestallers," as they were called, would have the animals butchered, dressed, and perhaps salted and barreled and then sell their meat to customers in Boston, or to exporting merchants or ships' captains. Sometimes they also passed live animals on down the supply chain, depending on what was most in demand at the time.[136]

In the eighteenth century, the New England livestock trade achieved strategic and political importance within the British Empire. During Queen

Anne's War, the Connecticut government took only five weeks during the summer of 1710 to raise provisions sufficient for its own troops and an additional two hundred head of cattle and six hundred sheep for the soldiers of New York as they prepared for an invasion of Canada.[137] Meat shortages and high prices for Boston consumers during times of war helped make livestock a political issue during the French and Indian Wars. Citizens grumbled against the commissary agents of the British army and navy, and against the forestallers and large merchants like Hancock who supplied them. Sheep raising took on new importance in the 1760s as colonists embargoed British goods in protest of imperial commercial policies and wearing domestically produced homespun wool clothing became an emblem of political activism. During the nonimportation movement of 1768–1771, Connecticut considered forbidding the export of pork and beef to New York as punishment for that colony's leniency toward the smuggling of British goods.[138] During the British embargo of Boston Harbor, following the Boston Tea Party, colonists from the Connecticut Valley and elsewhere sent livestock overland to help feed the city's destitute. By 1774, Connecticut (the whole state, though the river towns likely contributed more than their fair share) was exporting annually 15,000 head of livestock, 10,000 barrels of salted meat, and 150,000 pounds of cheese.[139]

During the Revolution, the livestock trade became a question of national security. Connecticut forbade the export by water of most agricultural goods for the duration of the war, lest these supplies be captured by the Royal Navy.[140] Joseph Trumbull, son of Connecticut governor Jonathan Trumbull, became commissary general of the Continental army in 1775 and organized the procurement and overland transportation of cattle and hogs from throughout New England to feed the army surrounding Boston.[141] The immense quantity of meat that Connecticut, especially the river towns, contributed to the Patriot cause highlights the extent to which the livestock trade had grown by the 1770s. In a single day in 1775, Connecticut's treasurer in Hartford was able to fill an order for six hundred barrels of salt pork to be dispatched to the militias of New Hampshire and Massachusetts as they marched toward the Siege of Boston. That same year, almost twelve hundred barrels of salted meat were gathered from the river towns to fill the reserve magazines of General Washington's army. Throughout the Revolution, herds of cattle poured from the valley to feed troops at Boston, at New York, and even farther afield, helping to earn Connecticut the sobriquet of the Provisions State.[142] That so little mutton flowed to Patriot troops merely underscores the continued political importance of domestic wool production during the Revolution[143]

The Red Meat of Empire

Meanwhile, farther north Colonel Timothy Bedel had his hands full. Reports filtered in that loyalist traitors from western Connecticut were using the river as a transit route to Canada where they were passing information to the British. Rumors swirled that Canadian and hostile Indian forces were planning to cross over Lake Champlain and fall upon the exposed American settlements of the northern valley. Local Indians friendly to the American cause were lobbying Bedel and their trading partners in the river towns for a fort to be built for their protection.[144] And then there was the cattle trade, threatening to split public opinion and siphon off much-needed manpower.

Livestock stood at the nexus of politics, the economy, and ecology for much of New England's colonial period. The desire for larger and greener pastures fueled the controversy that swirled over demands for the founding of new towns: pitting arguments for security and godly community against the expansion of the herds upon which New England's early economy depended. The developing commercial network of the livestock trade enabled farmers in the river towns to transform the richness of their valley soils into rum, sugar, and European manufactured goods at the same time that they helped feed the expanding populations of colonial ports like Boston and British colonies farther afield. Valley livestock provisioned the troops that fought Britain's eighteenth-century colonial wars and during the Revolution fed Patriots and supporters of the Crown alike.

For over a century, the livestock of the valley fed—both figuratively and more literally—the slave plantation system of the West Indies. Salted pork, and to a lesser extent beef, from the Connecticut Valley joined salted New England cod in providing cheap protein for slave diets. Horses and oxen from the valley and elsewhere in New England powered the sugar mills that processed the raw sugarcane. These draft animals carried the processed sugar, molasses, and rum to dockside ships for transport to consumers in Europe or North America (in Barbados, the public wharf was, tellingly, referred to as "New England Row"), and hauled the luxuries of Europe back to the plantations of the interior. Imported horses provided mounts for plantation owners, overseers, and slave catchers intent on maintaining the slave system that afforded them these luxuries.

Whatever their ultimate fate within the regional and Atlantic economy, livestock, and the English colonists working on their behalf, created a new environment, one directed toward the needs of raising meat and draft animals to support a growing economy up and down the valley and in the uplands that overlooked it. They created a landscape with fewer trees and more grass, much of it belonging to new imported species. This new environment was home to far fewer wild animals but populated with strange new domesticated (or semidomesticated) beasts. It was an environment created by the links of commerce that connected the inhabitants of the Connecticut Valley to the broader Atlantic World beyond.

A New Era
in the Life of the River

When the Montague Canal opened in 1800, it offered a memorable spectacle for at least one member of the Hoyt family of nearby Deerfield, Massachusetts. The aged patriarch of the family, Jonathan Hoyt Jr., recorded the event in his diary for the year: "Wensd [October] 29th—A fair, pleasant, warm day. Our Jack carted twenty load of dung. I went over to the New City [Montague, MA] & saw the first boats that ever went up the canals."[1]

Paternal authority, even over a grown son, brought certain privileges. While Jack (fifty-one-year-old Jonathan Hoyt III) stayed home tending to the business of the family farm, the elder Jonathan excused himself from what otherwise promised to be a busy day of hauling manure from the meadow where his cattle grazed to the fields where he would plant his crops.

Boats like the ones Hoyt watched going through the locks on that pleasant, warm autumn day had long tied farms like his to the wider world of Atlantic goods. While the lowest reaches of the river admitted small oceangoing ships, commerce above Hartford, and on the river's many tributaries, relied on smaller river-bound vessels. Early in the seventeenth century, this had meant canoes and bateaux. As the decades passed these gradually yielded to larger flat-bottomed sail vessels. So-called oak boats, constructed of stout oak planks, measured up to seventy-five feet in length and could carry up to forty tons. Oars aided in propelling the boats downriver while their crews pushed them upstream with long poles braced against the river's bottom. When a favorable wind could be found, the boat's one small, square sail helped ease the crew's burden. "Pine boats," built from the timber of the cold northern softwood forests, were designed for a one-way journey. Loaded with the various commodities of the upper valley (lumber, barreled meat, grain, etc.) traders set sail for the port towns of the lower valley, selling their vessel for lumber upon arrival.[2]

The rivermen who operated these craft—the historical actors who did the most to directly weave together the local markets of the valley with the wider Atlantic world beyond—remain largely beyond the grasp of history. Either they have left behind no records or those records have not survived the ravages of time. Only a single account book from an anonymous boatman operating in the mid-eighteenth century remains to offer a glimpse into the Great River's interior trade. The account tells of West Indies goods like rum, sugar, and molasses heading upriver and of country goods like flaxseed, grain, salted meat, and timber coming down. For example, during one voyage in 1753, the author carried a load of "English goods" from Hartford to Hatfield and fetched back barreled pork in return.[3] Although sparse in its style, this brief account book provides a picture of the sinews that tied together the commerce of the Connecticut Valley.

The watery highway these rivermen traversed was not always a smooth one. Which is why, in 1792, the state legislature of Massachusetts had granted a charter to a group of Hampshire County businessmen to form a new company: the Proprietors of the Locks and Canals on Connecticut River. Their intention was to build a system of canals and locks around Hadley Falls (at Holyoke) and Turners Falls (between Montague and Greenfield). For over a century, these two falls had presented an impediment to the commerce of the Connecticut Valley. Goods flowing up and down the river by flatboat had to be off-loaded at the falls, portaged around the rough waters, and reloaded onto another boat on the other side. Although local laborers benefitted from the wages earned portaging the traffic of the river, these excess costs in time and money annoyed the merchants of the valley. The Proprietors—a group drawn from among the wealthiest merchants, landowners, and professionals in the middle valley—pooled their own funds, raised money locally, and recruited financial backers from London to smooth away these natural obstructions to trade, completing the South Hadley Canal in 1795 and another canal around Turner Falls five years later.[4] Henceforth, boatmen on the Connecticut would be able to travel the length of Hampshire County. Goods would bypass the falls not by overland cart paths but through a system of canals and locks. Technology and capital would be brought to bear, the natural highway of the river would benefit from the hand of human improvement, and commerce would flourish.[5]

Investors in Hampshire County were not alone in their desire to overcome the cataracts that had so long delayed the passage and threatened the safety of these river vessels and their cargo. The watery highway of the Connecticut had always offered passengers and cargo a less than smooth ride.

Above Hartford, a series of natural fall lines broke up the river's path with numerous rapids and falls. To overcome these hindrances to commerce, the state of Vermont had chartered the Company for Rendering the Connecticut Navigable at Bellows Falls in 1791. Companies were formed to build canal and lock systems at Ottauquechee, Lebanon Falls, and Sumner's Falls in 1794, 1795, and 1796, respectively. This spate of canal building in the 1790s was only the beginning. More canals and locks were added—most notably at Enfield Falls (the first falls encountered as one traveled upriver on the Connecticut and also one of the largest) in 1828.[6]

New commodities flowed down the now (relatively) tamed Connecticut, on their way to new markets. The American Revolution disrupted the West Indies trade that had long supported New England's economic development. The British blockade and, after the war, Britain's prohibition on American trade took a heavy toll on the finances of Connecticut Valley farmers and merchants who had long orientated their production toward the imperial export market. The inhabitants of the sugar islands suffered even more profoundly from the rupturing of empire. Tens of thousands of slaves may have died from malnutrition during the war and in the years that followed. On some islands, the free population, too, faced hunger. Unable to feed their workforce, and without the lumber and draft animals they needed to run their sugar mills, planters curtailed production. During the war years, the British sugar trade experienced its lowest profits in a century. Gradually, planters shifted land toward greater subsistence agriculture, and sought out American smugglers and merchants on the French and Dutch Caribbean islands to help make up their shortfall in food, timber, and other essentials. Even after markets had settled and new suppliers been found, these substitutes often proved more costly than commodities that had formerly been freely imported from the erstwhile thirteen mainland colonies. Planters' and merchants' bottom lines suffered, but sugar remained a major source of wealth, even as its relative importance as a colonial import was eclipsed by cotton headed for British textile mills.[7] The New England economy, too, had begun a profound change by the time Britain once again opened the West Indies to American trade in 1794. New England merchants rushed to take up their old role as provisioners to the sugar islands, but within a decade or so New England had itself become a net importer of food and timber. The region's future lay with the new industries growing up to take advantage of the waterpower of rivers like the Connecticut and its tributaries.

As industrialization overtook the valley in the early nineteenth century, human designs on the natural world only multiplied. Manufacturing mills proliferated, and with them milldams. In the first half of the eighteenth century, almost every tributary river and stream in the Connecticut Valley large enough to support a waterwheel was dammed to provide power for a new textile mill. Paper mills, iron mills, and water-powered manufactories for a wide array of other consumer products likewise proliferated.[8]

The spread of canals and the growth of manufacturing mills reshaped the economy, as well as the land- and waterscapes, of the Connecticut Valley. The Northampton Cotton and Woolen Manufacturing Company offers an example of what industrialization meant for the region. In 1788, Northampton merchant Levi Shepard founded a mill to produce rope and canvas. Shepard's original mill was operated by hand crank, but by 1810 the company, now owned and run by Shepard's sons and nephew, had moved into a watermill located alongside Northampton's Mill River. The river, as its name suggests, had played host to a handful of sawmills and gristmills dating back to the seventeenth century. At the turn of the eighteenth century these were joined by a new larger sawmill, a mill for wood turning, a trip-hammer mill for metalworking, and a competing cotton mill, each with their own milldam, pond, and millrace. Within a few years the cotton and woolen manufactory run by the Shepherds (the spelling changed with the new generation) had grown into one of the largest textile mills in the United States. Although larger than most contemporary enterprises, the Shepherds' textile company represented the effect that industrialization was having on the economy of the valley, and of New England more generally.[9]

Upon opening his original manufactory in 1788, Levi Shepard began advertising in local newspapers to purchase flax from valley farmers, redirecting and increasing demand for a commodity that might otherwise have been used within the household or sold to neighboring colonies. His heirs' new manufactory on the Mill River expanded demand for this local raw material and added new lines of production for wool and cotton textiles. In the early nineteenth century, carding and spinning mills bought up regional wool, contributing to the expansion of sheep raising throughout the valley, but especially in the less fertile uplands and more recently settled portions of Vermont. Some mills, even in the early decades of the nineteenth century, imported wool from as far away as Saxony in order to produce superior quality yarn and cloth that could be sold at higher prices. Toward midcentury, New England woolen mills, including those in the valley, relied more and more on sheep raisers in the newly settled lands of the Ohio Valley for their wool supplies, a shift that increasingly squeezed out local suppliers. Other mills specialized in cotton or, like the Shepherds' mill in Northampton, produced cotton thread and/or cloth alongside their work with wool. For this new raw material, mill owners and the merchants from whom they purchased relied upon the slave plantations of the South. [10]

In 1848, the Connecticut River itself was dammed for the first time by the Hadley Falls Company. The *Springfield Republican* boasted that the dam was "the mightiest structure of the character that was ever built in this country." This triumph of nineteenth-century engineering proved short lived, however. As soon as the dam's final gate was secured, a leak appeared that grew in intensity until the entire structure gave way. "Just in the hour of triumph," the newspaper lamented, "the labor of hundreds of hands was swept away in an instant." The collapse provided a "magnificent and frightful" spectacle for the thousands of onlookers who had assembled to witness the dam's successful completion, but instead stood on the river's bank and watched as the Connecticut River's "waters hurried onwards over the ruins they had made." Despite this spectacular setback, the investors of the Hadley Falls Company proved undeterred. One short year later, workers completed a new dam across the Connecticut near the wreckage of the original. When the last gates on this second dam were closed—this time without any spectators in attendance—the structure held. In 1850, investors completed construction of a large cotton mill in Holyoke, Massachusetts, to take advantage of the power that the new dam supplied. [11]

As canals and new larger milldams spread through the region, the amount of standing water in the Connecticut Basin once again expanded. Water for filling canal locks and power waterwheels spread over fields and pastures, likely covering lands that had once—over a century and a half ago—been home to beaver ponds. Some fish species, like brook trout and yellow perch, likely benefitted from this expansion of habitat, but the obstructions posed by milldams placed further pressure on populations of anadromous fish like shad, alewives, and salmon. Indeed, salmon had entirely disappeared from the Connecticut Basin by approximately 1800. Canals and the new larger millponds also provided breeding habitat for mosquitoes, resulting in malaria's return to the Connecticut Valley. The inhabitants of Northampton, just upriver from the South Hadley Canal, were among the earliest afflicted (outside of long-suffering Deerfield, that is). Northamptonites began complaining of fever and chills even before the canal was completed and attempted to sue the canal company for introducing the "ague" into their town, to no avail. As canals and millponds spread and grew in size malaria once again laid hold of the Connecticut Valley, and of New England more generally. [12]

As manufacturing spread up and down the valley, from Connecticut to New Hampshire and Vermont, towns sprang up wherever a new mill was seated. These new mill towns drew surplus labor from farms and increased the regional demand for provisions. Declining soil fertility, from long cultivation, combined with the repeated division of older farms to provide an inheritance to multiple descendants, strained the sustainability of farming in the southern reaches of the valley. Combined with a growing population, these pressures on the land led at first to an exodus to still fertile lands farther north along the Connecticut, along its more northern tributaries, and to the uplands surrounding the valley. Here the children of the valley's original settlers, together with Scots-Irish newcomers, set to work clearing land to farm while allowing their livestock to roam free, in effect repeating the pattern practiced by the earliest European settlers of the Connecticut Valley. As the nineteenth century wore on, more and more emigrants from the valley would find their way to other regions like the Midwest, and, most importantly for the progress of American industrialization, to the manufacturing centers that were growing up throughout New England. Those valley farmers who remained on the land—whether in the north, the uplands, or on more established farms—still grew goods for sale in the market, but increasingly the end consumers of valley-raised agricultural produce lived not in the West Indies, England, Ireland, Madeira, or even in Boston, but in the Connecticut Basin itself.[13]

Farmers shifted their focus to accommodate the demands of the new manufacturing labor force. Grain became less important in many sections of the valley, in part due to declining soil fertility but also because farmers found they could make better money raising beef and dairy cattle. Feeding cattle in fenced-in pastures or in barns—the better to fatten them or collect their milk—allowed farmers to gather manure to spread over their often depleted soils. Croplands, in turn, were increasingly dedicated to growing provender for livestock or vegetables for sale to the mills. Local farmers thus came to specialize in perishable commodities—fresh meat, dairy products, and fresh vegetables that could only be sourced locally.[14]

For their daily bread, both valley farmers and the region's industrial workforce came more and more to rely upon imported grain and flour. The Connecticut Valley was importing appreciable quantities of grain at least as early as 1800, drawing first on crops grown in the mid-Atlantic states—New York, Pennsylvania, Maryland—and then, in later decades, the Ohio Valley. At first, flour came up the Connecticut on riverboats that boatmen poled against the river's current, by wagon along the often ill-maintained roads that ran parallel to the river, or overland via the rough highway that ran from Northampton west to the Hudson Valley. By the 1830s, the completion of a canal connecting New Haven to Northampton, by way of Farmington, allowed smooth travel for horse-drawn flatboats, and by the middle of the century railroad cars delivered Midwestern flour throughout New England.[15]

Initially the series of canals built during the 1790s and first decades of the nineteenth century proved a boon to the timber producers and sawmill owners of the valley. Farmers and timber contractors operating in New Hampshire and Vermont could place felled logs in the Connecticut River and send them south without having to worry they might become stuck on rapids or snap when going over falls. The lumbermen tasked with guiding log drives downriver might have complained that the tolls charged by canal companies seemed excessive, but there was little doubt that navigating loose logs or log rafts through the locks of the river's canals significantly reduced the drama and risk associated with drives. At the same time, canal construction, the construction of new and larger manufacturing mills, and the building of new towns to support those mills increased regional demand for the products of northern valley woodlands. In the early nineteenth century, new and larger sawmills sprang up to help satisfy this growing demand for lumber. In turn, landowners in the northern valley, and in the newly settled uplands, increased the number of trees they felled for sale to valley lumber mills and the rate of regional deforestation accelerated. At least until midcentury when a growing timber scarcity combined with competition from other parts of the United States—most notably Maine and the western portions of the mid-Atlantic states—to displace valley timber from even local markets. After midcentury most lumber used in the valley was cut and sawn elsewhere, then shipped to local builders by ship and canal, or by rail.[16]

In a sense, the early nineteenth century saw New England truly become a "new" England. In the seventeenth and eighteenth centuries, England had commanded an empire of goods that ultimately saw raw materials from the colonies flow to the metropole and manufactured goods flow out. (Indeed, Britain in the nineteenth century still commanded such an empire; that empire just no longer included the thirteen mainland American colonies.) In the nineteenth century, New England became the manufacturing center of a new American empire. To feed its workers, the region drew increasingly on flour from the mid-Atlantic States and flour and livestock from the Midwest. Likewise, it relied on midwestern wool and Southern cotton to feed its proliferating textile mills, and Maine and mid-Atlantic lumber to build those mills. In turn, a myriad of manufactured goods—yarn, thread, and cloth chief among them—flowed out of New England to satisfy consumers elsewhere in the Union.[17]

New England's industrialization was written on the landscape. Increasing acreage was flooded as dams and canals sequestered waters that once flowed freely. Cities expanded and new mill towns grew up. But this urbanization also brought an abandonment of parts of the countryside. Facing competition from elsewhere in the United States, farmers in the Connecticut Basin and elsewhere in New England stopped working marginal croplands on which they could no longer earn a living. These abandoned farms, in time, returned to woodlands. Deforestation, as a result of both timber harvesting and the clearing of lands for agriculture, reached its zenith in the Connecticut Basin sometime around midcentury—slightly earlier in the more settled portions of the southern valley and later farther north and in the uplands. From that point on, woodlands reclaimed more territory than was cleared by the axe. In 1600, as much as 90 percent of the land in present-day New England may have been covered in woods. By 1850, thanks in large part to the economic processes discussed in this book, that figure had fallen to about 30 percent of land in the heavily settled states of Connecticut and Massachusetts. Over the course of a century, as farms were abandoned and timber harvests fell off, Connecticut's woodlands recovered so that by the 1980s they made up approximately 70 percent of the state—less than what covered the region in 1600, but a substantial departure from the trend of deforestation that had characterized the seventeenth, eighteenth, and early nineteenth centuries.[18]

The closing years of the eighteenth century and the early decades of the nineteenth century, thus, marked a turning point in the relationship between the Connecticut River and the human communities that lined its banks. For the first time human ingenuity undertook, on a grand scale, the planned engineering of the river's face. But if such large-scale engineering of the river began only at the turn of the nineteenth century, the transformation of the river by human hands was not new. For over a century and a half prior to the construction of the first lock on the Connecticut River, commerce connected the settlements along its banks to an ever-expanding transatlantic market-place. For this entire period, stretching back to at least the 1630s, commerce had served as a driving force behind ecological change in the valley.

A full history of humanity's influence in shaping the Connecticut Valley would have to go back many millennia, to the arrival of the region's first human inhabitants. This book goes back only as far as the 1610s and the arrival of the first European explorers in the Connecticut Valley. This choice is not meant to marginalize the earlier environmental impact of the region's Native peoples. The 1610s are chosen because, like the 1790s, they mark a watershed (so to speak) in the relationship between the Connecticut

Valley and its human inhabitants. Environmental change in the valley did not begin with European settlement, but the arrival of, first, European traders and, then, European settlers increased the rate of change and directed its flow in revolutionary new directions. English settlement in the valley, for the first time, firmly integrated the region and its peoples—both Natives and newcomers—into the broader early modern world. The ecological impact of this integration was to be profound, if gradual compared to that seen in the second half of the nineteenth and in the twentieth centuries. The environmental consequences of valley inhabitants' market participation would be long felt, even if they were generally unintended and unforeseen at the time.

The Montague canal, bypassing Turner Falls, represented a new era when a resident of the valley could take a day off from the chores of the farm in order to witness and celebrate another milestone in humanity's conquest of nature. Canal building represented a new level of intentionality in humanity's struggle to control the natural land- and waterscapes of the valley. This was change that could be planned, scheduled, and then prosecuted on a set timetable (even if that timetable was not always met). But all of the fanfare that surrounds canals and other modern engineering projects, and all of the attention that has been given them by environmental historians and environmental activists, should not overshadow the ecological changes wrought during the preceding era that stretched from English settlement in the valley in the 1630s up through the end of the eighteenth century. This earlier era was not one characterized by ambitious projects capped by fanfare and celebration. At its heart lay the mundane daily production processes from which Jonathan Hoyt took a holiday to celebrate the passage of the first boats through the locks as they carried their cargo downriver toward the wider world of goods beyond.

NOTES

Introduction

1. Lisa Brooks, Donna Roberts Moody, and John Moody, "Native Space," in *Where the Great River Rises: An Atlas of the Upper Connecticut River Watershed in Vermont and New Hampshire*, ed. Rebecca A. Brown (Lebanon, NH: University Press of New England, 2009), 133; Margaret M. Bruchac, "Earthshapers and Placemakers: Algonkian Indian Stories and the Landscape," in *Indigenous Archaeologies: Decolonizing Theory and Practice*, ed. Claire Smith and H. Martin Wobst (New York: Routledge, 2005), 70; George Sheldon, *A History of Deerfield, Massachusetts*, 2 vols. (Greenfield, MA: E. A. Hall, 1895), 1: 29; Katherine Mixer Abbott, *Old Paths and Legends of the New England Border: Connecticut, Deerfield, Berkshire* (New York: G. P. Putnam's Sons; Knickerbocker Press, 1908), 164.

2. Brooks, Moody, and Moody, "Native Space," 133.

3. In juxtaposing the Pocumtuck legend of Ktsi Amiskw with the Euro-American story of a glacial origin for the Connecticut Valley, I follow the example of anthropologist Margaret Bruchac. Bruchac, "Earthshapers and Placemakers," 70–71.

4. Michael J. Caduto, *A Time Before New Hampshire: The Story of a Land and Native Peoples* (Lebanon, NH: University Press of New England, 2003), 54.

5. Examples: Teresa C. Crofton, "Through the Back Ages," *St. Nicholas* 18, no. 1 (November 1890–April 1891), 66–67; George Simon Roberts, *Historic Towns of the Connecticut River Valley* (Schenectady, NY: Robson & Adee, 1906), 3–6; Albert Van Dusen, *Puritans Against the Wilderness: Connecticut History to 1763* (Chester, CT: Pequot Press, 1975), 16; Michael Bell, *The Face of Connecticut: People, Geology, and the Land* (Hartford: State Geological and Natural History Survey of Connecticut, 1985), 169–170.

6. Connecticut (Colony), *The Public Records of the Colony of Connecticut*, ed. J. Hammond Trumbull and Charles J. Hoadley, 15 vols. (Hartford, CT: Case, Lockwood, 1850–1890), 3: 297.

7. Nuala Zahedieh, *The Capital and the Colonies: London and the Atlantic Economy, 1660–1700* (Cambridge: Cambridge University Press, 2010), 29.

8. Quoted in Richard B. Sheridan, *Sugar and Slavery: An Economic History of the British West Indies, 1623–1775* (Kingston: Canoe Press, 1994), 8.

9. Trevor Burnhard, *Planters, Merchants, and Slaves: Plantation Societies in British America, 1650–1820* (Chicago: University of Chicago Press, 2015), 110, 112; David W. Galenson, "The Settlement and Growth of the Colonies: Population, Labor, and Economic Development," in *The Cambridge Economic History of the United States*, ed. Stanley L. Engerman and Robert E. Gallman, 3 vols. (Cambridge: Cambridge University Press, 1996–2000), 1: 198.

10. B. W. Higman, "The Sugar Revolution," *Economic History Review* 53, no. 2 (May 2000), 213–236; Sheridan, *Sugar and Slavery*, 319; Eddy Stols, "The Expansion of the Sugar Market in

Western Europe," in *Tropical Babylons: Sugar and the Making of the Atlantic World, 1450–1680*, ed. Stuart B. Schwartz (Chapel Hill: University of North Carolina Press, 2004), 237–275; Kenneth Morgan, *Slavery and the British Empire: From Africa to America* (Oxford: Oxford University Press, 2007), 67; Burnhard, *Planters, Merchants, and Slaves*, 110.

11. Ronald Bailey, "The Slave(ry) Trade and the Development of Capitalism in the United States: The Textile Industry in New England," *Social Science History* 14, no. 3 (Autumn 1990), 374–375, 380; David Richardson, "Slavery, Trade, and Economic Growth in Eighteenth-Century New England," *Slavery and the Rise of the Atlantic*, ed. Barbara L. Solow (Cambridge: Cambridge University Press, 1991), 253; S. D. Smith, *Slavery, Family, and Gentry Capitalism in the British Atlantic: The World of Lascelles, 1648–1834* (Cambridge: Cambridge University Press, 2006), 21.

12. This line of historical interpretation has been hotly contested for decades, but has been rendered increasingly mainstream by recent scholarship showing that the trade in sugar contributed significantly to British industrialization, even if it was not the sole contributing factor. Eric Williams, *Capitalism & Slavery* (Chapel Hill: University of North Carolina Press, 1944); Ralph A. Austen and Woodruff D. Smith, "Private Tooth Decay as Public Economic Virtue: The Slave-Sugar Triangle, Consumerism, and European Industrialization," *Social Science History* 14, no. 1 (Spring 1990), 95–115; Bailey, "The Slave(ry) Trade," 373–414; Robin Blackburn, *The Making of New World Slavery: From the Baroque to the Modern 1492–1800* (London: Verso, 1997), 361–363, 448, chap. 12; Jacob M. Price, "The Imperial Economy, 1700–1776," in *The Oxford History of the British Empire*, ed. William Roger Louis et al., 5 vols. (Oxford: Oxford University Press, 1998–1999), 2: 99; David Eltis and Stanley L. Engerman, *Journal of Economic History* 60, no. 1 (March 2000), 123–144; Higman, "The Sugar Revolution," 213–236; Carole Shammas, "The Revolutionary Impact of European Demand for Tropical Goods," in *The Early Modern Atlantic Economy*, ed. John J. McCusker and Kenneth Morgan (Cambridge: Cambridge University Press, 2000), 163–166, 178–179; Kenneth Morgan, *Slavery, Atlantic Trade and the British Economy, 1660–1800* (Cambridge: Cambridge University Press, 2000), 67–73; Joseph E. Inikori, *Africans and the Industrial Revolution in England: A Study in International Trade and Economic Development* (Cambridge: Cambridge University Press, 2002), 2–7, chap. 3; Morgan, *Slavery and the British Empire*, 81–83; Ronald Findlay and Kevin H. O'Rourke, *Power and Plenty: Trade War and the World Economy in the Second Millennium* (Princeton: Princeton University Press, 2007), 130–131; Zahedieh, *The Capital and the Colonies*, 1–7, 15–16, 236–237, 288–292. Some scholars, meanwhile, seem conflicted on the point: Burnhard, *Planters, Merchants, and Slaves*, 262–264, 176.

13. Smith, *Slavery, Family, and Gentry Capitalism*, 21.1

14. Bernard Bailyn, *The New England Merchants in the Seventeenth Century* (Cambridge, MA: Harvard University Press, 1955), 85.

15. Quoted in Samuel Eliot Morison, *The Maritime History of Massachusetts, 1783–1860* (Boston: Houghton Mifflin Company, 1921), 17; Dorothy Burne Goebel, "The 'New England Trade' and the French West Indies, 1763–1774: A Study in Trade Policies," *William and Mary Quarterly* 20, no. 3 (July 1963), 331–372; Kenneth Morgan, "Anglo-Dutch Economic Relations in the Atlantic World, 1688–1783," in *Dutch Atlantic Connections, 1680–1800: Linking Empires, Bridging Borders*, ed. Gert Oostindie and Jessica V. Roitman (Leiden: Brill, 2014), 126–132; Thomas M. Truxes, *Defying Empire: Trading with the Enemy in Colonial New York* (New Haven: Yale University Press, 2008), 58–60.

16. John J. McCusker and Russell R. Menard, *The Economy of British America, 1607–1789* (Chapel Hill: University of North Carolina Press, 1985), 108.

17. Bailey, "The Slave(ry) Trade," 380; Blackburn, *Making of New World Slavery*, 459–461; Price, "The Imperial Economy, 1700–1776," 90–91; Gautham Rao, *National Duties: Custom Houses and the Making of the American State* (Chicago: University of Chicago Press, 2016), 21.

18. Burnhard, *Planters, Merchants, and Slaves*, 110; Bailey, "The Slave(ry) Trade," 374–375, 380–385; Smith, *Slavery, Family, and Gentry Capitalism*, 20–21; Shammas, "European Demand for Tropical Goods," 175–176.

19. William Cronon, *Nature's Metropolis: Chicago and the Great West* (New York: W. W. Norton, 1991), xxvii.

20. What conservationist Aldo Leopold termed "the biotic community." Aldo Leopold, *A Sand County Almanac: With Essays on Conservation from Round River* (New York: Ballantine Books, 1966) 177, 244–247.

21. David Armitage, "Three Concepts of Atlantic History," in *The British Atlantic World, 1500–1800*, ed. David Armitage and Michael J. Braddick (Basingstoke: Palgrave Macmillan, 2002), 23. This book is not the first to trace the economic development of the early Connecticut Valley, although the current study's emphasis on environmental change and its broad temporal focus serve to separate it from its predecessors. Richard L. Bushman, *From Puritan to Yankee: Character and the Social Order in Connecticut, 1690–1765* (Cambridge, MA: Harvard University Press, 1967); Christopher Clark, *The Roots of Rural Capitalism: Western Massachusetts, 1780–1860* (Ithaca, NY: Cornell University Press, 1990); Margaret E. Martin, "Merchants and Trade of the Connecticut River Valley, 1750–1820," *Smith College Studies in History* 24, nos. 1–4 (October 1938–July 1939); John T. Cumbler, *Reasonable Use: The People, the Environment, and the State, New England 1790–1930* (New York: Oxford University Press, 2001).

22. As Peter Mancall has recently noted, Cronon's *Changes in the Land* continues to dominate the historiography of early New England (indeed, all of early North American) environmental history—despite having been published over thirty years ago. Merchant's *Ecological Revolutions* is nearing the twenty-five-year mark. The only recent environmental history of New England which can unhesitatingly be placed alongside these foundational texts is Brian Donahue's *The Great Meadow* (2004), a local history of Concord, Massachusetts. Peter C. Mancall, "Pigs for Historians: Changes in the Land and Beyond," *William and Mary Quarterly* 67, no. 2 (April 2010), 347–375; William Cronon, *Changes in the Land: Indians, Colonists and the Ecology of New England* (New York: Hill and Wang, 1983); Carolyn Merchant, *Ecological Revolutions: Nature, Gender, and Science in New England* (Chapel Hill: University of North Carolina Press, 1989); Brian Donahue, *The Great Meadow: Farmers and the Land in Colonial Concord* (New Haven: Yale University Press, 2004).

23. Pekka Hämäläinen, "The Politics of Grass: European Expansion, Ecological Change, and Indigenous Power in the Southwest Borderlands," *William and Mary Quarterly* 67, no. 2 (April 2010), 173–174.

24. This tendency to approach capitalism as merely an abstraction rather than a process is one of the most notable shortcomings of the current historiography on the early New England environment. Many existing studies present capitalism as a teleological certainty that was somehow separate from the market forces that created it, and, indeed, as a historical force largely autonomous from human agency. William Cronon's *Changes in the Land*, for instance, presented "the transition to capitalism" as a historical force seemingly external to the economic and ecological systems it investigated. Carolyn Merchant, in her *Ecological Revolutions*, adopted a pseudo-Marxist model of economic and ecological change driven by society's shifting relationship to the means of production and reproduction. Unlike Cronon, who presented capitalism as

arriving in New England with the first English settlers and dates the advent of large-scale commercial agriculture (and consequently large-scale environmental change) to the mid-eighteenth
century, Merchant argued that the capitalist revolution and its ecological implications did not
really begin until the early nineteenth century. Brian Donahue in his history of agriculture in
colonial Concord, Massachusetts, sought to reconcile these viewpoints by suggesting that even
the earliest English colonial ventures were driven by capitalism ("a new force in the world")
and that colonial farmers "were committed to the market," but in a manner that was neither
"intensive" nor "thoroughly commercial." Like Merchant, Donahue argued that real ecological
deterioration only came after the American Revolution with a regional shift toward commercial
agriculture that followed in the wake of "a more thoroughly commercialized Atlantic World."
Cronon, *Changes in the Land*, 75–77, 160–162, 167; Merchant, *Ecological Revolutions*, 2–3, 113,
150, 153, 190–191; Donahue, *The Great Meadow*, xvi, 20–22, 72–73, 220.

25. This historical narrative of the "rise" or "transition to capitalism" has deep roots, but
gained a new ascendancy in the historiography of New England in the 1980s–1990s. Allan
Kulikoff, "The Transition to Capitalism in Rural America," *William and Mary Quarterly* 46,
no. 1 (January 1989), 120–144; John Frederick Martin, *Profits in the Wilderness: Entrepreneurship
and the Founding of New England Towns in the Seventeenth Century* (Chapel Hill: University of
North Carolina Press; published for the Institute of Early American History and Culture, 1991),
1–5, 127–128; Stephen Innes, *Creating the Commonwealth: The Economic Culture of Puritan New
England* (New York: W. W. Norton, 1995), 329–331 (notes); Naomi R. Lamoreaux, "Rethinking
the Transition to Capitalism in the Early American Northeast," *Journal of American History* 90,
no. 2 (September 2003), 437–461.

26. Brian Donahue's *Great Meadow* deserves special praise for the wonderfully detailed
manner in which it unravels the intricate interconnections of colonial agriculture. Still, Donahue shares with other scholars—including Cronon and Merchant—a tendency to marginalize
ecological transformations that did not occur within the "world of fields and fences" (Cronon's
phrase). Donahue, *The Great Meadow*, 21; Cronon, *Changes in the Land*, 127.

27. For a thorough analysis of the economic and political activities of early Springfield,
Massachusetts, see Stephen Innes, *Labor in a New Land: Economy and Society in Seventeenth-
Century Springfield* (Princeton, NJ: Princeton University Press, 1983).

28. Timothy Dwight, *Travels in New-England and New-York*, 4 vols. (New Haven: Timothy
Dwight, 1821–1822), 2: 338.

29. We can, to quote Donald Worster, try to "think like a river" or, in this case, a river
valley, to understand the internal logic at work within the natural systems that undergirded
the human history of the Connecticut Valley. Donald Worster, "Thinking Like a River," in *The
Wealth of Nature: Environmental History and the Ecological Imagination* (New York: Oxford
University Press, 1993), 131.

30. Dwight, *Travels*, 2: 292.

31. In choosing such criteria to define the regional focus of my work, I am following Peter
Mancall who, in his history of the Upper Susquehanna River, pointed out that it was "the contours of the valley inhabitants' world—their mountains and rivers and vales" that "defined
settlement patterns and trade routes." Peter Mancall, *Valley of Opportunity: Economic Culture
Along the Upper Susquehanna, 1700–1800* (Ithaca, NY: Cornell University Press, 1991), 9; see also
Strother E. Roberts, "Changes in the Genre: A Brief Survey of Early Mid-Atlantic Environmental Histories," *Pennsylvania History: A Journal of Mid-Atlantic Studies* 79, no. 4 (Autumn 2012),
348–349.

32. Lucianne Lavin, *Connecticut's Indigenous Peoples: What Archaeology, History, and Oral Traditions Teach Us About Their Communities and Culture* (New Haven: Yale University Press, 2013), 192–193, 201; Kathleen J. Bragdon, *Native People of Southern New England, 1500–1650* (Norman, OK: University of Oklahoma Press, 1996), 71, 78, 90–91; Lisa Brooks, *The Common Pot: The Recovery of Native Space in the Northeast* (Minneapolis: University of Minnesota Press, 2008), 12, 17.

33. Quoted in Edwin Munroe Bacon, *The Connecticut River and the Valley of the Connecticut: Three Hundred and Fifty Miles from Mountain to Sea* (New York: G. P. Putnam's Sons, 1906), 27.

34. John Winthrop, "General Observations for the Plantation of New England," in *The Winthrop Papers*, ed. Stewart Mitchell, 6 vols. (Boston: Massachusetts Historical Society, 1931), 2: 112; David J. Silverman, "We Chuse to Be Bounded: Native American Animal Husbandry in Colonial New England," *William and Mary Quarterly* 60, no. 3 (2003), 511–512.

35. For example, Virginia DeJohn Anderson, "King Philip's Herds: Indians, Colonists, and the Problem of Livestock in Early New England," *William and Mary Quarterly* 51, no. 4 (1994), 601–624. For a more general discussion, see Jean M. O'Brien, "'Divorced' from the Land: Resistance and Survival of Indian Women in Eighteenth-Century New England," in *After King Philip's War: Presence and Persistence in Indian New England*, ed. Colin. G. Calloway (Hanover, NH: University Press of New England, 1997), 144–161; Margaret Bruchac, "Native Presence in Nonotuck and Northampton," in *A Place Called Paradise: Culture and Community in Northampton, Massachusetts, 1654–2004*, ed. Kerry W. Buckley (Amherst, MA: Historic Northampton Museum and Education Center in association with the University of Massachusetts Press, 2004), 18–38; Jean O'Brien, *Firsting and Lasting: Writing Indians Out of Existence in New England* (Minneapolis: University of Minnesota Press, 2010); Margaret M. Bruchac, "Revisiting Pocumtuck History in Deerfield: George Sheldon's Vanishing Indian Act," *Historical Journal of Massachusetts* 39, no. 1/2 (Summer 2011), 30–77; Christine M. DeLucia, *Memory Lands: King Philip's War and the Place of Violence in the Northeast* (Yale University Press, 2018), esp. chap. 5.

36. For the valley, see John Winthrop, *The History of New England from 1630 to 1649*, ed. James Savage, 2 vols. (Boston: Little, Brown, 1853), 1: 146–147; William Bradford, *Of Plymouth Plantation, 1620–1647*, ed. Samuel Eliot Morison (New York: Knopf, 1959), 270–271; Neal Salisbury, *Manitou and Providence: Indians, Europeans, and the Making of New England, 1500–1643* (New York: Oxford University Press, 1982), 105–106; Dean R. Snow and Kim M. Lanphear, "European Contact and Indian Depopulation in the Northeast: The Timing of the First Epidemics," *Ethnohistory* 35, no. 1 (Winter 1988), 15–33.

37. Examples: Roderick Frazier Nash, *Wilderness in the American Mind*, 4th ed. (New Haven: Yale University Press, 2001), chaps. 1–2; Merchant, *Ecological Revolutions*, 39–42, 100–104; Alan Taylor, "'Wasty Ways': Stories of American Settlement," *Environmental History* 3, no. 3 (July 1998), 291–310; Jon T. Coleman, *Vicious: Wolves and Men in America* (New Haven: Yale University Press, 2004), 9–11.

38. Michael Wigglesworth, "God's Controversy with New-England," *Proceedings of the Massachusetts Historical Society* 12 (1871–1873), 83–84.

39. David Blackbourn has complained of a tendency in environmental history to preference the "imagined landscape," asking "are all topographies in the mind, is every river nothing more than a flowing symbol?" David Blackbourn, *The Conquest of Nature: Water, Landscape, and the Making of Modern Germany* (New York: W. W. Norton, 2006), 16.

40. On the important role that labor has historically played in shaping human understandings of nature: Richard White, *The Organic Machine: The Remaking of the Columbia River* (New York: Hill & Wang, 1995).

41. William Heywood, "William Heywood's Journal," accession number 1984-54(M), Manuscript Section, New Hampshire Historical Society, Concord, NH, 1–2, 6, 12, 13, 15, 20–21.

42. For a discussion of this lingering cultural hatred of woodlands see Taylor, "Wasty Ways," 291–310.

43. Cronon, *Changes in the Land*, 169.

44. For recent scholars who offer a similar interpretation of the role of indigenous economic agents in environmental change: Brooks, *The Common Pot*, 20–25; Christopher Pastore, *Between Land and Sea: The Atlantic Coast and the Transformation of New England* (Cambridge, MA: Harvard University Press, 2014), chap. 1; Andrea L. Smalley, *Wild by Nature: North American Animals Confront Colonization* (Baltimore: Johns Hopkins University Press, 2017), esp. 47–49, 55.

45. Hämäläinen has complained that "grand, large-scale" historical models, "preoccupied with global patterns . . . often distort the realities on the ground." Hämäläinen, "The Politics of Grass," 173.

46. The fact that Cronon recognizes that economic changes came about "as much through the agency of the Indians as the Europeans" makes it all the more puzzling that he should assert that Native American and European economies were somehow antithetical. Cronon seems to disregard the possibility that an "Indian economy" could be anything other than the sort of "traditional" economy characterized by hunting, gathering, and horticulture. The disturbing implication of such a view of Indian economics, an implication that Cronon surely never intended, is that there could be no "modern" Indian economy and that any acculturation or accommodation to European markets or production activities constituted the relinquishment of an Indian identity. Cronon, *Changes in the Land*, 169.

47. Cronon, *Changes in the Land*, 169.

48. Many accounts of the New England landscape published in the seventeenth and eighteenth century—Cronon's sources—support this image of America as a land of "limitless" resources. However, these published accounts, written primarily by colonial boosters and European visitors, ignore the lived experience of resource scarcity (and perceived scarcity) that characterizes the unpublished journals, account books, court proceedings, and town meeting records that more fully reflect the challenge of managing scarce resources during the colonial era. Cronon, in his assertion of colonial-era profligacy, reproduced a historical narrative born in the nineteenth century from the biases of reforming agriculturalists and woodland managers who decried what they perceived as the irrational wastefulness of their seventeenth- and eighteenth-century forebears. Brian Donahue has very successfully challenged this progressive narrative. Donahue, *The Great Meadow*, xiii–xix.

49. As Gregory T. Cushman observed in his recent history of the guano trade, colonizing societies had three options if they hoped to continue expanding after the initial rush of "ecological imperialism" had stripped settlements of their most easily exploited resources. The descendants of the earliest settlers could (1) leave to colonize new environments; (2) learn to live within their ecological limits; or (3) import goods, services, and energy from other ecosystems. Early modern New Englanders embraced all three strategies, but eventually came to rely most heavily on the third option. Gregory T. Cushman, *Guano and the Opening of the Pacific World: A Global Ecological History* (New York: Cambridge University Press, 2013), 76.

50. In this respect, colonial New England was—as Carolyn Merchant eloquently phrased it—"a mirror on the world," reflecting market-driven processes that had already depleted resources in England and would relatively quickly do so in New England as well before pushing into new markets. Merchant, *Ecological Revolutions*, 1–2.

51. Julian L. Simon, *The Ultimate Resource 2* (Princeton: Princeton University Press, 1996), passim, esp. 407–408.

52. For example, Cronon's *Changes in the Land* and Merchant's *Ecological Revolutions* ultimately presented a declensionist narrative of the New England environment—even though both authors suggested they wished to avoid doing so. Merchant, *Ecological Revolutions*, xiv–xxi; Cronon, *Changes in the Land*, 4–6.

Chapter 1

1. Despite being perhaps the greatest factor driving ecological and hydrological change in northeastern North America in the seventeenth century, the environmental impacts of precipitously declining beaver populations have received little previous attention from historians. Christopher Pastore's recent book on Narragansett Bay, which considers the impact that beaver extermination had upon the downstream ecosystem of that estuary, stands as an exception. William Cronon, *Changes in the Land: Indians, Colonists, and the Ecology of New England* (New York: Hill & Wang, 1983), 106–107, 155; Carolyn Merchant, *Ecological Revolutions: Nature, Gender, and Science in New England* (Chapel Hill: University of North Carolina Press, 1989), 36–37, 87; Brian Donahue, *The Great Meadow: Farmers and the Land in Colonial Concord* (New Haven: Yale University Press, 2004), 49; Christopher Pastore, *Between Land and Sea: The Atlantic Coast and the Transformation of New England* (Cambridge, MA: Harvard University Press, 2014), 34–49.

2. John Winthrop, *The History of New England from 1630 to 1649*, ed. James Savage, 2 vols. (Boston: Little, Brown, 1853), 1: 62–63.

3. Winthrop, *History of New England*, 1: 105.

4. Winthrop, *History of New England*, 1: 138–139.

5. Alfred A. Cave, *The Pequot War* (Boston: University of Massachusetts Press, 1996), 81.

6. Mark Fiege, *The Republic of Nature: An Environmental History of the United States* (Seattle: University of Washington Press, 2012), 32; Ian K. Steele, *Warpaths: Invasions of North America* (New York: Oxford University Press, 1994), 90.

7. Lucianne Lavin, *Connecticut's Indigenous Peoples: What Archaeology, History, and Oral Traditions Teach Us About Their Communities and Culture* (New Haven, CT: Yale University Press, 2013), 192–193, 201; Kathleen J. Bragdon, *Native People of Southern New England, 1500–1650* (Norman: University of Oklahoma Press, 1996), 71, 78, 90–91; Lisa Brooks, *The Common Pot: The Recovery of Native Space in the Northeast* (Minneapolis: University of Minnesota Press, 2008), 12, 17.

8. Dean R. Snow and Kim M. Lanphear, "European Contact and Indian Depopulation in the Northeast: The Timing of the First Epidemics," *Ethnohistory* 35, no. 1 (Winter 1988), 15–33, esp. 22; Cristobal Silva, "Miraculous Plagues: Epidemiology on New England's Colonial Landscape," *Early American Literature* 43, no. 2 (2008), 249–275.

9. Amy Schwartz's review of the scholarship on early New England agriculture offers a discussion of the various population figures proposed by previous scholars. Amy D. Schwartz, "Colonial New England Agriculture: Old Visions, New Directions," *Agricultural History* 69, no. 3 (Summer 1995), 460. Also, Bragdon, *Native People*, 25–26.

10. For a more detailed consideration of the mechanisms through which European diseases wrought devastation on Native American, see David S. Jones, "Virgin Soils Revisited," *William and Mary Quarterly* 60, no. 4 (October 2003), 727, 730–734.

11. William Bradford, *Of Plymouth Plantation, 1620–1647*, ed. Samuel Eliot Morison (New York: Knopf, 1959), 270–271.

12. Bragdon, *Native People*, 25; Peter A. Thomas, "Into the Maelstrom of Change," in *A Place Called Paradise: Culture and Community in Northampton, Massachusetts, 1654–2004*, ed. Kerry W. Buckley (Amherst: Historic Northampton Museum and Education Center in association with the University of Massachusetts Press, 2004), 6.

13. Jones, "Virgin Soils Revisited," 703–742; Neal Salisbury, *Manitou and Providence: Indians, Europeans, and the Making of New England, 1500–1643* (New York: Oxford University Press, 1982), 105–106; David S. Jones, *Rationalizing Epidemics: Meanings and Uses of American Indian Mortality Since 1600* (Cambridge, MA: Harvard University Press, 2004), 31–32; James D. Rice, *Nature & History in the Potomac Country: From Hunter-Gatherers to the Age of Jefferson* (Baltimore: John Hopkins University Press, 2009), 130–134.

14. John Smith, *The Generall Historie of Virginia, New-England, and the Summer Isles* (London: Printed by I. D. and I. H. for Michael Sparkes, 1624), 229.

15. Robert J. Naiman, Carol A. Johnston, and James C. Kelley, "Alteration of North American Streams by Beaver," *BioScience* 38, no. 11 (December 1988), 754, 760.

16. William Wood, *New England's Prospect* (London: Printed for John Bellamie, 1634), 13; for a description of beaver wetlands in the Hudson Valley see Pastore, *Between Land and Sea*, 35, 45.

17. Beaver make their homes in watercourses that range in size from second- to fifth-order streams. The Connecticut itself is a sixth-order stream. Its tributaries range in size from the first through fifth order. Robert J. Naiman, Jerry M. Melillo, and John E. Hobbie, "Ecosystem Alteration of Boreal Forest Streams by Beaver (*Castor canadensis*)," *Ecology* 67, no. 5 (October 1986), 1254.

18. These rough estimates are based on an assumption of an average of three beaver colonies per every square kilometer, as observed in flourishing modern beaver populations inhabiting major watersheds. The Connecticut watershed's 11,250 square miles (or about 29,138 square kilometers) could have provided habitat for nearly 90,000 colonies, with an average of six individuals per colony, or about 540,000 individual beaver. Each colony would have maintained at least one pond with an average pond size of 4 hectares (almost 10 acres). Beaver ponds, therefore, may have once covered approximately 900,000 acres (1,406 square miles) of the land contained within the Connecticut basin. For pond size and estimates of beaver population density, see Naiman, Johnston, and Kelley, "Alteration of North American Streams," 754; and Carol A. Johnston and Robert J. Naiman, "Aquatic Patch Creation in Relation to Beaver Population Trends," *Ecology* 71, no. 4 (1990), 1617.

This estimation that beaver ponds and related wetlands may have covered 12 percent of the pre–fur trade Connecticut watershed, approximates the estimate derived by Donald L. Hey and Nancy Philippi of the Watershed Initiative for the upper Mississippi watershed prior to the extirpation of beaver. Donald L. Hey and Nancy S. Philippi, "Flood Reduction Through Wetland Restoration: The Upper Mississippi River Basin as a Case History," *Restoration Ecology* 3, no. 1 (March 1995), 9, 13–14; Donald L. Hey and Nancy S. Philippi, *A Case for Wetland Restoration* (New York: Wiley, 1999), 14.

19. Ronald L. Ives, "The Beaver-Meadow Complex," *Journal of Geomorphology* 5, no. 3 (October 1942), 196, 198, 200–203; Jerry R. Miller, Dru Germanoski, and Mark L. Lord, "Geomorphic Processes Affecting Meadow Ecosystems," in *Geomorphology, Hydrology, and Ecology of Great Basin Meadow Complexes: Implications for Management and Restoration*, eds. Jeanne C. Chambers and Jerry R. Miller (Fort Collins, CO: U.S. Department of Agriculture, Forest Service, Rocky Mountain Research Station, 2011), 39; Natalie Kramer, Ellen E. Wohl, and Dennis L.

Harry, "Using Ground Penetrating Radar to 'Unearth' Buried Beaver Dams," *Geology* 40, no. 1 (January 2012), 46.

20. David R. Butler and George P. Malanson, "The Geomorphic Influences of Beaver Dams and Failures of Beaver Dams," *Geomorphology* 71 (2005), 49–50.

21. Ives, "The Beaver-Meadow Complex," 198.

22. Jesse M. Cunningham, Aram J. K. Calhoun, and William E. Glanz, "Patterns of Beaver Colonization and Wetland Change in Acadia National Park," *Northeastern Naturalist* 13, no. 4 (2006), 583, 593–594.

23. "For New England Indians," William Cronon has observed, "ecological diversity . . . meant abundance, stability, and a regular supply of the things that kept them alive." William Cronon, *Changes in the Land: Indians, Colonists and the Ecology of New England* (New York: Hill and Wang, 1983), 53; Michael J. Heckenberger et al., "Early Evidence of Maize Agriculture in the Connecticut River Valley of Vermont," *Archaeology of Eastern North America* 20 (Fall 1992), 135.

24. Naiman, Johnston, and Kelley, "Alteration of North American Streams," 756.

25. Naiman, Johnston, and Kelley, "Alteration of North American Streams," 759–760.

26. Cunningham, Calhoun, and Glanz, "Patterns of Beaver Colonization," 585.

27. Naiman, Johnston, and Kelley, "Alteration of North American Streams," 761.

28. James Edmund Harting, *British Animals Extinct Within Historic Times, with Some Account of British Wild White Cattle* (Boston: J. R. Osgood, 1880), 33–42; Dolly Jørgensen, "A Short History of Welsh Beavers," *The Return of Native Nordic Fauna: A Research Blog Exploring Animal Reintroduction History*, February 25, 2014, http://dolly.jorgensenweb.net/nordicnature /?p=1452.

29. Julia Emberley, *The Cultural Politics of Fur* (Ithaca, NY: Cornell University Press, 1997), 46–47; Raymond Henry Fisher, "The Russian Fur Trade, 1550–1700," *University of California Publications in History*, 83 vols. (Berkeley, CA: University Press of California, 1911–1972), 31: 3–7.

30. Fisher, "The Russian Fur Trade," 3–7, 9, 17–23.

31. E. E. Rich, "Russia and the Colonial Fur Trade," *Economic History Review, New Series* 7, no. 3 (1955), 307, 311; J. F. Crean, "Hats and the Fur Trade," *Canadian Journal of Economics and Political Science / Revue Canadienne d'économique et de science politique* 28, no. 3 (August 1962), 376.

32. A. Akin, "On Furs and the Fur Trade," *Transactions of the Society, Instituted at London, for the Encouragement of Arts, Manufactures, and Commerce* 49, part I (1831–1832), 199–200; Rich, "Russia and the Colonial Fur Trade," 307–309, 311; Merchant, *Ecological Revolutions*, 41–43; Emberley, *Cultural Politics of Fur*, 47, 66–67; R. Turner Wilcox, *The Mode in Hats and Headdress* (New York: Scribner, 1959), 113–114, 123–135, 138–139.

33. William Babcock Weeden, *Economic and Social History of New England, 1620–1789*, 2 vols. (Boston: Houghton, Mifflin, 1891), 1: 39.

34. Wood, *New England's Prospect*, 26, 89.

35. Tom Andersen, *This Fine Piece of Water: An Environmental History of Long Island Sound* (New Haven, CT: Yale University Press, 2002), 50.

36. Mark Meuwse, "The Dutch Connection: New Netherland, the Pequots, and the Puritans in Southern New England, 1620–1638," *The Worlds of Lion Gardiner, ca. 1599–1663: Crossings and Boundaries*, special issue, *Early American Studies* 9, no. 2 (Spring 2011), 309.

37. Quoted in Cave, *The Pequot War*, 50.

38. Neal Salisbury, "Toward the Covenant Chain: Iroquois and Southern New England Algonquians, 1637–1684," in *Beyond the Covenant Chain: The Iroquois and Their Neighbors in*

Indian North America, 1600–1800, ed. Daniel K. Richter and James H. Merrell (Syracuse, NY: Syracuse University Press, 1987), 64–67; William A. Starna and José António Brandão, "From the Mohawk-Mahican War to the Beaver Wars: Questioning the Pattern," *Ethnohistory* 51, no. 4 (Fall 2004), 731, 736–741; Francis Jennings, *The Ambiguous Iroquois Empire: The Covenant Chain Confederation of Indian Tribes With English Colonies* (New York W.W. Norton & Company, Inc., 1984), 102; Brooks, *The Common Pot,* 21–23.

39. Cronon, *Changes in the Land,* 96–97.

40. Peter A. Thomas, "The Fur Trade, Indian Land, and the Need to Define Adequate 'Environmental' Parameters," *Ethnohistory* 28, no. 4 (Autumn 1981), 363; Meuwese, "The Dutch Connection," 298–299, 309.

41. Winthrop, *History of New England,* 1:105.

42. Francis Jennings, *The Invasion of America: Indians, Colonialism, and the Cant of Conquest* (New York: Norton, 1976), 133.

43. Cave, *The Pequot War,* 81.

44. Winthrop, *History of New England,* 1: 167.

45. Winthrop, *History of New England,* 1: 177. The narrative of the Pequot War and its causes that is offered here and that continues in subsequent paragraphs draws extensively on Jennings, *The Invasion of America,* 188–227; Cave, *The Pequot War*; and Jenny Hale Pulsipher, *Subjects unto the Same King: Indians, English, and the Contest for Authority in Colonial New England* (Philadelphia: University of Pennsylvania Press, 2005), 21–24.

46. Winthrop, *History of New England,* 1: 148–149; Jennings, *The Invasion of America,* 188–190.

47. Jennings, *The Invasion of America,* 193; Meuwse, "The Dutch Connection," 317.

48. The historical factors that contributed to the outbreak of the Pequot War were complex and varied, but the current scholarly consensus suggests that economic competition to control the natural resources and trade networks of southern New England played a central role. The English colonies' "economic contest" with the Pequots centered on control of the regional fur trade and, by extension, control of the wampum supplies over which the Pequots exercised considerable authority. The English thus possessed an "economic motive" to interpret any events that could be construed as even slightly provocative as justifications for war. Lynn Ceci, "Native Wampum as a Peripheral Resource in the Seventeenth-Century World-System," in *The Pequots in Southern New England: The Fall and Rise of an American Indian Nation,* ed. Laurence M. Hauptman and James D. Wherry (Norman: University of Oklahoma Press, 1990), 48, 59–60; Katherine Grandjean, "New World Tempests: Environment, Scarcity, and the Coming of the Pequot War," *William and Mary Quarterly* 68, no. 1 (January 2011), 76–77, note 4 on 76–77, 86; Steven T. Katz, "The Pequot War Reconsidered," *New England Quarterly* 64, no. 2 (June 1991), 206–207, 209; Meuwse, "The Dutch Connection," 297, 318; Cave, *The Pequot War,* 9–11.

49. Winthrop, *History of New England,* 1: 122–123; Cave, *The Pequot War,* 72–75; Jennings, *The Invasion of America,* 189–190.

50. Cave, *The Pequot War,* 104–109; Meuwse, "The Dutch Connection," 318.

51. Jennings, *The Invasion of America,* 189–190, 194–195, 209–211.

52. Grandjean, "New World Tempests," 77–78, 80–83, 85–87, 90–94; Cave, *The Pequot War,* 169.

53. The exact status of the Mohegans as a people and nation at the beginning of the seventeenth century remains difficult to discern. They may have simply been a geographically distinct branch of the Pequot nation. Or the Mohegans may have been a separate nation allied with the

Pequots that had gradually slipped into a subordinate status. Either way, by the mid-1630s the Mohegan villages proved themselves ready to break from their erstwhile Pequot compatriots/ allies. Julie A. Fisher and David J. Silverman, *Ninigret, Sachem of the Niantics and Narragansetts: Diplomacy, War, and the Balance of Power in Seventeenth-Century New England and Indian Country* (Ithaca, NY: Cornell University Press, 2014), 32–33; Michael Leroy Oberg, *Uncas: First of the Mohegans* (Ithaca, NY: Cornell University Press, 2003), 16–18; Cave, *The Pequot War*, 66–68; Jennings, *The Invasion of America*, 202–203.

54. Josiah Gilbert Holland, *History of Western Massachusetts*, 2 vols. (Springfield, MA: Samuel Bowles, 1855), 1:66.

55. Edward Johnson, *Wonder-Working Providence*, 2 vols. (Andover, MA: Warren F. Draper, 1867), 2: 199.

56. Quoted in New York (Colony), *An Abridgment of the Indian Affairs Contained in Four Folio Volumes, Transacted in the Colony of New York, from the Year 1678 to the Year 1751*, ed. Peter Wraxall (Cambridge, MA: Harvard University Press, 1915), xxxi.

57. Thomas, "The Fur Trade," 363–364.

58. Thomas, "The Fur Trade," 365.

59. Kerry Wayne Buckley, *A Place Called Paradise: Culture and Community in Northampton, Massachusetts* (Amherst: Historic Northampton Museum and Education Center in association with the University Press of Massachusetts, 2004), 11.

60. Father Paul Le Jeune, quoted in Shepard Krech III, *The Ecological Indian: Myth and History* (New York: W. W. Norton, 2000), 181.

61. Colin G. Calloway, *The Western Abenakis of Vermont, 1600–1800* (Norman: University of Oklahoma Press, 1990), 72–73; Buckley, *Place Called Paradise*, 11.

62. In effect, hostile competition created uncertainty over "property rights" in beaver, resulting in a situation analogous to Garrett Hardin's "Tragedy of the Commons." Shepard Krech takes note of similar rationales for overexploitation of beaver among the Micmacs and the Montagnais during roughly the same period. Garrett Hardin, "The Tragedy of the Commons," *Science* 162, no. 3859, New Series (December 13, 1968), 1243–1248; Krech, *The Ecological Indian*, 181–182; Calloway, *Western Abenakis*, 45–46.

63. Sylvester Judd, *History of Hadley, Including the Early History of Hatfield, South Hadley, Amherst and Granby, Massachusetts* (Northampton, MA: Metcalf, 1863), 355.

64. Connecticut (Colony), *The Public Records of the Colony of Connecticut, from April 1636 to October 1776*, 15 vols. (Hartford, CT: Brown and Parsons, 1850–1890), 1: 20.

65. Thomas, "The Fur Trade," 368.

66. William Hubbard, *A Narrative of the Troubles with the Indians of New-England from the First Planting Thereof to the Present Time* (Boston: Printed by John Foster, 1677), 2–3.

67. Krech, *The Ecological Indian*, 176.

68. Brooks, *The Common Pot*, 20, 23.

69. For examples, see Nicole Eddy, "Beavers on the Run," *Medieval Manuscripts Blog*, British Library, November 7, 2012, http://britishlibrary.typepad.co.uk/digitisedmanuscripts/2012/11 /beavers-on-the-run.html.

70. Edward Topsell, *The Historie of Four-Footed Beastes* (London: William Jaggard, 1607), Huntington Library, Rare Books Collection, #17726, 47, 171.

71. For examples, Thomas Morton, *New English Canaan* (Amsterdam: Jacob Frederick Stam, 1637), Huntington Library, Rare Books Collection, #3389, 77–78; John Josselyn, *An Account of Two Voyages to New-England* (London: Printed for Giles Widdows, 1674), 92–93.

72. Wood, *New England's Prospect*, 24–26.

73. Emma Spary, "Political, Natural, and Bodily Economies," in *Cultures of Natural History*, ed. N. Jardine, J. A. Secord, and E. C. Spary (Cambridge: Cambridge University Press, 1996), 182.

74. Jeremy Belknap, *The Foresters, an American tale: Being a Sequel to the History of John Bull the Clothier, in a Series of Letters to a Friend* (Boston: I. Thomas & E. T. Andrews, 1792), 173–186.

75. Nicolas Denys, *The Description and Natural History of the Coasts of North America (Acadia)*, ed. and trans. William F. Ganong (Toronto: Champlain Society, 1908), 429; Peter Williamson, *The Travels of Peter Williamson, Among the Different Nations and Tribes of Savage Indians in America* (Edinburgh: R. Fleming, 1768), 68–71.

76. Jeremy Belknap, *The History of New-Hampshire*, 3 vols. (Boston: Belknap and Young, 1784–1792), 3: 159.

77. Joseph Peirce, quoted in Belknap, *The History of New-Hampshire*, 3: 159–161.

78. Cunningham, Calhoun, and Glanz, "Patterns of Beaver Colonization," 583.

79. J. M. Wilson, *Beaver in Connecticut: Their Natural History and Management* (Hartford: Connecticut Department of Environmental Protection, Wildlife Division, 2001), 6.

80. Wilson, *Beaver in Connecticut*, 6; Cunningham, Calhoun, and Glanz, "Patterns of Beaver Colonization," 583–584, 593–594; Isaac J. Schlosser and Larry W. Kallemeyn, "Spatial Variation in Fish Assemblages Across a Beaver-Influenced Successional Landscape," *Ecology* 81, no. 5 (May 2000), 1381; Willis D. Hanson and Robert S. Campbell, "The Effects of Pool Size and Beaver Activity on Distribution and Abundance of Warm-Water Fishes in a North Missouri Stream," *American Midland Naturalist* 69, no. 1 (January 1963), 136, 144–146, 148–149.

81. Sean C. Mitchell and Richard A. Cunjak, "Stream Flow, Salmon and Beaver Dams: Roles in the Structuring of Stream Fish Communities Within an Anadromous Salmon Dominated Stream," *Journal of Animal Ecology* 76, no. 6 (November 2007), 1062–1074; James G. MacCracken and Allen D. Lebovitz, "Selection of In-Stream Wood Structures by Beaver in the Bear River, Southwest Washington," *Northwestern Naturalist* 86, no. 2 (Autumn 2005), 49–50, 55.

82. P. Collen and R. J. Gibson, "The General Ecology of Beaver (*Castor* spp.), as Related to Their Influence on Stream Ecosystems and Riparian Habitats, and the Subsequent Effects on Fish: A Review," *Reviews in Fish Biology and Fisheries* 10, no. 4 (2001), 448, 449; Ethan Jay Nedeau, *Freshwater Mussels and the Connecticut River Watershed* (Greenfield, MA: Connecticut River Watershed Council, 2008), 9; Naiman, Melillo, and Hobbie, "Ecosystem Alteration," 1266.

83. Merchant, *Ecological Revolutions*, 66; Wilson, *Beaver in Connecticut*, 6.

84. Thomas, "The Fur Trade," 371–373.

85. Thomas, "The Fur Trade," 369–371.

86. Jean O'Brien, *Firsting and Lasting: Writing Indians out of Existence in New England* (Minneapolis: University of Minnesota Press, 2010), 106–107, 118; Lisa Brooks, "Introduction," in *Dawnland Voices: An Anthology of Indigenous Writing from New England*, ed. Siobhan Senier (Lincoln: University of Nebraska Press, 2014), 250.

87. Merchant, *Ecological Revolutions*, 36–37; Donahue, *Great Meadow*, 49; Naiman, Johnston, and Kelley, "Alteration of North American Streams," 754–757, 759; Robert J. Naiman et al., "Beaver Influences on the Long-Term Biogeochemical Characteristics of Boreal Forest Drainage Networks," *Ecology* 75, no. 5 (June 1994), 906; Isaac J. Schlosser, "Dispersal, Boundary Processes, and Trophic-Level Interactions in Stream Adjacent to Beaver Ponds," *Ecology* 76, no. 3 (April 1995), 908, 920–922; Angela M. Gurnell, "The Hydrogeomorphological Effects of Beaver Dam-Building Activity," *Progress in Physical Geography* 22, no. 2 (1998), 178.

88. Butler and Malanson, "Geomorphic Influences," 50; Naiman, Melillo, and Hobbie, "Ecosystem Alteration,"1254, 1266; Steven Stoll, *Larding the Lean Earth: Soil and Society in Nineteenth-Century America* (New York: Hill and Wang, 2002), 54–61.

89. For pond size and estimates of beaver population density, see Naiman, Johnston, and Kelley, "Alteration of North American Streams," 754; and Johnston and Naiman, "Aquatic Patch Creation," 1617.

90. Building upon estimates from previous authors, beaver dams in a river basin the size of the Connecticut (29,138 km²) may have been responsible for retaining as much as 138.5 million m³ of sediment within the watershed at any given time. Following the beaver's removal, much of this accumulated sediment, along with a far greater proportion of the sediment borne downstream annually, would have found its way out into the sound. Pastore, *Between Land and Sea*, 47–48; Scott W. Nixon, "Prehistoric Nutrient Inputs and Productivity in Narragansett Bay," *Estuaries* 2, no. 2 (June 1997): 255; Naiman, Melillo, and Hobbie, "Ecosystem Alteration," 1258.

91. Timothy Dwight, *Travels in New-England and New-York*, 4 vols. (New Haven, CT: Timothy Dwight, 1821–1822), 1: 236–237. See also, Lewis Evans, *Geographical, Historical, Political, Philosophical and Mechanical Essays* (Philadelphia, PA: B. Franklin and D. Hall, 1755), 20.

92. Butler and Malanson, "Geomorphic Influences," 50.

93. William J. Mitsch and James G. Gosselink, "The Value of Wetlands: Importance of Scale and Landscape Setting," *Ecological Economics* 35, no. 1 (October 2000), 28; Joy B. Zedler, "Wetlands at Your Service: Reducing Impacts of Agriculture at the Watershed Scale," *Frontiers in Ecology and the Environment* 1, no. 2 (March 2003), 65–67; Carol A. Johnston, Naomi E. Detenbeck, and Gerald J. Niemi, "The Cumulative Effect of Wetlands on Stream Water Quality and Quantity: A Landscape Approach," *Biogeochemistry* 10, no. 2 (July 1990), 130, 135; Arnold O'Brien, "Evaluating the Cumulative Effects of Alteration on New England Wetlands," *Environmental Management* 12, no. 5 (1988), 628, 630; Naiman, Johnston, and Kelley, "Alteration of North American Streams," 360–361; Hey and Philippi, "Flood Reduction," 9.

94. Belknap, *The History of New-Hampshire*, 3: 77, 154.

95. Gurnell, "Hydrogeomorphological Effects," 168.

96. Judd, *History of Hadley*, 355–356.

97. In doing so, he paraphrases from Edward Johnson's *Wonder-Working Providence*. Brian Donahue, *Great Meadow*, 77.

98. Springfield, Massachusetts (Town), *The First Century of the History of Springfield: The Official Records from 1636 to 1736*, ed. Henry M. Burt, 2 vols. (Springfield, MA: Henry M. Burt), 1: 165.

99. "Hartford Town Votes," *Collections of the Connecticut Historical Society*, 31 vols. (Hartford: Connecticut Historical Society, 1897), 6: 28.

100. Springfield (Town), *History of Springfield*, 1: 356.

101. William DeLoss Love, *The Colonial History of Hartford: Gathered from the Original Records* (Hartford, CT: William DeLoss Love, 1914), 135–137, 165.

102. Connecticut (Colony), *Public Records*, 3: 132, 132n, 179n, 185.

103. Love, *Colonial History of Hartford*, 211–212.

104. Springfield (Town), *History of Springfield*, 1: 165, 168, 274–275, 2: 60, 62–63.

105. Timothy Silver, *A New Face on the Countryside: Indians, Colonists, and Slaves in South Atlantic Forests, 1500–1800* (New York: Cambridge University Press, 1990), 100.

106. Charles C. Mann, *1493: Uncovering the New World Columbus Created* (New York: Knopf, 2011), 104–107, 112–113; John Duffy, *Epidemics in Colonial America* (Baton Rouge: Louisiana State University Press, 1953), 203.

107. Mann, *1493*, 112.

108. Edward William Hooker, *The Life of Thomas Hooker* (Boston: Massachusetts Sabbath School Society, 1870), 47.

109. Duffy, *Epidemics in Colonial America*, 206–207; Darrett B. Rutman and Anita H. Rutman, "Of Agues and Fevers: Malaria in the Early Chesapeake," *William and Mary Quarterly* 33, no. 1 (January 1976), 50–51; Gerald N. Grob, *The Deadly Truth: A History of Disease in America* (Cambridge, MA: Harvard University Press, 2002), 86; Virginia Dejohn Anderson, "Thomas Minor's World: Agrarian Life in Seventeenth-Century New England," *Agricultural History* 82, no. 4 (Fall 2008), 509; A. W. Barrows, "President's Address on Malarial Fever in New England," *Proceedings of the Connecticut Medical Society, Eighty-Fifth Annual Convention* (Hartford: Connecticut Medical Society, 1876), 24; Mann, *1493*, 112; Edward Ward, *A Trip to New-England with a Character of the Country and People, Both English and Indians* (London, 1699), 9. Ward, a satirical author who never visited any of England's mainland colonies, presumably borrowed his opinion of malaria's prevalence in New England from other authors.

110. Charles H. Levermore, "Witchcraft in Connecticut," *New England Magazine* 6 (March–August 1892), 639–640.

111. "The Winthrop Papers, Part IV" in *Collections of the Massachusetts Historical Society,* Fifth Series (Boston: Massachusetts Historical Society, 1882), 6: 144.

112. N. N., *A Short Account of the Present State of New-England* ([London?], 1690), 4.

113. J. F. A. Adams, "Malaria in New England," in *Public Health: Papers and Reports: Vol. VII: Presented at the Ninth Annual Meeting of the American Public Health Association (Savannah, GA, Nov. 28 to Dec. 3) 1881* (Boston: Houghton, Mifflin, 1883), 170.

114. Darrett B. Rutman and Anita H. Rutman suggest that perhaps malaria was never well established in New England and simply died out after the end of the Great Migration cut off a fresh supply of infected hosts. This fails to explain why new malaria outbreaks persisted after 1640—apparently up until the 1690s. It also evades the question of why the considerable exchange of population that took place because of the New England slave trade and the region's commerce with the West Indies did not result in a reintroduction through the movement of infected hosts. Rutman and Rutman, "Of Fevers and Agues," 51. See also Richard Tren and Donald W. Roberts, *The Excellent Powder: DDT's Political and Scientific History* (Indianapolis, IN: Dog Ear Publications, 2010), 349; Grob, *Deadly Truth*, 86; Margaret Humphreys, *Malaria: Poverty, Race, and Public Health in the United States* (Baltimore: Johns Hopkins Press, 2001), 138.

115. Oliver Wendell Holmes, "Dissertation of Intermittent Fever in New England," in *Boylston Prize Dissertations for the Years 1836 and 1837* (Boston: Charles C. Little and James Brown, 1838), 89–90, 93–94.

116. Holmes, "Dissertation," 86.

117. Adams, "Malaria in New England," 168–169, 170; N. S. Shaler, "Environment and Man in New England," *North American Review* 162, no. 475 (June 1896), 733–734; Marcus L. Hansen, "The Second Colonization of New England," *New England Quarterly* 2, no. 4 (October 1929), 557.

118. Adams, "Malaria in New England," 170; Curtis R. Best, "A History of Mosquitoes in Massachusetts," Northeastern Mosquito Control Association (November 1993), http://www.nmca.org/Nmca93-4.htm.

Chapter 2

1. David Pieterszen de Vries, *Voyages from Holland to America, A.D. 1632 to 1644*, trans. Henry C. Murphy (New York: Billin and Bros., 1853), 126.

2. Haynes' view on the matter closely mirrors that of his fellow governor, John Winthrop of Massachusetts, for example. John Winthrop, "General Observations for the Plantation of New England," in *The Winthrop Papers*, ed. Stewart Mitchell, 6 vols. (Boston: Massachusetts Historical Society, 1931), 2: 112.

3. John Winthrop, *The History of New England from 1630 to 1649*, ed. James Savage, 2 vols. (Boston: Little, Brown, 1853), 1: 138–139.

4. de Vries, *Voyages from Holland*, 126–128.

5. Edward Johnson, *A History of New-England . . . [Wonder-Working Providence of Sions Saviour . . .]* (London: Printd for Nath. Brooke, 1654), 199.

6. Thomas Breedon, "Narrative and Deposition of Capt. Bredon," in *Documents Relative to the Colonial History of the State of New-York*, 15 vols. (Albany, NY: Weed, Parsons, 1853–1887), 3: 40.

7. For a more detailed discussion of the importance of Native American women's agency in introducing maize cultivation and breeding new species better suited to the cool New England climate, see Carolyn Merchant, *Ecological Revolutions: Nature, Gender, and Science in New England* (Chapel Hill: University of North Carolina Press, 1989), 75–81, and Kathleen J. Bragdon, *Native People of Southern New England, 1500–1650* (Norman: University of Oklahoma Press, 1996), 50–53.

8. Neal Salisbury, *Manitou and Providence: Indians, Europeans, and the Making of New England, 1500–1643* (New York: Oxford University Press, 1982), 18; Bragdon, *Native People*, 31, 55–79, 90–91; Lucianne Lavin, *Connecticut's Indigenous Peoples: What Archaeology, History, and Oral Traditions Teach Us About Their Communities and Culture* (New Haven, CT: Yale University Press, 2013), 193; Bragdon, *Native People*, 31, 55–79.

9. Lavin, *Connecticut's Indigenous Peoples*, 192, 201.

10. Howard S. Russell, *Indian New England Before the* Mayflower (Hanover, NH: University of New England Press, 1980), 14; Bragdon, *Native People*, 91–92; Lisa Brooks, *The Common Pot: The Recovery of Native Space in the Northeast* (Minneapolis: University of Minnesota Press, 2008), 12, 17.

11. John Smith, *A Description of New England* (London: Printed by Humfrey Lownes for Robert Clerke, 1616), Huntington Library, Rare Books Collection, #32514-PHOTOSTAT, 17.

12. Winthrop, *History of New England*, 1: 62–63.

13. For a full discussion of this groundbreaking thesis of the causes of the Pequot War, see Katherine Grandjean, "New World Tempests: Environment, Scarcity, and the Coming of the Pequot War," *William and Mary Quarterly* 68, no. 1 (January 2011), 75–100 passim; and Katherine Grandjean, *American Passage: The Communications Frontier in Early New England* (Cambridge, MA: Harvard University Press, 2015), 34–40.

14. Grandjean, "New World Tempests," 77, 80–81, 83; Grandjean, *American Passage*, 20; William Pynchon et al., *Colonial Justice in Western Massachusetts (1639–1702): The Pynchon Court Record, An Original Judges' Diary of the Administration in the Springfield Courts in the Massachusetts Bay Colony*, ed. Joseph H. Smith (Cambridge, MA: Harvard University Press, 1961), 14.

15. Grandjean, "New World Tempests," 78; Grandjean, *American Passage*, 25–26, 30, 33, 38, 144; Connecticut (Colony), *The Public Records of the Colony of Connecticut, from April 1636 to October 1776*, 15 vols. (Hartford, CT: Brown and Parsons, 1850–1890), 1: 3–4;

16. Grandjean, "New World Tempests," 92, 94, 100.

17. This impulse to control the market in corn offers a reminder that for the English, just as for Native American trading partners, trade operated within a "socio-cultural world," as Peter A. Thomas has put it. For English leaders, enforcing a "just price" meant ensuring the welfare

of colonists while also exerting social control over Indian trading partners. Peter A. Thomas, "The Fur Trade, Indian Land, and the Need to Define Adequate 'Environmental' Parameters," *Ethnohistory* 28, no. 4 (Autumn 1981), 360, 363.

18. William Pynchon et al., *Colonial Justice in Western Massachusetts*, 14–15; John Mason, "A Brief History of the Pequot War," in *History of the Pequot War: The Contemporary Accounts of Mason, Underhill, Vincent and Gardener*, ed. Charles Orr (Cleveland, OH: Helman-Taylor, 1897), 46; Peter A. Thomas, "Into the Maelstrom of Change," in *A Place Called Paradise: Culture and Community in Northampton, Massachusetts, 1654–2004*, ed. Kerry W. Buckley (Amherst: Historic Northampton Museum and Education Center in association with the University of Massachusetts Press, 2004), 9.

19. Thomas, "The Fur Trade," 363–369.

20. Thomas, "Into the Maelstrom," 13; Thomas, "The Fur Trade," 372.

21. Harry Andrew Wright, ed., *The Indian Deeds of Hampden County* (Springfield, MA, 1905) 26–27; Margaret Bruchac, "Native Presence in Nonotuck and Northampton," in *A Place Called Paradise: Culture and Community in Northampton, Massachusetts, 1654–2004*, ed. Kerry W. Buckley (Amherst: Historic Northampton Museum and Education Center in association with the University of Massachusetts Press, 2004), 24.

22. John Pynchon, *The Pynchon Papers*, ed. Carl Bridenbaugh and Juliette Tomlinson, 2 vols. (Boston: Colonial Society of Massachusetts, distributed by the University Press of Virginia, 1985), 2: 26–27, 278, 286–288; Alice Nash, "Quanquan's Mortgage of 1663," in *Cultivating a Past: Essays on the History of Hadley, Massachusetts*, ed. Marla R. Miller (Amherst: University of Massachusetts Press, 2009), 33–35; Thomas, "The Fur Trade," 372–373.

23. Thomas, "The Fur Trade," 366–366.

24. John Pynchon, *The Pynchon Papers*, 2: 26–27, 278, 286–288; Margaret M. Bruchac, "Revisiting Pocumtuck History in Deerfield: George Sheldon's Vanishing Indian Act," *Historical Journal of Massachusetts* 39, no. 1/2 (Summer 2011), 25; Nash, "Quanquan's Mortgage," 33–35.

25. Thomas, "The Fur Trade," 372–373, 375.

26. Peter A. Thomas, "Contrastive Subsistence Strategies and Land Use Factors for Understanding Indian-White Relations in New England," *Ethnohistory* 23, no. 1 (Winter 1976), 4.

27. Margaret Ellen Newell, *Brethren by Nature: New England Indians, Colonists, and the Origins of American Slavery* (Ithaca, NY: Cornell University Press, 2015), 136.

28. Massachusetts (Colony), *The Acts and Laws of the Province of Massachusetts Bay*, 21 vols. (Boston: Wright & Potter, 1869), 1: 152; Virginia DeJohn Anderson, *Creatures of Empire: How Domestic Animals Transformed Early America* (New York: Oxford University Press, 2004), 175–199; William Cronon, *Changes in the Land: Indians, Colonists, and the Ecology of New England* (New York: Hill & Wang, 1983), 129–132, 136–137.

29. James D. Drake, *King Philip's War: Civil War in New England, 1675–1676* (Amherst: University of Massachusetts Press, 1999), 55–56, 85–90; Daniel R. Mandell, *King Philip's War: Colonial Expansion, Native Resistance and the End of Indian Sovereignty* (Baltimore: Johns Hopkins University Press, 2010), 30, 60–65, 71–77; Lavin, *Connecticut's Indigenous Peoples*, 331–335; Eric B. Schultz and Michael J. Tougias, *King Philip's War: The History and Legacy of America's Forgotten Conflict* (Woodstock, VT: Countryman Press, 1999), 46–47, 50–52; Yasuhide Kawashima, *Igniting King Philip's War: The John Sassamon Murder Trial* (Lawrence: University Press of Kansas, 2001), 147–148; Newell, *Brethren by Nature*, 50, 175.

30. This process often led not only to the seizure of Native land but to the seizure of Native individuals as slaves through a system of colonial debt-peonage that Margaret Ellen

Newell has termed "judicial enslavement." Margaret Ellen Newell, "Indian Slavery in Colonial New England," in *Indian Slavery in Colonial America*, ed. Alan Gallay (Lincoln: University of Nebraska Press, 2009), 52–57; and Newell, *Brethren by Nature*, 215–236.

31. Massachusetts (Colony), *The Acts and Laws of the Province of Massachusetts Bay*, 21 vols. (Boston: Wright & Potter, 1869–1922), 1: 152; Connecticut (Colony), *Public Records*, 4: 248–249; Jean M. O'Brien, "'Divorced' from the Land: Resistance and Survival of Indian Women in Eighteenth-Century New England," in *After King Philip's War: Presence and Persistence in Indian New England*, ed. Colin. G. Calloway (Hanover, NH: University Press of New England, 1997), 145–146, 149–151; Drake, *King Philip's War*, 94–96; Newell, *Brethren by Nature*, 119; Joshua Micah Marshall, "'A Melancholy People': Anglo-Indian Relations in Early Warwick, Rhode Island, 1642–1675," in *New England Encounters: Indians and Euroamericans, ca. 1600–1850*, ed. Alden T. Vaughn (Boston: Northeastern University Press, 1999), 102.

32. Thomas L. Doughton, "Unseen Neighbors: Native Americans of Central Massachusetts, a People Who Had 'Vanished,'" in *After King Philip's War: Presence and Persistence in Indian New England*, ed. Colin. G. Calloway (Hanover, NH: University Press of New England, 1997), 207–280, 218–221; Daniel R. Mandell, *Tribe, Race, History: Native Americans in Southern New England, 1780–1880* (Baltimore: Johns Hopkin University Press, 2008), 153, 214; Newell, "Indian Slavery," 45; Linford D. Fisher, *The Indian Great Awakening: Religion and the Shaping of Native Cultures in Early America* (Oxford: Oxford University Press, 2012), 11; Donna Keith Baron, J. Edward Hood, and Holly V. Izard, "They Were Here All Along: The Native American Presence in Lower-Central New England in the Eighteenth and Nineteenth Centuries," *William and Mary Quarterly* 53, no. 3 (July 1996), 573.

33. "Wangunk," *Yale Indian Papers Project*, Yale University, accessed June 29, 2016, http://yipp.yale.edu/tribe/83.

34. Quotation from Connecticut (Colony), *Public Records*, 1: 19–20. Sherman W. Adams, "Wethersfield," in *The Memorial History of Hartford County, Connecticut, 1633–1884*, ed. James Hammond Trumbull, 2 vols. (Boston: Edward L. Osgood, 1886), 2: 319; R. W. Bacon, "Native Americans in Middletown: Who Called It 'Home' Before Our 'First Settlers'?" *The Middler: Newsletter of the Society of Middletown First Settlers Descendants, Part I* 10, no. 1 (Spring 2010), 8.

35. William DeLoss Love, *The Colonial History of Hartford: Gathered From the Original Records* (Hartford, CT: William DeLoss Love, 1914), 96–97; Lavin, *Connecticut's Indigenous Peoples*, 332–333; Connecticut (Colony), *Public Records*, 2: 378–379.

36. "The Memorial of Job Bates and Isaac Waterman," *Yale Indian Papers Project*, Yale University, accessed June 29, 2016, http://yipp.yale.edu/annotated-transcription/digcoll2434.

37. Thomas, "Contrastive Subsistence Strategies," 8–9.

38. Wright, *Indian Deeds*, 57–60; Bruchac, "Revisiting Pocumtuck History," 47.

39. Claudia Mason Chicklas, "A Profile in Courage," in *Dawnland Voices: An Anthology of Indigenous Writing from New England*, ed. Siobhan Senier (Lincoln: University of Nebraska Press, 2014), 297–299; Bruchac, "Revisiting Pocumtuck History," 61–62; Mali Keating and Gregory L. Sharrow, "North American Passage: The 19th-Century Odyssey of an Abenaki Family," *Visit'n: Conversations with Vermonters* 7 (November 2001), 29–31; Alice Nash, "Odanak Durant les Années 1920, Un Prisme Reflétant l'Histoire des Abénaquis," trans. Claude Gélinas, *Recherches Amérindiennes au Québec* 32, no. 2 (2002), 27–28; Keene, NH (city), Twenty-Second Annual Report of the City of Keene (Keene, NH: Sentinel Printing Company, 1895), 55; Keene, NH (city), Forty-Seventh Annual Report of the City of Keene (Keene, NH: Sentinel Printing

Company, 1921), 449; Hamilton Child, *The First Gazetteer of Cheshire County, N.H. 1736–1885* (Syracuse, NY: Journal Office, 1885), 118.

40. Doughton, "Unseen Neighbors," 207–280, 218–221. Mandell, *Tribe, Race, History*, 153, 214; Newell, "Indian Slavery," 45; Fisher, *Indian Great Awakening*, 11; Baron, Hood, and Izard, "'They Were Here All Along,'" 573.

41　James McSparran, "A Reprint of *America Dissected, Being a Full and True Account of All the American Colonies*," in Wilkins Updike, *A History of the Episcopal Church in Narragansett, Rhode Island*, ed. Daniel Goodwin, 3 vols. (Boston: D. B. Updike, 1907), 3: 29.

42. Max George Schumacher, *The Northern Farmer and His Markets During the Late Colonial Period*, Dissertations in American Economic History (New York: Arno Press, 1975), 30, 32.

43. Cronon, *Changes in the Land*, 47–51.

44. Marc D. Abrams and Gregory J. Nowacki, "Native Americans as Active and Passive Promoters of Mast and Fruit Trees in the Eastern USA," *Holocene* 18, no. 7 (2008), 1124, 1130, 1132; Cronon, *Changes in the Land*, 51.

45. For examples: Judd, *History of Hadley*, 46; Springfield (Town), *History of Springfield*, 2: 155; Temple, *Town of Palmer*, 20.

46. "Reverend J. H. Temple's Address," *History and Proceedings of the Pocumtuck Valley Memorial Association, 1870–1879*, 2 vols. (Deerfield, MA: Pocumtuck Valley Memorial Association, 1890), 1: 116.

47. Temple, *Town of Palmer*, 20; Judd, *History of Hadley*, 106; Connecticut (Colony), *The Code of 1650, Being the Compilation of the Earliest Laws and Orders of the General Court of Connecticut* (Hartford: Andrus & Judd, 1833), 47.

48. Judd, *History of Hadley*, 106.

49. For examples: Springfield (Town), *History of Springfield*, 1: 429; "Hartford Town Votes," in *Collections of the Connecticut Historical Society*, 31 vols. (Hartford: Connecticut Historical Society, 1860–1967), 6: 283, 316; Judd, *History of Hadley*, 106; and Connecticut (Colony), *Public Records*, 3: 30.

50. Cronon, *Changes in the Land*, 144–146.

51　Brian Donahue, *The Great Meadow: Farmers and the Land in Colonial Concord* (New Haven, CT: Yale University Press, 2004), 4, 88–89; Jelle Zeilinga de Boer, *Stories in Stone: How Geology Influenced Connecticut History and Culture* (Middletown, CT: Wesleyan University Press, 2009), 88–90.

52. Thomas Lechford, *Plain Dealing, or Nevves from New England* (London: Printed for Nath. Butter, 1642), 47.

53. John Winthrop Jr., quoted in Fulmer Mood, "John Winthrop, Jr., on Indian Corn," *New England Quarterly* 10, no. 1 (March 1937), 125.

54. Howard S. Russell, *A Long Deep Furrow: Three Centuries of Farming in New England* (Hanover: University of New Hampshire Press, 1976), 41; Merchant, *Ecological Revolutions*, 179–180.

55. Quotation from Russell, *A Long Deep Furrow*, 133, and Stephen Innes, *Labor in a New Land: Economy and Society in Seventeenth-Century Springfield* (Princeton, NJ: Princeton University Press, 1983), 33. See also Vern Grubinger, "Winter Rye: A Reliable Cover Crop," *Cultivating Healthy Communities: A Publication of UVM Extension's Vermont Vegetable and Berry Program*, University of Vermont (October 2010), accessed August 16, 2016, https://www.uvm.edu/vtvegandberry/factsheets/winterrye.html; E. A. Oelke et al., "Rye," *Corn Agronomy: Where Science Meets the Field*, UW Extension, University of Wisconsin, accessed August 16, 2016,

http://corn.agronomy.wisc.edu/Crops/Rye.aspx; Sustainable Agriculture Research & Education (SARE), "Winter Wheat: *Triticum aestivum*," *Managing Cover Crops Profitably*, USDA, accessed August 16, 2016, http://www.sare.org/Learning-Center/Books/Managing-Cover-Crops -Profitably-3rd-Edition/Text-Version/Nonlegume-Cover-Crops/Winter-Wheat.

56. Russell, *A Long Deep Furrow*, 42; Christopher Clark, *The Roots of Rural Capitalism: Western Massachusetts, 1780–1860* (Ithaca, NY: Cornell University Press, 1990), 42.

57. Russell, *A Long Deep Furrow*, 42.

58   The price was first adjusted downwards in May before being raised to two shillings and eight pence in December of the same year. The official price was returned to two shillings and six pence in February of the next year. Connecticut (Colony), *Public Records*, 1: 72, 79, 118, 205.

59. For example, Samuel Martin of Wethersfield and William Andrews of Hartford were charged in 1645 with exporting grain without the permission of the monopoly, but only after their fully laden ship had sailed away. Connecticut (Colony), *Public Records*, 1: 116–117, 119–121, 140, 170, 379, 392.

60. John Winthrop Jr. to Unknown, September 19 1660, "The Winthrop Papers (Continued), Part IV)," in *Collections of the Massachusetts Historical Society*, Fifth Series, vol. 8 (Boston: Massachusetts Historical Society, 1882), 65–66.

61. Connecticut (Colony), *Public Records*, 2: 270–270, 277–278.

62. Connecticut (Colony), *Public Records*, 3: 297; Great Britain, Public Records Office, *Calendar of State Papers, Colonial Series*, ed. William Noel Sainsbury, J. W. Fortescue, and Cecil Headlam, 45 vols. (London: Mackie and Co. Ld. and His Majesty's Stationery Service, 1860–1926), 10: 576–577.

63. Boston (city), *Documents of the City of Boston for the Year 1876*, 3 vols. (Boston: Rockwell and Churchill, 1877), 3: 4; Ian K. Steele, *The English Atlantic, 1675–1740: An Exploration of Communication and Community* (New York: Oxford University Press, 1986), 337n44; United States, Bureau of the Census, *Historical Statistics of the United States: Colonial Times to 1970*, 2 vols. (Washington, DC: U.S. Department of Commerce, Bureau of the Census, 1975), 2: 1168.

64. Great Britain, Public Records Office, *Calendar of State Papers*, 26: 258.

65. For a detailed account of how mainland traders parlayed West Indies exports into credit with English and other European merchants, or into bills of exchange for paying those merchants, see Richard Pares, *Yankees and Creoles: The Trade Between North America and the West Indies Before the American Revolution* (New York: Archon Books, 1968), 153–161.

66. Richard S. Dunn, *Sugar and Slaves: The Rise of the Planter Class in the English West Indies, 1624–1713* (Chapel Hill: Published for the Omohundro Institute of Early American History and Culture by the University of North Carolina Press, 1972), 87; United States, Bureau of the Census, *Historical Statistics*, 2: 1168.

67. Connecticut (Colony), *Public Records*, 3: 297.

68. Pares, *Yankees and Creoles*, 2; Innes, *Labor In a New Land*, 33; Richard B. Sheridan, *Sugar and Slavery: An Economic History of the British West Indies, 1623–1775* (Baltimore: Johns Hopkins University Press, 1973), 106, 220–221; Richard B. Sheridan, "The Crisis of Slave Subsistence in the British West Indies During and after the American Revolution," *William and Mary Quarterly* 33, no. 4 (October 1976), 615–641; David Watts, "Cycles of Famine in Islands of Plenty," in *Famine as a Geographical Phenomenon*, ed. B. Currey and G. Hugo (Dordrecht, the Netherlands: D. Reidel, 1984), 58; Andrew Jackson O'Shaughnessy, *An Empire Divided: The American Revolution and the British Caribbean* (Philadelphia: University of Pennsylvania Press, 2000), 161–163, 174.

69. Great Britain, Public Records Office, *Calendar of State Papers*, 24: 207.

70. Connecticut (Colony), *Public Records*, 7: 582–583.

71. Connecticut (Colony), *Public Records*, 7: 583

72. Great Britain, Public Records Office, *Calendar of State Papers*, 41: 12.

73. Frank Wesley Pitman, *The Development of the British West Indies, 1700–1763* (New Haven, CT: Yale University Press, 1917), 288–290, 326.

74. Dorothy Burne Goebel, "The 'New England Trade' and the French West Indies, 1763–1774: A Study in Trade Policies," *William and Mary Quarterly* 20, no. 3 (July 1963), 332, 126–132; Thomas M. Truxes, *Defying Empire: Trading with the Enemy in Colonial New York* (New Haven, CT: Yale University Press, 2008), 58–60; Sheridan, *Sugar and Slavery*, 319; Trevor Burnhard and John Garrigus, *The Plantation Machine: Atlantic Capitalism in French Saint-Dominique and British America* (Philadelphia: University of Pennsylvania Press, 2016), 113–115.

75. Great Britain, Public Records Office, *Calendar of State Papers*, 38: 384–386.

76. Wim Klooster and Gert Oostindie, *Realm Between Empires: The Second Dutch Atlantic, 1680–1815* (Ithaca, NY: Cornell University Press, 2018), 40–42; John Bonnett, *Emergence and Empire: Innis, Complexity, and the Trajectory of History* (Montreal, QC: McGill-Queen's University Press, 2013), 114–115; Pitman, *Development of the British West Indies*, 272–296; Pares, *Yankees and Creoles*, 56–57.

77. Lords Commissioners for Trade and Plantation, "Official Transcripts of Reports on the State of the British Colonies in North America and the West Indies: 1721–1766," British Library, Western Manuscripts Collection, Kings MS 205, f. 220–220b.

78. Schumacher, *The Northern Farmer*, 143.

79. Merchant, *Ecological Revolutions*, 6–8; Donahue, *The Great Meadow*, 56–58.

80. de Boer, *Stories in Stone*, 96–98; Jane Mt. Pleasant, "A New Paradigm for Pre-Columbian Agriculture in North America," *Early American Studies: An Interdisciplinary Journal* 13, no. 2 (Spring 2015), 381–2, 30—3, 400, 411; Donahue, *The Great Meadow*, 43; Cronon, *Changes in the Land*, 150; Merchant, *Ecological Revolutions*, 6–8, 165.

81. Arthur L. Brandegee and Eddy N. Smith, *Farmington, Connecticut: The Village of Beautiful Homes* (Farmington, CT: A.L. Brandegee and E.N. Smith, 1906), 79; Josiah Howard Temple, *History of the Town of Palmer Massachusetts* (Springfield, MA: Town of Palmer, 1889), 40.

82. Russell, *A Long Deep Furrow*, 133.

83. Judd, *History of Hadley*, 362–363.

84. Grant Powers, *Historical Sketch of the Coos Country, 1754–1785* (Haverhill, NH: Henry Merrill, 1880), 75.

85. Quotations from John Josselyn, *An Account of Two Voyages to New-England . . .* (London: Printed for Giles Widdows, 1674), 188–189; Oxford English Dictionary, "blast, *n.¹*," *OED Online*, Oxford University Press, http://www.oed.com/view/Entry/19936?rskey=7XbqiU&result=1&isAdvanced=false (accessed 09 Aug 2016).

86. Quotation from Connecticut (Colony), *The Public Records of the Colony of Connecticut, From April 1636 to October 1776*, 15 vols. (Hartford: Brown and Parsons, 1850–1890), 2: 129–130.

87. Josselyn, *Account of Two Voyages*, 189.

88. John Hull, "The diaries of John Hull, Mint-master and Treasurer of the Colony of Massachusetts Bay," in *Transactions and Collections of the American Antiquarian Society*, 12 vols. (Worcester, MA: American Antiquarian Society, 1820–1911), 3: 218.

89. Quoted in Percy Wells Bidwell and John I. Falconer, *History of Agriculture in the Northern United States, 1620–1860* (Washington, DC: The Carnegie Institute, 1925), 13–14.

90. The "wormes" may also have been an import, possibly the pea leaf weevil whose eggs and/or larvae could have hitched a ride across the Atlantic in peapods brought as provisions or seed. Or, these worms may have been native pests—such as the armyworm, wireworm, or cutworm—that had long plagued Indian fields. Connecticut (Colony), *Public Records*, 3: 297.

91. Connecticut (Colony), *Public Records*, 7: 10–11.

92. Richard N. Mack, "Plant Naturalizations and Invasions in the Eastern United States: 1634–1860," Annals of the Missouri Botanical Garden 90, no. 1 (Winter 2003), 84.

93. Clark, *Roots of Rural Capitalism*, 42; Cronon, *Change in the Land*, 153;

94. Great Britain, Public Records Office, *Calendar of State Papers, Colonial Series*, ed. William Noel Sainsbury, J. W. Fortescue, and Cecil Headlam, 45 vols. (London: Mackie and Co. Ld. and His Majesty's Stationery Service, 1860–1926), 12: 350.

95. Great Britain, Public Records Office, *Calendar of State Papers*, 13: 255.

96. Great Britain, Public Records Office, *Calendar of State Papers*, 23:191.

97. Ronald Bailey, "The Slave(ry) Trade and the Development of Capitalism in the United States: The Textile Industry in New England," *Social Science History* 14, no. 3 (Autumn 1990),374–375, 380; Jacob M. Price, "The Imperial Economy, 1700–1776," in *The Oxford History of the British Empire*, ed. William Roger Louis et al., 5 vols. (Oxford: Oxford University Press, 1998–1999), 2: 90–91; B. W. Higman, "The Sugar Revolution," *The Economic History Review* 53, no. 2 (May 2000), 225–226; Gilman M. Ostrander, "The Colonial Molasses Trade," *Agricultural History* 30, no. 2 (Apr. 1956), 82–84; Lizzie Collingham, *The Taste of Empire: How Britain's Quest for Food Shaped the Modern World* (New York: Basic Books, 2017), 132–133.

98. Cronon, *Changes in the Land*, 147, 150; Merchant, *Ecological Revolutions*, 153–165, 153–156; Donahue, *The Great Meadow*, 166, 208–210; Russell, *A Long Deep Furrow*, 42, 133.

99. Sylvester Judd, *History of Hadley, Including the Early History of Hatfield, South Hadley, Amherst and Granby, Massachusetts* (Northampton, MA: Metcalf & Company, 1863), 363; Russell, *A Long Deep Furrow*, 132–133.

100. Hartford (Town), "The Original Distribution of the Lands in Hartford Among the Settlers, 1639," *Collections of the Connecticut Historical Society*, 31 vols. (Hartford: Connecticut Historical Society, 1912), 14: 20, 58, 300.

101. Russell, *A Long Deep Furrow*, 91.

102. Dean Albertson, "Puritan Liquor in the Planting of New England," *New England Quarterly* 23, no. 4 (December 1950), 480.

103. Richard L. Bushman, From *Puritan to Yankee: Character and the Social Order in Connecticut, 1690–1765* (Cambridge, MA: Harvard University Press, 1967), 108; Sarah. F. McMahon, "A Comfortable Subsistence: The Changing Composition of Diet in Rural New England, 1620–1840," *William and Mary Quarterly* 42, no. 4 (January 1985), 42; Russell, *A Long Deep Furrow*, 91.

104. Judd, *History of Hadley*, 72–73; Hartford County, Connecticut, *Hartford County, Connecticut, County Court Minutes Volumes 3 and 4 1663–1687, 1697*, ed. Helen Schatvet Ullman (Boston: New England Genealogical Society, 2005), 121, 321.

105. Great Britain, Public Records Office, *Calendar of State Papers*, 10: 576

106. Russell, *A Long Deep Furrow*, 114, 142; John Chauncey Pease and John Milton Niles, *Gazetteer of the States of Connecticut and Rhode-Island* (Hartford, CT: William S. Marsh, 1819), 89; Thomas F. De Voe, *The Market Assistant* (New York: Hurd and Houghton, 1867), 338.

107. Edmund Delaney, *The Connecticut River: New England's Historic Waterway* (Guilford, CT: Globe Pequot, 1983), 31.

108. Russell, *A Long Deep Furrow*, 142.

109. Great Britain, Public Records Office, *Calendar of State Papers*, 10: 576.

110. J. Q. Bittinger, *History of Haverhill, N.H.* (Haverhill, NH: Cohos Steam, 1888), 368.

111. Connecticut (Colony), *Public Records*, 1: 61.

112. "Hartford Town Votes," 75; Russell, *A Long Deep Furrow*, 139.

113. Great Britain, Public Records Office, *Calendar of State Papers*, 10: 528, 576.

114. Schumacher, *The Northern Farmer*, 30.

115. Thomas Fitch, "The Fitch Papers: Correspondence and Documents During Thomas Fitch's Governorship of the Colony of Connecticut, 1754–1766, Volume I," in *Collections of the Connecticut Historical Society*, 31 vols. (Hartford: Connecticut Historical Society, 1860–1967), 17: 212.

116. John Smith, *Advertisements for the Unexperienced Planters of New-England* (London: John Haviland, 1631), 4; Great Britain, Public Records Office, *Calendar of State Papers*, 9: 73; New Hampshire (colony), *The Provincial Papers of New Hampshire*, ed. Nathaniel Bouton et al., 39 vols. (Concord and Nashua, NH: various printers, 1867–1941), 3: 780.

117. Great Britain, Public Records Office, *Calendar of State Papers*, 2: 348.

118. John Holroyd, Earl of Sheffield, *Observations on the Commerce of the American States* (London: J. Debrett, 1784), 103.

119. Timothy Dwight, *Travels in New-England and New-York*, 4 vols. (New Haven, CT: Timothy Dwight, 1821–1822), 1: 49–50, 109, 3: 73.

120. Russell, *A Long Deep Furrow*, 117; Thomas M. Truxes, "Connecticut in the Irish-American Flaxseed Trade, 1750–1775," Éire-Ireland: A Journal of Irish Studies 12, no. 2 (1977), 39–40.

121. Judd, *History of Hadley*, 385.

122. Stuart Bruchey, *The Colonial Merchant: Sources and Readings* (New York: Harcourt, Brace, & World, 1966), 172–173; Truxes, "Connecticut in the Irish-American Flaxseed Trade," 35.

123. Thomas M. Truxes, *Irish-American Trade, 1660–1783* (Cambridge: Cambridge University Press, 1988), 194–196, 198; Sheffield, *Observations*, 103.

124. Jared Eliot, *A Continuation on the Essay Upon Field-Husbandry, As It Is, or May Be Ordered in New England* (New London, CT: T. Green, 1751), 10.

125. Quoted in Truxes, "Connecticut in the Irish-American Flaxseed Trade," 36.

126. Connecticut (Colony), *Public Records*, 14: 344–345, 498.

127. Truxes, "Connecticut in the Irish-American Flaxseed Trade," 57.

128. Victor S. Clark, *History of the Manufactures in the United States, 1697–1860* (Washington, DC: Carnegie Institution of Washington, 1916), 82; Russell, *A Long Deep Furrow*, 117; Truxes, "Connecticut in the Irish-American Flaxseed Trade," 38–40, 57.

129. John Adams, *The Works of John Adams*, ed. Charles Francis Adams, 10 vols. (Boston: Charles C. Little and James Brown, 1850–1856), 2: 342; Michelle M. Mormul, "The Linen and Flaxseed Trade of Philadelphia, 1765 to 1815," (PhD diss., University of Delaware, 2010), 89–90.

130. Judd, *History of Hadley*, 385; Charles Hopkins Clark "The Growth of the County," in *The Memorial History of Hartford County, Connecticut, 1633–1884*, ed. James Hammond Trumbull, 2 vols. (Boston: Edward L. Osgood, 1886), 1: 210.

131. New Hampshire (colony), *The Provincial Papers of New Hampshire*, 24: 387, 395, 433, 474, 535, 552, 558, 561, 608, etc.

132. See for examples Jonathan Chase Financial Papers, New Hampshire Historical Society, Manuscript Section, M 1878-001, passim; Samuel Blodgett Waste Book No. 2, accession number

1996-004, New Hampshire Historical Society, Manuscript Section, passim; John Saunders to Richard Lang, February 2, 1793, Richard Lang Papers, Box 1, Folder 1, "Correspondence, July 1791–Aug 1795," New Hampshire Historical Society, Manuscript Section.

133. Sheffield, *Observations*, 103n.

134. Great Britain, Public Records Office, *Calendar of State Papers*, 41: 18–19; Truxes, "Connecticut in the Irish-American Flaxseed Trade," 47.

135. *The Connecticut Courant*, September 2, 1765, 3.

136. *The Connecticut Courant*, September 8, 1766, 4; John Bidwell, *American Paper Mills, 1690–1832* (Hanover, NH: Dartmouth College Press, 2013), 85, 171, 196.

137. Truxes, "Connecticut in the Irish-American Flaxseed Trade," 50–55. Many trading ventures were not as simple as the straightforward exchanges between Ireland and the colonies or the triangular trade described above. Colonial vessels often made multiple stops between delivering flaxseed to Ireland and returning to the colonies with Irish, English, or Caribbean salt. Mormul, "Linen and Flaxseed Trade," 88, 101–102.

138. Great Britain, Public Records Office, *Calendar of State Papers*, 20: 273.

139. Great Britain, Public Records Office, *Calendar of State Papers*, 24:175.

140. Charles Byron Kuhlmann, *The Development of the Flour-Milling Industry in the United States, with Special Reference to the Industry in Minneapolis* (Boston: Houghton Mifflin, 1929), 64–65; Bidwell and Falconer, *History of Agriculture in the Northern United States*, 93; Clark, *Roots of Rural Capitalism*, 150–152.

Chapter 3

1. William DeLoss Love, *The Colonial History of Hartford: Gathered from the Original Records* (Hartford: William DeLoss Love, 1914), 107–113; and John Winthrop, *The History of New England from 1630 to 1649*, ed. James Savage, 2 vols. (Boston: Little, Brown, 1853), 2: 38–39.

2. Timothy Dwight, *Travels in New-England and New-York*, 4 vols. (New Haven, CT: Timothy Dwight, printed by S. Converse, 1821–1822), 1: 144.

3. Marc D. Abrams and Gregory J. Nowacki, "Native Americans as Active and Passive Promoters of Mast and Fruit Trees in the Eastern USA," *Holocene* 18, no. 7 (2008), 1123–1137; Brian Donahue, *The Great Meadow: Farmers and the Land in Colonial Concord* (New Haven, CT: Yale University Press, 2004), 38–39.

4. Richard Judd, *Second Nature: An Environmental History of New England* (Amherst and Boston: University of Massachusetts Press, 2014), 36–38; D. Foster et al., "The Environmental and Human History of New England," in *Forests in Time: Environmental Consequences of 1,000 Years of Change in New England*, ed. David R. Foster and John D. Aber (New Haven, CT: Yale University Press, 2004), 66–68.

5. Harriet Beecher Stowe, *Old Town Folks* (Boston: Fields, Osgood, 1869), 275.

6. Francis M. Thompson, *History of Greenfield*, 2 vols. (Greenfield, MA: Press of T. Morrey & Son, 1904), 2: 961; Priscilla J. Brewer, *From Fireplace to Cookstove: Technology and the Domestic Ideal in America* (Syracuse, NY: Syracuse University Press, 2000), 8.

7. Brewer, *Fireplace to Cookstove*, 14.

8. Charles William Manwaring, ed., *A Digest of the Early Connecticut Probate Records: Hartford District, 1635–1700*, 3 vols. (Hartford: R. S. Peck & Co., 1904–1906), 1: 353.

9. Brewer, *Fireplace to Cookstove*, 9.

10. Samuel Curwen, *The Journal and Letters of Samuel Curwen: An American in England, from 1775 to 1783*, ed. George Atkinson Ward (Boston: Little, Brown, 1864), 47.

11. Benjamin Franklin, *An Account of the New Invented Pennsylvanian Fire-Places* (Philadelphia: Printed and Sold by B. Franklin, 1744), 5, 38–39, 41.

12. Judith A. McGaw, "So Much Depends upon a Red Wheelbarrow: Agricultural Tool Ownership in the Eighteenth-Century Mid-Atlantic," in *Early American Technology: Making and Doing Things from the Colonial Era to 1850*, ed. Judith A. McGaw (Chapel Hill: Published for the Institute of Early American History and Culture by the University of North Carolina Press, 1994), 353–354.

13. This commonly accepted figure boasts an impressive pedigree. William Cronon, in his classic *Changes in the Land*, suggested that the typical New England household probably consumed somewhere in the range of thirty to forty cords of firewood per year. As his source, Cronon cites a 1923 article by Austin F. Hawes, Connecticut's second state forester. Hawes himself suggests twenty to forty cords as a possible range for annual household firewood consumption, unfortunately without providing the provenance of his estimate. The context of the paragraph suggests that Hawes may have used the wood allotment granted by colonial towns to their ministers as his source, although this seems odd since many towns allowed their ministers far in excess of this amount. Moreover, ministers' wood supplies offer a poor proxy for average household consumption for two reasons: ministers were often expected to provide wood to heat the town's meetinghouse during winter services and may also have been expected to sell some portion of their wood allowance to help supplement their annual salaries. Carolyn Merchant, in *Ecological Revolutions*, quotes the figure of thirty cords for annual household consumption. Merchant takes the figure of thirty cords from Brian Donahue's honors thesis, written while Donahue was a senior at Brandeis University and later published in an edited volume of undergraduate research papers all focusing on different facets of the colonial history of Concord, Massachusetts. Donahue, in his senior honors thesis, cites Max George Schumacher's *The Northern Farmer and His Markets*. Schumacher actually places consumption in the range of thirty to fifty cords, offering no analysis regarding the figure, but rather, through his footnotes, pointing the reader to the mid-nineteenth-century *History of Hadley* written by the inexhaustible amateur historian Sylvester Judd. Schumacher presumably takes his upper bound from Judd's discussion of the large amounts of firewood sometimes paid to ministers by colonial towns. The lower bound comes from Judd's estimate of firewood consumption in mid-eighteenth-century Hadley, Massachusetts. Judd's basis for this estimate: "When Hadley had only 100 families, about 1765, the consumption of wood was not much less than 3000 cords annually." Unfortunately Judd, who is quite good about providing citation in other parts of his *History*, offers no clues to how he came by his data; neither for the population of Hadley nor for the town's total wood consumption. William Cronon, *Changes in the Land: Indians, Colonists, and the Ecology of New England* (New York: Hill and Wang, 1983), 120–121; Austin F. Hawes, "New England Forests in Retrospect," *Journal of Forestry* 21, no. 3 (March 1923), 220; Carolyn Merchant, *Ecological Revolutions: Nature, Gender, and Science in New England* (Chapel Hill: University of North Carolina Press, 1989), 157; Brian Donahue, "The Forests and Fields of Concord: An Ecological History, 1750–1850," in David Hackett Fisher, ed., *Concord: The Social History of a New England Town, 1750–1850* (Waltham, MA: Brandeis University, 1983), 30; and Sylvester Judd, *History of Hadley, Including the Early History of Hatfield, South Hadley, Amherst and Granby, Massachusetts* (Northampton, MA: Metcalf & Company, 1863), 107–108.

14. Account books offer one obvious source for determining firewood consumption, though surviving records of this sort for the Hartford area date back only to the turn of the eighteenth century and contain only spotty data. The account book of Samuel Catlin, a Hartford

farmer who sometimes earned extra money by selling wood to his neighbors, offers a roughly representative example. In 1700, Catlin sold William Worthington only about eleven cords of firewood, suggesting an annual firewood consumption lower than commonly thought for the period. On the other hand, it is very likely that Worthington had other sources for firewood besides Catlin. In the following year Catlin sold Worthington only three cords of wood. In later years, Catlin sold wood to a wide array of Hartford citizens in amounts ranging from less than a cord to up to about six cords for a given year. Households likely depended both upon wood cut from their own lands and wood purchased from a variety of suppliers. Unfortunately, self-procurement provides no transaction records for historical study. As for Catlin's Hartford contemporaries, either they were not as fastidious in keeping their accounts or their account books simply have not survived the ensuing three centuries.

Colonial wills offer another possible avenue for exploring household firewood consumption, but these also often prove frustratingly vague. It was common for a husband to provide in his will that his widow be provided with an annual supply of firewood either by his heirs or by his executor. John Wilcock's 1651 will required that his wife Mary "should have wood enough for her expense Laid in the yard in Season," failing to proscribe a precise amount to be delivered. Samuel Steele made similar arrangements in his 1685 will, stipulating that his two sons provide their widowed mother with "her firewood brought home ready cut." Further examples exist but, like these, fail to specify just how many cords might be considered "necessary firewood" for a widow's comfortable maintenance.

Some wills and probate records provide more concrete clues. In 1694, Margaret Thompson paid four pounds to cover the debt owed by her recently deceased husband John for their winter's supply of wood. Using the price paid for a cord of wood in the account book of one of Thompson's Hartford contemporaries (nine shillings per cord), this sum would have purchased only about nine cords. Possibly, this four pounds represented only the residual debt that the deceased Thompson still owed to his firewood supplier or represented a payment to only one supplier among many, suggesting the possibility that his household's total winter wood consumption may have been higher. The figure also leaves open the question of annual consumption. What proportion of a household's total yearly fuel wood supply was consumed during the winter months? Assuming that the Thompsons maintained only a kitchen fire, which required a constant supply of wood year-round, then they might have used about twenty-seven to thirty-six cords for the entire year (depending on whether a New England "winter" is taken to last a quarter of the year or a full third), approximating the twenty-to-forty-cord figure commonly quoted in the literature.

Where wills or probate records set aside a specific number of cords for a widow's support, the total consumption of a household still requires some careful guesstimation. In 1738, Thomas Seymour of Hartford left his wife Mary "the north room of my now dwelling house" and "10 cords of wood a year during her natural life" to heat it. Assuming a two- or three-room house, the entire household might be assumed to use twenty to thirty cords a year. But since a parlor fireplace would not consume as much as the near-constantly burning kitchen fire this may be an underestimation. In 1750, John Willington left his wife, another Mary, "the use of the south room in my dwelling house, and the use of one-half of the chamber over the said room" and directed his executor to "find her 25 cords of wood a year." Again, assuming a two to three room house, the Willington's total annual household consumption might be expected to be in excess of fifty to seventy-five cords a year—a spectacular sum.

One of the great drawbacks of relying on surviving wills and probate records as sources for estimating early modern levels of consumption is their tendency to represent only the wealthier members of a community. During the winters of colonial New England, warmth was a luxury. Those who could afford to stack the wood high in the kitchen fireplace or to maintain fires in multiple rooms could be accounted lucky. A roaring parlor fire and a generous spirit of hospitality earned a man the respect and admiration of his chill-nipped neighbors. The two examples given above, the only two examples of husbands proscribing a hard figure for the number of cords to be provided for their widows in the probate records of colonial Hartford County, seem especially likely to represent the firewood consumption of only the exceptionally wealthy members of mid-eighteenth-century Connecticut society. Both Seymour and Willington held estates inventoried at nearly two thousand pounds following their deaths. For reference, the next inventoried estate in the records after Seymour's, that of Deacon John Skinner of Colchester, was valued at only a little over four hundred pounds.

The fairly late dates of these two records, 1738 and 1750, also suggests that perhaps the number of cords burned by a given household over the course of a year may have been increasing as the decades passed. In part, this may also be considered a function of wealth. As towns became established, lager houses, with more rooms and consequently more fireplaces, replaced the ruder habitations of the seventeenth-century pioneers. As the clearing and breaking of land placed relatively fewer constraints on the labor of those lucky enough to inherit improved farmland, and as these improvements began to pay off, some town inhabitants would have been able to devote more resources to the comforts of life—including more firewood.

So how much wood might the "average" Hartford household have used over the course of a year? The records referenced so far, with all their caveats, suggest somewhere between eleven cords (the amount William Worthington bought from Samuel Catlin) and seventy-five cords (the possible upper bound of consumption in the household of the late John Willington): a range far too broad to be considered analytically useful. A more realistic and more practical estimate (and the one used henceforth in this chapter) would be twenty to thirty cords.

See Judd, *History of Hadley,* 107; Samuel Catlin, "Account Book, 1700–1737," Connecticut Historical Society, Hartford, CT, 5, 8, 19, 43, 44, 54, 56; Manwaring, *Probate Records,* 1: 145, 164, 512, 365–366, 3: 335, 339, 548.

15. John Francis et al., "Account Book, 1708–1787," Connecticut Historical Society, Hartford, CT.

16. The account book also contained one reference to carting candlewood (pitch pine) for a neighbor. Since candlewood was most commonly used for lighting rather than as heating fuel (its high pitch content made it a poor choice for the hearth) this entry is excluded from the count. Joseph Olmsted, "Account Book, 1685–1747," Connecticut Historical Society, Hartford, CT, 6–7, 9, 12–16, 18–19, 24, 34, 38.

17. R. V. Reynolds and Albert H. Pierson, "Fuel Wood Used in the United States, 1630–1930," Circular No. 641, U.S. Department of Agriculture, Washington, D.C., February 1942, 6.

18. Reynolds and Pierson, "Fuel Wood," 6.

19. William Wood, *New Englands Prospect* (London: Printed by the Cotes for John Bellamie, 1635), 16–17.

20. William Douglass, *A Summary, Historical and Political of the First Planting, Progressive Improvements, and Present State of the British Settlements in North-America,* 2 vols. (Boston: Printed by Daniel Fowle, 1750), 1: 65.

21. Dwight, *Travels,* 1: 16.

22. Catlin, "Account Book," 45.

23. John Talcott, "Record Book, 1635–1742," Connecticut Historical Society, Hartford, CT, 19, 53, 71.

24. Many seventeenth-, eighteenth-, and nineteenth-century accounts list wood in terms of "loads" rather than cords. The number of cords contained in a single "load" might vary greatly. Crèvecoeur, writing in the late eighteenth century, estimated the "load" and the cord as roughly equal. Sylvester Judd in his history of Hadley estimated that a "load" represented between two-thirds and three-quarters of a cord. I make use of this last estimate. The Ashby example is taken from Brewer, *Fireplace to Cookstove*, 86. [J. Hector] St. John de Crève-coeur, *Sketches of an Eighteenth Century America: More Letters from an American Farmer*, ed. Stanley T. Williams (Whitefish, MT: Kessinger Publishing, 2006), 144; Judd, *History of Hadley*, 416n.

25. Royal Philosophical Society, *The Philosophical Transactions and Collections to the End of Year MDCC: Abridged, and Disposed Under General Heads*, ed. John Lowthorp, 5 vols. (London: Printed for J. and J. Knapton et al., 1732), 2: 668.

26. One sixteenth-century English poet urged landowners to remember to "Sell bark to the tanner, ere timber ye fell." Thomas Tusser, *Five Hundred Points of Good Husbandry*, ed. William Mavor (London: Printed for Lackington, Allen, 1812), 137.

27. "Hartford Town Votes," in *Collections of the Connecticut Historical Society*, 31 vols. (Hartford: Connecticut Historical Society, 1860–1967), 6: 251.

28. Gordon G. Whitney, *From Coastal Wilderness to Fruited Plain: A History of Environmental Change in Temperate North America from 1500 to the Present* (Cambridge: Cambridge University Press, 1994), 219; Aldren A. Watson, *The Blacksmith: Ironworker and Ferrier* (New York: Norton, 2000), 18; Nelson Courtlandt Brown, *Forest Products: Their Manufacture and Their Use* (New York: John Wiley & Sons, 1919), 189; Ralph Chipman Hawley and Austin Foster Hawes, *Manual of Forestry for the Northeastern United States* (New York: John Wiley & Sons, 1918), 183; Alf J. Mapp Jr., *Thomas Jefferson, Passionate Pilgrim: The Presidency, the Founding of the University, and the Private Battle* (Lanham, MD: Madison Books, 1991), 225.

29. Thomas R. Cox at al., *This Well-Wooded Land: Americans and Their Forests from Colonial Times to the Present* (Lincoln: University of Nebraska Press, 1985), 13.

30. "Hartford Town Votes," 2, 218; Love, *History of Hartford*, 15, 155.

31. "Hartford Town Votes," 16–20; Love, *History of Hartford*, 152.

32. Mary Babson Fuhrer, *A Crisis of Community: The Trials and Transformations of a New England Town, 1815–1848* (Chapel Hill: University of North Carolina Press, 2014), 256; Ken Lancaster et al., *Improve Your Woodlot by Cutting Firewood* (Upper Darby, PA: USDA Forest Service Northeastern Area State and Private Forestry, 1977), 9; Douglas D. McCreary and Glenn Nader, "Small-Parcel Landowner's Guide to Woodland Management," ANR Publication 8263, University of California Division of Agriculture and Natural Resources (2007), 7.

33. Betty Flanders Thomson, *The Changing Face of New England* (New York: Macmillan, 1958), 63–64.

34. Bureau of Soils, "Soil Map: Conn-Mass, Springfield Sheet," and Milton Whitney, "Description of a Soil Map of the Connecticut Valley," Circular No. 7, U.S. Department of Agriculture, Washington, D.C., June 29, 1942, 4.

35. Dwight, *Travels*, 1: 80–81.

36. Cronon, *Changes in the Land*, 144–146.

37. "Hartford Town Votes," 283, 316.

38. "The Original Distribution of the Lands in Hartford Among the Settlers, 1639," *Collections of the Connecticut Historical Society*, 31 vols. (Hartford: Connecticut Historical Society, 1912), 14: 256–257, 411–413, 438.

39. "Hartford Town Votes," 9, 16–20.

40. In regulating the commons, the early town government of Hartford mirrored what had been left behind in old England. Indeed, such systems for governing commonly property in lands and resources were standard in the villages and towns of early modern northern Europe. It is this system, which through local governance made the users of a resource into its managers, that helped prevent the "Tragedy of the Commons" that Garrett Hardin predicted should lead to the rapid depletion of common resources. Historical commons were never the "open-access" systems that Hardin modeled. By denying the use of the commons to some inhabitants, and by carefully limiting the use that commoners could make of the town's corporately held lands, Hartford's local government successfully husbanded the shared resources of the town for several generations. See Robert T. Deacon, "Deforestation and Ownership: Evidence from Historical Accounts and Contemporary Data," *Land Economics* 75, no. 3 (August 1999), 341–359; Tine de Moor, "Avoiding Tragedies: A Flemish Common and Its Commoners Under the Pressure of Social and Economic Change During the Eighteenth Century," *Economic History Review* 62, no. 1 (2009), 1–22.

41. "Hartford Town Votes," 220–221.

42. "Hartford Town Votes," 220–221, 271, 312, 322.

43. Love, *History of Hartford*, 145.

44. "Hartford Town Votes," 312.

45. Catlin, "Account Book," 5; Manwaring, *Probate Records*, 1: 512.

46. In 1788, for example, a party of wintertime merrymakers learned the foolishness of testing the limits of the frozen river when their one-horse open sleigh broke through the ice and sank into the river. Its occupants barely escaped with their lives. The fate of the horse went unrecorded. Ezekiel Price, "Ezekiel Price Diary, 1787–1788," Ms. N-1013, Massachusetts Historical Society, Boston, MA.

47. "Original Distribution," 492–494; Jay Mack Holbrook, *Connecticut 1670 Census* (Oxford, MA: Holbrook Institute, 1977), iii.

48. These men were William Pitkin, John Crow, and Thomas Hosmer. Pitkin and Crow jointly owned a sawmill at a site on the Hoccanum River that would eventually come to be known as Pitkin Falls. Thomas Hosmer, along with his son and heir Stephen, built their own sawmill on the river's west side. "Original Distribution," 280, 485–486, 529–534, 536–538.

49. Dwight, *Travels*, 1: 201.

50. "Original Distribution," 568.

51. Forty of those who received lands in the West Division (about 30 percent of total households) received fewer than thirty acres. "Original Distribution," 562–566.

52. "Original Distribution," 551.

53. Love, *History of Hartford*, 145–146.

54. This excludes the lots granted within "the Bridgefield," the only lands between the Little River and the West Division that had been divided prior to the 1670s, which embraced about 285 acres. Love, *History of Hartford*, 144–145.

55. Love, *History of Hartford*, 292–293.

56. Mary K. Talcott, "General History to the Revolution," in *The Memorial History of Hartford County, Connecticut, 1633–1884*, ed. James Hammond Trumbull, 2 vols. (Boston: Edward L. Osgood, 1886), 1: 297.

57. Quoted in Charles M. Andrews, *River Towns of Connecticut: A Study of Wethersfield, Hartford, and Windsor*, (Baltimore, MD: Isaac Friedenwald, 1889), 50–51.

58. Windsor (Town), Connecticut, *First Book of Records of Town Acts*, 58, January 9, 1693.

59. Windsor, *First Book of Records*, 71, May 17, 1697.

60. Windsor, *First Book of Records*, 86, February 11, 1701.

61. Love, *History of Hartford*, 152.

62. This figure excludes lands lying either on the east bank of the Connecticut River or in the parish of West Hartford. By the turn of the eighteenth century, both of these areas boasted population centers of their own which would have required their own firewood supplies.

63. Henry Gannett, *A Geographic Dictionary of Connecticut*, U.S. Geographical Survey, no. 117 (Washington, D.C.: Government Printing Office, 1894), 31.

64. Arthur H. Cole, "The Mystery of Fuel Wood Marketing in the United States," *Business History Review* 44, no. 3 (Autumn 1970), 339.

65. "Hartford Town Votes," 137.

66. Catlin, "Account Book," 5, 8, 19, 43, 44, 54, 56.

67. John Smith, "Account Book, 1726–1741," Connecticut Historical Society, Hartford, CT, 1, 9.

68. Pehr Kalm, *Travels into North America*, trans. John Reinhold Forster, 3 vols. (London: Printed by W. Eyres, 1770, 1: 93.

69. Cole, "The Mystery of Fuel Wood Marketing in the United States," 346–347; Carl Bridenbaugh, *Cities in the Wilderness: The First Century of Urban Life in America, 1625–1742* (New York: Knopf, 1955), 151–152, 311–313; Blake McKelvey, *Snow in the Cities: A History of America's Urban Response* (Rochester, NY: University of Rochester Press, 1995), 11–12.

70. Henry Flanders, *The Lives and Times of the Chief Justices of the Supreme Court of the United States*, 2 vols. (Philadelphia: J. B. Lippincott, 1858), 2: 58–60.

71. Anya Zilberstein, *A Temperate Empire: Making Climate in Early America* (New York: Oxford University Press, 2016), 4–5, 148–151, 164–167.

72. Both Wood and Johnson are quoted in Karen Ordahl Kupperman, "Climate and Mastery of the Wilderness in Seventeenth-Century New England," *Seventeenth-Century New England: A Conference Held by the Colonial Society of Massachusetts, June 18 and 19, 1982* (Boston: Colonial Society of Massachusetts; distributed by the University Press of Virginia, 1984), 20.

73. John Evelyn, *Silva: Or, a Discourse of Forest-Trees* (London: Printed for J. Walthoe et al., 1729), 11.

74. William Howard Tucker, *History of Hartford, Vermont* (Burlington, VT: Free Press Association, 1889), 14–15.

75. Richard A. Anthes, "Enhancement of Convective Precipitation by Mesoscale Variations in Vegetative Covering in Semiarid Regions," *Journal of Climate and Applied Meteorology* 23, no. 4 (1984), 545–547; Vinod Raina, "Do Forests Affect Rainfall?" *Economic and Political Weekly* 25, no. 30 (1990), 1633.

76. Woodward quoted and Hale, Monceau, and Poivre discussed in Richard Grove, *Green Imperialism: Colonial Expansion, Tropical Island Edens and the Origins of Environmentalism, 1600–1860* (Cambridge: Cambridge University Press, 1995), 156–168.

77. Samuel Williams, *The Natural and Civil History of Vermont* (Walpole, NH: Printed by Isaiah Thomas and David Carlise Jr., 1794), 57.

78. William Burke, *An Account of the European Settlements in America*, 2 vols. (London: Printed for R. and J. Dodsley, 1757), 2: 183.

79. Ibid.

80. Samuel Williams, *The Natural and Civil History of Vermont*, 2 vols (Burlington, VT: Samuel Mills, 1809), 2: 357–358. This is a new, expanded edition of Williams' *History*, originally published in 1794.

81. Lewis Evans, *Geographical, Historical, Political, Philosophical and Mechanical Essays* (Philadelphia: Printed by B. Franklin and D. Hall, 1755), 20.

82. Dwight, *Travels*, 1: 203–204.

Chapter 4

1. Benning Wentworth to Roger Wolcott, June 25, 1753, "The Wolcott Papers: Correspondence and Documents During Roger Wolcott's Governorship of the Colony of Connecticut, 1750–1754, with Some of Earlier Date," *Collections of the Connecticut Historical Society*, 31 vols. (Hartford: Connecticut Historical Society, 1916), 16: 310.

2. On the Molasses Act of 1733 see John J. McCusker and Russell R. Menard, *The Economy of British America, 1607–1789* (Chapel Hill: University of North Carolina Press, 1985), 163–164; Arthur M. Schlesinger, *The Colonial Merchants and the American Revolution, 1763–1776* (New York: Atheneum, 1968), 42–49; and Gilman M. Ostrander, "The Colonial Molasses Trade," *Agricultural History* 30, no. 2 (1965), 77–84.

3. E. P. Thompson, *Whigs and Hunters: The Origin of the Black Act* (New York: Pantheon Books, 1975).

4. Thompson, *Whigs and Hunters*; J. A. Sharpe, *Crime in Early Modern England, 1550–1750* (London: Longman, 1984), 122–124, 131–134, 139–142; Norbert Schindler and Pamela E. Selwyn, *Rebellion Community and Custom in Early Modern Germany* (Cambridge: Cambridge University Press, 2002), 75; "Preface," in *Albion's Fatal Tree: Crime and Society in Eighteenth-Century England*, ed. Douglas Hay et al. (New York: Pantheon Books, 1975), 13–14; Douglas Hay, "Property, Authority and the Criminal Law," in *Albion's Fatal Tree*, 55; Dirk Hoerder, *People and Mobs: Crowd Action in Massachusetts During the American Revolution, 1765–1780* (Berlin: Freie Univeristät Berlin, 1971), 129–138; and Paul A. Gilje, *The Road to Mobocracy: Popular Disorder in New York City, 1763–1834* (Chapel Hill: University of North Carolina Press, 1987), 8–10.

5. E. W. Cooney, "Eighteenth Century Britain's Missing Sawmills: A Blessing in Disguise?" *Construction History* 7 (1991), 30, 34–35, 40, 42.

6. Thomas R. Cox, *The Lumberman's Frontier: Three Centuries of Land Use, Society, and Change in America's Forests* (Corvallis: Oregon State University Press, 2010), 2; Charles F. Carroll, *The Timber Economy of Puritan New England* (Providence, RI: Brown University Press, 1973), 70; Sylvester Judd, "The Judd Manuscripts," Miscellaneous Series, Forbes Library, Northampton, MA, 9: 329; John A. Stoughton, *"Windsor Farmes": A Glimpse of an Old Parish* (Hartford, CT: Clark & Smith, 1883), 118; James Elliott Defebaugh, *History of the Lumber Industry of America*, 2 vols. (Chicago: American Lumberman, 1907), 195.

7. Sylvester Judd, *History of Hadley, Including the Early History of Hatfield, South Hadley, Amherst and Granby, Massachusetts* (Northampton, MA: Metcalf & Company, 1863), 109.

8. Great Britain, Public Records Office, *Calendar of State Papers, Colonial Series*, ed. William Noel Sainsbury, J. W. Fortescue, and Cecil Headlam, 45 vols. (London: Mackie and Co. Ld. and His Majesty's Stationery Service, 1860–1926), 12: 140, 247–248, 260, 444–445, 517, 536; Richard Grove, *Green Imperialism: Colonial Expansion, Tropical Island Edens and the Origins of Environmentalism, 1600–1860* (Cambridge: Cambridge University Press, 1995).

9. Great Britain, Public Records Office, *Calendar of State Papers*, 15: 84.

10. Quotations from Edmund S. Morgan and Helen M. Morgan, *The Stamp Act Crisis: Prologue to Revolution* (New York: Collier Books, 1962), 215, and Andrew Jackson O'Shaughnessy, *An Empire Divided: The American Revolution and the British Caribbean* (Philadelphia: University of Pennsylvania Press, 2000), 98–99.

11. William Cronon, *Changes in the Land: Indians, Colonists, and the Ecology of New England* (New York: Hill and Wang, 1983), 12, 121–122.

12. Connecticut (Colony), *The Public Records of the Colony of Connecticut*, ed. J. Hammond Trumbull and Charles J. Hoadley, 15 vols. (Hartford, CT: F. A. Brown; Lockwood & Brainard, 1850–1890), 3: 298.

13. Massachusetts (Colony), *Records of the Governor and Company of Massachusetts Bay in New England*, ed. Nathaniel Bradstreet Shurtleff, 5 vols. (Boston: W. White, 1853), 1: 172.

14. Judd, "Judd Manuscripts," Miscellaneous Series, 12: 188.

15. Windsor (Town), Connecticut, *Book of Records of Town Acts*, 3 vols., 1: fo. 63, January 9, 1693, 3: fo. 20, December 15, 1720.

16. Hezekiah Spencer Sheldon, *Documentary History of Suffield in the Colony and Province of Massachusetts Bay in New England, 1660–1749* (Springfield, MA: Clark W. Bryan, 1879), 100.

17. Connecticut (Colony), *Public Records*, 3: 235, 4: 316, 5: 434, 499, 6: 60, 7: 80.

18. This figure is taken from Howard S. Russell, *A Long Deep Furrow: Three Centuries of Farming in New England* (Hanover, NH: University Press of New England, 1976), 59.

19. Connecticut (Colony), *Public Records*, 1: 67–68.

20. Thomas Fitch, "The Fitch Papers: Correspondence and Documents During Thomas Fitch's Governorship of the Colony of Connecticut, 1754–1766, Volume I," *Collections of the Connecticut Historical Society* (Hartford: Connecticut Historical Society, 1918), 17: 277–278.

21. William Burt to Mr. Dummer, June 25, 1703, in Great Britain, Public Records Office, *Calendar of State Papers,* 21: 515.

22. Michael Williams, *Deforesting the Earth: From Prehistory to Global Crisis* (Chicago: University of Chicago Press, 2003), 222; Marsha L. Hamilton, *Social and Economic Networks in Early Massachusetts: Atlantic Connections* (University Park, PA: University of Pennsylvania Press, 2009), 73; Thomas R. Cox et al., *This Well-Wooded Land: Americans and Their Forests from Colonial Times to the Present* (Lincoln: University of Nebraska Press, 1985), 20.

23. Connecticut (colony), *Public Records*, 5: 434.

24. Massachusetts (colony), *Journals of the House of Representatives of Massachusetts*, 50 vols. (Boston: Massachusetts Historical Society, 1919–1990), 1: 148.

25. Connecticut (colony), *Public Records*, 5: 499.

26. Ellsworth S. Grant, *"Thar She Goes!" Shipbuilding on the Connecticut River* (Lyme, CT: Greenwich Publishing Group, 2000), 12.

27. W. D. Wetherell, *This American River: Five Centuries of Writing about the Connecticut* (Hanover, NH: University Press of New England, 2002), 19; Wick Griswold, *A History of the Connecticut River* (Charleston, SC: History Press, 2012), 55.

28. Edmund Delaney, *The Connecticut River: New England's Historic Waterway* (Guilford, CT: Globe Pequot Press, 1983), 32, 47; Carroll, *The Timber Economy of Puritan New England*, 123; Grant, *Thar She Goes*, 13.

29. Joseph Cullon, "Colonial Shipwrights and Their World: Men, Women, and Markets in Early New England" (PhD diss., University of Wisconsin–Madison, 2003), 22.

30. Grant, *Thar She Goes*, 13.

31. Lord Bellomont quoted in Thomas R. Cox et al., *This Well-Wooded Land*, 23–24; Cullon, "Colonial Shipwrights," 15–17.

32. Massachusetts (Colony), *Journals of the House of Representatives*, 1: 148.

33. Great Britain, Public Records Office, *Calendar of State Papers*, 41: 21.

34. Connecticut State Archives, *Trade and Maritime Affairs,* Reel I, fo. 70a.

35. Connecticut State Archives, *Trade and Maritime Affairs,* Reel I, fo. 71a.

36. Connecticut (Colony), *Public Records,* 5: 499.

37   Great Britain, Public Records Office, *Calendar of State Papers,* 41: 347–348; G. Terry Sharrer, "Naval Stores, 1781–1881," in *Material Culture of the Wooden Age,* ed. Brooke Hindle (Tarrytown, NY: Sleepy Hollow Press, 1981), 243.

38. Quotation from Great Britain, *Calendar of State Papers,* 21: 559–560, see also 22: 488; Windsor (Town), Connecticut, *Book of Records of Town Acts,* 3 vols., Windsor Town Clerk's Office, 1: fo. 71, January 19, 1697; Francis Olcott Allen and John C. Pease, eds., *The History of Enfield, Connecticut,* 2 vols. (Lancaster, PA: Wickersham Print, 1900), 1: 297–299, 301, 307–312, 315, 318–319; Mikko Airaksinen, "Tar Production in Colonial North America," *Environment and History* 2, no. 1 (February 1996), 115–125.

39. Airaksinen, "Tar Production," 115; Great Britain, Public Records Office, *Calendar of State Papers,* 31: 3, 33: 423, 37: 74, 241, 41: 323; Judd, *History of Hadley,* 301n.

40. Roger Wolcott, *Poetical Meditations, Being the Improvement of Some Vacant Hours* (New London, CT: Printed by L. Green, 1725), 34.

41. Cronon, *Changes in the Land,* 30.

42. "The Town of Suffield Connecticut," *White Pine Series of Architectural Monographs* 7, no. 6 (1921), 12, 16.

43. Edwin J. Perkins, *The Economy of Colonial America* (New York: Columbia University Press, 1988), 22–23.

44. Joseph J. Malone, *Pine Trees and Politics* (New York: Arno Press, 1979), 6.

45. Robert Greenhalgh Albion, *Forests and Sea Power: The Timber Problem of the Royal Navy, 1652–1862* (Cambridge, MA: Harvard University Press, 1926), 236.

46. Malone, *Pine Trees,* 112, 122–123.

47. Andrew Wietze, *White Pine: American History and the Tree That Made a Nation* (Guilford, CT: Globe Pequot, 2018), xix.

48. Brief references to Pine Act resistance in the Connecticut Valley can be found sprinkled here and there throughout the relevant historical literature, but no sustained study has ever been conducted. The most recent history of Massachusetts' eighteenth-century Hampshire County devotes but a single sentence to the Pine Acts despite its explicit focus on social conflict, saying only that resistance to the unpopular laws was "a fairly old and fairly common reaction among New England woodsmen." Malone, *Pine Trees,* 131, 215; Albion, *Forests and Sea Power,* 251–273; Russell, *A Long Deep Furrow,* 174; Judd, *History of Hadley,* 304–305; and Gregory H. Nobles, *Divisions throughout the Whole: Politics and Society in Hampshire County, Massachusetts, 1740–1775* (Cambridge: Cambridge University Press, 1983), 157.

49. Judd, "Judd Manuscripts," Connecticut Series, 5: 225.

50. Great Britain, Public Records Office, *Calendar of State Papers,* 15: 54.

51. James Birket, *Some Cursory Remarks Made by James Birket in His Voyage to North America, 1750–1751* (New Haven, CT: Yale University Press, 1916), 4.

52. Lawrence Henry Gipson, *Jared Ingersoll: A Study of American Loyalism in Relation to British Colonial Government* (New Haven, CT: Yale University Press, 1920), 94.

53. Gipson, *Jared Ingersoll,* 92–94.

54. Roger Wolcott to Benning Wentworth, February 5, 1753, "The Wolcott Papers," 235.

55. Benning Wentworth to Roger Wolcott, June 25, 1753, "The Wolcott Papers," 309.

56. Wentworth to Wolcott, June 25, 1753, "The Wolcott Papers," 310.

57. Moreover, Daniel's son Gurdon Whitmore owned a share in at least one Middletown sawmill in the 1790s, proving that the Whitmore's lumber business was in fact a multigenerational affair. It therefore seems likely that Daniel, like his father before him and son afterwards, would also have been involved in the lumber trade and might even have been part owner of the sawmill where he encountered Blake in 1753. Connecticut State Archives, *Trade and Maritime Affairs*, Reel I, fo. 70a–b; Connecticut State Archives, *Private Controversies*, 2nd Series, fo. 65–68; "MIDDLETOWN, February 23," *Middlesex Gazette*, February 23, 1793, 3.

58. Blake met with considerable disappointment in his attempts to have Whitmore punished for this assault. He encountered a great deal of official foot-dragging from Connecticut governor Roger Wolcott. Wolcott proved far more interested in protecting the interests of his constituents than in cooperating in the enforcement of an unpopular imperial policy. Wolcott ignored repeated letters from General Surveyor Wentworth calling for action in the Blake case. In 1754, Wentworth sent Wolcott a new copy of Blake's commission as deputy surveyor, along with a letter demanding that Daniel Whitmore be prosecuted for his "indignity to the King's authority." No trial ever took place. Benning Wentworth to Roger Wolcott, January 17, 1753, "The Wolcott Papers," *Collections of the CHS*, 16: 231; Wentworth to Wolcott, June 25, 1753, "The Wolcott Papers," *Collections of the CHS*, 16: 310; Benning Wentworth to Roger Wolcott, May 15, 1754, "The Fitch Papers: Correspondence and Documents During Thomas Fitch's Governorship of the Colony of Connecticut, 1754–1766, Volume I," *Collections of the Connecticut Historical Society* (Hartford: Connecticut Historical Society, 1918) 17: 1–2; *Journal of the Commissioners for Trade and Plantations from January 1759 to December 1763*, ed. K. H. Ledward (London: His Majesty's Stationery Office, 1935), 28.

59. Judd, "Judd Manuscripts," Connecticut Series, 5: 190, 240.

60. Quoted in Colin G. Calloway, *Dawnland Encounters: Indians and Europeans in Northern New England* (Hanover, NH: University Press of New England, 1991), 121–123; Colin G. Calloway, *The Western Abenakis of Vermont: War, Migration, and the Survival of an Indian People* (Norman: University of Oklahoma Press, 1990), 142, 160–182; Lisa Brooks, *The Common Pot: The Recovery of Native Space in the Northeast* (Minneapolis: University of Minnesota Press, 2008), 45; Albion, *Forests and Sea Power*, 237; Henry H. Saunderson, *History of Charlestown, New Hampshire; The Old No. 4* (Claremont, NH: Claremont Manufacturing, 1876), 25–26.

61. Jared Ingersoll to John Pownal, June 2, 1760, "The Fitch Papers, Volume II," 18: 69.

62. Ingersoll to Pownal, June 2, 1760, in "The Fitch Papers, Volume II," 18: 69–70.

63. Jared Ingersoll to Benning Wentworth, December 18, 1761, in *Papers of the New Haven Colony Historical Society* (New Haven: Printed for the New Haven Historical Society, 1918), 9: 256; Gipson, *Jared Ingersoll*, 100, 107.

64. Samuel Wyllys and Matthew Talcott to Jared Ingersoll, April 9, 1764, in *Papers of the NHCHS*, 9: 267.

65. Jared Ingersoll to the Navy Board, June 8, 1763, and Jared Ingersoll to the Navy Board, February 7, 1764, in *Papers of the NHCHS*, 9: 262–263.

66. Jared Ingersoll to the Commisioners of the Navy, May 13, 1762, and Jared Ingersoll to Col. Symes, March 3, 1763, in *Papers of the NHCHS*, 9: 259–261; Edwin S. Lines, "Jared Ingersoll, Stamp Master, and the Stamp Act," in *Papers of the NHCHS*, 9: 178.

67. Gideon Lyman, "Affidavit of Gideon Lyman," in *Papers of the NHCHS*, 9: 264–265; Samuel Wyllys and Matthew Talcott to Jared Ingersoll, April 9, 1764, in *Papers of the NHCHS*, 9: 267–268.

68. Eliphet Dyer to Jared Ingersoll, April 14, 1764, in *Papers of the NHCHS*, 9: 290; Gipson, *Jared Ingersoll*, 104–107.

69. Benning Wentworth to the Lords Commissioners for Trade and Plantations, October 21, 1763, Wentworth Family Papers, 1720–1940, Acc. #1939-6(V), 2 Boxes, New Hampshire Historical Society, Manuscript Section, Box 1, Folder 2: 1739–1766.

70. Calloway, *Western Abenakis*, 185.

71. Benning Wentworth to Thomas Fitch, July 1, 1763, Jared Ingersoll Papers, Connecticut Historical Society, Hartford, Connecticut.

72. Judd, "Judd Manuscripts," Miscellaneous Series, 9: 106.

73. Judd, "Judd Manuscripts," Massachusetts Series, 5: 131.

74. Judd, *History of Hadley*, 305.

75. *Massachusetts Gazette and Boston News-Letter*, July 21, 1763, 1.

76. Judd, "Judd Manuscripts," Massachusetts Series, 5: 131.

77. For more on Israel Williams' political connections and personal authority in Hampshire County, see Nobles, *Divisions Throughout the Whole*, 30–35. Also, see William Lawrence Welch Jr., "River God: The Public Life of Israel Williams, 1709–1788," PhD diss., University of Maine, 1975; and Kevin Michael Sweeney, "River Gods and Related Minor Deities: The Williams Family and the Connecticut River Valley, 1637–1790," PhD diss., 2 vols., Yale University, 1986, 2: ch. 7.

78. Judd, "Judd Manuscripts," Massachusetts Series, 5: 131; Josiah Gilbert Holland, *History of Western Massachusetts*, 2 vols. (Springfield, MA: Samuel Bowles, 1855), 1: 183.

79. E. R. Ellis, *Biographical Sketches of Richard Ellis, the First Settler of Ashfield, Mass., and His Descendants* (Detroit, MI: Wm. Graham, 1888), 281.

80. George Sheldon and J. M. Arms Sheldon, *The Rev. John Williams House* (Deerfield, MA: Deerfield, 1918), 14.

81. Hampshire County, Massachusetts, Hampshire County Court Common Pleas/General Sessions, vol. 17, microfilm, Henry N. Flynt Library, Historic Deerfield, Massachusetts, February 11, 1766; Judd, *History of Hadley*, 305.

82. Hampshire County, Court Common Pleas/General Sessions, vol. 17, February 11, 1766.

83. Twenty-two rioters were indicted in all. Eleven pled no contest and were fined three pounds each, plus the costs of the court. Four pled not guilty and the king's attorney chose to drop their cases, presumably for lack of evidence and corroborating witnesses. One man pled not guilty, was found guilty by a jury, and was fined two pounds plus the costs of the court. The legal fate of the remaining six who faced indictment went unrecorded. Hampshire County, Court Common Pleas/General Sessions, vol. 17, February 11, 1766, May 20–26, 1766; Nobles, *Divisions Throughout the Whole*, 32–33.

84. Hampshire County, Court Common Pleas/General Sessions, vol. 17, February 11, 1766, May 20–26, 1766; *New Hampshire Provincial and State Papers*, ed. Nathaniel Bouton et al., 40 vols. (Concord, NH: Edward A. Jenks; State of New Hampshire, 1867–1943), 26: 106, 306.

85. Cox, *The Lumberman's Frontier*, 5.

86. Hampshire County, Court Common Pleas/General Sessions, vol. 17, February 11, 1766, May 20–26, 1766.

87. In Hampshire County in the 1760s, the poaching of white pines could be considered a "social crime." J. A. Sharpe, *Crime in Early Modern England, 1550–1750* (London and New York: Longman, 1984), 121–124, 127, 133, 139–140; Douglas Hay, "Preface" and "Property, Authority and the Criminal Law," in Douglas Hay et al., *Albion's Fatal Tree: Crime and Society in*

Eighteenth-Century England (New York: Pantheon Books, 1975), 13–14, 55; Judd, "Judd Manuscripts," Massachusetts Series, 5: 131.

88. The notes of Sylvester Judd offer evidence of this for the Hadley area. Judd, "Judd Manuscripts," Miscellaneous Series, 9: 93.

89. This old yarn has been repeated in twentieth-century histories of colonial New England as well. For example, see Albion, *Forests and Sea Power*, 260, and Russell, *Long Deep Furrow*, 174.

90. Gipson, *Jared Ingersoll*, 110n.

91. *Journals of the Continental Congress, 1774–1789*, ed. Worthington Chauncey Ford, 34 vols. (Washington, D.C.: U.S. Government Printing Office, 1907), 9: 1002.

92. Connecticut (Colony), *Public Records*, 1: 175–176, 517–518.

93. Judd, *History of Hadley*, 303.

94. Judd, "Judd Manuscripts," Connecticut Series, 5: 190, 240.

95. *The Boston Weekly News-Letter*, September 7–14, 1732, 2; *The New-England Weekly Journal*, September 11, 1732, 2.

96. William Heywood, "William Heywood's Journal," Acc. #1984-54(M), Manuscript Section, New Hampshire Historical Society, Concord, New Hampshire, 17–20.

97. Jared Ingersoll to Benning Wentworth, December 18, 1761, Jared Ingersoll Papers, Connecticut Historical Society, Hartford, Connecticut.

98. Atecouando quoted in Lisa Brooks, *The Common Pot: The Recovery of Native Space in the Northeast* (Minneapolis: University of Minnesota Press, 2008), 45; Albion, *Forests and Sea Power*, 237; Saunderson, *History of Charlestown*, 25–26.

99. W. Barrett, "The Northeastern Region," *Regional Silviculture of the United States*, ed. John W. Barrett (New York: Ronald Press, 1962), 41; John Kricher, *Eastern Forests: A Field Guide to Birds, Mammals, Trees, Flowers, and More*, Peterson Field Guides Series (Boston and New York: Houghton Mifflin, 1998), 72–75, 81; Carroll, *The Timber Economy of Puritan New England*, 24; Betty Flanders Thomson, *The Changing Face of New England* (New York: Macmillan, 1958), 102–104.

100. Lisa Brooks, "Introduction," in *Dawnland Voices: An Anthology of Indigenous Writing from New England*, ed. Siobhan Senier (Lincoln: University of Nebraska Press, 2014), 250.

101. Dwight is quoted in John T. Cumbler, *Reasonable Use: The People, the Environment, and the State, New England, 1790–1930* (Oxford: Oxford University Press, 2001), 22.

102. Lyme (Town), Connecticut, *Lyme Records, 1667–1730*, ed. Jean Chandler Burr (Stonington, CT: Pequot Press, 1968), 169.

103. Lyme (Town), *Lyme Records*, 171.

104. Connecticut (Colony), *Public Records*, 12: 498–499.

105. Connecticut (Colony), *Public Records*, 5: 506, 7: 281–82, 9: 409–10, 12: 133, 498–499, 13: 126–27.

106. Strother Roberts, "'Esteeme a Little of Fish': Fish, Fishponds and Farming in Eighteenth-Century New England and the Mid-Atlantic," *Agricultural History* 82, no. 2 (Spring 2008), 154.

107. Birket, *Some Cursory Remarks*, 7, 14.

108. This figure is based upon estimates from A. P. Knight's *Sawdust and Fish Life*. In his study, Knight determines that 375 logs of the average approximate dimensions sixteen feet in length by twelve inches in diameter would produce a grand total of 27,000 pounds of sawdust during the milling process. These 375 logs would yield approximately 24,000 board feet; a quantity 20 percent greater than the board feet of pine sold to Hartford from Springfield sawmills in 1698. Assuming

a constant sawdust-to-board-feet ratio, the 20,000 boards sawn by the Springfield mills would have produced approximately 22,500 pounds of sawdust. Knight's 1903 study, of course, provides an imperfect proxy for the estimation of sawdust production by colonial mills. The up-and-down saws of colonial sawmills were considerably less efficient than the turn-of-the-twentieth-century saws of Knight's time, producing more sawdust and other wood waste—as Knight notes. Knight's figures can be used to gain some idea of the water-polluting potential of colonial sawmill operations. A. P. Knight, *Sawdust and Fish Life* (Toronto, ON: Murray, 1903), 14, 39.

109. Knight, *Sawdust and Fish Life*, 4–5, 13–14, 39–40; Francis O. Arimoro, Robert B. Ikomi, and Efe C. Osalor, "The Impact of Sawmill Wood Wastes on the Water Quality and Fish Communities of Benin River, Niger Delta Area, Nigeria," *International Journal of Science & Technology* 2, no. 1 (2007), 2, 11; James A. Lichatowich, *Salmon Without Rivers: A History of the Pacific Salmon Crisis* (Washington, D.C.: Island Press, 1999), 60; David Jenkins, "Atlantic Salmon, Endangered Species, and the Failure of Environmental Policies," *Comparative Studies in Society and History* 45, no. 4 (2003), 847; Arch E. Cole and Louis F. Warrick, "Water Pollution Studies in Wisconsin: Effects of Industrial (Pulp and Paper Mill) Wastes on Fish," *Sewage Works Journal* 7, no. 2 (1935), 301–302.

110. Carolyn Merchant, *Ecological Revolutions: Nature, Gender, and Science in New England* (Chapel Hill: University of North Carolina Press, 1989), 37; P. Collen and R. J. Gibson, "The General Ecology of Beavers (*Castor* spp.), as Related to Their Influence on Stream Ecosystems and Riparian Habitats, and the Subsequent Effects on Fish—A Review," *Reviews in Fish Biology and Fisheries* 10 (2001), 453.

111. J. Mark Shrimpton, Joseph D. Zydlewski, and John W. Heath, "Effect of Daily Oscillation in Temperature and Increased Suspended Sediment on Growth and Smolting in Juvenile Chinook Salmon, *Oncorhynchus tshawytscha*," *Aquaculture* 273 (2007), 274–275.

112. Timothy Dwight, *Travels in New-England and New-York*, 4 vols. (New Haven, CT: Timothy Dwight, 1824), 2: 325.

113. Cox, *The Lumberman's Frontier*, 47–48, passim.

Chapter 5

1. Jacob Bayley to Timothy Bedel, September 25, 1778, "Timothy Bedel Papers, 1771–1787" Acc. #1180-1, Box 1 of 1, Folder 1C, "Correspondence, 1777," New Hampshire Historical Society, Concord, NH; Timothy Bedel to General Schuyler, February 16, 1777, "Timothy Bedel Papers," Folder 1C.

2. Quotation from John Quincy Bittinger, *History of Haverhill* (Haverhill, NH: Cohos Steam Press, 1888), 175. See also Frederic Wells, *History of Newbury, Vermont: From the Discovery of the Coös Country to Present Time* (St. Johnsbury, VT: Caledonian Company, 1902), 8. Bedel's correspondence bears out this observation: Bayley to Bedel, September 25, 1778, and Bedel to Schuyler, February 16, 1777, "Timothy Bedel Papers," Folder 2, "Correspondence, 1778."

3. Max Schumacher cites custom records showing that of goods shipped legally out of colonial customs ports, Connecticut exported a third of all the preserved meat, almost half of all sheep and hogs, two-thirds of all cattle, and three-quarters of all the horses exported from the thirteen colonies from 1768 to 1773. Max George Schumacher, *The Northern Farmer and His Markets During the Late Colonial Period*, Dissertations in American Economic History (New York: Arno Press, 1975), 30.

4. Timothy Dwight, *Travels in New-England and New-York*, 4 vols. (New Haven, CT: Timothy Dwight, 1822–1824), 1: 144, 316, 2: 77, 89, 3: 500.

5. Stephen Innes, *Creating the Commonwealth: The Economic Culture of Puritan New England* (New York: Norton, 1995), 280.

6. Ibid.

7. John Winthrop, *The History of New England from 1630 to 1649*, ed. James Savage, 2 vols. (Boston: Little, Brown, 1853), 1: 138; Francis J. Bremer, *John Winthrop: America's Forgotten Founding Father* (Oxford: Oxford University Press, 2003), 316.

8. Virginia DeJohn Anderson, *Creatures of Empire: How Domestic Animals Transformed Early America* (Oxford: Oxford University Press, 2004), 167; Sumner Chilton Powell, *Puritan Village: The Formation of a New England Town* (Middletown, CT: Wesleyan University Press, 1963), 76.

9. Quoted in Anderson, *Creatures of Empire*, 168.

10. William Bradford, *Of Plymouth Plantation: 1620–1647*, ed. Samuel Eliot Morison (New York: Knopf, 1959), 244.

11. Massachusetts (Colony), *Records of the Governor and Company of the Massachusetts Bay in New England*, ed. Nathaniel B. Shurtleff, 6 vols. (Boston: William White, 1853–1854), 1: 358–359; Winthrop, *History of New England*, 1: 206–207; David Grayson Allen, *In English Ways: The Movement of Societies and the Transferal of English Local Law and Custom to Massachusetts Bay in the Seventeenth Century* (Chapel Hill: University of North Carolina Press, 1981), 3–4.

12. Winthrop, *History of New England*, 1: 167.

13. Winthrop, *History of New England*, 1: 204.

14. David Grayson Allen, "Both Englands," in *Seventeenth-Century New England: A Conference Held by the Colonial Society of Massachusetts, June 18 and 19, 1982*, ed. David D. Hall and Philip Chadwick Foster Smith (Boston: Colonial Society of Massachusetts, distributed by the University Press of Virginia, 1984), 63, 66.

15. W. Harwood Long, "Regional Farming in Seventeenth-Century Yorkshire," *Agricultural History Review* 8 (1960), 105, 113.

16. See Innes, *Creating the Commonwealth*, 281.

17. Earl Hayter, "Livestock-Fencing Conflicts in Rural America," *Agricultural History* 37, no. 1 (January 1963), 11–12.

18. Quoted in Henry R. Stiles, *The History of Ancient Windsor* (New York: Charles B. Norton, 1859), 63.

19. Anderson, *Creatures of Empire*, especially 163–164.

20. Springfield (Town), Massachusetts, *The First Century of the History of Springfield: The Official Records from 1636 to 1736*, ed. Henry M. Burt, 2 vols. (Springfield, MA: Henry M. Burt), 1: 60.

21. William Cronon, *Changes in the Land: Indians, Colonists, and the Ecology of New England* (New York: Hill & Wang, 1983), 129; Carl Bridenbaugh, *Fat Mutton and Liberty of Conscious: Society in Rhode Island, 1636–1690* (New York: Antheneum, 1976), 49.

22. Connecticut (Colony), *The Public Records of the Colony of Connecticut*, ed. J. Hammond Trumbull and Charles J. Hoadley, 15 vols. (Hartford, CT: F. A. Brown; Lockwood & Brainard, 1850–1890), 2: 139.

23. See Karen Ordahl Kupperman, "Climate and Mastery of the Wilderness in Seventeenth-Century New England," in *Seventeenth-Century New England: A Conference Held by the Colonial Society of Massachusetts, June 18 and 19, 1982*, ed. David D. Hall and Philip Chadwick Foster Smith (Boston: Colonial Society of Massachusetts, distributed by the University Press of Virginia, 1984).

24. William DeLoss Love, *The Colonial History of Hartford* (Hartford, CT: William DeLoss Love, 1914), 2–3.

25. Kupperman, "Climate and Mastery," 7.

26. Winthrop, *History of New England*, 1: 219, 246.

27. Innes, *Creating the Commonwealth*, 283.

28. Darrett B. Rutman, "Governor Winthrop's Garden Crop: The Significance of Agriculture in the Early Commerce of Massachusetts Bay," *William and Mary Quarterly*, 3rd Series, 20, no. 3 (July 1963), 396, 398; Anderson, *Creatures of Empire*, 168.

29. Winthrop, *History of New England*, 2: 37.

30. Innes, *Creating the Commonwealth*, 281.

31. Sylvester Judd, *History of Hadley* (Northampton, MA: Metcalf & Company, 1863), 367.

32. Bridenbaugh, *Fat Mutton*, 90–92; Innes, *Creating the Commonwealth*, 281.

33. Judd, *History of Hadley*, 369.

34. Connecticut (Colony), "Regulation of Meat Packing," in *Foundations of Colonial America: A Documentary History*, ed. W. Keith Kavenagh, 3 vols. (New York: Chelsea House, 1973), 1: 462.

35. Springfield (Town), *History of Springfield*, 1: 251.

36. George Sheldon, *A History of Deerfield, Massachusetts*, 2 vols. (Deerfield, MA: Pocumtuck Valley Memorial Association, 1895), 1: 222.

37. Judd, *History of Hadley*, 370–371.

38. Bernard Bailyn, *The New England Merchants in the Seventeenth Century* (Cambridge, MA: Harvard University Press, 1979), 88–89, 95–96; Richard L. Bushman, *From Puritan to Yankee: Character and the Social Order in Connecticut, 1690–1765* (Cambridge, MA: Harvard University Press, 1967), 28.

39. Thomas M. Truxes, "Connecticut in the Irish-American Flaxseed Trade, 1750–1775," *Éire-Ireland: A Journal of Irish Studies* 12, no. 2 (1977), 50–55; Margaret Ellen Newell, *From Dependency to Independence: Economic Revolution in Colonial New England* (Ithaca, NY: Cornell University Press, 2016), 189–190.

40. Joseph Cullon, "Colonial Shipwrights and Their World: Men, Women, and Markets in Early New England," (PhD diss., University of Wisconsin–Madison, 2003), 12–13; James E. McWilliams, *Building the Bay Colony: Local Economy and Culture in Early Massachusetts* (Charlottesville: University of Virginia Press, 2007), 145–150; Howard S. Russell, *A Long Deep Furrow: Three Centuries of Farming in New England* (Hanover, NH: University Press of New England, 1976), 60–61.

41. McWilliams, *Building the Bay Colony*, 145–150; Daniel Vickers, *Farmers and Fishermen: Two Centuries of Work in Essex County, Massachusetts, 1630–1850* (Chapel Hill: University of North Carolina Press, 1994), 100; Great Britain, Public Records Office, *Calendar of State Papers, Colonial Series*, ed. William Noel Sainsbury, J. W. Fortescue, and Cecil Headlam, 45 vols. (London: Mackie and Co. Ld. and His Majesty's Stationery Service, 1860–1926), 5: 532; Raymond McFarland, *A History of the New England Fisheries* (New York: University of Pennsylvania Press, 1911), 67; Walter S. Dunn Jr., *The New Imperial Economy: The British Army and the American Frontier, 1764–1768* (Westport, CT: Praeger, 2001), 39; Bushman, *Puritan to Yankee*, 28; Julian Gwyn, "Comparative Economic Advantage: Nova Scotia and New England, 1720s–1860s," in *New England and the Maritime Provinces: Connections and Comparisons*, ed. Stephen J. Hornsby and John G. Reid (Montreal, QC: McGill-Queen's University Press, 2005), 95–96.

42. Connecticut (Colony), *Public Records*, 2: 558; Hartford County, Connecticut, *Hartford County, Connecticut, County Court Minutes: Volumes 3 and 4, 1663–1687, 1697*, trans. Helen Schavert Ullman (Boston: New England Historic Genealogical Society, 2005), 153–154.

43. Local legend, however, adds an additional piece of drama to this tale of competing resource claims. Both sides agreed that the value of the lands did not justify the costs of further litigation (or the fines that might result from subsequent rioting). Instead, so the legend goes, the two towns agreed to have the issue decided through private combat among four combatants, two from each town, "leaving it to the Lord" to decide to whom the meadows belonged. *Harper's New Monthly Magazine: December, 1875, to May, 1876* (New York: Harper & Brothers, 1876), 52: 324; Katherine M. Abbott, *Old Paths and Legends of the New England Border: Connecticut, Deerfield, Berkshire* (New York: Knickerbocker Press, 1907), 48; Frances Manwaring Caulkins, *History of New London, Connecticut* (New London, CT: H. D. Utley, 1895), 168.

44. Joseph Peirce quoted in Jeremy Belknap, *The History of New-Hampshire*, 3 vols. (Boston: Belknap and Young, 1784–1792), 3: 159–161.

45. Timothy Dwight, *Travels*, 4: 50.

46. Cronon, *Changes in the Land*, 144–146.

47. Carolyn Merchant, *Ecological Revolutions: Nature, Gender, and Science in New England* (Chapel Hill: University Press of North Carolina, 1989), 165–166.

48. Cronon, *Changes in the Land*, 141–142; Merchant, *Ecological Revolutions*, 165–166.

49. Judd, *History of Hadley*, 362.

50. Stiles, *Ancient Windsor*, 147.

51. No relation to the Virginia rebel of the same name. "The Original Distribution of the Lands in Hartford Among the Settlers, 1639," *Collections of the Connecticut Historical Society*, 31 vols. (Hartford: Connecticut Historical Society, 1912), 14: 553.

52. Benjamin H. Hall, *History of Eastern Vermont* (New York: D. Appleton, 1858), 59; Henry H. Saunderson, *History of Charlestown, New Hampshire; The Old No. 4* (Claremont, NH: Claremont Manufacturing, 1876), 5.

53. Samuel Deane, *The New-England Farmer: Or, Georgical Dictionary* (Worcester, MA: Isaiah Thomas, 1790), 4–5.

54. Chester M. Destler, *Connecticut: The Provisions State* (Chester, CT: Pequot Press, 1973), 8.

55. J. Ritchie Garrison, "Farm Dynamics and Regional Exchange: The Connecticut Valley Beef Trade, 1670–1850," *Agricultural History* 61, no. 3 (Summer 1987), 1–17.

56. For examples, see Joseph Barnard, "Account Book, 1739–1768," Henry N. Flynt Library, Historic Deerfield, MA; Robert Miller, "Robert and Elisha Miller Account Book, 1710–1771," Connecticut Historical Society, Hartford, CT; Jonathan Hoyt, "Jonathan Hoyt Journal, 1800," Henry N. Flynt Library, Historic Deerfield, MA; Edward Bucknam, "Ledger, 1776–1787," Lancaster Acc. #1994-028, New Hampshire Historical Society, Concord, NH; William Heywood, "William Heywood's Journal," Acc. #1984-54(M), Manuscript Section, New Hampshire Historical Society, Concord, NH.

57. Deerfield (Town), *The Deerfield Town Book, 1670–1707*, transcribed by Richard I. Melvoin, Pioneer Valley Memorial Association, Historic Deerfield, MA, 31, passim.

58. Brian Donahue, *The Great Meadow: Farmers and the Land in Colonial Concord* (New Haven, CT: Yale University Press, 2004), 159–160.

59. Judd, *History of Hadley*, 367, 369; Garrison, "Farm Dynamics," 2–3; John Montague Smith, *History of the Town of Sunderland, Massachusetts* (Greenfield, MA: E. A. Hall, 1899), 181.

60. Garrison, "Farm Dynamics," 3; Gregory H. Nobles, *Divisions Throughout the Whole: Politics and Society in Hampshire County, Massachusetts, 1740–1775* (Cambridge: Cambridge University Press, 1983), 107.

61. Quoted in Peter Bolles Hirtle, "Agrarian Economy in Flux: Agricultural History of Deerfield, 1670–1760," (unpublished Historic Deerfield summer fellowship paper, 1973), 18–19.

62. Garrison, "Farm Dynamics," 3.

63. Great Britain, Public Records Office, *Calendar of State* Papers, 10: 577; Stiles, *Ancient Windsor*, 481, 483; Deane Phillips, *Horse Raising in Colonial New England* (Ithaca, NY: Cornell University, 1922), 906, 918.

64. Quotation from David Watts, *The West Indies: Patterns of Development, Culture and Environmental Change* (New York: Cambridge University Press, 1987), 197, see also 163, 198–199, 407–409; Phillips, *Horse Raising*, 909–918; Destler, *The Provisions State*, 11.

65. Richard S. Dunn, "A Tale of Two Plantations: Slave Life at Mesopotamia in Jamaica and Mount Airy in Virginia, 1799 to 1828," *William and Mary Quarterly* 43, no. 1 (January 1977), 32–65; Richard S. Dunn, *Sugar and Slaves: The Rise of the Planter Class in the English West Indies, 1624–1713* (Chapel Hill: University of North Carolina Press, 2012), 320; Michael Tadman, "The Demographic Cost of Sugar: Debates on Slave Societies and Natural Increase in the Americas," *American Historical Review* 105, no. 5 (December 2000), 1534–1575; Watts, *The West Indies*, 408.

66. "PORTSMOUTH, March 11" *The Boston News-Letter and New-England Chronicle*, March 24, 1768, 4.

67. William Cronon, *Nature's Metropolis: Chicago and the Great West* (New York: Norton, 1991), 225–226.

68. Daniel Lang to Richard Lang, September 10, 1796, Richard Lang Papers, Box 1, Folder 2A, "Correspondence, August 1796–Oct 1796," New Hampshire Historical Society, Concord, NH.

69. Nathaniel Lang to Richard Lang, October 25, 1796, Richard Lang Papers, Box 1, Folder 2A.

70. Nathaniel Lang to Richard Lang, October 25, 1796, Richard Lang Papers, Box 1, Folder 2A; *New Hampshire Provincial and State Papers*, ed. Nathaniel Bouton et al., 40 vols. (Concord: Edward A. Jenks; State of New Hampshire, 1867–1943), 14: 257–258; William Allen Wallace, *The History of Canaan, New Hampshire*, ed. James Burns Wallace (Concord, NH: Rumford Press, 1910), 20, 42, 346, 353.

71. Wallace, *History of Canaan*, 77.

72. Nathaniel Lang to Richard Lang, October 25, 1796, Richard Lang Papers, Box 1, Folder 2A.

73. Frank Wilkeson, "Cattle-Raising on the Plains," *Harper's New Monthly Magazine*, ed. Henry Mills Alden (New York: Harper & Brothers, 1886), 72: 791; I. F. King, "The Coming and Going in Ohio Droving," *Ohio Archaeological and Historical Publications* 17 (1908), 250; "On the Preparation of Livestock and Meat in Reference to their Exportation by Steam-Vessels," *Farmer's Magazine* 7, no. 1 (1837), 447.

74. William Heywood, "William Heywood's Journal," Acc. #1984-54(M), Manuscript Section, New Hampshire Historical Society, Concord, NH, 14.

75. Henry Colman, *Fourth Report on the Agriculture of Massachusetts: Counties of Franklin and Middlesex* (Boston: Dutton and Wentworth, 1841), 93.

76. Destler, *The Provisions State*, 31, 43; Nathaniel Lang to Richard Lang, October 25, 1796, Richard Lang Papers, Box 1, Folder 2A; Heywood, "William Heywood's Journal," 14.

77. For the effects of cattle drives on western ecosystems: James E. Sherow, *The Grasslands of the United States: An Environmental History*, Nature and Human Societies Series, ed. Mark R. Stoll, (Santa Barbara, CA: ABC-CLIO, 2007), 67–69.

78. See Tine de Moor, "Avoiding Tragedies: A Flemish Common and Its Commoners Under the Pressure of Social and Economic Change Curing the Eighteenth Century," *Economic History Review* 62, no. 1 (2009).

79. J. H. Temple, *History of North Brookfield, Massachusetts* (Boston: Town of North Brookfield, 1887), 188–189.

80. For the routes taken by these paths see Love, *History of Hartford*, 39n; Katharine Mixer Abbott, *Old Paths and Legends of New England: Saunterings over Historic Roads* (New York: G. P. Putnam's Sons, 1908), 274n.

81. George F. Daniels, *History of the Town of Oxford, Massachusetts* (Oxford, MA: George F. Daniels with the cooperation of Oxford, MA, 1892), 222.

82. Donahue, *Great Meadow*, 57.

83. The introduction of white clover to the valley by the 1650s has already been mentioned. Turnips were being grown in the valley at least as early as 1706. Judd, *History of Hadley*, 362; Joseph Olmstead, "Account Book 1685–1747, East Hartford," MS 83562, Connecticut Historical Society, Hartford, CT, unnumbered first page.

84. Massachusetts (Colony), *Records of the Governor and Company*, 1: 87.

85. Ibid., 1: 182.

86. Connecticut (Colony), *Public Records*, 2: 51.

87. "Hartford Town Votes," in *Collections of the Connecticut Historical Society*, 31 vols. (Hartford: Connecticut Historical Society, 1860–1967), 6: 334.

88. Connecticut (Colony), *Public Records*, 2: 51.

89. Ibid., 2: 245.

90. Massachusetts (Colony), *Records of the Governor and Company*, 1: 215; Connecticut (Colony), *Public Records*, 1: 130.

91. Richard B. Taylor and Eric C. Hellgren, "Diet of Feral Hogs in the Western South Texas Plains," *Southwestern Naturalist* 42, no. 1 (March 1997), 37.

92. Donald M. Waller and William S. Alverson, "The White-Tailed Deer: A Keystone Herbivore," *Wildlife Society Bulletin* 25, no. 2 (Summer 1997), 222; Robert Hayes et al., "Survival and Habitat Use of Feral Hogs in Mississippi," *Southeastern Naturalist* 8, no. 3 (2009), 411.

93. Taylor and Hellgren, "Diet of Feral Hogs," 38.

94. Jeffery T. Wilcox and Dirk H. Van Vuren, "Wild Pigs as Predators in Oak Woodlands of California," *Journal of Mammalogy* 90, no. 1 (2009), 114–118.

95. For example, Judd, *History of Hadley*, 378.

96. David R. Foster et al., "Wildlife Dynamics in the Changing New England Landscape," *Journal of Biogeography* 29, no. 10/11 (2002), 1339, 1342, 1345; David R. Foster, "Thoreau's Country: A Historical-Ecological Perspective on Conservation in the New England Landscape," *Journal of Biogeography* 29, no. 10/11 (2002), 1543; David R. Foster and Glenn Motzkin, "Ecology and Conservation in the Cultural Landscape of New England: Lessons from Nature's History," *Northeastern Naturalist* 5, no. 2 (1998), 118, 121; N. L. Chadwick, D. R. Progulske, and J. T. Finn, "Effects of Fuelwood Cutting on Birds in Southern New England," *Journal of Wildlife Management* 50, no. 3 (July 1986), 401.

97. Windsor (Town), Connecticut, *First Book of Records of Town Acts*, 1, August 21, 1650.

98. "Hartford Town Votes," 11.

99. Mason A. Green, *Springfield, 1636–1886: History of Town and City* (Springfield, MA: C. A. Nichols, 1888), 73; Springfield (Town), *History of Springfield*, 1: 175–176.

100. Judd, *History of Hadley*, 352.

101. Connecticut (Colony), *Public Records*, 1: 149.

102. Judd, *History of Hadley*, 353–354.

103. New Hampshire (Colony), *New Hampshire Provincial and State Papers*, 1: 398; Vermont (State), *Vermont State Papers*, ed. William Slade Jr. (Middlebury, VT: J. W. Copeland, 1823), 322.

104. For examples, see Lyman Simpson Hayes, *History of the Town of Rockingham, Vermont* (Bellows Falls, VT: Town of Rockingham, 1907), 104; Amos Newton Somers, *History of Lancaster, New Hampshire* (Concord, NH: Rumford Press, 1899), 67, 373; Francis M. Thompson, *History of Greenfield*, 2 vols. (Greenfield, MA: T. Morey & Son, 1904), 2: 991–993; the early Springfield records suggest that John and Joseph Harman were such men, Springfield (Town), *History of Springfield*, 1: 361, 365, 390, 391, 394; J. H. Temple and George Sheldon, *A History of the Town of Northfield, Massachusetts* (Albany, NY: Joel Munsell, 1875), 444.

105. Springfield (Town), *History of Springfield*, 1: 218. Thompson, *History of Greenfield*, 2: 992; Jon T. Coleman, *Vicious: Wolves and Men in America* (New Haven, CT: Yale University Press, 2004), 60.

106. Edward Howes to John Winthrop Jr., April 18, 1634, "Letters of Edward Howes," *Collections of the Massachusetts Historical Society*, 4th Series (Boston: Printed for the Massachusetts Historical Society, 1863), 6: 498.

107. Stiles, *Ancient Windsor*, 149n; Judd, *History of Hadley*, 353; Coleman, *Vicious*, chap. 5.

108. Connecticut (Colony), *Public Records*, 1: 367, 561, 3: 422; Massachusetts (Colony), *Records of the Governor and Company*, 2: 103; Roger Williams, *A Key into the Language of America* (London: Gregory Dexter, 1643), 163–166; Coleman, *Vicious*, 47–48.

109. Springfield (Town), *History of Springfield*, 1: 442.

110. "Hartford Town Votes," 205.

111. Thompson, *History of Greenfield*, 2: 987.

112. Judd, *History of Hadley*, 353n, 354n.

113. Cronon, *Changes in the Land*, 130; Judd, *History of Hadley*, 155, 298, 353, 356n; Connecticut (Colony), *Public Records*, 2: 443, 5: 86, 7: 288–289, 374, 12: 356–357; George W. Ellis and John E. Morris, *King Philip's War* (New York: Grafton Press, 1906), 238n; Massachusetts (Colony), *Acts and Resolves, Public and Private, of the Province of Massachusetts Bay*, 21 vols. (Boston: Wright and Potter, 1869–1922), 1: 589, 2: 26, 136, 501, 3: 208.

114. England (Parliament), "Woolen Act of May 4, 1699," in *Foundations of Colonial America: A Documentary History*, ed. W. Keith Kavenagh, 3 vols. (New York: Chelsea House, 1973), 1: 462.

115. Massachusetts (Colony), *The Acts and Laws of the Province of Massachusetts Bay*, 21 vols. (Boston: Wright & Potter, 1869), 1: 152.

116. Hampshire County, Massachusetts, Hampshire County Court Common Pleas/General Sessions, vol. 17, microfilm, Henry N. Flynt Library, Historic Deerfield, MA, February 12–15, 1765–August 27, 1765.

117. Anderson, *Creatures of Empire*, 148–149.

118. P. E. Hosten, H. Whitridge, and M. Broyles, "Diet Overlap and Social Interactions Among Cattle, Horses, Deer and Elk in the Cascade-Siskiyou National Monument, Southwest Oregon," U.S. Department of the Interior, Bureau of Land Management, Medford District,

2007, https://www.blm.gov/or/resources/recreation/csnm/files/dietoverlap.pdf, 2–4; Hudson A. Glimp, "Multi-Species Grazing and Marketing," *Rangelands* 10, no. 6 (December 1988), 275–276; Rich Olson, "Deer Habitat Requirements and Management in Wyoming," B-964, Wyoming Department of Renewable Resources (February 1992), 17; Susan M. Cooper et al., "Distribution and Interaction of White-Tailed Deer and Cattle in a Semi-Arid Grazing System," *Agriculture Ecosystems and Environment* 127 (2008), 85; Jeffery T. Wilcox and Dirk H. Van Vuren, "Wild Pigs as Predators in Oak Woodlands of California," *Journal of Mammalogy* 90, no. 1 (2009), 117; Catherine Menard et al., "Comparative Foraging and Nutrition of Horses and Cattle in European Wetlands," *Journal of Applied Ecology* 39, no. 1 (February 2002), 120; John E. MacDonald, Daniel Clark, and William A. Woytek, "Reduction and Maintenance of a White-Tailed Deer Herd in Central Massachusetts," *Journal of Wildlife Management* 71, no. 5 (July 2007), 1592; William J. Shea and Georg Schwede, "Variable Acorn Crops: Responses of White-Tailed Deer and Other Mast Consumers," *Journal of Mammalogy* 74, no. 4 (November 1993), 999.

119. Timothy Dwight, *Travels*, 1: 26.

120. A. J. Belsky, A. Matzke, and S. Uselman, "Survey of Livestock Influences on Stream and Riparian Ecosystems in the Western United States," *Journal of Soil and Water Conservation* 54 (1999), 3–4, 8–10.

121. Matthew Noble, "Ledger," MSS 403, 1766-1840 N 751, Baker Library, Harvard Business School, Boston, MA.

122. V. M. Christy, "Industrial Development and Its Relation to Town Planning: IV: The Leather Industry," *Town Planning Review* 11, no. 3 (June 1925), 174.

123. L. A. Clarkson, "The Organization of the English Leather Industry in the Late Sixteenth and Seventeenth Centuries," *Economic History Review* 13, no. 2 (1960), 246.

124. Michal McMahon, "'Publick Service' versus 'Mans Properties': Dock Creek and the Origins of Urban Technology in Eighteenth-Century Philadelphia," in *Early American Technology: Making and Doing Things from the Colonial Era to 1850*, ed. Judith A. McGaw (Chapel Hill: published for the Institute of Early American History and Culture by the University of North Carolina Press, 1994), 114–147.

125. Strother E. Roberts, "'Esteeme A Little of Fish': Fish, Fishponds and Farming in Eighteenth-Century New England and the Mid-Atlantic," *Agricultural History* 82, no. 2 (Spring 2008), 143–163.

126. John Pynchon, *The Pynchon Papers*, ed. Carl Bridenbaugh, 2 vols. (Boston: Colonial Society of Massachusetts; distributed by the University Press of Virginia, 1982), 1: 79, 80; Anderson, *Creatures of Empire*, 15–17.

127. For instance, the Indians who took Mary Rowlandson prisoner during King Philip's War relied on groundnut to sustain them on their winter journey up the Connecticut Valley toward Canada. Mary Rowlandson, *The Sovereignty and Goodness of God*, ed. Neal Salisbury (Boston: Bedford/St. Martin's, 1997), passim.

128. Pynchon, *Pynchon Papers*, 1: 79, 80; Anderson, *Creatures of Empire*, 15–17.

129. Connecticut (Colony), *Public Record*, 2: 371.

130. Virginia DeJohn Anderson, "King Philip's Herds: Indians, Colonists, and the Problem of Livestock in New England," *William and Mary Quarterly* 51, no. 4 (October 1994), 602, 606–607, 609, 615–617, 618.

131. Quotation from Jill Lepore, *In the Name of War: King Philip's War and the Origins of American Identity* (New York: Vintage, 1998), 96; George W. Ellis and John E. Morris, *King Philip's War* (New York: Grafton Press, 1906), 125–127; Edwin Monroe Bacon, *The Connecticut River*

and the Valley of the Connecticut: Three Hundred and Fifty Miles From Mountain to Sea (New York: G. P. Putnam's Sons, 1907), 121, 153, 157, 177; Eric B. Schultz and Michael J. Tougias, *King Philip's War: The History and Legacy of America's Forgotten Conflict* (Woodstock, VT: Countryman Press, 1999), 62–63.

132. Colin G. Calloway, *The Western Abenakis of Vermont: War, Migration, and the Survival of an Indian People* (Norman: University of Oklahoma Press, 1990), 142, 150–152, 235; Bacon, *The Connecticut River*, 214, 240, 243; David L. Ghere, "The 'Disappearance' of the Abenaki in Western Maine: Political Organization and Ethnocentric Assumptions," in *After King Philip's War: Presence and Persistence in Indian New England*, ed. Colin. G. Calloway (Hanover, NH: University Press of New England, 1997), 81–82.

133. James Hoffman Lewis, "Farmers, Craftsmen and Merchants: Changing Economic Organization in Massachusetts, 1730 to 1775," (PhD diss., Northwestern University, 1984), 145, 148.

134. For a few examples: *New-England Weekly Journal*, January 27, 1741, 4; *Boston New-Letter*, July 23–30, 1741, 2; *Boston Post-Boy*, October 26, 1746, 2; *Boston Evening Post*, May 28, 1750, 2; *Boston Post-Boy*, April 20, 1752, 2; *Boston Evening-Post*, May 3, 1756, 2; *Boston Gazette*, May 29, 1758, 3; *Boston Evening-Post*, December 21, 1761, 4; *Boston Post-Boy*, June 13, 1763, 4; *Boston News-Letter*, April 30, 1767, 3; *Boston Gazette*, February 11, 1771, 4; *Boston Evening-Post*, April 11, 1774, 1.

135. For examples: *Boston Evening-Post*, October 6, 1746, 2; *Boston Post-Boy*, March 23, 1752, 2; *Boston Post-Boy*, April 6, 1752, 2; *Boston Evening-Post*, October 15, 1753, 4; *Boston Evening-Post*, September 20, 1756, 2; *Boston News-letter*, November 28, 1765, 3; *Boston Evening-Post*, December 2, 1765, 3; *Boston Evening-Post*, March 9, 1767, 4; *Essex Gazette*, October 11–18, 1774, 4.

136. James Hoffman Lewis, "Farmers, Craftsmen and Merchants: Changing Economic Organization in Massachusetts, 1730 to 1775," (PhD diss., Northwestern University, 1984), 165, 176–177, 191; Karen J. Friedmann, "Victualling Colonial Boston," *Agricultural History* 47, no. 3 (July 1973), 200–201.

137. Theodore Dwight Jr., *The History of Connecticut from the First Settlement to the Present Time* (New York: Harper & Brothers, 1859), 247.

138. *Massachusetts Spy*, January 24–28, 1771, 4.

139. Destler, *The Provisions State*, 13.

140. Connecticut (Colony), *Public Records*, 15: 135.

141. David C. Hsiung, "Food, Fuel and the New England Environment in the War for Independence, 1775–1776," *New England Quarterly* 80, no. 4 (2007), 624.

142. Destler, *The Provisions State*, 19, 23, 31, 43.

143. Hsiung, "Food, Fuel, and the New England Environment," 626.

144. Bayley to Bedel, March 17, 1777, "Timothy Bedel Papers," Folder 1C; Bedel to Schuyler, February 16, 1777, "Timothy Bedel Papers," Folder 1C.

Epilogue

1. Jonathan Hoyt, "Jonathan Hoyt Journal, 1800," Henry N. Flynt Library, Historic Deerfield, MA, 38.

2. George Sheldon, "Old Time Traffic and Travel on the Connecticut," in *Proceedings of the Pocumtuck Valley Memorial Association, 1890–1891* (Deerfield, MA: Pocumtuck Valley Memorial Association, 1901), 122–123.

3. Anonymous, "Account Book: List of Shipments on the Connecticut River, 1752–1754," Jones Library, Amherst, MA.

4. Josiah Gilbert Holland, *History of Western Massachusetts*, 2 vols. (Springfield, MA: Samuel Bowles, 1855), 1: 304; Lyman S. Hayes, "The Navigation of the Connecticut River: Address Before the Vermont Historical Society," in *The Proceedings of the Vermont Historical Society for the Years 1913–1914* (Barre: Vermont Historical Society, 1915), 74.

5. Connecticut Valley Waterway Board, *Report of the Connecticut Valley Waterway Board on an Investigation of the Connecticut River* (Boston: Wight & Potter, 1913), 34, 36; Margaret E. Martin, "Merchants and Trade of the Connecticut River Valley, 1750–1820," *Smith College Studies in History* 24, nos. 1–4 (October 1938–July 1939), 9–10; John T. Cumbler, *Reasonable Use: The People, the Environment, and the State, New England, 1790–1930* (Oxford: Oxford University Press, 2001), 28.

6. Cumbler, *Reasonable Use*, 28–29.

7. "Copy of the Petition of the West India Planters and Merchants, Presented to the King Dec. 16, 1778," *Annual Register* (1778), 312; Richard B. Sheridan, "The Crisis of Slave Subsistence in the British West Indies During and after the American Revolution," *William and Mary Quarterly* 33, no. 4 (October 1976), 615–641; Andrew Jackson O'Shaughnessy, *An Empire Divided: The American Revolution and the British Caribbean* (Philadelphia: University of Pennsylvania Press, 2000), 161–174; Trevor Burnhard and John Garrigus, *The Plantation Machine: Atlantic Capitalism in French Saint-Dominique and British America* (Philadelphia: University of Pennsylvania Press, 2016), 227–233.

8. Cumbler, *Reasonable Use*, 33–36; Christopher Clark, *The Roots of Rural Capitalism: Western Massachusetts, 1780–1860* (Ithaca, NY: Cornell University Press, 1990), 233.

9. Cumbler, *Reasonable Use*, 21–22; Christopher Clark, "The Roots of Rural Capitalism: Distant Trade and Local Exchange," in *A Place Called Paradise: Culture and Community in Northampton, Massachusetts, 1654–2004*, ed. Kerry W. Buckley (Amherst: Historic Northampton Museum and Education Center in association with the University of Massachusetts Press, 2004), 202; Clark, *Roots of Rural Capitalism*, 112.

10. Clark, *Roots of Rural Capitalism*, 81, 202, 233–234, 287; Cumbler, *Reasonable Use*, 21–22; Carolyn Merchant, *Ecological Revolutions: Nature, Gender, and Science in New England* (Chapel Hill: University Press of North Carolina, 1989), 237–239; Richard W. Judd, *Second Nature: An Environmental History of New England* (Amherst: University of Massachusetts Press, 2014), 136–137.

11. "Destruction of the Great Dam on the Connecticut River," *New-Bedford Mercury*, November 24, 1848, 1; "Springfield Republican Office, Oct. 22," *Boston Semi-Weekly Atlas*, October 24, 1849, 1; Cumbler, *Reasonable Use*, 43.

12. For the disappearance of salmon: Timothy Dwight, *Travels in New-England and New-York*, 4 vols. (New Haven, CT: Timothy Dwight, 1824), 2: 325. For malaria: Oliver Wendell Holmes, "Dissertation of Intermittent Fever in New England," in *Boylston Prize Dissertations for the Years 1836 and 1837* (Boston: Charles C. Little and James Brown, 1838), 89–90, 93–94; Frederick Newton Kneeland, *Northampton: The Meadow City* (Northampton, MA: F. N. Kneeland and L. P. Bryant, 1894), 106; Massachusetts State Board of Health, Lunacy, and Charity, *Second Annual Report of the State Board of Health, Lunacy, and Charity of Massachusetts, 1880: Supplement Containing the Report and Papers on Public Health* (Boston: Rand, Avery, 1881), 51–52; James Russell Trumbull, *History of Northampton, Massachusetts, from Its Settlement in 1654*, 2 vols. (Northampton, MA: Gazette Printing, 1902), 577–581. For a discussion of the (re)flooding

of the landscape in a different region of New England, see Theodore Steinberg, *Nature Incorporated: Industrialization and the Waters of New England* (Amherst: University of Massachusetts Press, 1991), esp. 99–102.

13. Cumbler, *Reasonable Use*, 13–14, 19; Steinberg, *Nature Incorporated*, 55–56, 119–120.

14. Clark, *Roots of Rural Capitalism*, 81–82, 233–234, 287; Cumbler, *Reasonable Use*, 22–23, 33–36; Judd, *Second Nature*, 123, 135–137.

15. Charles Byron Kuhlmann, *The Development of the Flour-Milling Industry in the United States, with Special Reference to the Industry in Minneapolis* (Boston: Houghton Mifflin, 1929), 64–65; Percy Wells Bidwell and John I. Falconer, *History of Agriculture in the Northern United States, 1620–1860* (New York: Peter Smith, 1941), 93; Clark, *Roots of Rural Capitalism*, 150–152; John C. Hudson and Christopher R. Laingen, *American Farms, American Food: A Geography of Agriculture and Food Production in the United States* (Lanham, MD: Lexington Books, 2016), 39–40.

16. Clark, *Roots of Rural Capitalism*, 258, 291–292; Cumbler, *Reasonable Use*, 36; Edward Pearson Pressey, *History of Montague: A Typical Puritan Town* (Montague, MA: New Clairvaux Press, 1910), 151–152; Alan C. Swedlund, *Shadows in the Valley: A Cultural History of Illness, Death and Loss in New England, 1840–1916* (Amherst: University of Massachusetts Press, 2010), 44; Thomas R. Cox, *The Lumberman's Frontier: Three Centuries of Land Use, Society, and Change in America's Forests* (Corvallis: Oregon State University Press, 2010), 47–100.

17. Caroline Farrar Ware, *The Early New England Cotton Manufacture: A Study in Industrial Beginnings* (New York: Russell & Russell, 1966), 190; Timothy Leunig, "A British Industrial Success: Productivity in the Lancashire and New England Cotton Spinning Industries a Century Ago," *Economic History Review* 56, no. 1 (February 2003), 93.

18. Clark, *Roots of Rural Capitalism*, 292; Cumbler, *Reasonable Use*, 161–162; Steve Grant, "When Forests Covered the Connecticut Landscape," *Hartford Courant*, July 5, 2014, http://articles.courant.com/2014-07-05/news/hc-250-connecticut-landscape-20140705_1_connecticut-river-connecticut-forest-connecticut-courant; Pontus Olofsson et al., "Time Series Analysis of Satellite Data Reveals Continuous Deforestation of New England Since the 1980s," *Environmental Research Letters* 11, no. 6 (May 2016), 1–2.

INDEX

Abenakis, 35, 40, 42, 68–69, 71, 146, 148, 155, 196
Act for the Preservation of Shiptimber and Plank (1715) (Connecticut), 138
agriculture, 55–96; American Revolution and, 198; beaver and, 29, 31, 43, 51–52; capitalism and, 9; climate change and, 121, 123; deforestation and, 164, 208; diseases/insect pests and, 83–85, 95, 121; diversification and, 86–94; English settlers and, 14, 15–16, 21, 51–52, 57–60, 67, 69–75, 81–84, 86–96, 121, 165–66; export trades and, 5–7, 19, 60–62, 76, 78, 88, 90–91, 95, 203, 206; fire and, 73–75, 82; firewood and, 97, 99, 132, 174; Hartford (CT) and, 87, 100–101, 109–10, 116; Hitchcock, Justin on, 178; industries and, 161; livestock and, 82, 87, 164–65, 167–68, 176, 184, 206; manure and, 49, 176–77; meadows and, 52, 73, 86, 176; Native Americans and, 14, 15, 19, 23, 24, 29, 47–48, 58–72, 73, 82, 101; *The New-England Farmer* (Deane), 176; pines and, 155, 160; river vessels and, 201; salt and, 93–94; sawmills and, 156; shipbuilding and, 136; slave trade and, 5–7, 60, 79, 95; soils and, 49, 75, 81–82, 206; staves and, 134; timber and, 127; Wethersfield (CT) and, 88; wetlands and, 52, 55–56; woodlands and, 97, 101, 121, 126, 164, 173, 174, 208. *See also* crops; grains; *individual crops*
American Revolution, 79, 92, 148, 153, 163–64, 197–99, 203
Anderson, Virginia DeJohn, 196
Andros, Edmund, 84–85
Anglo-Dutch Wars, 63, 98–99
apples, 86, 87–88, 192
Atiwaneto (Abenaki spokesman), 146
Atlantic World, 3–11

barley, 75, 76, 77, 79, 84, 86, 87
beaver (*C. canadensis*), 21–57; agriculture and, 29, 31, 43, 51–52; Dutch and, 25, 32, 33–34, 42; ecology and, 21, 25–30, 43–47, 50, 53, 58; England and, 43–44; extirpation of, 18, 25, 41–43, 45–48, 51–56, 68; fashion and, 30–32, 34; fish species and, 45–47, 158, 159; French and, 25, 41, 42, 44; in *Historie of Four-Footed Beastes* (Topsell), 43; in *History of New Hampshire* (Belknap) and, 44, 50; malaria and, 53, 55–56; meadows and, 2, 27, 29, 30, 44–45, 47, 48, 174; Native Americans and, 21, 25, 28–30, 32–42, 44–48, 57, 59–60, 66–67, 69; natural resources and, 22, 25–26; Peirce, Joseph and, 44–45; property rights and, 66; Pynchon, John and, 39–40, 41–42; soils and, 29, 30, 124, 126; timber and, 29, 49–50; tree species and, 27, 29, 49–50; wetlands and, 25, 26–27, 30, 49–53, 55, 68. *See also* fur trade; Ktsi Amiskw (Great Beaver)
beaver (*C. fiber*), 30–31, 43
Bedel, Timothy, 151–52, 155, 163–64, 199
Belknap, Jeremy, 44, 50
Bellomont, Lord (Coote, Richard), 90, 137
Bernard, Francis, 149, 150
bird species, 45, 186–87
Birket, James, 143, 157
Blake, Daniel, 127–28, 144–45
Block, Adriaen, 32–33, 34–35, 49, 125
Boston: cattle and, 181–83; as entrepôt, 4, 6–7, 78–81, 84–85, 89, 91, 95, 170–72; firewood and, 99, 119–20, 125, 127; fish species and, 157; grains and, 78; livestock and, 162–64, 170–72, 176, 177, 178–79, 181–82, 198–99; meat and, 197, 198; shipbuilding and, 137; timber and, 132; West Indies and, 7; white pine and, 143
Boston News-Letter, 181

ACKNOWLEDGMENTS

No historian is an island, complete unto him/herself. When finally composing my acknowledgments, after over a decade of researching and writing, it seemed only appropriate to return to—and to repurpose—the words with which this book begins. To understand an ecosystem, I have argued, one must understand the networks that connect it to other regions and markets. To understand a scholar, one must understand the networks of people and institutions that have connected that scholar's work to the knowledge, expertise, and generosity of others. The list of generous individuals and institutions to whom I am indebted is long.

Timothy Breen was a mentor and, perhaps more importantly, a professionalizing force in my life. Joel Mokyr helped steer a mere history student through the labyrinths of economic history, as did Regina Grafe. Michael Sherry's seminars offered an invaluable arena for presenting writing, some of which was not yet ready for prime time, and having it torn apart by my peers. For their constructive feedback, I would especially like to thank Andrew Wehrman, James Coltrain, Charlotte Cahill, Michael Green, and Meghan Roberts (whose name, I'm sure, will come up again). I also owe thanks to several other scholars who have had all or some large part of this manuscript inflicted upon them, and who were kind enough to respond to this imposition by generously offering comments and advice that improved the book immeasurably. Thank you, Seth Rothman, for offering your mentorship; to Linford Fisher for your help framing my introductory arguments; to Walter Woodward for being an early source of encouragement; to Dan Richter for the laundry list of excellent suggestions you offered in your role as series editor for the University of Pennsylvania Press; to my anonymous reader during the press' review process, and to Jenny Hale Pulsipher, a no-longer-anonymous reviewer for all of your advice on how to transform a raw manuscript into a publication-worthy book. Thank you, as well, to all of my supportive colleagues at both Brown and Bowdoin.

Much of the material in this book has, at some point in time, been presented elsewhere, either in print or as a spoken word performance (of sorts). Many thanks to the anonymous reviewers who helped shape the *New England Quarterly* article ("Pines, Profits, and Politics") upon which Chapter 4 of this book is based. I have had the opportunity to present much of the material that appears in this book at a wide variety of conferences, workshops, and seminars over the years. I have never failed to come away with my understanding honed and my analysis sharpened. I greatly appreciate the efforts of all those who ever took me to task at these scholarly meetings, and of the administrators and organizers of the Omohundro Institute, the American Historical Association, the Society for Early America, the Massachusetts Historical Society's Early America and Environmental History Seminars, the McNeill Center, the USC–Huntington EMSI's American Origins Seminar, and the Chabraja Center for Historical Studies.

One interesting fact I learned while at Northwestern University conducting the research that eventually grew into this book is that many of the most valuable archival resources for studying the colonial Connecticut Valley are, in fact, located at quite a distance from Chicago. Which brings me back to my point about the generosity of institutions. First, I must take a moment to thank Elizabeth Pardoe, my guide to some of the more lucrative funding opportunities I was lucky enough to enjoy during the course of my research. Thank you to the American Council for Learned Societies (ACLS), the Andrew W. Mellon Foundation, and the Dolores Zohrab Liebmann Fund. Together these institutions afforded me the time and resources needed to begin researching and writing this book. The ACLS, in particular, was doubly kind in awarding me a New Faculty Fellowship, allowing me to learn the ropes of teaching while also having time to continue work on this book. Thank you to the American Philosophical Society for its Phillips Fund Grant for Native American Research, to the New England Regional Fellowship Consortium, to Harvard Business School for its Alfred D. Chandler Jr. Travel Fellowship, to the Henry E. Huntington Library, to the Chabraja Center, to the Fort Dearborn Chapter of the Daughters of the American Revolution, the Illinois Chapter of the National Society of the Colonial Dames of America, and the Society of Colonial Wars in the State of Illinois. Without their support, the research for this book would not have been possible.

Of course, getting to the archives was a far less daunting challenge than actually navigating them once I was there. The help and kindness I experienced everywhere I conducted research made this book project not only possible, but also a pleasure. I offer my gratitude to the staffs of Historic Deerfield's Henry N. Flint Library and the Pocumtuck Valley Memorial Association Library, the Massachusetts Historical Society, the Connecticut Historical

Society, the Connecticut Valley Historical Museum, the Connecticut State Library and State Archives, Special Collections at Smith College, the New Hampshire Historical Society, the Huntington Library, and the British Library.

Finally, I would like to thank my parents, Susan and Terry, and all of my family for their support in a prolonged process that I am sure they did not always fully understand. Thank you to Ciro and Hugo for bringing light to my life and for sparing me at least a little bit of time for getting work done. I offer my most heartfelt gratitude to Meghan Roberts (I told you she would come up again) for reading countless drafts, enduring myriad conversations on early modern historiography, and picking up books at the library when I forgot to do it myself. Thank you, Meghan, for teaching me ambition and providing me a model of scholarly excellence toward which to strive—this book is for you.